Professional Visual Basic Interoperability – COM and VB6 to .NET

Billy Hollis

Rockford Lhotka

Wrox Press Ltd. ®

Professional Visual Basic Interoperability – COM and VB6 to .NET

Published by Wrox Press Ltd,
Arden House, 1102 Warwick Road, Acocks Green,
Birmingham, B27 6BH, UK
Printed in the United States
ISBN 1-861005-65-2

Trademark Acknowledgements

Wrox has endeavored to provide trademark information about all the companies and products mentioned in this book by the appropriate use of capitals. However, Wrox cannot guarantee the accuracy of this information.

Credits

Authors
Billy Hollis
Rockford Lhotka

Additional Material
Kevin Ford

Technical Reviewers
Mike Apostal
Maxime Bombardier
Martin Beaulieu
Damien Foggon
Mark Horner
David Schultz
Thearon Willis

John Rivard
. *(Microsoft Visual Basic
Development team)*
Ed Robinson
*(Microsoft Visual Basic
Program Management
Team)*

Technical Architect
Paul Jeffcoat

Technical Editors
Alessandro Ansa
Caroline Robeson

Author Agents
Laura Jones
Cilmara Lion

Project Administrators
Rob Hesketh
Cilmara Lion

Managing Editor
Louay Fatoohi

Production Coordinator
Natalie O'Donnell

Index
Andrew Criddle

Proof Reader
Chris Smith

Cover
Chris Morris

About the Authors

Billy Hollis

Billy Hollis first learned BASIC over twenty-five years ago, and is co-author of the first book ever published on Visual Basic .NET, *VB.NET Programming with the Public Beta*, from Wrox Press. He is a frequent speaker at conferences, including Comdex and the Visual Basic Insiders' Technical Summit (VBITS), often talking about the topics of software design and specification, object-based development in Visual Basic, and Microsoft .NET. Billy is MSDN Regional Director of Developer Relations in Nashville, Tennessee for Microsoft, and has hosted Developer Days in Nashville for the last three years. He has his own consulting company in Nashville that focuses on training, consultation, and software development for the Microsoft .NET platform.

Rockford Lhotka

Rockford Lhotka has authored several Wrox Press titles, including *VB.NET Programming with the Public Beta*, *VB6 Business Objects*, and *VB6 Distributed Objects*, and is a regular columnist for *MSDN Online* and *Visual Studio Magazine*. He regularly presents at major conferences around the world, including Microsoft PDC, Tech Ed, VS Live!, and VS Connections. He has over fourteen years of experience in software development and has worked on many projects in various roles, including software architecture, design and development, network administration, and project management. Rockford is the Principal Technology Evangelist for Magenic Technologies, one of America's premiere Microsoft Gold Certified Partners dedicated to solving today's most challenging business problems using 100% Microsoft tools and technology.

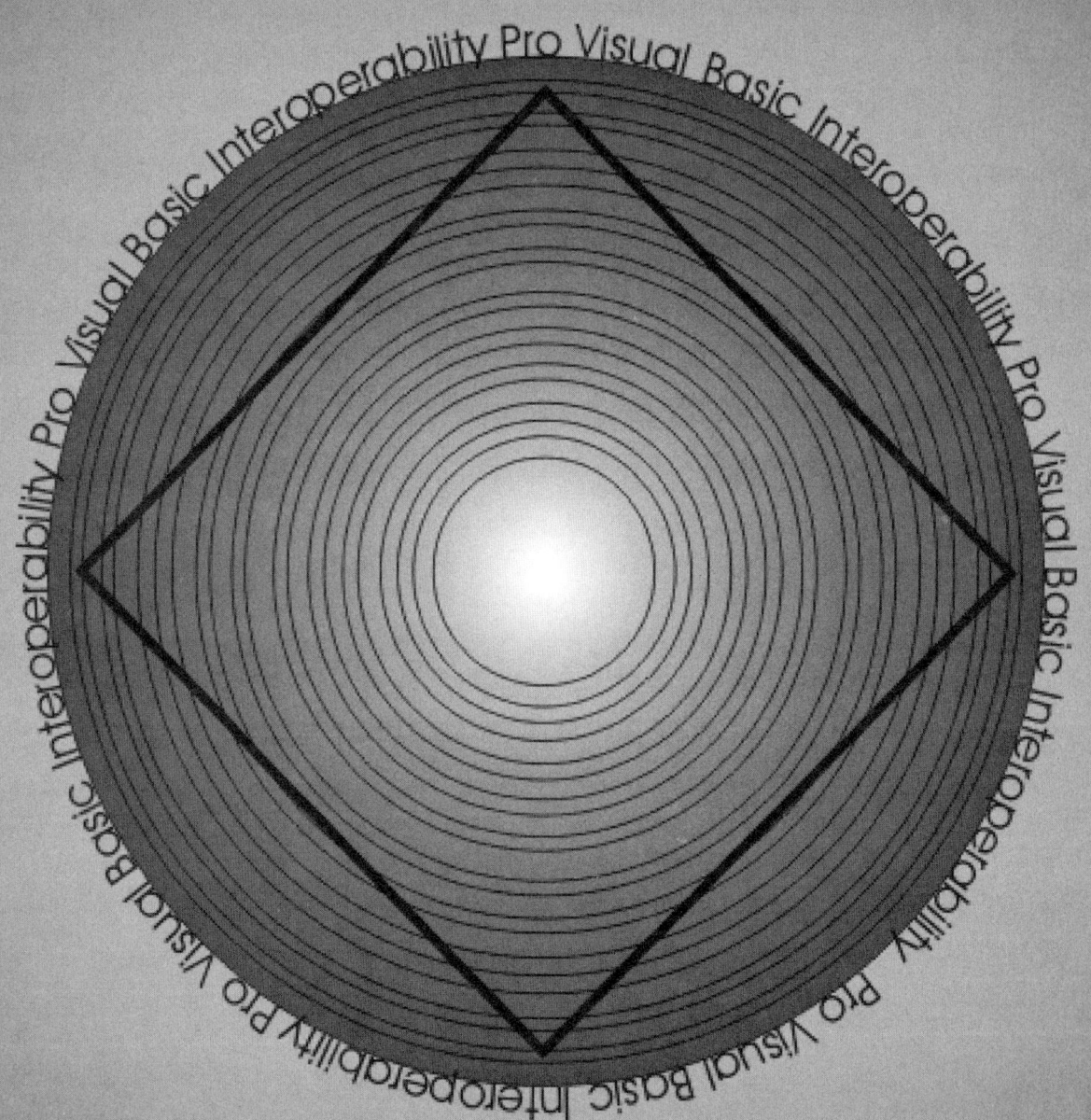

Table of Contents

Table of Contents

Table of Contents

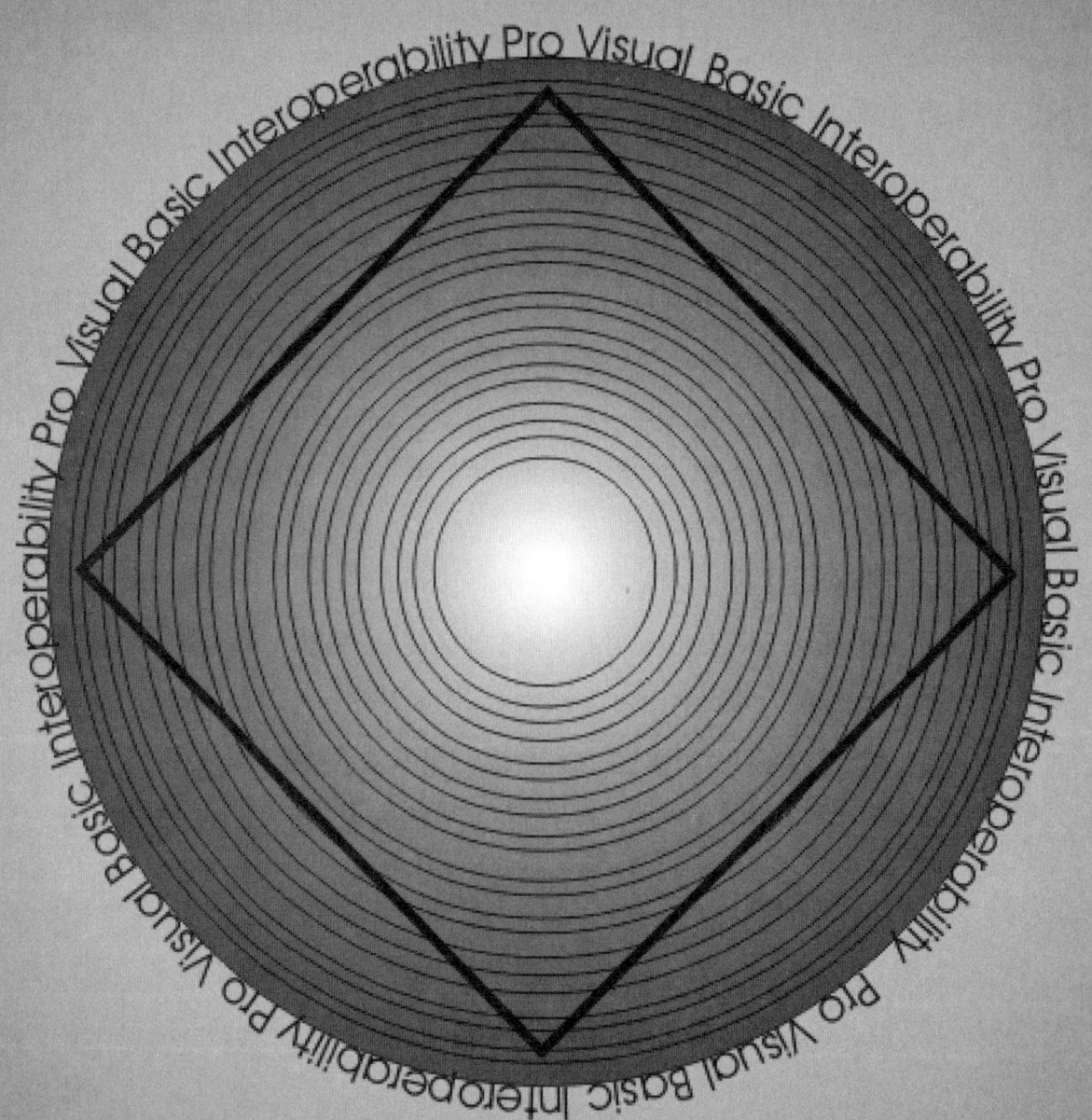

Introduction

Who is this Book for?

This book is written for programmers who are experienced in VB6, and who need to understand how VB6 and Visual Basic .NET can interoperate.

It is expected that the reader has already become reasonably familiar with the overall structure of .NET and the syntactical differences between VB6 and Visual Basic .NET. The book is not a tutorial in the changes between VB6 and Visual Basic .NET, nor is it an introduction to .NET technologies. If you are interested in learning about .NET in general, or Visual Basic .NET in particular, you may wish to consult the following books from Wrox Press:

- ❑ *Professional .NET Framework*, ISBN 1-861005-56-3
- ❑ *Professional VB.NET*, ISBN 1-861004-97-4

What's Covered in this Book?

Chapter 1, *The Importance of Interoperability*, looks at why interoperability between VB6 and COM and the new .NET platform will be necessary.

Chapter 2, *Using COM Components from .NET*, shows how to import a COM component into the .NET platform, making it available for use from .NET even though it remains a COM component running in COM. It also covers how to design COM components and interfaces to make them easier to deal with from a .NET perspective.

Chapter 3, *Using .NET Assemblies from COM*, looks at the reverse scenario – the issues involved in creating a .NET assembly for use by COM applications, and how to use it effectively.

Chapter 4, *Calling COM Components in MTS and COM+ from .NET*, focuses on the use of COM+ or MTS-based COM components by Visual Basic .NET client applications.

Chapter 5, *Visual Basic .NET and COM in COM+*, shows how a Visual Basic .NET assembly running in COM+ interacts with VB6 components also running in COM+, and visa versa.

Chapter 6, *Custom Marshaling*, gives an overview of the different mechanisms for using marshaling – moving information bi-directionally from unmanaged code to managed code.

Chapter 7, *Threading Issues*, looks at the threading issues that are likely to arise when interoperating between Visual Basic .NET and VB6. We show how threading works in VB6 with COM, and then in Visual Basic .NET on the .NET platform.

Chapter 8, *DCOM, Remoting, and Web Services*, covers using DCOM via COM interop, and the alternatives to DCOM provided by the .NET platform – XML Web Services and .NET Remoting.

Chapter 9, *Sharing Configuration Information*, looks at using private INI files, the Windows registry, and XML-based configuration files to share configuration information in both VB6 and Visual Basic .NET.

Chapter 10, *Flat File Access in .NET*, shows how binary, random, and sequential access to flat files has changed from VB6 to Visual Basic .NET.

Chapter 11, *Using ADO in .NET*, compares ADO and ADO.NET and discusses situations where ADO should still be used, even for new projects in Visual Basic .NET. We also examine some of the differences between using ADO in .NET as opposed to VB6.

Chapter 12, *Calling API or Static DLL Functions from .NET*, looks at interoperability with DLLs that do not have COM interfaces, and which are generally used to allow VB programs to work with the Windows API.

Chapter 13, *Interoperability of ActiveX Controls in .NET*, looks at one kind of COM component that requires special treatment – ActiveX controls.

Chapter 14, *How Do I Prepare VB6 Code for Migration?*, provides some general guidelines that, if implemented while maintaining and enhancing existing VB6 code, will ease the eventual migration of the code to Visual Basic .NET.

What Do I Need to Use this Book?

All you'll need is a PC running:

- ❏   Windows 2000 or XP

- ❏   Visual Studio .NET Professional edition (or higher versions)

- ❏   Visual Studio 6.0 with Visual Basic 6.0

Conventions

We have used a number of different styles of text and layout in the book to help differentiate between the different kinds of information. Here are examples of the styles that we use and an explanation of what they mean.

Bullets appear indented, with each new bullet marked as follows:

❑ **Important words** are in a bold type font

❑ Words that appear on the screen in menus like the File or Window are in a similar font to the one that you see on screen

❑ Keys that you press on the keyboard, like *Ctrl* and *Enter*, are in italics

❑ If you see something like Object, you'll know that it's a filename, object name, or function name

Code in a gray box is new, important, pertinent code:

```
Dim objMyClass as New MyClass("Hello World")

Debug.WriteLine(objMyClass.ToString)
```

Sometimes you'll see code in a mixture of styles, like this:

```
Dim objVar as Object

objVar = Me

CType(objVar, Form).Text = "New Dialog Title Text"
```

The code on a white background is code that we've already looked at and that we don't wish to examine further.

Advice, hints, and background information come in an italicized, indented font like this.

> **Important pieces of information come in boxes like this.**

Customer Support

We always value hearing from our readers, and we want to know what you think about this book: what you liked, what you didn't like, and what you think we can do better next time. You can send us your comments, either by returning the reply card in the back of the book, or by e-mail to feedback@wrox.com. Please be sure to mention the book title in your message.

How to Download the Sample Code for the Book

When you visit the Wrox site, http://www.wrox.com/, simply locate the title through our Search facility or by using one of the title lists. Click on Download in the Code column, or on Download Code on the book's detail page.

The files that are available for download from our site have been archived using WinZip. When you have saved the attachments to a folder on your hard drive, you need to extract the files using a de-compression program such as WinZip or PKUnzip. When you extract the files, the code is usually extracted into chapter folders. When you start the extraction process, ensure that your software (WinZip, PKUnzip, etc.) is set to use folder names.

Errata

We've made every effort to make sure that there are no errors in the text or in the code. However, no one is perfect and mistakes do occur. If you find an error in one of our books, like a spelling mistake or a faulty piece of code, we would be very grateful for feedback. By sending in errata, you may save another reader hours of frustration and, of course, you will be helping us to provide even higher quality information. Simply e-mail the information to support@wrox.com. Your information will be checked and, if correct, posted on the errata page for that title or used in subsequent editions of the book.

To find errata on the web site, go to http://www.wrox.com/ and simply locate the title through our Advanced Search or title list. Click on the Book Errata link, which is below the cover graphic on the book's detail page.

E-mail Support

If you wish to directly query a problem in the book with an expert who knows the book in detail, then e-mail support@wrox.com with the following information:

- ❑ The **title of the book**, **last four digits of the ISBN**, and **page number** of the problem in the Subject field
- ❑ Your **name**, **contact information**, and the **problem** in the body of the message

We *won't* send you junk mail. We need the details to save your time and ours. When you send an e-mail message, it will go through the following chain of support:

- ❑ Customer Support – Your message is delivered to our customer support staff who are the first people to read it. They have files on the most frequently asked questions and will answer anything general about the book or the web site immediately.

- ❑ Editorial – Deeper queries are forwarded to the technical editor responsible for that book. They have experience with the programming language or particular product, and are able to answer detailed technical questions on the subject.

- ❑ The Authors – Finally, in the unlikely event that the editor cannot answer your problem, they will forward the request to the author. We do try to protect the authors from any distractions to their writing; however, we are quite happy to forward specific requests to them. All Wrox authors help with the support on their books. They will e-mail the customer and the editor with their response and, again, all readers should benefit.

The Wrox Support process can only offer support to issues that are directly pertinent to the content of our published title. Support for questions that fall outside the scope of normal book support is provided via the community lists of our http://p2p.wrox.com/ forum.

p2p.wrox.com

For author and peer discussion, join the P2P mailing lists. Our unique system provides **programmer to programmer**™ contact on mailing lists, forums, and newsgroups, all in addition to our one-to-one e-mail support system. If you post a query to P2P, you can be confident that the many Wrox authors and other industry experts who are present on our mailing lists are examining it. At p2p.wrox.com, you will find a number of different lists that will help you, not only while you read this book, but also as you develop your own applications. Particularly appropriate to this book are the pro_vb, pro_vb_dotnet, and vb_dotnet lists.

To subscribe to a mailing list, just follow these steps:

1. Go to http://p2p.wrox.com/

2. Choose the appropriate category from the left menu bar

3. Click on the mailing list you wish to join

4. Follow the instructions to subscribe and fill in your e-mail address and password

5. Reply to the confirmation e-mail you receive

6. Use the subscription manager to join more lists and set your e-mail preferences

Why this System Offers the Best Support

You can choose to join the mailing lists or you can receive them as a weekly digest. If you don't have the time, or facility, to receive the mailing list, then you can search our online archives. Junk and spam mails are deleted, and your own e-mail address is protected by the unique Lyris system. Queries about joining or leaving lists, and any other general queries about lists, should be sent to listsupport@p2p.wrox.com.

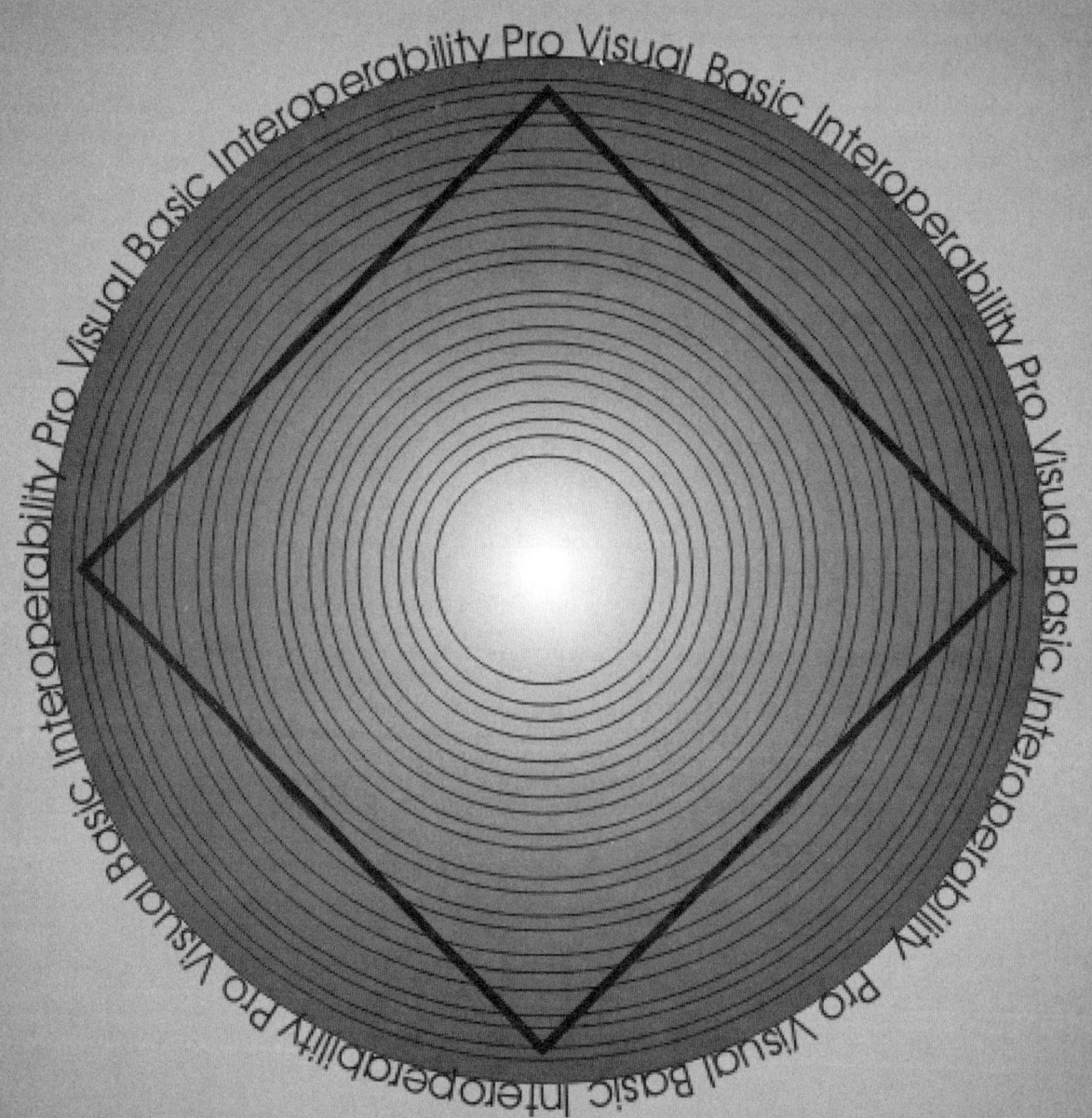

The Importance of Interoperability

At this time, we face the biggest transition in software development in the last ten years. Finally, a platform designed from scratch for an Internet-enabled world has been produced. It's called Microsoft .NET, and it is a huge advance for any software development project that requires Internet integration.

However, new platforms suffer from an inherent problem. Organizations have already invested heavily in their software infrastructure. It is not financially possible to merely throw away such an investment in favor of a new platform. A transition period is necessary (perhaps a very long one), in which the new platform must work side-by-side with software already being used.

Often, simple co-existence is not enough. New systems must interact with old systems, communicating information back and forth. This capability, in which there is a high level of integration between disparate platforms, is called **interoperability**.

VB6 is the most popular programming language in the world, and Visual Basic .NET is likely to be the most commonly-used language in .NET for at least some period of time (more on that below). Therefore, the most important interoperability situation when moving to .NET is getting programs in Visual Basic .NET to interoperate with pre-existing VB6 programs, and with the data used by those programs. That's what this book is about.

Going Forward with Visual Basic .NET

Right now, VB is the most popular programming tool in existence. Based on surveys commissioned by Microsoft, the aggregate number of lines of code written in VB surpassed the number of lines of code written in COBOL during the year 2001. Microsoft has sold more than eight million licenses for VB worldwide.

Indications are that the popularity of VB will continue into the .NET era. In fact, the argument can be made that VB may become even more popular. .NET removes many of the historical limitations of VB, taking away some of the reasons other languages were used in the past.

Developers moving to .NET also have no solid reason to choose another language over VB. .NET-enabled languages do not vary much in their raw capabilities. They have about the same functionality and performance characteristics. VB can even be used for the bulk of their web programming needs, displacing other languages and tools. The probable result is that most organizations moving to .NET will choose a language based on what their developers already know. Why take on the dual challenges of a new platform and a different language at the same time?

This has two main implications:

❑   VB is the most popular and prevalent development tool currently used

❑   VB is likely to be the most popular development tool used in .NET for some period of time

That means many organizations will be grappling with the challenges in moving from their current VB6 programming environment into one based on Visual Basic .NET.

Two Strategies – Migration and Interoperability

The reasons for moving to .NET are sufficiently compelling that many organizations will make the change. For those organizations currently using VB and planning to use Visual Basic .NET as their new development tool, there are two possible strategies to use when making the transition:

1.   Migrate their existing VB code to Visual Basic .NET.

2.   Continue to use existing VB programs, and develop new projects in Visual Basic .NET. Arrange for new (.NET) programs to **interoperate** with old (non-.NET) ones.

Of course, these strategies may be combined so that some old code is migrated while some is retained. In fact, such a combination will probably be the used more often than either strategy alone.

The Migration Option

The last VB version before .NET was 6.0. VB 1.0 came out in 1991, and 6.0 came out in 1998. That's five new versions in only seven years. How did VB shops cope with that?

It actually wasn't difficult. Migrating from early versions of VB to later versions was relatively painless. New syntax was added with each version, but syntax changes were minimal. Old projects were simply opened in the new version and saved. That was the sum total of migration efforts in most previous VB versions.

The exception was the change from VB3, which generated 16-bit code for Windows 3.1, to VB4, which created 32-bit programs for Windows 95 and NT 3.1. Microsoft also did away with the VBX form of add-in controls, and replaced it with COM-based OCX controls. This made the VB3-to-VB4 migration the toughest of the previous shifts that VB developers have needed to make.

But even that one was not too bad. After obtaining replacement controls, the migration required modest manual changes for most projects. As an example, the team I was on at the time was made up of eight developers, and there were some thirty large programs to migrate. We did it all in less than a week.

It was too good to last. Microsoft worked hard at upward compatibility in previous versions, but there comes a time when the underlying technological changes force radical readjustment. It was simply not possible to bring VB onto the .NET platform while retaining the degree of upward compatibility previously experienced.

Major Areas of Incompatibility Between VB6 and Visual Basic .NET

Most of the incompatibilities between VB6 and Visual Basic .NET are a consequence of fitting Visual Basic .NET into the .NET Framework. A few are "cleaning up" a language whose syntactical roots go back over 35 years.

It is important to understand that Microsoft did not make changes just for the sake of change. There were many debates about what to keep in the new VB and what to remove. The changes were necessary to get VB into .NET, and that was necessary because the advantages of .NET will take VB forward into a new generation of development. The negative consequences of incompatibility must be balanced against the hugely positive consequences of getting VB into the .NET world.

Books are available on the subject of moving to Visual Basic .NET, and they offer details on all of the changes. We will not repeat that information here. But it is important to understand the magnitude of the changes to enable a good comparison between the migration and interoperability options. Here are the major areas of incompatibility, with some examples of each.

Changes in Data Types

The .NET Framework has a consistent set of data types used by all languages that run in .NET. It is called the Common Type System, or CTS.

The CTS includes all the data types common to traditional languages, such as integer types, floating-point types, Booleans, and so forth. It also includes variable length strings, which have long been a part of BASIC, but were not present in many other programming languages such as C++.

As you might expect, generating a set of types to be used in all languages requires compromises. The CTS was adapted to VB by adding variable length strings, for example. But some changes required VB to adapt instead.

Integer types have their name changed, and a new type is added. Here is a table summarizing these changes:

Old (VB6) type	New (Visual Basic .NET) type	Size	Range	Name for type in .NET Framework
Integer	Short	16 bits	-32,768 to 32,767	Int16
Long	Integer	32 bits	-2,147,483,648 to 2,147,483,647	Int32
(N/A)	Long	64 bits	-9,223,372,036,854,775,808 to 9,223,372,036,854,775,807	Int64

This change is not a huge migration roadblock, because old code can be easily converted to compensate. Even if the code is not changed, it will still run – the variables will just hold higher values than they did before.

The other change is more radical. All arrays in .NET are zero-based. You can do the following in VB6:

```
Dim sMyArray(10 To 20) As String        ' VB6 code
```

No analogue to this exists in .NET. Therefore any VB6 code that takes advantage of such arrays must be significantly recoded to work in Visual Basic .NET.

Another missing data type is the fixed-length string. In VB6, you can declare a string as fixed length like this:

```
Dim sMyFixedLengthString As String*16        ' VB6 code
```

In this case, the string is exactly 16 characters. No such data type exists in Visual Basic .NET. To compensate, Microsoft provides a "compatibility class", which is a class in the Framework libraries that simulates the behavior of a fixed-length string. This works in most instances, but it fails in at least one situation. The compatibility class cannot be used in structures (the replacement for User Defined Types), so structures cannot have fixed-length strings in them in Visual Basic .NET. There are a number of workarounds, but all require manual adjustment of code.

Changes Related to Object-Oriented Programming

Those of us who use VB for object-based development have long complained about the limitations of VB compared to other pure object-oriented languages such as Java, C++, or SmallTalk. Those limitations are removed in Visual Basic .NET. However, the cost of their removal is making VB work in the .NET Framework, which is itself a pure object environment. That again required compromises with other languages.

As a result, Visual Basic .NET no longer has default properties, unless they are indexed. The Set keyword is no longer used for setting object references. And property procedures have a different syntax.

These are fairly minor issues that can be automatically fixed by conversion software. Strangely enough, the conversion issues have more to do with new capabilities. In many cases, lack of inheritance, parameterized constructors, and other object capabilities caused VB developers to write a variety of workarounds. An example is wrapper classes for collections to enforce type-safety. This should be done with inheritance, but VB6 didn't have it, so several techniques were used to simulate it.

Those techniques can be migrated to .NET in most cases, but they are considerably less than optimal techniques to use in .NET. Migrating code that uses such techniques may result in a system that does not have much value. It may be better to continue to use the old system in VB6, and rewrite at some point in the future in .NET.

Radically Different Means for Creating a Web Interface

VB6 had two means of creating a web-based user interface – WebClasses and DHTML Pages. Neither proved particularly popular, but some installations did use them because the alternative (Active Server Pages) was arguably not much better.

.NET offers Web Forms in ASP.NET as the preferred way to do web interfaces. Web Forms are not very compatible with either WebClasses or DHTML Pages. The VB6 Upgrade Wizard attempts to convert WebClasses, but manual work is necessary. It will not automatically convert DHTML Pages at all.

If an existing project uses these obsolete technologies, then migration of the project will involve extensive manual work.

Functionality Moved from Keywords to the Underlying Framework

VB6 was the culmination of a decade of effort to add more functionality to VB. The preferred way to add such functionality in the VB world was through the use of keywords. This made the functionality highly accessible to the developer.

.NET uses a different philosophy. Much functionality in .NET is expressed in the .NET Framework classes rather than through language keywords. While these are arguably a bit harder to learn to use, they are accessible to all languages, and also extensible through inheritance (which VB6 did not have).

Keywords such as `Circle` and `Line` do not exist in Visual Basic .NET. There are drawing objects to accomplish these functions. Other keywords that have been removed in favor of .NET Framework classes include `Sqr`, `Rnd`, `Lset`, `Rset`, and `VarType`.

These keywords all have replacements but, in some cases, the replacement is not an exact match. That leads to situations requiring manual changes to logic to compensate.

Removal of Obsolete Syntax

VB began as a BASIC variant, and supported many old syntactical elements that have long since gone out of style. `Gosub`, for example, is no longer recommended as a programming technique, but VB6 included support for it in the interests of upward compatibility.

Seeing that they would be unable to provide total upward compatibility, the Visual Basic .NET team decided to use this opportunity to remove some of the most archaic of the old BASIC-style syntax. Removed keywords include:

❑   `Gosub`

❑   `On x GoTo` ... (computed `GoTos`)

❑   `Let`

❑   `VarPtr`, `ObjPtr`, `StrPtr`

❑   `DefBool`, `DefByte`, `DefInt`, `DefLng`, `DefCur`, `DefSng`, `DefDbl`, `DefDec`, `DefDate`, `DefStr`, `DefObj`, `DefVar`

Any systems that use any of this syntax will require manual adjustment when converting code to .NET. Some of these, such as Gosub, require substantial modification since there is no element in .NET that provides anything close to equivalent functionality.

> *You can get a complete list of keyword-related changes by looking up the topic* 'Programming Element Support Changes Summary " *in the .NET Help system.*

Good Candidates for Migration to Visual Basic .NET

Current VB projects should be evaluated as candidates for converting to Visual Basic .NET in light of the above issues. Some will be good candidates, while others are probably not worth migration but should instead be rewritten from scratch.

Even with well designed and well written applications, moving to Visual Basic .NET will not be a transparent conversion. But systems with certain characteristics will be better choices to attempt a migration.

Any tiered design will transfer more easily to Visual Studio.NET. In general, classes and components will migrate more easily than user interface modules. Given the object-oriented nature of .NET, it is not surprising that code that implements good object-oriented design principles will move more easily than code that does not.

Bad Candidates for Migration

Fat VB clients, where all the business logic is mixed up with the UI code, will probably not be practical candidates for migration. But even well written user interface code may have issues.

The migration tool can convert VB forms to Windows Forms, but the capabilities of Windows Forms and the new .NET controls are not an exact one-to-one match with older forms and controls. This means manual work in migrating many VB forms applications, especially those that render sophisticated user interfaces or use third-party controls extensively. It will be easier with many of these applications to simply redevelop the user interface from scratch in Windows Forms, or to leave the applications in VB6.

But the biggest danger signal that a system is not suitable for migration is significant presence of old, obsolete syntax (such as Gosub or the other removed keywords listed earlier) and/or sloppy programming techniques such as using lots of GoTos. Such code may require a large amount of manual intervention to work at all, and the resulting code may be very difficult to maintain. (If the current code is a nightmare to maintain, the converted version is not likely to be any better!)

Impossible Migration

Some organizations will face situations in which migration is not a choice. For example, if the organization is using COM-based software for which it does not have access to the sourcecode, then that software cannot be migrated into .NET. Such software must either be replaced, or the new software developed in .NET must be interoperable with it.

Examples of such situations include:

- ❑ Third-party COM-based software for which the .NET upgrade is not yet available

- ❑ Third party COM-based software for which a .NET upgrade will never be available (because a vendor went out of business, for example)

- ❑ In-house COM-based software for which the sourcecode has been lost (don't laugh – it's more common than you might think)

Implications for Interoperability

The bottom line is that some fraction of systems will be impractical or impossible to migrate from VB6 to Visual Basic .NET. And if any part of an organization's systems is not to be migrated, it may be necessary to leave other supporting parts in VB6 also, even if those parts could be migrated.

An organization that wants to use .NET, but decides that some old systems can't be migrated, must find a way to make newly developed software work with older systems. The existing systems may be in place indefinitely, but a forward-thinking organization will not want to allow that fact to limit their ability to respond with new Internet-enabled software in .NET.

Even if the decision is made to migrate everything in an organization, this is more likely to be a long-term strategic decision. It will usually be impractical in large organizations to migrate everything at once. Some pieces will be migrated before other pieces and, during the transition period, interoperability will be necessary between old (unmigrated) systems, systems migrated to .NET, and systems newly written in .NET.

Design Situations that Need Interoperability

Given the expense of migration to .NET, some organizations may question whether it makes sense. But this must be balanced against the immense advantages that .NET confers. .NET offers several architectural options that are difficult or impractical to implement with existing tools. Foregoing these options can seriously risk an organization's competitive position.

.NET makes available architectural options that sometimes require interoperability with older systems. Here is a sampling of such cases.

Web Services

Microsoft has declared Web Services to be the most important single reason to use .NET. Even if you disagree with that assertion (as I do), there is no doubt that Web Services are going to be extremely important to many organizations.

The actual code inside a typical Web Service module is not likely to involve extensive processing or computation. Just as many Active Server Pages are mere wrappers for functionality in components running elsewhere, Web Services are also likely to be wrappers for other components. That way, the components performing the actual work can be on an application server, and are not weighing down the web server with their resource requirements.

The component used to supply the actual data exposed by a Web Service could easily be a COM component. There are many existing COM components that do useful processing of data for internal purposes, and the results may be appropriate to expose to external business partners through Web Services.

Web Services can be produced in Visual Studio 6 with the SOAP Toolkit. However, the amount of work required is significantly more than that needed to create a Web Service in .NET. Web Services in .NET also have access to the built-in capabilities of ASP.NET, such as security and caching. Any organization getting into Web Services in a big way will probably want to do so using .NET.

This may very well create a situation in which the best option for creating the Web Service is using .NET, but the best option for doing the actual processing is a COM component. In that case, interoperability between .NET and COM will be necessary.

Smart Clients

One of the lesser-known implications of .NET is the fact that it makes it much more practical to return to smart client architectures. In recent years, smart clients have given up considerable ground to browser-based interfaces. The main reason for this is the deployment cost of smart clients based on COM technologies. Deployment of COM-based software to client machines is quite expensive compared to the minimal deployment costs of web-based software viewed through a browser.

However, HTML-driven browsers are a major step back in terms of usability and friendliness. There are also fewer options for security. And creating browser-based interfaces with tools such as Active Server Pages requires more development effort than creating forms-based interfaces with VB.

.NET changes the economics of this situation by dramatically reducing the cost of deployment of forms-based interfaces. Once the .NET Framework is installed on a client, there are a number of inexpensive deployment options for forms-based smart client software. For a simple system, executable programs and DLLs can just be copied into a directory and run. Systems can also be run from a shared drive on a network. It is even possible for such software to be deployed completely from a web server, and to be version-checked and redeployed whenever changes are made.

In a sense, that means .NET offers the best of both worlds. Client software can be intelligent and usable, and can offload processing from the server, while still keeping deployment costs to acceptable levels.

The smart client capability of .NET will probably first be used in intranet scenarios. As the .NET Framework becomes more ubiquitous over the next year or two, smart clients can be extended to extranets and the general public.

Some of the earliest of these smart clients will need to access functionality that already exists. Existing n-tier systems may simply need a new presentation layer. These smart clients would then need to interoperate with a COM-based middle tier.

New ASP.NET Front Ends

One of the most impressive innovations in .NET is ASP.NET. As a means of creating web-based interfaces, ASP.NET is light years ahead of Active Server Pages. Some organizations are already reporting that they can produce a web front end in one third to one fifth of the time in ASP.NET that an equivalent project using Active Server Pages would require.

But, as with the smart client scenario, some ASP.NET front ends may need to be implemented on top of existing n-tier systems. The ASP.NET pages will therefore need to access a COM middle tier.

Extending Old Components

COM has no provision for inheritance. In the COM world, the only way to use inheritance is to go back to a source language such as C++. The inheritance capabilities are actually in the language, not in COM.

That means that extending an existing COM component with inheritance using VB6 is impossible. Various workarounds exist to wrap COM objects and create an entire new interface for them, but these techniques are clumsy, expensive to develop, and may impact on performance.

.NET, on the other hand, is completely object-oriented, and supports inheritance at the execution level. The wrapper assemblies used to provide COM interoperability in .NET can be inherited and extended. This gives new software the ability to use inheritance to extend the capabilities of COM components. (More detail on wrapper assemblies, called Runtime Callable Wrappers, is available in several later chapters in this book.)

Distributed Processing of Data

A major liability of server-based web-oriented software is the need for most data processing to take place on the server. Browser-based clients have limited capability to process or manipulate sets of data.

.NET includes a new data access and manipulation technology called ADO.NET. Combined with Web Services and smart clients, a new data manipulation architecture becomes available. It includes the following:

- ❑ Smart clients (on systems containing the .NET Framework) handle the user interface.
- ❑ Smart clients access data on the server via Web Services.
- ❑ Smart clients manipulate the data locally using ADO.NET.
- ❑ Data can be persisted on the client if necessary by saving it in XML.
- ❑ The changes in the data are communicated back to the server via another Web Service.

The databases involved in such an architecture may also need to serve older software through access technologies such as ADO. Or it may be necessary for middle-tier COM objects to access data via ADO, and then for Web Services to expose the data via ADO.NET. These scenarios would require interoperability for accessing and manipulating data.

Major Areas of Interoperability

As we've seen above, there are various types of interoperability that may be important in various circumstances. This book covers the most common interoperability situations, with technical advice on how to handle them.

Let's go over the major areas of interoperability covered in the book.

Calling COM Components from .NET

Using an existing middle tier in COM while developing new modules in .NET requires the .NET modules to call the COM components. This type of access is also needed to use ActiveX controls (OCX controls). In this type of interoperability, the COM interface must be wrapped within .NET and exposed as a .NET interface.

Chapters 2, 4, and 5 go over various aspects of this type of interoperability. Some of the more advanced topics concerned with such interoperability – threading, custom marshaling, and DCOM versus .NET Remoting – are covered in Chapters 6 to 8.

Calling .NET Components from COM

In some cases, it may be necessary to develop components in .NET that replace existing COM components. The old programs that used the COM components cannot then access the new .NET component directly. The new .NET component must expose a COM interface to enable these old programs to work with the new replacement component. Another kind of wrapper is used to provide this interface, known as a COM Callable Wrapper.

This type of interoperability is covered in Chapter 3.

Sharing Data Access Between Old Code and New

When new programs in .NET must operate at the same time as old COM programs, the two often must share the same underlying data stores. This is a form of interoperability. Some of these data sources may be relational, while others may involve older flat-file structures.

Also, while .NET offers a new data access model in the form of ADO.NET, this new model does not completely replace ADO. There are some capabilities of ADO that are not available in ADO.NET, such as pessimistic locking. If these capabilities are needed by new .NET programs, those programs must access ADO, which is COM-based. Developers need to understand how to use ADO inside .NET, and the minor differences that exist from using ADO in VB6.

Chapters 10 and 11 go into interoperability topics related to data access.

Sharing Configuration Information

A system that contains older COM-based modules and new .NET modules may need to have a central source of configuration information. It would be undesirable, for example, for the different types of software to use different activity logs. Both need to find out the location of activity logs from a single configuration source. Chapter 9 discusses the sharing of configuration information between .NET and COM, using either the Windows Registry, INI files, or XML-based configuration files.

Calling Non-COM DLLs with Static Entry Points

Some existing software is not COM-based. Older DLLs exist that use static entry points to their functions. The most prevalent examples are the DLLs containing the Windows API.

Using such DLLs from .NET is fairly straightforward. The syntax resembles that used in VB6 (although different operations are being carried out underneath). However, there are a few issues that developers need to be aware of for this type of interoperability, and Chapter 12 goes over these.

Wrapping Up

Migration strategies for organizations moving to Visual Basic .NET will vary a lot. In some cases, a wholesale conversion will be quite practical, and the organization can move totally to .NET-based software in a reasonable period of time.

However, the majority of organizations will need a more complex strategy. The transition period may be quite long, with a need for new software to interoperate with old during that period. In some cases, old COM-based software may be used indefinitely, requiring a long period of interoperability with .NET. For that majority of organizations, this book should provide some needed technical guidance on implementing interoperability between older software and .NET.

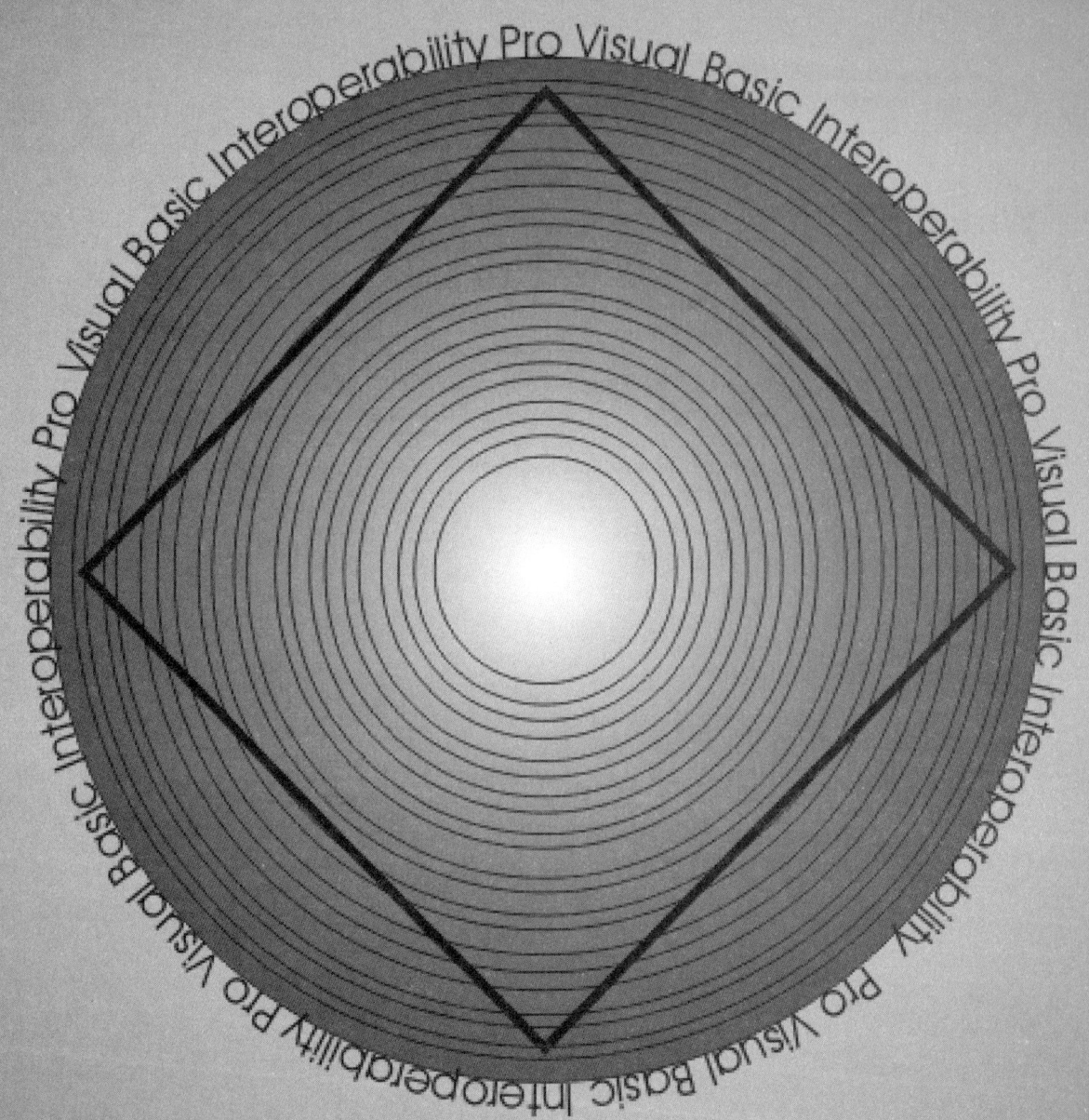

2

Using COM Components from .NET

As we move into the world of .NET, we leave behind a large amount of COM components and code. In most cases, we'll be unable to rewrite all of our existing COM code into .NET, and so we'll be left with the requirement to continue to use that COM code from within our new .NET applications and components. As we migrate VB6 code to Visual Basic .NET, we'll also have the need to call .NET assemblies from our existing VB6 applications.

The .NET environment provides extensive support for COM components, allowing us to take a COM component and expose it to our .NET applications as though it were a .NET component. This allows us to easily use our COM code while we move into the world of .NET. The .NET runtime also supports the reverse, allowing us to expose our .NET assemblies for use by VB6 applications – a topic we'll cover in Chapter 3.

Since COM and .NET are different technologies, the process of calling a COM component from within .NET means that we are communicating from the .NET platform back to the older COM platform. This imposes an overhead on our communication in terms of performance. It also puts some restrictions on the design of both the COM and .NET components involved in such interoperability, but is often well worth it in order to reuse existing code.

In this chapter we'll see how we can import a COM component into the .NET platform – making it available for use from .NET even though it remains a COM component running in the COM platform. We'll also see how we can examine the COM component's interfaces from our code. For most COM components and .NET applications, these capabilities will be sufficient.

Given the opportunity, however, we can design our COM components and interfaces to make them easier to deal with from a .NET perspective. In some cases, where we can't adapt our COM interfaces, we may need to manually perform some data marshaling between the two platforms by creating our own intermediate **wrapper** component – hopefully a rare occurrence, but one that we'll discuss in this chapter as well.

> *As we'll see, Visual Basic .NET can make use of most COM components. In theory, this means that any DLL we've created with VB4 or higher should be accessible from Visual Basic .NET. Obviously, code written in VB3 or earlier won't be accessible, because those versions of VB couldn't create COM components.*

VB developers are fortunate in that many of the truly complex issues that can arise when interacting with COM components from .NET won't typically occur if the COM components are built with VB. Unlike many components built with C++, VB tends to create components that are easily used from within .NET because they are OLE Automation-compliant.

COM Component Creation

The.NET environment, and Visual Studio .NET in particular, provide very good support for interoperability from .NET applications back to COM components. Using Visual Studio .NET, we can reference a COM DLL in much the same manner that we reference a .NET DLL – making the use of many COM DLLs almost transparent to our application.

In most cases, this built-in support will be sufficient to allow our new applications to use our existing components. There are some data types, especially when working with Variants in VB6, which may not work automatically. In such cases, we either need to create our own intermediate wrapper components so that Visual Basic .NET can receive supported data types, or we need to employ custom marshaling as discussed in Chapter 6.

Building a COM Component

Before we can use a COM component from within .NET, we need to have an existing COM component. In this section, we'll create a COM component by using VB6. During this process, we'll discuss some of the basic design decisions that we can make in our COM components that will make interoperability with .NET easier. Later in this chapter we'll discuss some of the more advanced – and less common – design issues that may come up.

Creating the Project

To start with, let's create a VB6 ActiveX DLL project named `Chapter2COM`. We could also create ActiveX EXE or ActiveX Control type projects, which also create COM components. These components can be made accessible to our .NET applications in much the same way as an ActiveX DLL. ActiveX EXE projects are discussed more completely in Chapter 7, while the use of ActiveX controls is covered in Chapter 13.

Project Properties

Use the Project | Properties menu option to change the project's name to Chapter2COM:

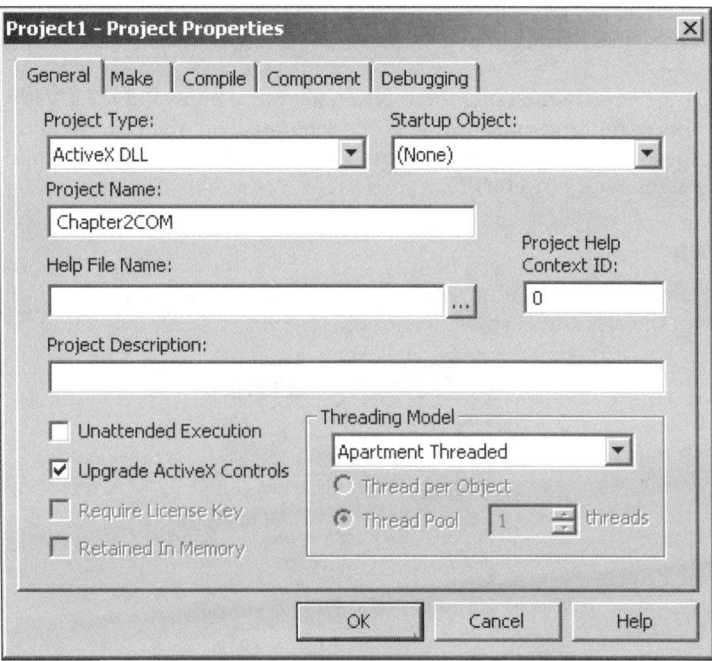

This dialog also includes some other options worth discussing from an interoperability perspective. When our COM component is invoked from .NET, it will still be running within the context of the COM platform, meaning that it will still be subject to the same rules and constraints as any other COM component. This means that our component will still be loaded into a COM apartment, and will be running on a thread initialized by COM – just as it would be were it invoked from a regular Windows application. For more information on threading and how it impacts interoperability, please refer to Chapter 7.

The Unattended Execution checkbox is useful for server-side components where we want to ensure that our component cannot bring up a dialog box to be displayed on the screen. In fact, any MsgBox statements will be written to the system's Application Log file automatically rather than being displayed on the screen. This box should be checked if our component will be used by server-side .NET applications as well. Whether the application using our component is a COM application or a .NET application, if it will be running on a server, we should check this box.

The Threading Model selection defaults to Apartment Threaded, meaning that our component can be used from a host process that has one or more COM apartments. This is the correct setting for use from .NET as well, since it provides the greatest flexibility and performance for our component. The other option is Single Threaded, which will *work* but does not offer the best functionality since it will cause all objects created from the component to run on one singe thread in one single COM apartment.

ActiveX EXE Considerations

If we were creating an ActiveX EXE project instead of an ActiveX DLL, we would have a couple of other options in the Project Properties dialog. In particular, in the Threading Model area, we could indicate that we want to have a Thread per Object, or we could choose to define a thread pool to contain a certain number of threads on which to run our objects. Again, we'll discuss this in more detail in Chapter 7.

These options operate exactly the same for a .NET client as they would for a VB6 client. Since an ActiveX EXE is always running in its own process, separate from the process of the application invoking the components, these threading options have no special impact on the client application – regardless of whether it is running in COM or in .NET.

Class Properties

By default, our project is started with a single class named Class1. Using the Properties window, change the name of the class to SimpleClass:

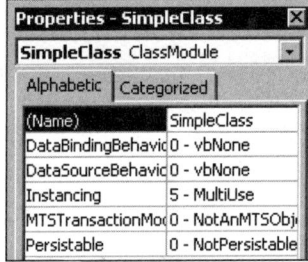

This means that the full name of our class will be Chapter2COM.SimpleClass, since the full name of a COM component is always the COM server name combined with the class name.

The DataBindingBehavior and DataSourceBehavior properties have no meaning for .NET, since data binding in .NET is different from data binding under COM. The value we set here will have no impact on how our component is used by Visual Basic .NET.

Likewise, the MTSTransactionMode property is used by MTS or COM+ as the component is put into a Package or Application, and has no impact on how .NET interacts with the component. Again, the value we set here will have no impact on how our component is used by Visual Basic .NET.

The Persistable property is used to indicate that our class should participate in COM-based serialization and allows us to create code within our class that converts our data into and out of a byte stream. This type of serialization is not the same as .NET serialization, and so this property is ignored as our class is imported into .NET. Again, the value we set here will have no impact on how our component is used by Visual Basic .NET.

The .NET Framework includes a concept called **serialization** *which is somewhat like the Persistable property from VB6. It is important to remember, however, that persistence in VB6 and serialization in Visual Basic .NET are two very different solutions to a similar problem and they can't directly interoperate.*

The Instancing property provides the same functionality from a .NET client as it does from a COM client. The following table indicates the how this option impacts on.NET:

Instancing	Description
Private	Not usable from .NET.
PublicNotCreatable	Usable from .NET, but only if created by code within the COM component. This is the same as when this component is used by a VB6 client, where the client cannot create an instance of the object, but the client can use it if the object is created by other code within the DLL.
Multiuse	Creatable and usable from .NET just like a regular .NET class.
GlobalMultiuse	Creatable and usable from .NET just like a regular .NET class. The normal behavior of a Global class in VB6 does *not* carry through – in .NET this is the same as regular Multiuse.

Typically, we'll want to use Multiuse – the default – when creating COM classes for use from within .NET.

Sub, Function, and Property Methods

We can now write the code that will provide the functionality of our class. Later in the chapter, we'll discuss multiple interfaces and how they impact on the process but, for now, let's work with the native interface of the class. The native interface of a class in VB6 is composed of the Sub, Function, and Property routines marked as Public within the class.

For instance, add the following code to the class:

```
Option Explicit

Public Function GetString() As String
  GetString = "A VB6 COM string"
End Function
```

This code defines GetString as being part of our native interface since it is declared as Public. It also provides implementation code for the function – in this case simply returning a fixed string as a result.

Routines that are scoped as Private or Friend are not part of the native interface of our class, and thus will not be available for use from our .NET client code. This makes sense, since those methods would not be available for use from a VB6 client application either.

The same scoping rules apply to both Sub and Property type methods. For instance, we can add a subroutine with the following code:

```
Public Sub DoSomething()
  Dim intIndex As Integer
  Dim lngSum As Long

  For intIndex = 1 To 1000
    lngSum = lngSum + intIndex
  Next
End Sub
```

Since it is declared as Public, it will be available for use by our .NET client.

Property Methods

The same is true for the following `Property` methods:

```
Private mintValue As Integer

Public Property Get Number() As Integer
   Number = mintValue
End Property

Public Property Let Number(value As Integer)
   mintValue = value
End Property
```

However, `Property` methods have some other interesting differences from VB6, since the concept of a `Property` method in .NET is not quite the same as it is in COM. In particular, this `Number` property defines a read-write `Integer` property on our class. If we want a read-only property, then only the `Get` part of the code should be `Public`:

```
Public Property Get Number() As Integer
   Number = mintValue
End Property

Friend Property Let Number(value As Integer)
   mintValue = value
End Property
```

By changing the `Let` to be of `Friend` scope, it is removed from the native interface of our class and so will not be available to .NET, just as though there were no `Let` routine at all. As we import this component into .NET, this property will be marked as a read-only property.

The same is true for write-only properties – where the `Get` part of the code must *not* be `Public`:

```
Friend Property Get Number() As Integer
   Number = mintValue
End Property

Public Property Let Number(value As Integer)
   mintValue = value
End Property
```

By making the `Get` inaccessible, but having the `Let` be `Public`, we've created a write-only property from the perspective of our .NET code.

For the purposes of our example code, let's make sure that both `Get` and `Let` are `Public`:

```
Public Property Get Number() As Integer
   Number = mintValue
End Property

Public Property Let Number(value As Integer)
   mintValue = value
End Property
```

This ensures that we are creating a read/write property for use by our .NET client application.

Events

We can also raise events from within our code. For instance, we can declare an event within our `SimpleClass`:

```
Public Event COMevent()
```

Then we can add a method that will raise the event:

```
Public Sub RaiseTheEvent()
   RaiseEvent COMevent
End Sub
```

This provides us with a way to trigger the raising of the event from our .NET client application to illustrate how events work.

As we'll see, the process of importing the COM component for use by .NET code will automatically translate the COM events back into the .NET event model, providing us with transparency – the COM events will appear as though they were raised by a normal .NET object.

Passing Data

Our `GetString` method returns a `String` value as a result. Most methods accept or return some sort of data, and there are rules that govern how that data is moved from .NET to COM and back again.

Data Passing Rules

Some data types are **blittable** types, meaning that they require no data conversion between the COM and .NET platforms. They are sometimes referred to as **isomorphic** types, since they have the same representation in memory in COM as they do in .NET.

Other data types *do* require conversion, as they are not represented in the same way in .NET as they are in COM. These are called **non-blittable** or **non-isomorphic** types. Since they may have different representations in memory between COM and .NET, they often require conversion as the data is moved from one platform to the other.

Though we'll discuss the intricacies of these types later in the chapter, it is important to understand the basics now.

Blittable types offer substantially better performance for interoperation than non-blittable types. This is because a blittable type can be simply copied, while a non-blittable type might need conversion from the COM representation into a .NET representation and visa versa before the data can be transferred across platforms.

Blittable types available to VB programmers include:

VB6	Visual Basic .NET
Byte	Byte
Integer	Short
Long	Integer
Single	Single
Double	Double

Remember that the VB6 Integer is a Visual Basic .NET Short, and the VB6 Long is a Visual Basic .NET Integer.

Visual Basic .NET also includes the Long data type, which represents a 64-bit integer value. This data type is also blittable, though there is no equivalent to the data type in VB6. 64-bit integer values are supported by some other unmanaged languages, and so may be used when working with COM components built with those languages.

Additionally, single-dimension arrays of a blittable type are considered blittable. This means that we could declare the following in VB6:

```
Public arData(5) As Integer
```

and this would be blittable data, offering the same performance benefits.

Common non-blittable data types used by VB programmers include:

VB6	Visual Basic .NET
String	String
Date	Date
Boolean	Boolean
User-defined type	Structure
Variant	Object
Object	Object
<specific class>	<specific class>

Basically, any data type that is non-numeric or contains two or more data elements will be non-blittable, and will require conversion as the data is moved from one platform to the other. This includes any multi-dimensional array, regardless of the underlying data type of the data within the array.

Non-blittable types are represented differently in memory in COM from in .NET or, sometimes, they have multiple representations in memory in COM and so it is ambiguous as to how they would be converted or represented in .NET. For instance, a `String` data type in .NET may be represented in Windows or COM using a wide variety of formats – some ANSI, some UNICODE, some following the BSTR format used by VB6, and some following a null-terminated format favored by C-style languages. Given this ambiguity, the `String` data type often requires some conversion.

Completing the Code

To see how each of the blittable and non-blittable VB6 types is represented in .NET, we'll add code to exercise every option. First off, add the following code to return all of the various blittable data types:

```
' Blittable types
Public Function GetByte() As Byte
   GetByte = 65
End Function

Public Function GetInteger() As Integer
   GetInteger = 42
End Function

Public Function GetLong() As Long
   GetLong = 4242
End Function

Public Function GetSingle() As Single
   GetSingle = 42.42
End Function

Public Function GetDouble() As Double
   GetDouble = 4242.4242
End Function

Public Function GetSimpleArray() As Integer()
   Dim ar(5) As Integer

   ar(0) = 5
   ar(1) = 4
   ar(2) = 3
   ar(3) = 2
   ar(4) = 1
   ar(5) = 0
   GetSimpleArray = ar
End Function
```

Then we'll add a user-defined type (UDT) declaration so we can see how a complex data type is handled. Add the following to the top of the class:

```
Option Explicit

' User-defined type declaration
Public Type ComplexData
   Name As String
```

```
    Birthdate As Date
End Type
```

Finally, we'll add code to return all the common non-blittable data types, including returning data of type ComplexData:

```
' Non-blittable types
Public Function GetString() As String
   GetString = "A VB6 COM string"
End Function

Public Function GetDate() As Date
   GetDate = Now
End Function

Public Function GetBoolean() As Boolean
   GetBoolean = False
End Function

Public Function GetComplex() As ComplexData
   Dim var As ComplexData

   var.Name = "Fred"
   var.Birthdate = "1/1/1960"
   GetComplex = var
End Function

Public Function GetVariant() As Variant
   GetVariant = Now
End Function

Public Function GetObject() As Object
   Set GetObject = New SimpleClass
End Function

Public Function GetSimpleClass() As SimpleClass
   Set GetObject = New SimpleClass
End Function

Public Function GetComplexArray() As Integer()
   Dim ar(1, 1) As Integer

   ar(0, 0) = 5
   ar(1, 0) = 4
   ar(0, 1) = 3
   ar(1, 1) = 2
   GetComplexArray = ar
End Function
```

At this point, we have a COM component with a single class that returns all of the types of data that are typically used in a VB6 application.

ByVal and ByRef

So far, we've been looking at data returned from functions. However, we can also accept data as parameters to our methods. The data *types* remain the same and are subject to the same conversion rules that we discussed earlier for blittable and non-blittable data. Obviously, they are faster if they are blittable than if they are non-blittable. However, with parameters, we also need to take into account whether the data will be passed by value or by reference.

> *Remember that VB6 defaults to passing parameters by reference (ByRef), while Visual Basic .NET defaults to passing parameters by value (ByVal).*

Blittable data types that are passed using the ByVal keyword cause the data to be *copied* across the platform boundary.

The following VB6 code illustrates this syntax:

```
Public Sub BlittableByValue(ByVal Value As Long)

End Sub
```

In this case, the COM code gets a copy of the original value and has no access to the memory containing the actual underlying data. Even if the data is changed by the code in the method, the value is not copied back and so it is not possible for this code to alter the original value.

Blittable data types that are passed using the ByRef keyword provide the COM code with a pointer to the actual memory location of the underlying data, as illustrated by the following code:

```
Public Sub BlittableByReference(ByRef Value As Long)

End Sub
```

This means that any change to the data made by the COM code will directly and immediately alter the value of the underlying data for both the COM and .NET code in our application.

In either case, the .NET code passes data to the COM code – either the data itself or a pointer to the data, which is itself essentially a 32-bit integer value under Win32 or a 64-bit value under Win64. This means that there is no significant performance difference between passing blittable data types by value as opposed to by reference.

The rules for non-blittable data are a bit different, and there can be a performance gain by using ByVal when possible.

When a non-blittable data value is passed using the ByVal keyword, the data is copied across the platform boundary, just as it was with a blittable data type. The following code shows the syntax for such a method:

```
Public Sub NonblittableByValue(ByVal Value As String)

End Sub
```

The COM code gets a copy of the original value – after any necessary conversions from .NET format to COM format have occurred. Since any changes to `ByVal` data are ignored, the data is *not* copied back from the COM platform to the .NET platform when the method call is complete – the copy process is a one-way thing from .NET to COM.

Since the underlying data structure or format of non-blittable data may be different between COM and .NET, it is not possible to pass a pointer to the memory containing the underlying data. This means that, even when a non-blittable data value is passed by reference, the underlying data is copied – and possibly converted – before a pointer is created. The pointer then points to the memory that contains the converted data.

We can pass a non-blittable data element with code such as:

```
Public Sub NonblittableByReference(ByRef Value As String)

End Sub
```

This copy process is essentially the same as when the data is passed by value – with the important difference that the data is *also copied back* to .NET, and is converted again if necessary. When a non-blittable value is passed by reference, it will be copied twice – a copy from .NET to COM and then another copy to get the potentially changed value back from COM to .NET. The data is copied back to the calling code whether it has been changed or not, so it is important to only pass data by reference when we really need the value returned.

This process is highly optimized, but there is a performance impact. For most client applications this will be a non-issue but, for server-side components or other applications where thousands of method calls are being made within a loop, this could become problematic. In such cases, it may be necessary to consider migrating the code entirely into .NET to avoid the overhead of the conversion process.

Modules

In VB6 COM components, we often place `Public` constants, `Types`, `Enums`, or even `Public` variable declarations in a Module. Code in a Module is not part of the COM type library of the component and so it is not made available for use from .NET, though, obviously, it remains available for use by code within the COM component itself. For any of these items to be available for use by a .NET client, the declarations must be made within a class module in our project.

For instance, if we want to create an `Enum` to be useable from within .NET, we need to add it to a class.

> *Keep in mind that such a change will alter the component's interface and could lead to version compatibility issues.*

We could add the following code to `SimpleClass`:

```
Public Enum Depth
  VeryDeep
  Deep
  Shallow
End Enum
```

This Enum will be made available as a data type within .NET when our COM component is imported.

Now build the project to create the DLL.

Binary Compatibility

One of the big advantages that .NET offers over COM is that it gets away from central registration of components and classes, and the use of GUID values such as CLSIDs, and generally avoids a lot of the fragility that exists with COM components. This fragility expresses itself to the VB6 developer through the use of Binary Compatibility in the Project Properties dialog:

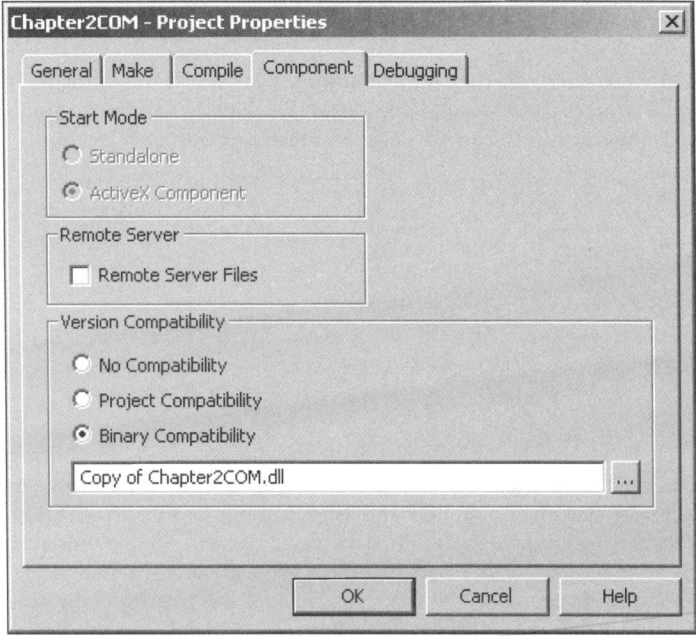

If we don't set this option properly then, every time we recompile our COM DLL, it will be assigned new GUID values – meaning that any early bound client applications using the component will cease to function until they are updated to recognize the new GUID values.

Before we can turn on Binary Compatibility, we need to have compiled our component at least once. This is because binary compatibility will ensure that our code is compatible with an existing DLL – and so we need a pre-compiled DLL against which to make this comparison.

When we do set Binary Compatibility, it should be set against a *copy* of the DLL, not against the DLL we'll be compiling over. By setting it to a copy, we are ensuring that our CLSID and component interface data will remain consistent, compile after compile. Were we to set compatibility to the DLL that we're overwriting with our compile, there would be a danger of overwriting the DLL with an incompatible version – creating incompatible versions from there onwards.

It is important to remember to update the copy in the case that we *do* choose to break compatibility and change the interface. We also need to update the copy any time we add new classes or methods to the DLL so that those new elements remain compatible from there on.

> Binary compatibility is very import for .NET interoperability, since the CLSID values that identify our component will be captured when we import the component into .NET. Any subsequent changes to the component's CLSID values will cause our .NET applications to fail when they attempt to access the component – meaning we'll need to re-import the COM DLL for use by .NET.

Importing COM Components

Now that we've explored the issues involved in creating a VB6 COM component for use by .NET, let's move on and see what options exist for actually importing that component into the .NET environment.

Of course, the COM component itself never actually runs in the .NET platform – the import process merely creates a .NET wrapper class that allows our .NET code to call back into the COM platform to interact with the component. The following diagram illustrates this:

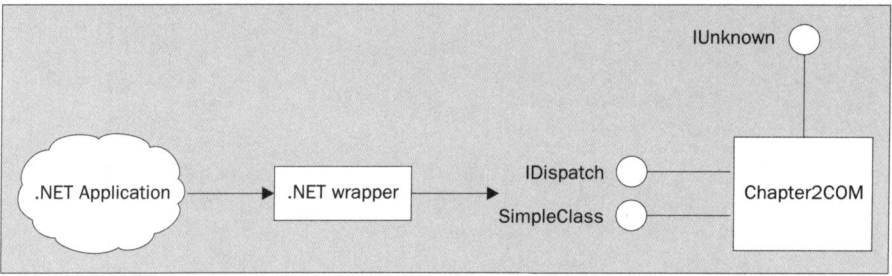

Our .NET application can't talk directly to the COM component. Instead, a **runtime-callable wrapper** (RCW) assembly is created that gives our .NET application the illusion that the COM component is actually a .NET assembly. This wrapper exposes all of the data types, classes, and methods available from the COM component, but they are exposed as .NET data types, classes, and methods. Any time that our application makes calls to these classes and methods, the wrapper assembly delegates the calls back into the COM platform and invokes the underlying COM component on our behalf. It also invokes any code necessary to perform conversions of the data as it is moved from one platform to the other.

The key to making a COM component available for use by a .NET application is the creation of the RCW. We can do this at design time, when we are building our application, or dynamically at run time when our application is being used. Generating the RCW at run time can provide us with a higher degree of flexibility since we can invoke DLLs that we don't have access to at design time.

In most cases, we'll create the wrapper at design time, so let's look at the ways that this is supported.

Importing During Design

There are three ways to import a COM component at design time.

❑   We can use Visual Studio .NET to import the COM component

❑   We can use a command-line utility to create the RCW

❑   We can create a primary interop assembly for the COM DLL

Using Visual Studio .NET is the easiest and most direct approach, and is good when we plan only to use the COM DLL from a single .NET application. If we plan to use the component from many .NET applications, we should create a primary interop assembly.

The command-line approach requires some extra work on our part, but allows us to tap into more options and functionality – something we'll use extensively later in the book. This option is typically used if we're not using Visual Studio .NET at all, but rather are using a text editor such as Notepad. Again, if we plan to use the COM component from many .NET applications, we should create a primary interop assembly for the component.

Primary interop assemblies provide a centralized location where any .NET application can reference the COM component. They are listed in the **Add Reference** dialog in Visual Studio .NET, so they are simple to use once they are created.

Let's walk through each of these options.

Visual Studio .NET

Visual Studio .NET provides very strong built-in support for working with COM components from our .NET applications. In fact, using a COM component is typically as simple as adding a reference to the component to our project.

To see this in action, open up Visual Studio .NET and create a new Windows Application named `Chapter2Net`.

Choose the **Project | Add References** menu option to bring up the references dialog. This dialog has three tabs – including one for COM. Click that tab and then wait. It takes a while for the dialog to scan the Windows registry to find all of the COM components on a machine. Once the list is populated, we can scroll down to our `Chapter2COM` component and double-click it to add it to our new reference list:

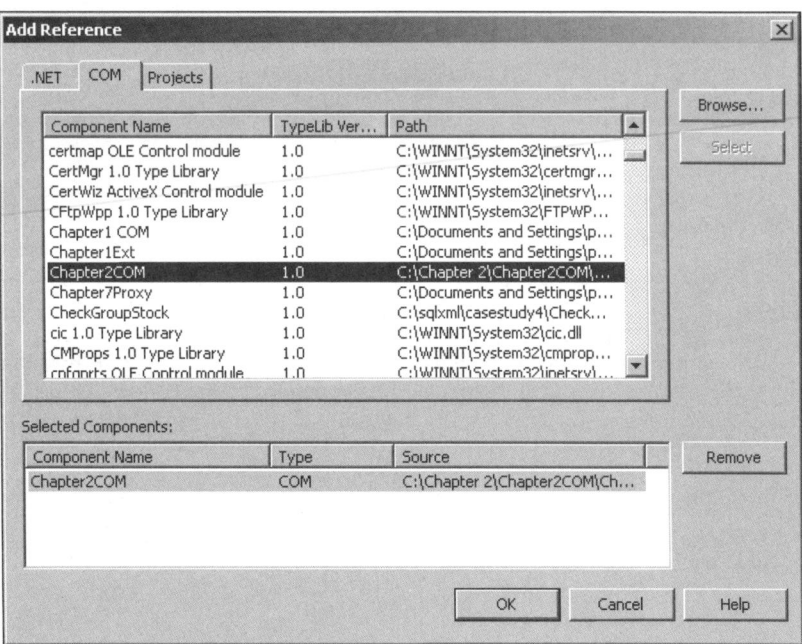

Notice that the version number of the component's type library is listed. The version number we typically think of when we think of a COM component is the component version number that we find in the VB6 Project Properties dialog. When referencing a component, however, the more important version number is the one that we don't typically see – and that is the automatically generated type library version number. This is created when our component is compiled, and reflects the number of revisions made to our component's interface.

> **Any time that our COM component's interface is changed, the existing RCW will become invalid and will need to be recreated. This is the reason why it is so important to use Binary Compatibility on our COM component to ensure that its CLSID, interface, and type library don't change over time.**

When we click OK, a reference to the component will be added to our project. Behind the scenes, Visual Studio .NET also creates and compiles the RCW and adds it to our project as a hidden file. We can see the DLL that is created within the Solution Explorer if we turn on the option to see all files. This is done via the Show All Files icon in the Solution Explorer's toolbar:

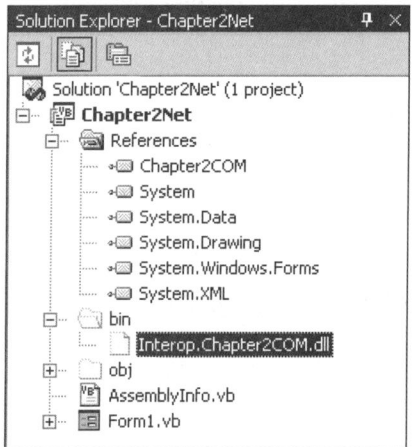

Here we see the Solution Explorer with Chapter2COM as one of our project's references. Since the Show All Files button is selected, we can also see files that would normally be hidden, such as a DLL. This means that we can see the Interop.Chapter2COM.dll file, which is the .NET wrapper for our COM component.

Now that the COM component has been referenced by our project, we can use it from within our code. We can also use the standard Object Browser to look at the component. Use the View | Other Windows | Object Browser menu option to bring up the browser and navigate to the Interop.Chapter2COM assembly:

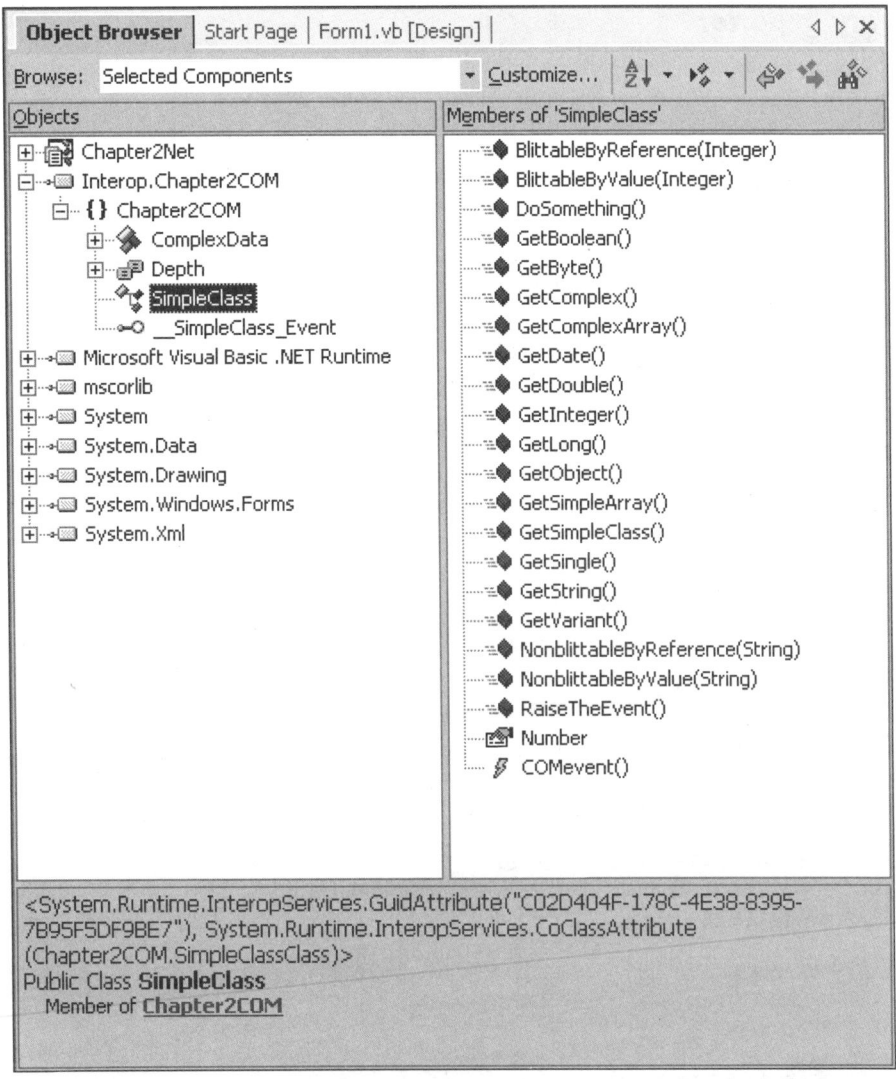

Within the assembly, we see a Chapter2COM namespace that contains our SimpleClass. It also contains the Depth Enum and a Structure representing our ComplexData UDT, along with an interface for our event. This event interface is an implementation detail that doesn't concern us directly but, rather, is used by the .NET interop mechanism to handle event processing on our behalf.

While we're now ready to write code to use our COM component, let's remove this reference and take a look at the command-line approach to importing a COM component for use by .NET. To remove the reference, right-click on the Chapter2COM reference in the Solution Explorer and choose Remove.

Type Library Importer

While most people will probably use the built-in capabilities of Visual Studio .NET when importing a COM component, there is an alternative in the form of a command-line utility named TlbImp.exe. This program can be used to create a wrapper DLL just like the one automatically created by Visual Studio .NET.

> *As we'll see in Chapter 6, sometimes it is necessary to use this manual approach because it allows us to tap into features that aren't available directly through Visual Studio .NET.*

One advantage to using the command-line utility rather than the Visual Studio .NET support is that we can create a single .NET wrapper DLL that can be used by any .NET application that uses the COM component. When Visual Studio .NET creates the wrapper, it is created as part of our specific .NET project but, when we create the wrapper DLL by hand, we can more easily share it across all of our .NET projects.

> *It is also possible to simply copy the wrapper DLL created by Visual Studio .NET into a central location and use it as well, but we lose the advantages of control and the ability to create a primary interop assembly, as we'll discuss shortly.*

Another advantage to the command-line utility approach is that we can use the COM component from .NET applications that we are creating without the use of Visual Studio .NET. We might be using a simple text editor or some other specialized development tool outside of Visual Studio .NET, and it is reassuring to know that we can still easily access COM components when needed.

The TlbImp.exe utility is typically located in:

```
C:\Program Files\Microsoft Visual Studio .NET\FrameworkSDK\Bin\TlbImp.exe
```

To avoid having to worry about this path, there is a special menu option that we can use to open the command window. Look under Start | Programs | Microsoft Visual Studio .NET | Visual Studio .NET Tools | Visual Studio .NET Command Prompt.

To import a COM DLL using TlbImp, we need to navigate to the directory where the DLL resides on disk. For instance, the following screenshot shows a command window where we've navigated to the directory containing our Chapter2COM project:

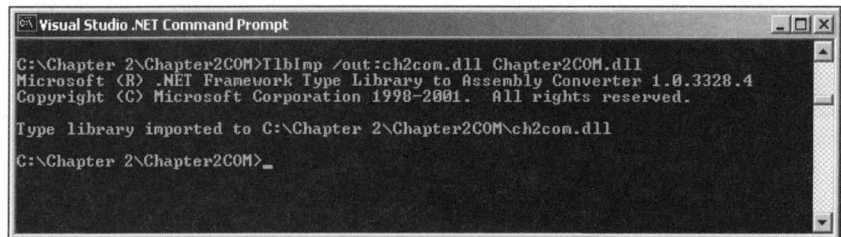

The TlbImp application is run with a simple command-line entry:

```
tlbimp /out:ch2com.dll Chapter2COM.dll
```

There are a number of other options available as well, but this is the command that creates a simple wrapper similar to that created automatically by Visual Studio .NET – in this case the wrapper is named ch2com.dll.

We can add a reference to this wrapper assembly within Visual Studio .NET or from the command-line compiler.

Using the Wrapper from Visual Studio .NET

Visual Studio .NET allows us to add references to any .NET assembly on disk. Within the Chapter2Net project, choose **Project | Add Reference**. Then click the **Browse** button and navigate to the ch2com.dll assembly file and select it.

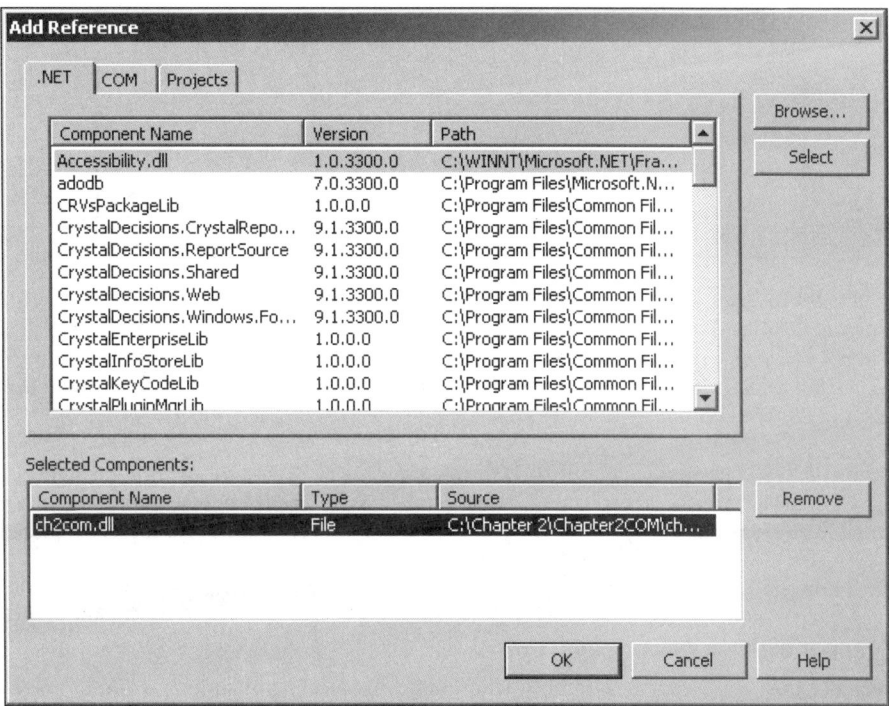

When we click **OK**, a reference to ch2com.dll will be added to our project. Notice that we are adding a reference to a .NET assembly here, not to a COM component. This is because we've already created the RCW and we're simply using it from our application, rather than having Visual Studio .NET create a new one on our behalf.

The ch2com.dll file will be copied to our project's bin directory automatically by Visual Studio .NET. We know that Visual Studio .NET is automatically making a copy of the assembly for our application's use due to the Copy Local property. If we select the **ch2com** entry in the Solution Explorer we can see its properties:

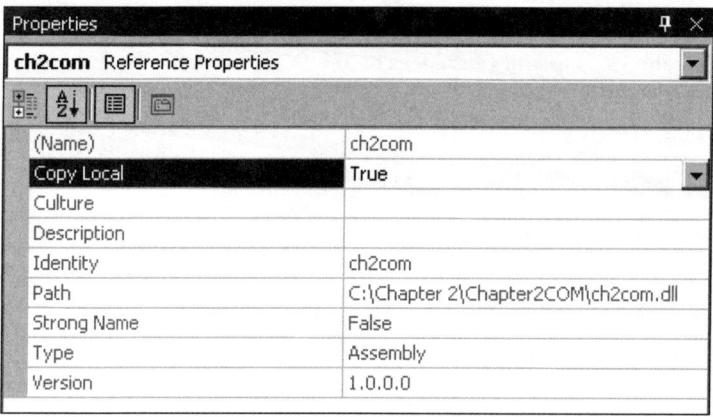

Copy Local is set to True – indicating that our application will get a copy of the assembly for its use. This setting needs to be True unless the assembly is in the .NET Global Assembly Cache – a topic we'll discuss when we create a primary interop assembly. This has no impact on the location of the COM DLL *itself*, as that DLL is located through the use of the Windows registry just like any other COM DLL. Only the RCW is copied.

Since ch2com.dll is a pre-built assembly on our machine, we can reuse this wrapper assembly from any number of .NET projects, rather than having Visual Studio .NET create a new wrapper for each project. Keep in mind, however, that each project will get its own copy of the DLL, so it isn't really shared.

Now let's see how we can reference a wrapper assembly in the case that we are not using Visual Studio .NET.

Using the Wrapper without Visual Studio .NET

We can also use this new wrapper assembly when building .NET applications without Visual Studio .NET. For instance, we could create a simple command-line application in Notepad (or any other text editor) with the following code:

```
Imports System.Console
Imports ch2com

Public Class TheApp
  Public Shared Sub Main()
    Dim obj As New SimpleClass()

    WriteLine(obj.GetString)
  End Sub

End Class
```

Notice the statement that imports the ch2com namespace. The namespace is named the same as the wrapper assembly we created with the TlbImp command-line utility, so it will vary if we change the output name on the command line.

Save this into a file named cmdtest.vb.

Before we can make use of the RCW, we need to copy it to the directory where we saved the `cmdtest.vb` file. We can then use the VB command-line compiler to compile the application with the following line:

```
vbc cmdtest.vb /r:ch2com.dll
```

The key to success here is the `/r` switch, which indicates that we're referencing another assembly as we compile – in this case the `ch2com.dll` assembly.

Primary Interop Assemblies

The wrapper we just created is virtually identical to the wrapper that would be created by Visual Studio .NET automatically. If we know that we'll be using a COM DLL from a number of .NET applications, we may want to be able to create a wrapper once and reuse it across several applications. In such a case, we want to create a special type of wrapper assembly called a **primary interop assembly**.

A primary interop assembly provides a shared and more reliable wrapper for the COM DLL. This type of assembly is identified as coming from the publisher of the COM DLL and is automatically listed within Visual Studio .NET in the Add References dialog.

> **It is highly recommended that any widely used COM component have a primary interop assembly to help manage the RCW and more easily keep it in sync with the underlying component.**

Though we must do some extra work to create a primary interop assembly, it is well worth it. By taking these steps, we are creating an assembly that is strongly linked to the underlying COM component and that is centrally available and shared by all .NET applications that wish to use that component.

This assembly should only be created by the publisher of the original COM DLL, as it must be signed using a publisher key, which should correspond to the publisher of the COM DLL. This type of signing gives the assembly a **strong name** – meaning it can be uniquely identified not only by version number, but also by publisher.

To create a primary interop assembly, we must take the following steps:

- ❑ Find or create a key file for strong naming
- ❑ Create the RCW as a primary interop assembly
- ❑ Place the RCW in the `Primary Interop Assemblies` directory
- ❑ Register the RCW in the Global Assembly Cache

Let's walk through these steps.

Creating a Strong Name

A strong name allows the .NET runtime to uniquely identify the assembly – even if there are other assemblies with the same filename and version on the system.

A strong name consists of the assembly's file name, its version number, and the public key of the publisher. This public key is part of a public-private key pair and is the same basic technology used to sign electronic mail, ActiveX components, and so forth. Unlike with ActiveX control signing, however, the public-private keys used for signing in .NET aren't verified by a reliable third party such as Versign.

The purpose of signing an assembly with our key is not to guarantee our identity to others but, rather, it is done to ensure a unique strong name for our assembly.

When we reference a COM component in Visual Studio .NET, we have very little control over the process of generating the wrapper assembly. However, when we use the `TlbImp` command-line utility, we can easily ensure that the wrapper assembly has a strong name so it can be inserted into the GAC.

Before we can build our assembly with a strong name, we need to have a public-private key pair with which to sign the assembly. The .NET Framework SDK comes with a command-line utility that we can use to generate keys for this purpose – `sn.exe`.

> **It is recommended that every organization generate a single public-private key pair and consistently use that private key to sign all of their assemblies.**

The command to create a keyfile containing a public-private key pair is:

```
sn -k outfile
```

The private key that this generates can be used to sign our assemblies, providing a unique strong name for them even when another publisher uses the same filename for an assembly.

The key file generated by this process should be kept in a safe place and only used by the organization that generated it. It is the uniqueness of this key that ensures that no other publisher can create the same strong name for an assembly as we do with our key.

In our case, we can generate a key for use in signing the `ch2com.dll` assembly with the following command:

```
sn -k mykey.snk
```

This will create a file named `mykey.snk`, which we can use as a parameter to `TlbImp` so it creates our wrapper class with a strong name. The command to do this is:

```
tlbimp /out:ch2com.dll chapter2com.dll /keyfile:mykey.snk
```

When we execute this command, we will generate a wrapper assembly named `ch2com.dll` with a strong name that incorporates our newly generated key. Again, we should store this key in a safe place and use it to sign any future assemblies that require a strong name – it uniquely identifies us as the publisher for any assembly.

Creating a Primary Interop Assembly

Now our RCW has a strong name – but it isn't a primary interop assembly yet. The TlbImp utility also includes the /primary switch, which will cause the assembly to be marked as a primary interop assembly. To use this, invoke the following command:

```
tlbimp /out:ch2com.dll chapter2com.dll /keyfile:mykey.snk /primary
```

This not only gives the assembly a strong name, but also marks it as a primary interop assembly.

The Primary Interop Assemblies Directory

Primary interop assemblies are typically located in a specific directory. By being placed in this directory, Visual Studio .NET will automatically list the assemblies when we bring up the Add Reference dialog.

Copy ch2com.dll to C:\Program Files\Microsoft.NET\Primary Interop Assemblies.

> *Obviously, the specific location of this directory may vary depending on the configuration of individual machines.*

At this point, we have a fully functional primary interop assembly, but it is not yet configured to be shared by all .NET client applications. To share an assembly we need to make use of the Global Assembly Cache.

The Global Assembly Cache

As we've discussed, importing a COM component for use by .NET doesn't really make the COM code run in the .NET environment – it still runs in the COM platform and is bound by the rules of that environment.

One key element of the COM environment is that COM components are registered at the machine level. This means that all applications on the machine will always invoke exactly the same DLL from the same directory. This is true for COM components when we call them from a .NET application as well – all .NET applications call into the same underlying COM component – whichever one is registered on the machine where the application is running.

> *If it hasn't been clear to this point – the COM component must be registered on the machine for a .NET application to use it. This is the same as if any other client tried to use the component – it won't work if it isn't registered.*

Normally, .NET assemblies follow different rules. A typical .NET assembly resides in the same physical directory as the application that is using it. Each application using an assembly has its own copy of the assembly – each independent from the others, which is why we've been copying the ch2com.dll file into our project directory so far.

.NET does have a concept that is similar to the COM idea of a component being available machine-wide, however. This is the **Global Assembly Cache** (GAC), which is a machine-wide repository of .NET assemblies. These assemblies are shared across all applications on the machine and all applications use the same assembly – just like all COM applications on a machine use the same COM component.

When we create a .NET wrapper class for a COM component, that wrapper class always refers to the underlying COM component. If we create several applications, each with their own wrapper assembly, all of those wrapper assemblies will refer back to exactly the same COM component.

Essentially, we are mixing conceptual models. Our .NET applications *think* that they each have an independent assembly (the wrapper) when, in reality, they are all sharing the same underlying COM component. To avoid any confusion, it is a good idea to put the .NET wrapper assembly into the .NET GAC – thus providing a single wrapper assembly for use by all applications on the machine. This single wrapper assembly then refers to the single underlying COM component.

Before an assembly can be placed in the GAC, it must have a strong name so that it can be uniquely identified, not only by filename, but also by publisher and version number. Our primary interop assembly already has a strong name, so we are all set in that regard.

To register the RCW in the GAC, we use the `gacutil.exe` command-line utility. Open a Visual Studio .NET command prompt and navigate to the `Primary Interop Assemblies` directory. Then enter the following:

```
gacutil /i ch2com.dll
```

This will register the assembly with the GAC, making it available for use by all applications on this machine.

> *It is often a good idea to create a BAT file that contains the instructions necessary to create the RCW, copy it to the* `Primary Interop Assemblies` *directory, and register it with the GAC – making it easier to update the files in the case that the COM component's interface needs to be changed.*

We'll also need to add the assembly to the GAC on any machine where our application will be installed.

Adding an assembly to the GAC is very comparable to registering a COM component in the registry – it becomes a machine-wide shared resource.

We can now use the assembly from the GAC without having to have a local copy of the DLL in our application's directory. This makes a lot of sense, since we don't have a local copy of the underlying COM component, so why should we have a local copy of the wrapper assembly?

Using the Primary Interop Assembly from Visual Studio .NET

We can now use `ch2com.dll` as a primary interop assembly from within a .NET application. Within Visual Studio .NET, we can directly reference this wrapper DLL from our projects. This is a bit different from referencing the COM component itself, since now we're referencing a pre-built .NET assembly.

Return to Visual Studio .NET and the `Chapter2Net` project. Remove any existing reference to `ch2com.dll` and then use the Project | Add References menu option to bring up the references dialog:

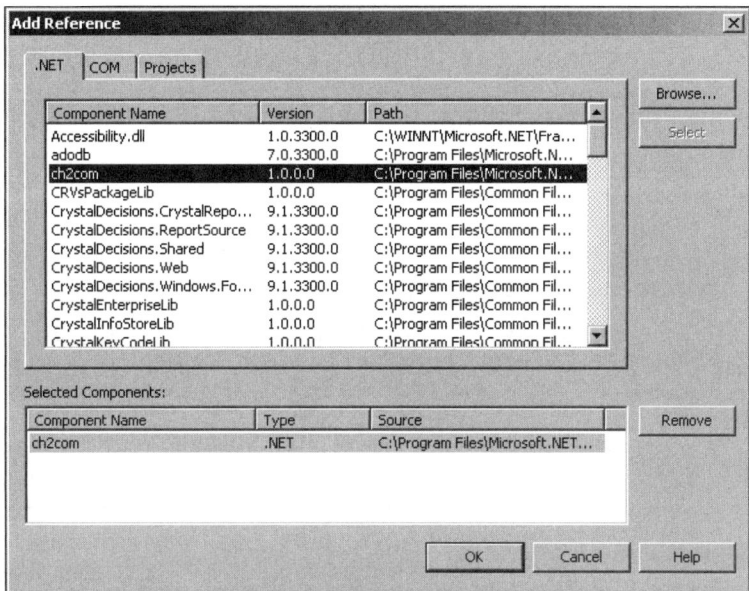

The **.NET** tab in this dialog lists the .NET assemblies available for use in our application. Since ch2com.dll is a primary interop assembly, it is listed right here in the dialog – requiring no extra work on our part to locate and use.

With ch2com.dll as one of our selected components, when we click **OK**, a reference to this assembly will be added to our project. At this point, we are ready to use the component from within our code – the same as if we'd imported the COM component directly using Visual Studio .NET.

However, we are now using a *shared* version of the assembly. If we click on the reference in the Solution Explorer, we can see the properties listed:

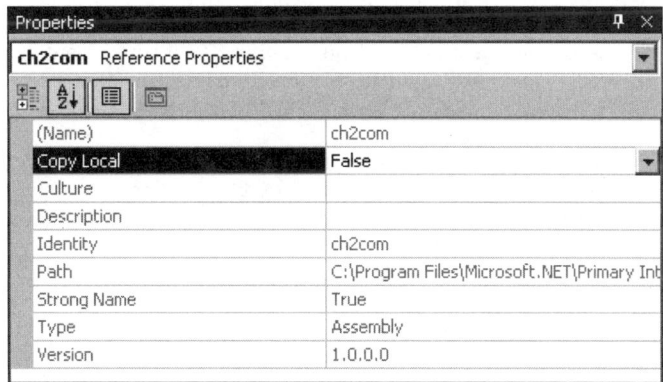

Notice that the **Copy Local** property is set to **False** – indicating that no local copy is made but, rather, that we are using the shared version in the GAC.

Using the Primary Interop Assembly without Visual Studio .NET

Earlier, we created a file named `cmdtest.vb` that made use of our `ch2com.dll` RCW, but we had to copy that DLL into our application directory for it to work. This is no longer the case since `ch2com.dll` is now a primary interop assembly that is registered in the GAC.

In a command window, navigate to the directory that contains `cmdtest.vb` and delete the `ch2com.dll` file located there. Then enter the following command:

```
vbc cmdtest.vb /r:ch2com.dll /libpath:"c:\program files\microsoft.net\primary
interop assemblies"
```

This is very similar to the command we entered earlier, with the addition of a `libpath` option. This is needed so that the compiler can find the `ch2com.dll` assembly to use as a reference. It doesn't copy it to the local directory, however, but, since it is shared in the GAC, our application will work just fine.

While there is some extra work involved in creating a primary interop assembly, it is typically worth it. A primary interop assembly is more integrated into Visual Studio .NET so it is simpler to use. More importantly, it provides a central point where we can update the RCW if our COM component's interface changes over time.

Handling Dependencies

So far, we've been looking at the simple case – a COM component that is not dependent on any other COM components. Most projects involve COM components that do have dependencies on other COM components, however, and we have to be aware of this when importing these components.

If we reference a COM component that has dependencies, things can get a bit more complex. Sometimes, the COM component we are talking to will make use of other COM components behind the scenes – with our Visual Basic .NET code never directly interacting with the other components. Other times, the COM component we're talking to may provide us with references to objects that come from other COM components.

When we talk to a COM component and it, in turn, talks to other COM components behind the scenes, we don't need a reference from our .NET application to the other components – nor do they need an RCW.

In the case where we get a reference to an object from another COM component, that component must have a wrapper assembly and our Visual Basic .NET project needs to reference that wrapper. This makes sense, since an RCW is needed any time that we want to make use of a COM component from .NET.

Visual Studio .NET will automatically add appropriate references – including creating appropriate wrapper assemblies – if we use it to directly reference a COM component that returns references to objects from another component. If we are creating the wrapper assemblies manually, then we'll need to create the appropriate RCW for each component.

Creating a Dependency

Make a second VB6 ActiveX DLL project named `Chapter2Ext`, which contains a single class named `ExtClass` with the following code:

```
Option Explicit

Public Function GetString() As String
```

```
     GetString = "This is an external string"
   End Function
```

If we compile this into a DLL – making sure to use binary compatibility as discussed earlier – we can change our `Chapter2COM` project to make use of this new component.

Open `Chapter2COM` and use the **Project | References** menu option to bring up the references dialog. Add a reference to the **Chapter2Ext** component and click OK:

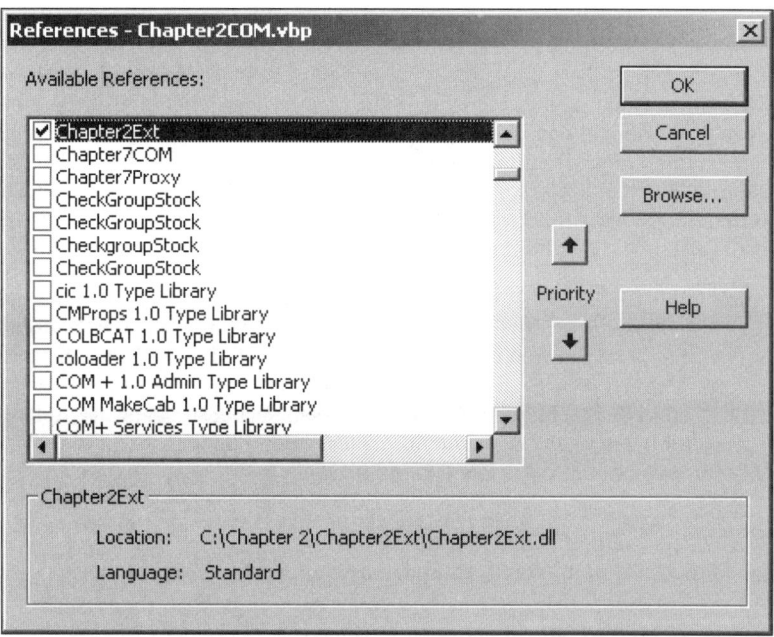

Now we can add a method to `SimpleClass` to use this new component:

```
Public Function GetExtString() As String
   Dim obj As ExtClass

   Set obj = New ExtClass
   GetExtString = obj.GetString
End Function
```

This method does not return a reference to any external object – it merely makes use of the object behind the scenes. This type of method does *not* require that our Visual Basic .NET project have any reference to, or knowledge of, the `Chapter2Ext.dll` component.

However, let's also add another method to `SimpleClass`:

```
Public Function GetExternal() As ExtClass
   Set GetExternal = New ExtClass
End Function
```

This method returns a reference to an object that comes from `Chapter2Ext.dll`, and thus means that our Visual Basic .NET project must be aware of the `Chapter2Ext.dll` component. Methods of this type, which return object references, force us to create an RCW for not only the component containing `SimpleClass`, but also for the component containing `ExtClass`.

While we haven't broken compatibility with the previous `Chapter2COM` component, we *have* changed its interface with these new methods. This means that we need to not only update the copy of the component we made earlier for binary compatibility, but also update the RCW so that it is aware of the new methods.

Earlier in this chapter, we discussed the importance of binary compatibility and we set the `Chapter2COM` component to be compatible with a copy of the DLL. Adding a method doesn't break compatibility, but it does change the interface of our component. Since these new methods are not in the copy with which we remain compatible, each time that we compile the DLL going forward, the methods will get assigned new ID values – causing early bound clients to be unable to use the component properly. To avoid this, we must update the copy of the DLL with which we are set to be compatible, so that the information for the new methods is locked and remains consistent from compile to compile. This is not new – this has been a best practice for VB6 development for years.

Update the compatibility DLL now. With this change, our `Chapter2COM` component has a dependency on the `Chapter2Ext` component. If we are not using a primary interop assembly but, rather, are directly referencing the COM component from within Visual Studio .NET, we can simply remove and re-add the reference within Visual Studio .NET and it will automatically also add a reference to the `Chapter2Ext.dll` component. However, as we discussed earlier, it is always preferable to use a primary interop assembly for COM components, so let's take a look at the process of creating a primary interop assembly for a component that has dependencies.

Creating the Dependent Primary Interop Assembly

We can attempt to run `TlbImp` to create an updated wrapper for `Chapter2COM`:

```
tlbimp /out:ch2com.dll chapter2com.dll /primary /keyfile:mykey.snk
```

Unfortunately, this will result an error since this component requires a reference to an RCW for `Chapter2Ext.dll`.

What we need to do is first create a primary interop assembly for `Chapter2Ext.dll`. To do this, we need to follow the same steps as we did earlier for `Chapter2COM.dll`.

First, create the RCW:

```
tlbimp /out:ch2ext.dll chapter2ext.dll /primary /keyfile:"C:\Chapter
2\Chapter2COM\mykey.snk"
```

Then copy it to the `Primary Interop Assemblies` directory and register it in the GAC:

```
gacutil /i ch2ext.dll
```

This completes the process of building a primary interop assembly for the dependant component, so we can return to the process of recreating the RCW for `Chapter2COM.dll`.

Recreating the RCW for Chapter2COM

To create a new wrapper assembly for `Chapter2COM.dll`, we need to use a slightly different `TlbImp` command:

```
tlbimp /out:ch2com.dll chapter2com.dll /primary /keyfile:mykey.snk
/reference:"c:\program files\microsoft.net\primary interop assemblies\ch2ext.dll"
```

Notice the use of the `/reference` switch, which indicates that this component references another component for which we have a primary interop assembly named `ch2ext.dll`. If we have multiple dependencies, we'll use a `/reference` switch for each dependent file.

We now have an updated wrapper assembly for `Chapter2COM.dll` that reflects our updated interface and the dependency that we just added.

We'll also need to update the GAC and copy this new version of `ch2com.dll` to the `Primary Interop Assemblies` directory.

First though, we should remove the current `ch2com` entry from the GAC. The GAC is quite capable of having multiple versions of the same assembly registered all at once but, when we are working with COM components, this is a problem. The underlying COM component *doesn't* support the concept of having multiple versions registered at the same time. It can become confusing and even cause application failures if we keep multiple versions of the RCW for a component, since some .NET clients might try to use an old wrapper assembly that is no longer valid if the COM component has been updated.

To unregister the existing `ch2com` RCW, use the following command:

```
gacutil /u ch2com
```

Now copy the new `ch2com.dll` to the `Primary Interop Assemblies` directory and then use `gacutil` to register this new version:

```
gacutil /i ch2com.dll
```

This makes the updated version available for use on our system so we can develop against it.

When we reference the `ch2com.dll` wrapper assembly from a project, either through Visual Studio .NET or by using the `/r` switch on the VB command line compiler, we will automatically gain access to the `Chapter2Ext` component's objects as well, since they are now referenced from within the `ch2com.dll` assembly.

It is also worth noting that primary interop assemblies, and any assemblies on which they depend, must be deployed to the `Primary Interop Assemblies` directory and registered in the GAC on client workstations where the components will be used. Of course, we'll have to deploy and register the COM components as well. Any time that we use COM components from .NET applications, we must contend with the requirement to register the COM component and, if we are using a primary interop assembly, that also must be registered in the GAC.

Importing Dynamically

Typically, we'll be adding references to our COM components at design time – as we're writing our application. However, there are cases where we'll need more dynamic access to the components – loading them while the application is actually running rather than while we're doing development. This is very similar to the way that we can dynamically access a component in VB6 using `CreateObject` or in ASP using `Server.CreateObject`.

CreateObject Function

To meet this need, we can use the `CreateObject` function built into the `Microsoft.VisualBasic` namespace. This namespace is automatically available to Visual Basic .NET applications, as it contains a great many functions and methods commonly used in VB applications.

The `CreateObject` function in Visual Basic .NET is essentially the same as the function of the same name in previous versions of VB – it creates instances of COM objects based on the PROGID of the class. The COM PROGID consists of the COM server name combined with the class name. For instance, the PROGID of our `SimpleClass` is `Chapter2COM.SimpleClass`.

This means that we can write a simple line of code to create an instance of this class *without* having to reference the COM component via a .NET wrapper class. The line of code would be:

```
Dim obj As Object = CreateObject("Chapter2Late.LateClass")
```

This appears to return a reference to the COM object. Behind the scenes, the `CreateObject` function is dynamically creating a .NET wrapper class that allows our code to interact with the underlying COM object via its `IDispatch` interface. This `IDispatch` interface is also used by any late bound COM clients such as Active Server Pages script code.

This means that we can interact with the underlying COM object's native interface. We won't have access to any secondary interfaces that it may have implemented by using the `Implements` keyword in VB6. There is also a performance impact here – late bound access to an object is substantially slower than the early bound techniques that we've used so far in this chapter, but this approach is more flexible and doesn't require us to manually create and deploy the RCW.

.NET System Class Library Support

If we don't want to use the `CreateObject` function, we can also choose to use the `Type.GetTypeFromProgID` and `Activator.CreateInstance` methods:

```
Dim t As Type = Type.GetTypeFromProgID("Chapter2COM.SimpleClass")
Dim obj As Object = Activator.CreateInstance(t)
```

This is functionally equivalent to the `CreateObject` function – resulting in a reference to a dynamically created COM object that we can call via late binding. There's no real advantage to this approach and simply using the `CreateObject` function is typically more intuitive and readable.

However, there is a variation on this technique where we call `Type.GetTypeFromCLSID`, which creates an instance of a COM class based on its CLSID rather than its PROGID:

```
Dim g As New Guid("{797D55B7-A792-47FA-9464-08C0DB550252}")
Dim t As Type = Type.GetTypeFromCLSID(g)
Dim obj As Object = Activator.CreateInstance(t)
```

This code creates a GUID variable to contain the CLSID for `Chapter2.SimpleClass`, and then calls `Type.GetTypeFromCLSID` to retrieve that type so we can create an instance of the class. Of course, the CLSID for this component will be different on your machine, but should remain consistent from compile to compile as long as we observe proper use of binary compatibility and don't change the interfaces of the component.

If we don't know the PROGID but *do* know the CLSID value, this is a very valuable technique to know. Also, this technique can be a tiny bit faster than using the PROGID, since it avoids one lookup in the Windows registry – at the obvious cost of losing readability in our code since a GUID value is far less humanly readable than a PROGID.

Using COM Components

At this point, we've discussed how to create a COM component using VB6, and we've explored how we can reference components from within Visual Studio .NET, create wrapper assemblies by using the `TlbImp` command-line utility, and create and register a primary interop assembly. Our system is now set up with a primary interop assembly for both the `Chapter2COM` and `Chapter2Ext` components.

Now let's move on and explore how we can use the classes and data types exposed by our COM components within our Visual Basic .NET code.

From a simple coding viewpoint, we can treat a COM object just like we would treat a .NET object. The wrapper assemblies that sit between our .NET code and the COM code make interaction with the COM objects largely transparent. However, there are some key issues to keep in mind when working with COM objects, especially those that consume important or limited system resources such as memory, file handles, or database connections.

Early Binding

If we are using a .NET wrapper assembly created either by Visual Studio .NET or through the `Tlbimp` utility, we can use early binding to interact with the COM component. This is preferable, since early binding offers significant advantages.

First off, early binding is much faster than late binding. Each early bound method call is made in the most efficient manner possible, without the overhead of dynamically locating and then invoking a method that comes with late binding.

Also, since the type information for early bound classes is available at design time, the IntelliSense features built into Visual Studio .NET are available for our use. This means that we can take advantage of auto-completion, tool-tip help, and compile-time syntax checking for our code.

Calling Simple Methods

Return to our `Chapter2Net` application in Visual Studio .NET and make sure that it is referencing the `ch2com` primary interop assembly:

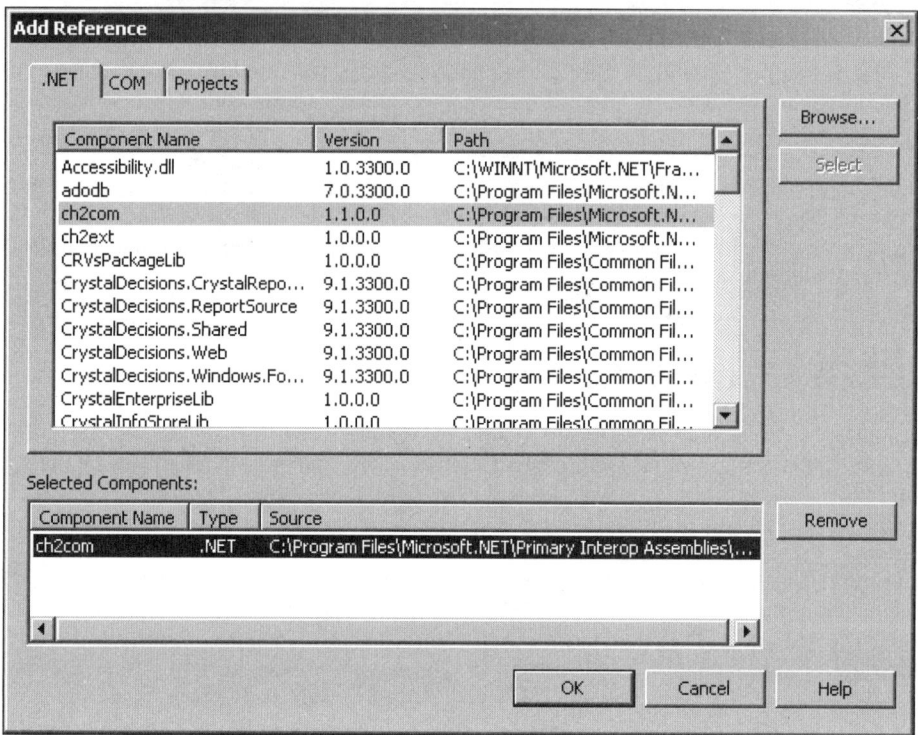

Note that we don't need to reference the `ch2ext` assembly as it is already pre-referenced by the `ch2com` assembly, and so we have all the information that we need from this one reference.

We can now write some code to interact with our COM component. For instance, we can add five `Label` controls to the form and write the following code to invoke some of the methods on our object:

```
Private Sub Form1_Load(ByVal sender As System.Object, _
    ByVal e As System.EventArgs) Handles MyBase.Load

  Dim obj As New ch2com.SimpleClass()

  Label1.Text = obj.GetBoolean
  Label2.Text = obj.GetString
  Label3.Text = obj.GetInteger
  Label4.Text = obj.GetLong
  Label5.Text = obj.GetDate

End Sub
```

This code creates an instance of `SimpleClass` and then populates the `Label` controls with various data returned from the methods on that object.

Classes and Interfaces and COM

When we create the instance of the class, IntelliSense lists several options of classes available for our use. This can be a bit confusing since `SimpleClass` is not listed as a class but, rather, is listed as an interface:

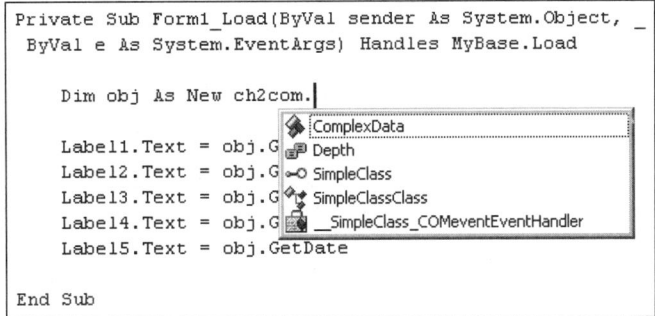

In fact, our options include:

Option	Description
ComplexData	The .NET Structure corresponding to the VB6 UDT we defined
Depth	The Enum we defined in VB6
SimpleClass	The interface defined by our VB6 class
SimpleClassClass	The class corresponding to our VB6 class
_SimpleClass_COMeventEventHandler	Used internally by the .NET runtime for event support

Note that this display is quite different from that which we see in the Object Browser window, where `SimpleClass` appears as a class and `SimpleClassClass` is not visible at all. Presumably, one of these displays has a bug that will be fixed in a future version of Visual Studio .NET.

When working with .NET classes and interfaces, we always create instances of a class, so things are pretty straightforward.

COM, however, works differently (though that fact has always been hidden from us by VB6). In COM, we never *really* create instances of objects directly. Instead, we are always working with an interface that in turn interacts with an underlying object.

> **VB6 gives us the *illusion* of working directly with an object, but the reality is that our code actually invokes methods on the object's native interface.**

In fact, VB6 creates our class by using the name we provide (in this case `SimpleClass`) and it also creates a formal interface for the class by prefixing an underscore to the name (so we get `_SimpleClass`). Though we never see the `_SimpleClass` interface in VB6, all of our method calls are actually routed to `_SimpleClass` behind the scenes.

Visual Basic .NET doesn't normally have to worry about that sort of thing, because the .NET platform allows us to create and interact with objects directly. However, we are currently attempting to write .NET code that interacts with a COM object and so the two models come into conflict. From the perspective of a VB6 developer, it is like the curtain is being pulled back and we're seeing what has been going on behind the scenes all of this time.

To help ease the transition and make our code appear more "normal", the RCW renames the class by appending the word `Class` on the end, and it renames the native interface by removing the underscore – so we end up with a class named `SimpleClassClass` and an interface named `SimpleClass`.

In normal coding, we don't make use of `SimpleClassClass` – though, later in this chapter, we will see the one case where it is of value. Instead, whenever we want to use an instance of our COM class, we make use of the interface.

This is why our Visual Basic .NET code creates an instance of the `SimpleClass` *interface*, not the class itself. In COM, we never create instances of a class – we can only interact with objects via an interface – so our Visual Basic .NET code follows that same model by creating an instance of the interface instead of the class.

Running the Application

We can run the application and see that it works as intended – illustrating the level of transparency as our .NET code calls back into COM.

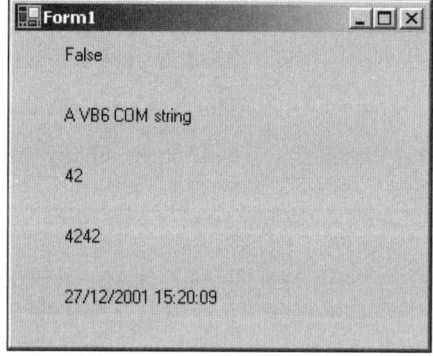

Using Complex Data Types

We can also make use of the `ComplexData` structure by changing the code as follows:

```
Private Sub Form1_Load(ByVal sender As System.Object, _
    ByVal e As System.EventArgs) Handles MyBase.Load

  Dim obj As New ch2com.SimpleClass()

  Dim data As ch2com.ComplexData = obj.GetComplex

  Label1.Text = data.Name
  Label2.Text = data.Birthdate

End Sub
```

The `ComplexData` UDT from VB6 is automatically translated into a Visual Basic .NET Structure, providing us with a directly comparable data type for use within our .NET application.

We can also make use of the `Enum` we declared in `SimpleClass` with the following change:

```
Private Sub Form1_Load(ByVal sender As System.Object, _
    ByVal e As System.EventArgs) Handles MyBase.Load

  Dim obj As New ch2com.SimpleClass()

  Dim data As ch2com.ComplexData = obj.GetComplex

  Label1.Text = data.Name
  Label2.Text = data.Birthdate

  Dim depth As ch2com.Depth

  depth = ch2com.Depth.VeryDeep

  Label3.Text = depth.ToString
End Sub
```

This new code declares a variable of type `Depth` and sets its value. As we enter this code, notice that we get automatic IntelliSense for the enumerated type – a list of valid options appears for our convenience:

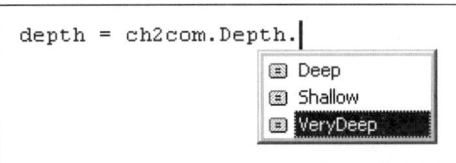

Even better, the `ToString` method on an enumerated type displays the text equivalent of the value rather than the numeric value, so the text in `Label3` will end up being **VeryDeep**.

Handling Events

Our `SimpleClass` object is designed with an event – `COMevent`. We can handle this event from within our code just like we would an event from a regular .NET object. First off, we need to declare the object variable at the class level and use the `WithEvents` keyword:

```
Public Class Form1
  Inherits System.Windows.Forms.Form

  Private WithEvents obj As ch2com.SimpleClass
```

Then we can add a method to handle the event. This can be done by using the drop-down menus at the top of the code window, just like we would for any other event, or the code can be entered by hand:

```
Private Sub obj_COMevent() Handles obj.COMevent
  MsgBox("COMevent fired")
End Sub
```

Finally, we need to update the code in our form's `Load` event to properly create the object and to call the `RaiseTheEvent` method, including removal of the `Dim` statement for the `obj` variable:

```
Private Sub Form1_Load(ByVal sender As System.Object, _
    ByVal e As System.EventArgs) Handles MyBase.Load

    obj = New ch2com.SimpleClass()

    Dim data As ch2com.ComplexData = obj.GetComplex

    Label1.Text = data.Name
    Label2.Text = data.Birthdate

    Dim depth As ch2com.Depth

    depth = ch2com.Depth.VeryDeep

    Label3.Text = depth.ToString

    obj.RaiseTheEvent()
End Sub
```

Now, when we run the application, we'll be presented with a message box displaying the event text, and we'll see that the `ComplexData` and `Enum` data are displayed in our form.

The early bound behavior that we are experiencing here is the same whether we've referenced the component from within Visual Studio .NET or we've created the wrapper assembly using `TlbImp`.

We can also use late binding to access the component.

Late Binding

Late binding is slower than early binding, and we lose the IntelliSense features of the Visual Studio .NET IDE, so development is often slower and debugging is harder. We also lose the ability to receive events that are raised by the component that we're calling, and it becomes difficult if not impossible to use complex data types such as a UDT.

However, late binding can offer substantial flexibility in how we create and work with our COM components – especially if we're creating a very dynamic application where the specific COM DLLs that we'll be using aren't available or known until the application is actually running.

Late binding is accomplished simply by using variables of type `Object`. A variable of type `Object` can hold any value or any data type in the .NET environment – including holding a reference to any kind of object in our application. This includes COM objects or, at least, their .NET wrapper objects.

> *To use late binding, we need to make sure that* `Option Strict` *is turned off in our code module. This is the default setting, so we won't typically need to worry about it. If* `Option Strict` *is turned on, the VB compiler will prevent us from calling methods on a variable of type* `Object` *– thus preventing the use of late binding.*

When dealing with COM objects and late binding, there are two approaches – one slow, the other slower.

Late Binding with a Wrapper Assembly

We can use late binding to interact with the .NET wrapper assembly objects that, in turn, interact with the underlying COM objects. This involves just one layer of late binding – between our code and the wrapper objects. The wrapper objects themselves are still early bound to the underlying COM objects. This is illustrated by the following diagram:

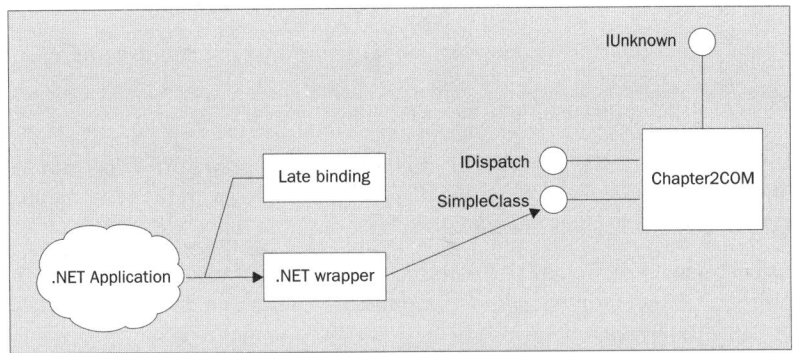

Although we might use late binding within our .NET code, the .NET wrapper code will directly invoke the `SimpleClass` component via its interface – using early binding within COM.

To do this in our code, we can change the `Chapter2Net` application. Remove the `Private WithEvents` declaration of the `obj` variable and the `obj_COMevent` method from the code. Then make the following changes to the form's `Load` event:

```
Private Sub Form1_Load(ByVal sender As System.Object, _
    ByVal e As System.EventArgs) Handles MyBase.Load

    Dim obj As Object = New ch2com.SimpleClass()

    Label1.Text = obj.GetBoolean
    Label2.Text = obj.GetString
    Label3.Text = obj.GetInteger
    Label4.Text = obj.GetLong
    Label5.Text = obj.GetDate
End Sub
```

Notice that this is virtually the same as the code that we wrote originally – calling a set of methods on our object – except that this time the object is of type `Object`.

As we enter the code, we'll see that there is no IntelliSense and no automatic capitalization of the method names. The Visual Studio .NET IDE can't provide these services because it has no idea about the real type of the variable – all it knows is that it is a generic object.

User-Defined Types

It also turns out that .NET's ability to marshal data back and forth from COM to .NET is crippled when we use late binding. Anything other than basic data types will not work automatically. For instance, we cannot use UDTs, so we can no longer call the `GetComplex` method:

```
Dim data As ch2com.ComplexData

data = obj.GetComplex
```

This method returns a UDT, which is properly marshaled when .NET knows that our object is of type `SimpleClass`. However, when our object is of type `Object`, .NET has no reference by which to understand this UDT and so is unable to marshal it into our application.

If we need to get a UDT from COM, we must explicitly indicate the data type of our object:

```
data = CType(obj, ch2com.SimpleClass).GetComplex
```

The `CType` function converts the generic object into the data type we provide – `ch2com.SimpleClass` – and we then call the `GetComplex` method. This provides .NET with the information it needs to properly marshal the UDT into our application.

Of course, this is also an early bound technique so it will only work if our project has a reference to the wrapper assembly for the underlying COM component. What we've done is used the `CType()` function to provide a strongly typed reference to the object for this one method call.

Late Binding with Dynamic Creation

Earlier in the chapter, we discussed how we can use the `CreateObject` function to create a COM object dynamically as our application is running. In this case, the .NET wrapper assembly is created for us on the fly – and it is a generic wrapper that will invoke the COM object using its `IDispatch` interface rather than any strongly typed interface. Essentially, this wrapper uses late binding in COM to interact with the component.

We can use late binding from our .NET application to interact with this generic wrapper class – in which case we're using "double" late binding, as illustrated by the following diagram:

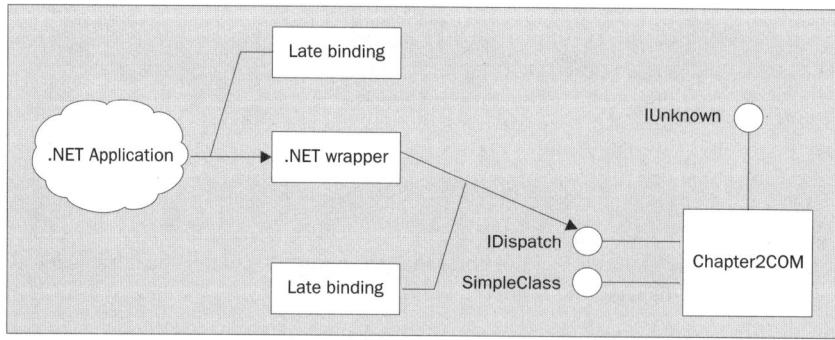

In the Solution Explorer, expand the **References** node and then right-click on **ch2com** and click **Remove**. This will remove the reference from our project. At this point our `Chapter2Net` project has no explicit knowledge of the COM components at all.

Now we can update our code in the form's `Load` event:

```
Private Sub Form1_Load(ByVal sender As System.Object, _
    ByVal e As System.EventArgs) Handles MyBase.Load
```

```
Dim obj As Object = CreateObject("Chapter2COM.SimpleClass")

    Label1.Text = obj.GetBoolean
    Label2.Text = obj.GetString
    Label3.Text = obj.GetInteger
    Label4.Text = obj.GetLong
    Label5.Text = obj.GetDate

End Sub
```

Since we no longer have a reference to `Chapter2COM`, we must use the `CreateObject` function to create an instance of the object. Notice that we're using the full `Chapter2COM` component name in the `CreateObject` call. This is because `CreateObject` takes the COM PROGID of the component, not the .NET wrapper name. This use of `CreateObject` is identical to VB6.

Our series of basic method calls to the object are unaffected by this change – they were late bound before and they continue to be late bound. However, we know that behind the scenes they are now also causing late bound calls to the COM object itself, so each method call is doubly late bound.

Also note that it is no longer possible to call the `CType` function to temporarily use early binding to access a UDT, as we demonstrated in the previous section. We have no access to the data types of the underlying COM component and so we have no data type to use in the `CType` function. There is no workaround for this. If we need to use a UDT, we'll need to use an early bound technique.

Manual Invocation of Methods

We can also do the late bound method calls by hand if we desire. Visual Basic .NET does this on our behalf so, typically, we can simply use its late binding capabilities but, if we want to manually call the methods, we can do so by using the `InvokeMember` method on the `Type` object. We might choose to do this if we need to not only dynamically load the COM component but, also, dynamically call methods based on metadata or some external information that we are provided with at run time. This technique can also allow us to do late binding while having `Option Strict` turned on.

```
Private Sub Form1_Load(ByVal sender As System.Object, _
    ByVal e As System.EventArgs) Handles MyBase.Load

    Dim t As Type = Type.GetTypeFromProgID("Chapter2COM.SimpleClass")
    Dim obj As Object = Activator.CreateInstance(t)

    Label1.Text = CStr(t.InvokeMember("GetLong", _
        Reflection.BindingFlags.InvokeMethod, Nothing, obj, Nothing))
End Sub
```

In this code, we're getting the type from our COM component and storing that in a variable named `t`. We then use it to create an instance of the COM object. We discussed this technique earlier in the chapter. This creates an early bound .NET wrapper object, so the only late binding that will occur as we call methods in this scenario will take place in our .NET code.

Of course, with `Option Strict` turned off, we can still call methods directly against the `obj` variable using normal late binding.

With that done, we are using the `InvokeMember` method to call the `GetLong` method on our object. The `InvokeMember` method takes a few parameters and provides a return value. The return value of `InvokeMember` is the return value of the underlying method – in this case, an `Integer` value (`Long` in VB6).

The parameters for `InvokeMember` are:

Parameter	Description
Method name	The name of the method to be invoked.
Invoke attributes	What action to take – in this case, we're indicating that we want to simply invoke the method.
Binder object	An object to handle data binding – not needed in our case.
Target object	A reference to the actual object to be invoked – in this case, our COM object.
Method arguments	An array of argument values passed to the method. Since our method accepts no parameters, we are passing `Nothing`.

The result is the same as the late bound call:

```
Label1.Text = obj.GetLong()
```

However, by using `InvokeMember`, we can choose to have `Option Strict On` and avoid the native late binding support built into Visual Basic .NET, if we desire.

Object Lifetimes

When interacting with COM components from within .NET applications, we need to keep in mind that we are working with two different platforms. Object lifetimes are managed very differently in .NET when compared to COM. Since we're bridging from one model to another, there can be issues with this.

In COM, object lifetimes are managed by a technique called **reference counting**. Every time we establish a reference to an instance of a COM object, a counter is incremented. Every time we release a reference to an object, that counter is decremented. When the counter reaches zero, the object knows that no code is referencing it and so the object is immediately destroyed.

Since the exact conditions under which a COM component will be destroyed are known, we can know specifically when an object is destroyed. This is called **deterministic finalization**.

In .NET, object lifetimes are managed by a technique called **garbage collection**. No effort is made to track the number of references to any object at any given point in time. Instead, on a periodic basis, the garbage collection algorithm runs through our application – tracing all object references from top to bottom. All of the objects that can still be referenced by our code are kept, while all of the objects that can no longer be referenced from our code are destroyed.

There's no way to predict exactly when the garbage collection will run, so an object with no references might sit in memory for some time before it is finally destroyed. Since we can't specifically predict when the object will be destroyed, .NET uses **non-deterministic finalization**.

Technically, it is possible to force the garbage collection process to run by invoking it directly. This is not a recommended practice, however, as the garbage collector is optimized to run such that it balances the need to reclaim memory and resources against the processing overhead of running the collection algorithm.

Both of these approaches have their good and bad points. Reference counting incurs some overhead in tracking the number of references against each object but, then, garbage collection incurs some overhead as all of the objects are traced to see if they are still referenced by our code. Reference counting is very susceptible to memory leaks when a counter isn't incremented or decremented, but there's an expense with garbage collection since objects hang around in memory for a while after they are no longer needed.

On the whole, the garbage collection approach is simpler to work with and is typically faster in most cases. *This is why .NET uses this approach instead of the reference counting scheme used by COM.*

The fact that objects may stay in memory for some time after they are no longer needed can impact on our .NET applications as they interact with COM objects. The .NET wrapper assembly for a COM component contains the code to increment and decrement the reference count on the COM object, so we don't have to worry about that from within our .NET code. As soon as we reference a COM object from within our .NET code, the reference count is incremented. This is true regardless of the technique we use to instantiate the object.

When our .NET code is done with the object – either because we explicitly set the object reference to Nothing, or because the variable goes out of scope at the end of a method call – then the .NET wrapper object is no longer referenced by our code.

This is where it gets tricky. Just because the .NET wrapper object is not referenced by our code *does not* mean that the object is destroyed. Remember that .NET objects aren't destroyed until the garbage collector gets around to finding out that the object is no longer referenced by our application. And it isn't until the .NET wrapper object is destroyed that it decrements the reference counter on the underling COM object.

The benefit we get from this is that the COM object reference count is automatically decremented by .NET, which helps eliminate the possibility of memory leaks. Of course, this is not much different from VB6, which would also automatically decrement the reference count when an object was released.

This means that our .NET application will keep the underlying COM object alive until the corresponding .NET wrapper object is garbage-collected. We're imposing .NET object lifetime semantics on our COM objects.

In most cases, this doesn't matter. Typically there's no harm in having a COM object sit in memory for a while after we're done with it. However, if our COM object is holding expensive resources during that time, then it can become an issue.

What is an expensive resource? Large regions of memory, unique items like a lock on a file, or limited resources like a database connection are examples of expensive resources. Most objects don't hold files or database connections open for their entire lifetime, but those that do must be handled with special care.

If our COM object holds an expensive resource until it is destroyed, our .NET application code will need to take extra steps to ensure that the object releases those resources as early as possible. Conceptually, this is no different from when we deal with .NET objects that hold expensive resources.

In either case, we can **dispose** of the object by implementing appropriate disposal behaviors. In the case of a .NET object, we can implement the `IDisposable` interface and then call the `Dispose` method to cause the object to release its expensive resources. In the case of a COM object, we need to use a special method that releases the reference to a COM object even though the .NET wrapper object itself is not destroyed until the garbage collector runs.

This is the `ReleaseComObject` method on the `Marshal` class, which is found in the `System.Runtime.InteropServices` namespace. When this method is called on a COM wrapper object, the reference count is immediately decremented on the underlying COM object. If that causes the reference count to reach zero, then that object will be destroyed immediately – thus releasing its expensive resources.

Again, this is only important for those COM objects that hold onto expensive resources until they are destroyed so, in most cases, we don't need to worry about this at all.

Before we call the `ReleaseComObject` method, it is typically easiest to add an `Imports` statement to the top of our code:

```
Imports System.Runtime.InteropServices
```

This makes the classes in the `InteropServices` namespace more easily available to our code. We can then call the `ReleaseComObject` method when we are done using the object – causing the reference count to be immediately decremented.

For instance, if our project is using early binding to interact with the `Chapter2COM` component as we did earlier in the chapter (you will need to add the `ch2com` reference again for this), our form's `Load` event could have code such as:

```
Private Sub Form1_Load(ByVal sender As System.Object, _
    ByVal e As System.EventArgs) Handles MyBase.Load

  Dim obj As New ch2com.SimpleClass()

  Label1.Text = obj.GetBoolean
  Label2.Text = obj.GetString
  Label3.Text = obj.GetInteger
  Label4.Text = obj.GetLong
  Label5.Text = obj.GetDate

  Marshal.ReleaseComObject(obj)
  obj = Nothing
End Sub
```

Rather than waiting for the garbage collector to destroy the .NET object, and thus decrement the reference count on the COM object, we are explicitly indicating that the reference count of the underlying COM object should be decremented immediately. The garbage collection process will still destroy the wrapper object at some point in the future, but the underlying COM object can be destroyed now.

Also note that the `obj` variable is set to `Nothing` immediately following the call to `ReleaseComObject`. This is not strictly necessary, but is a good practice as it prevents us from accidentally attempting to interact with the variable after we've released the underlying COM object.

The same `ReleaseComObject` method can be used if we're using late binding or dynamic creation of the COM object and its associated .NET wrapper. For instance, earlier in the chapter we used a dynamic creation technique in our form's `Load` event. We could enhance that code to release the reference with the following code:

```
Private Sub Form1_Load(ByVal sender As System.Object, _
    ByVal e As System.EventArgs) Handles MyBase.Load

    Dim obj As Object = CreateObject("Chapter2COM.SimpleClass")

    Label1.Text = obj.GetBoolean
    Label2.Text = obj.GetString
    Label3.Text = obj.GetInteger
    Label4.Text = obj.GetLong
    Label5.Text = obj.GetDate

    Marshal.ReleaseComObject(obj)
End Sub
```

The `CreateObject` function returns a reference to a .NET wrapper object for the underlying COM object. We can then make late bound calls against that object and, when we are done with the object, we call the `ReleaseComObject` method. This causes the reference count on the underlying COM object to be decremented – causing the COM object to be immediately destroyed if the count reaches zero.

Multiple Interfaces

So far, we've been working with simple COM classes that only expose their native interface for our use. Many applications include objects that implement multiple interfaces. We can make use of these other interfaces within our .NET applications.

Before we can see how to work with secondary interfaces, we need to enhance our `Chapter2COM` component to actually implement multiple interfaces. Open up the `Chapter2COM` project in VB6.

Add a new class module to the project and name it `ISecondary`. This class module won't contain any implementation code – just the definition for a secondary interface. Add the following code to the class:

```
Option Explicit

Public Function GetSecondaryValue() As String

End Function

Public Function GetString() As String

End Function
```

This defines a couple of methods for the interface – both functions that return `String` values.

> There are other ways to define an interface to be implemented by a VB6 class. We can create a type library by hand, from another VB application, or from a C++ application. In any case, we end up with a clearly defined interface that we can implement in our class by using the `Implements` keyword.

Now that we have a defined interface, we can enhance `SimpleClass` to implement this interface in addition to the native interface that it already implements. To do this, we'll use the `Implements` keyword. Open up the code window for `SimpleClass` and add the following:

```
Option Explicit

Implements ISecondary
```

Then we need to provide an actual implementation for all of the methods defined on that interface. In this case, we need to implement the `GetSecondaryValue` and `GetString` methods. Add the following code to `SimpleClass`:

```
Private Function ISecondary_GetSecondaryValue() As String
   ISecondary_GetSecondaryValue = "Secondary value"
End Function

Private Function ISecondary_GetString() As String
   ISecondary_GetString = "Secondary string value"
End Function
```

Notice that the `GetString` method from `ISecondary` has the same name as a method on the native interface of `SimpleClass`. Due to the way that interface methods are named in VB6, there's no naming conflict since the interface version of the method has `ISecondary` prefixed to the method name.

We can now compile the `Chapter2COM` project to create our updated component.

> *Don't forget to also update the copy of `Chapter2COM.dll` that we made for the purpose of binary compatibility. Though our change didn't raise any warning about incompatibility with the previous version, we did just add a new class to our project, and the interface to `SimpleClass` will become out of sync in the future unless we update the DLL against which we are compatible.*

Since we've changed the component, we will need to re-create the primary interop assembly.

Use `TlbImp` to recreate the RCW, with:

```
tlbimp /out:ch2com.dll chapter2com.dll /primary /keyfile:mykey.snk
/reference:"c:\program files\microsoft.net\primary interop assemblies\ch2ext.dll"
```

Use `gacutil` to unregister the existing `ch2com` entry, with:

```
gacutil /u ch2com
```

Copy the new `ch2com.dll` to the `Primary Interop Assemblies` directory and use `gacutil` to register the new version of `ch2com.dll`, with:

```
gacutil /i ch2com.dll
```

This is described in detail earlier in the chapter.

Design-Time References

Using multiple interfaces when we're referencing the COM component at design time is very easy. Whether we're importing the component directly from within Visual Studio .NET or by using the `TlbImp` utility, the .NET wrapper assembly will contain not only the information about our base class, but also information about its secondary interfaces and their definitions.

Because we've changed the `ch2com.dll` wrapper, you should remove the current `ch2com` reference from your `Chapter2Net` project and re-reference it to make sure that the reference is up to date.

If we view the `ch2com` assembly in the Object Browser now, we'll see the new interface:

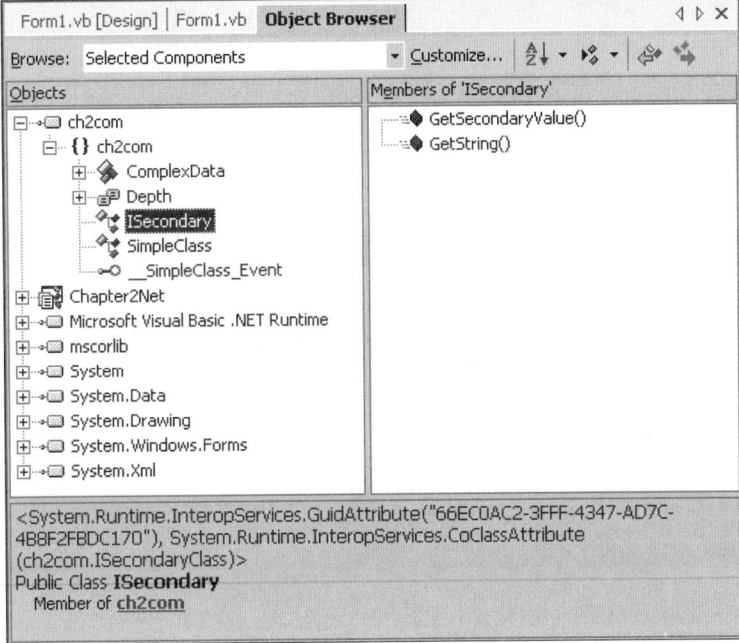

We can now update the code in the form's `Load` event to make use of not only the native interface of `SimpleClass`, but also the methods implemented on its `ISecondary` interface:

```
Private Sub Form1_Load(ByVal sender As System.Object, _
    ByVal e As System.EventArgs) Handles MyBase.Load

  Dim obj As New ch2com.SimpleClass()
  Dim sec As ch2com.ISecondary = obj

  Label1.Text = obj.GetBoolean
  Label2.Text = obj.GetString
  Label3.Text = obj.GetInteger

  Label4.Text = sec.GetSecondaryValue
  Label5.Text = sec.GetString

End Sub
```

The highlighted lines indicate where we're calling methods on the secondary interface. From a coding perspective, this is the same thing that we would do in VB6. We declare a variable of the interface type and assign it to the object that implements the interface. That new variable gives us access to the methods implemented on that interface.

Late Binding

Things are a bit different when we use late binding to access the COM object. With late binding, we are using the `IDispatch` interface of the COM object to invoke the methods – and only the methods on the object's native interface are available. This means that we have no access to secondary interfaces on COM components when we are using late binding or dynamic instantiation of the objects.

Inheritance

If we are using early binding to access our COM component, we can use it as a base for inheritance. This can be very powerful, as it allows us to transparently extend or alter the behavior of an existing COM class by subclassing it with a .NET class – this brings a new level of object-oriented programming capabilities to our COM classes.

We won't review all of the benefits and capabilities offered by inheritance and object-oriented programming here. However, it is worth taking a look at how we can inherit from a COM object to create a .NET class.

In Visual Studio .NET, open the `Chapter2Net` project and make sure it has an up-to-date reference to the `ch2com` primary interop assembly. The code in the form's `Load` event should currently appear as:

```
Private Sub Form1_Load(ByVal sender As System.Object, _
    ByVal e As System.EventArgs) Handles MyBase.Load

  Dim obj As New ch2com.SimpleClass()
  Dim sec As ch2com.ISecondary = obj

  Label1.Text = obj.GetBoolean
  Label2.Text = obj.GetString
  Label3.Text = obj.GetInteger

  Label4.Text = sec.GetSecondaryValue
  Label5.Text = sec.GetString

End Sub
```

Add a new class to the project by using the **Project | Add Class** menu option. Name the class **NetClass**. To make this class inherit from `SimpleClass` in our COM component, we can simply add a line of code:

```
Public Class NetClass
  Inherits ch2com.SimpleClassClass

End Class
```

Notice that, here, we are using the actual *class*, not the interface. Earlier in the chapter, we discussed how we never really create instances of COM classes but, rather, only work with their interfaces. When we go to implement inheritance, however, we need to make use of the class itself, not the interface.

> At this point, **NetClass** is identical to **SimpleClass**, since it automatically gains all of the methods, properties, and events exposed by **SimpleClass**. This includes not only the methods on the native interface of **SimpleClass**, but also any methods from secondary interfaces. When a COM class is made available for use by .NET, all of the interfaces are "flattened" into a single interface for the class.

We can then move on to extend this interface by adding any new methods, properties, or events. It is also possible to alter the behavior of methods in SimpleClass by replacing them with new implementations in NetClass. For instance:

```
Public Class NetClass
   Inherits ch2com.SimpleClassClass

   Public Shadows Function GetString() As String
     Return MyBase.GetString & " and my new string from .NET"
   End Function

   Public Function GetNETString() As String
     Return "My .NET string"
   End Function
End Class
```

This code replaces the GetString method with a new implementation that utilizes the GetString method of the COM object and appends more text to it. It also adds an entirely new method named GetNETString.

Note the use of the Shadows keyword in our implementation of GetString. Shadowing a method is similar to overriding the method with the Overrides keyword, in that we are replacing the original behavior with the code in our subclass.

We can also use the Overrides keyword to override methods from the COM class but, if we do that, we are forced to override all of the methods or we will receive a run-time error when we attempt to instantiate our object.

> If we override one method on a COM class, we must override *all* of the methods on that class.

If we return to the form and update the Load method, we can use this new class:

```
Private Sub Form1_Load(ByVal sender As System.Object, _
     ByVal e As System.EventArgs) Handles MyBase.Load

   Dim obj As New NETclass()
   Dim sec As ch2com.ISecondary = obj

   Label1.Text = obj.GetBoolean
   Label2.Text = obj.GetString
   Label3.Text = obj.GetNETString
```

```
        Label4.Text = sec.GetSecondaryValue
        Label5.Text = sec.GetString
    End Sub
```

This code illustrates how our newly derived class continues to expose the events raised by `SimpleClass` while, at the same time, altering the behavior of `GetString`. It also shows how we can use the new `GetNETString` method that we added in our subclass. We also see that the `ISecondary` interface remains valid for the object, even though it is based on the newly created subclass.

The ability to extend and alter the behavior of a COM object within the context of our .NET applications through inheritance is very powerful.

Inspecting a COM Component from .NET

The .NET development environment includes some very powerful tools for examining our assemblies from the command line, from Visual Studio .NET, and even from within our application code. We can apply these tools to any COM components that we reference within our applications as well.

These tools are designed to operate within the .NET platform and rely heavily on the metadata available that describes each .NET assembly. When we reference a COM component, either with Visual Studio .NET or with the `TlbImp` utility, there will be metadata that describes the COM component just like any other .NET assembly.

On the other hand, if we are instantiating the COM component dynamically at run time, using the `CreateObject` function or the `Type` and `Activator` classes, then there will not be any .NET metadata available. This means that the tools for examining the component will be relatively useless.

ildasm.exe

.NET assemblies, whether EXE or DLL, consist of metadata and **Intermediate Language** (IL). IL is the code to which all .NET applications are compiled, until they are run by the .NET runtime engine. The .NET Framework SDK includes a graphical utility named `ildasm.exe`, which disassembles the IL and metadata in an assembly and allows us to browse through the contents. `ildasm` can usually be found at `C:\Program Files\Microsoft Visual Studio .NET\FrameworkSDK\Bin`.

We can use `ildasm` to examine the .NET wrapper assembly created for a COM component either by Visual Studio .NET or the `TlbImp` utility. For instance, we can use `ildasm` to examine the `ch2com.dll` RCW that we created earlier in the chapter. At the command line, navigate to the `Primary Interop Assemblies` folder and enter the following command:

```
ildasm ch2com.dll
```

This screenshot shows the display with the ch2com namespace node expanded:

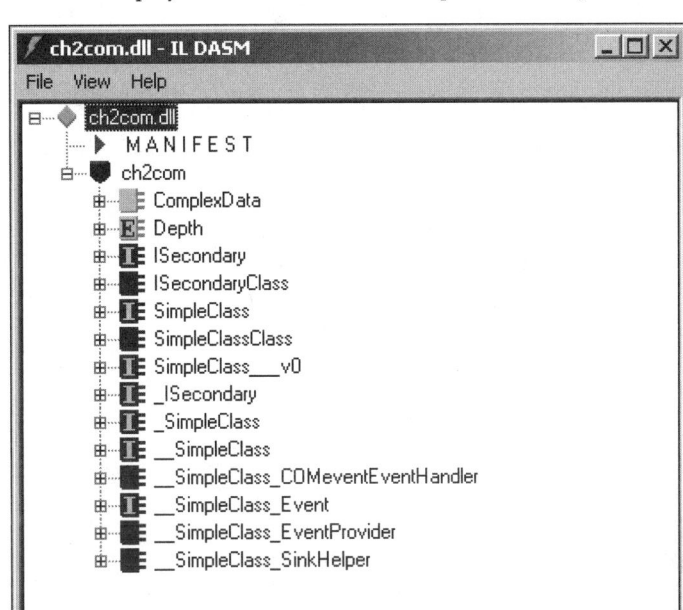

We can see that all of our data types are listed, along with some extras. Of all of these, the ones that we directly use when building our .NET client applications are those with no leading underscore. Those with an underscore or double underscore exist for internal use by the COM interop services classes on our behalf.

The following table lists the meanings of the various entries that we interact with directly:

Data Type	Description
ComplexData	This is the .NET Structure representing the user-defined type
Depth	This is the .NET Enum representing the original Enum
ISecondary	This is the ISecondary interface – as defined by our ISecondary class in VB6 – which is used when we want to interact with an object via this interface
ISecondaryClass	This is the ISecondary class that we use for inheritance to subclass the ISecondary class
SimpleClass	This is the native interface for our VB6 SimpleClass class – as defined in VB6 – which is used to create an instance of the class and then to interact with it via the native interface
SimpleClassClass	This is the SimpleClass class that we use for inheritance to subclass the SimpleClass class

We can take a look at the details behind each of the nodes. For instance, if we expand the SimpleClass node, we'll see that it is merely a pointer to the real _SimpleClass interface, as we discussed earlier in the chapter:

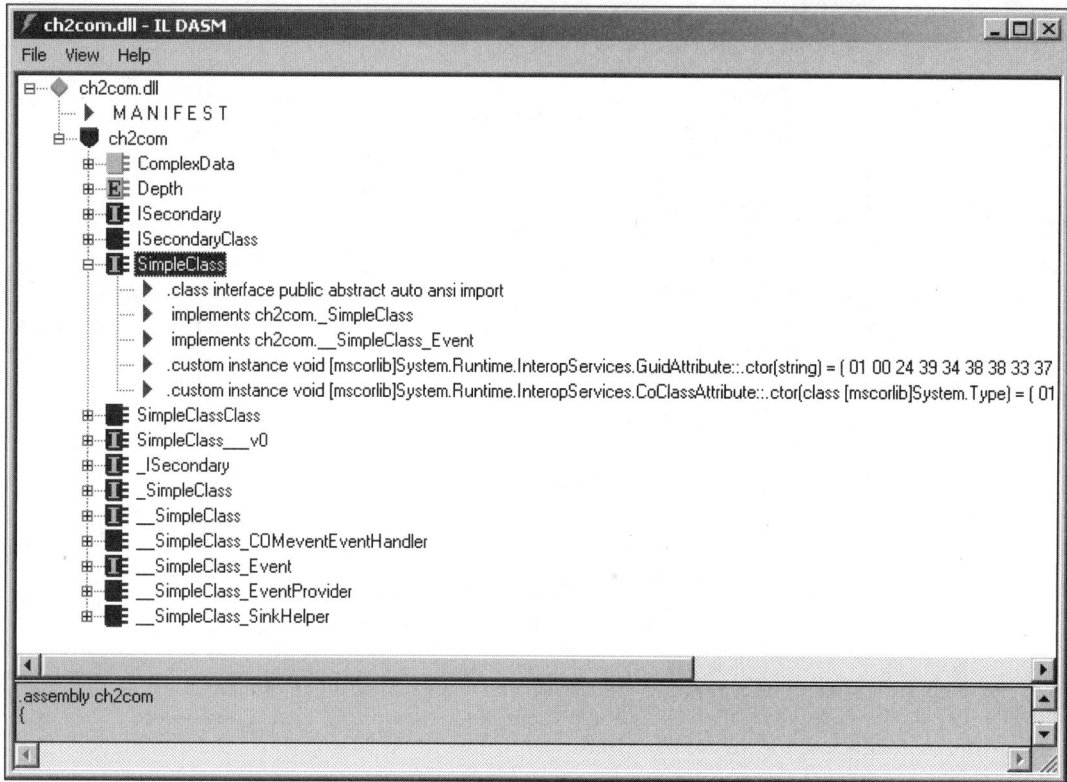

The fact that it is a pointer to another interface is indicated by the:

    implements ch2com._SimpleClass

line of text.

We can also expand the _SimpleClass node, where we'll see the list of methods available on that interface:

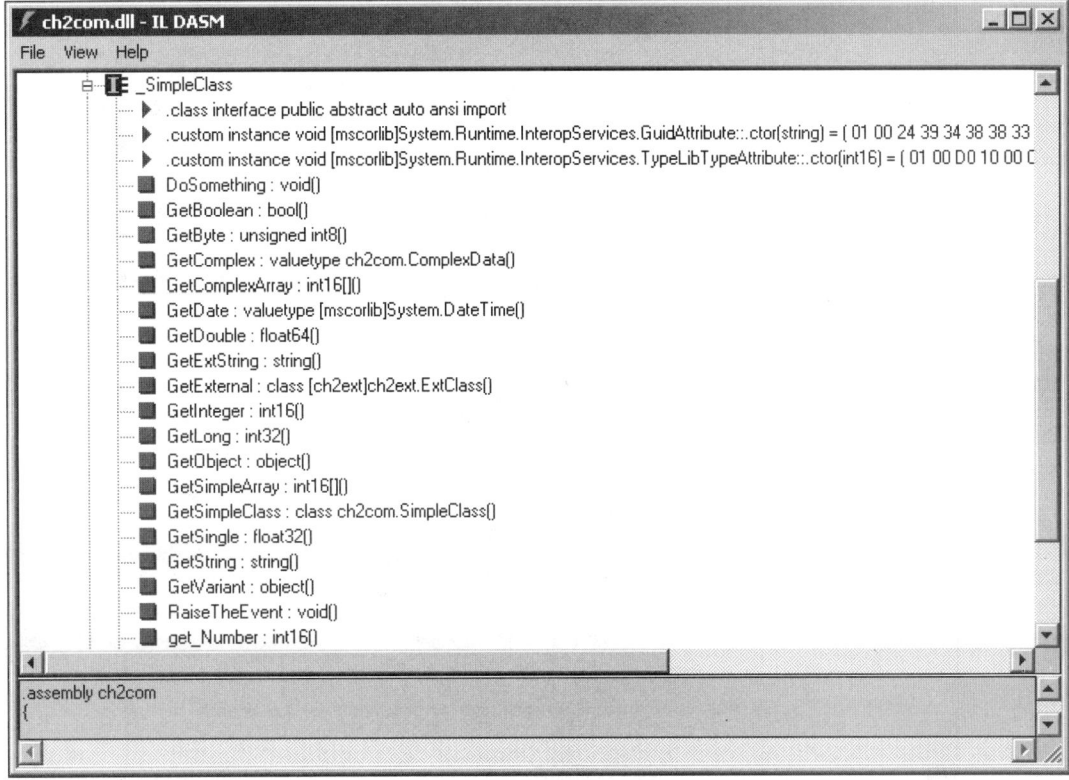

This shows all of the methods that we've defined as part of the native interface of SimpleClass in VB6.

We can see that ildasm gives us a deeper, behind-the-scenes view into the construction of the .NET wrapper assembly than we see when using the typical Object Browser or Class View windows in Visual Studio .NET.

Object Browser

Within Visual Studio .NET, we can use the Object Browser window to examine the assemblies referenced by our project. This includes any COM components that we've referenced via a .NET wrapper assembly, by directly referencing the COM component in Visual Studio .NET or by referencing the wrapper assembly generated by the TlbImp utility.

In our Chapter2Net project, with the ch2com assembly referenced, bring up the Object Browser and expand the ch2com node. Within that node, we'll find a node representing the namespace contained within the assembly – {} ch2com. We can expand that namespace node and our display will appear similar to the following:

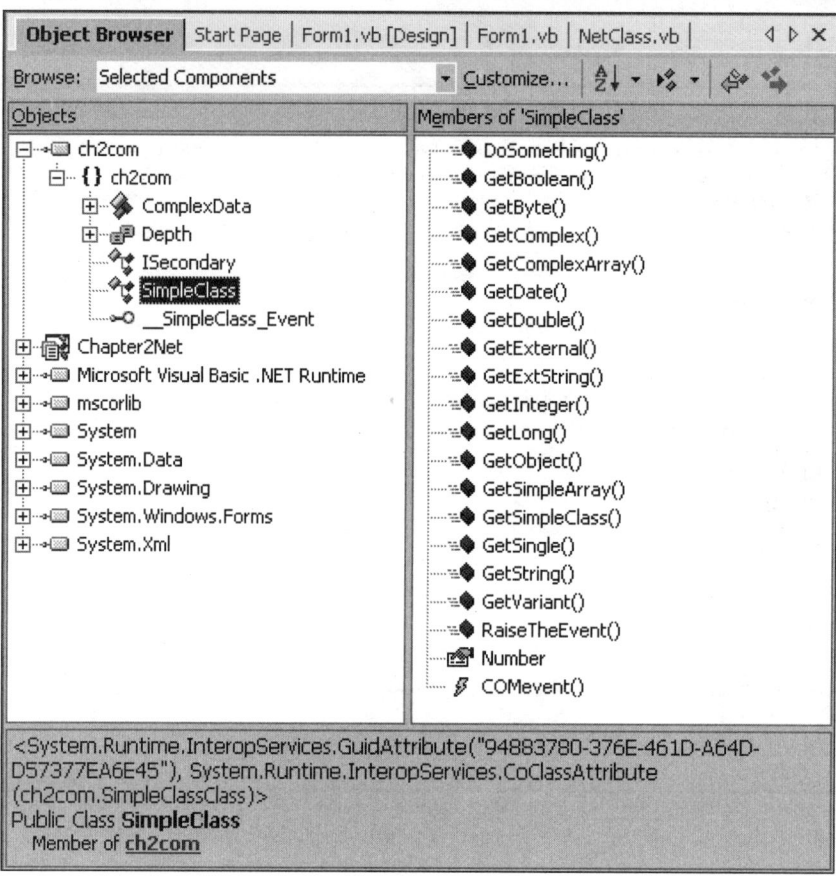

Unlike the `ildasm` display, the Object Browser automatically hides the internal elements in the assembly, only showing us the elements that we typically care about – the ones representing data types or classes that we can use within our .NET code. If we want to see the hidden members, we can right-click on the display and choose **Show Hidden Members**:

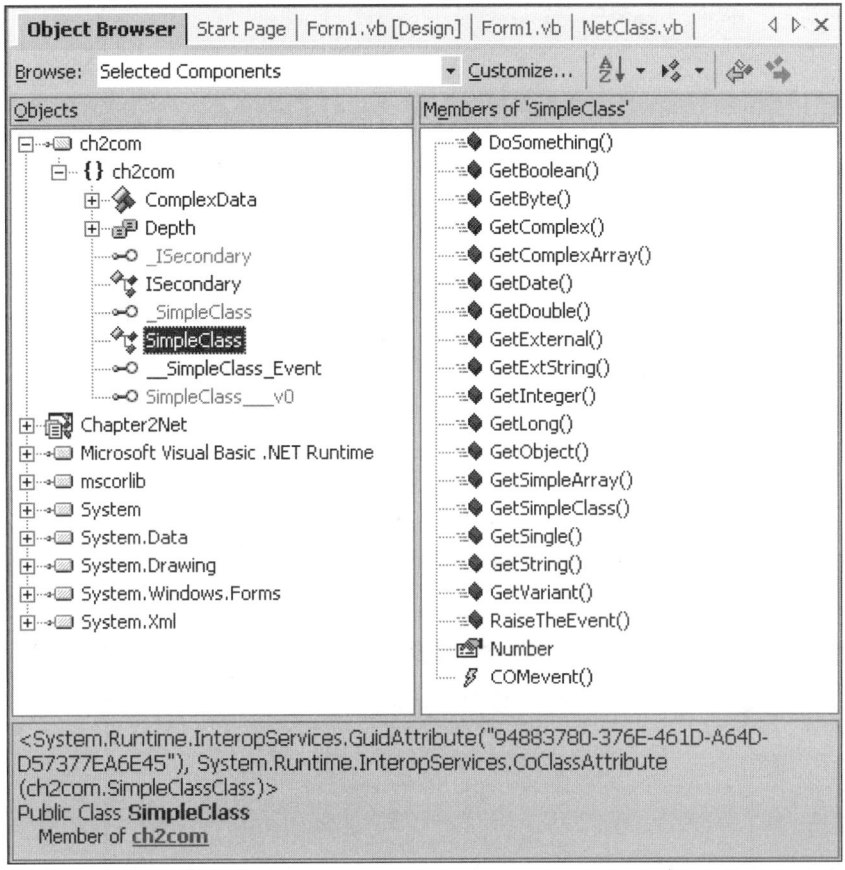

Note that the `ISecondary` and `SimpleClass` interfaces show here as classes, not interfaces as they do elsewhere. Also, the `ISecondaryClass` and `SimpleClassClass` elements are not listed at all, even though they are available for our use when implementing inheritance. This can be confusing and is hopefully something that will be resolved in future versions of Visual Studio .NET.

We can zoom in to see the details beneath each element. Though what we are examining here is the .NET wrapper assembly, it reflects all of the methods and data types available in the underlying COM component.

Class View

The Class View window in Visual Studio .NET is somewhat similar to the Object Browser, but it only lists information about the classes and modules that directly make up our application, rather than listing details about all of the assemblies that we have referenced.

Earlier in the chapter, we implemented some inheritance in our Chapter2Net project. We have a class named NetClass, which inherits from SimpleClass, and the Class View can provide us with an interesting display. Open the Class View window by selecting the View | Class View menu option. If we then expand the **NetClass** node, we'll get a display similar to this:

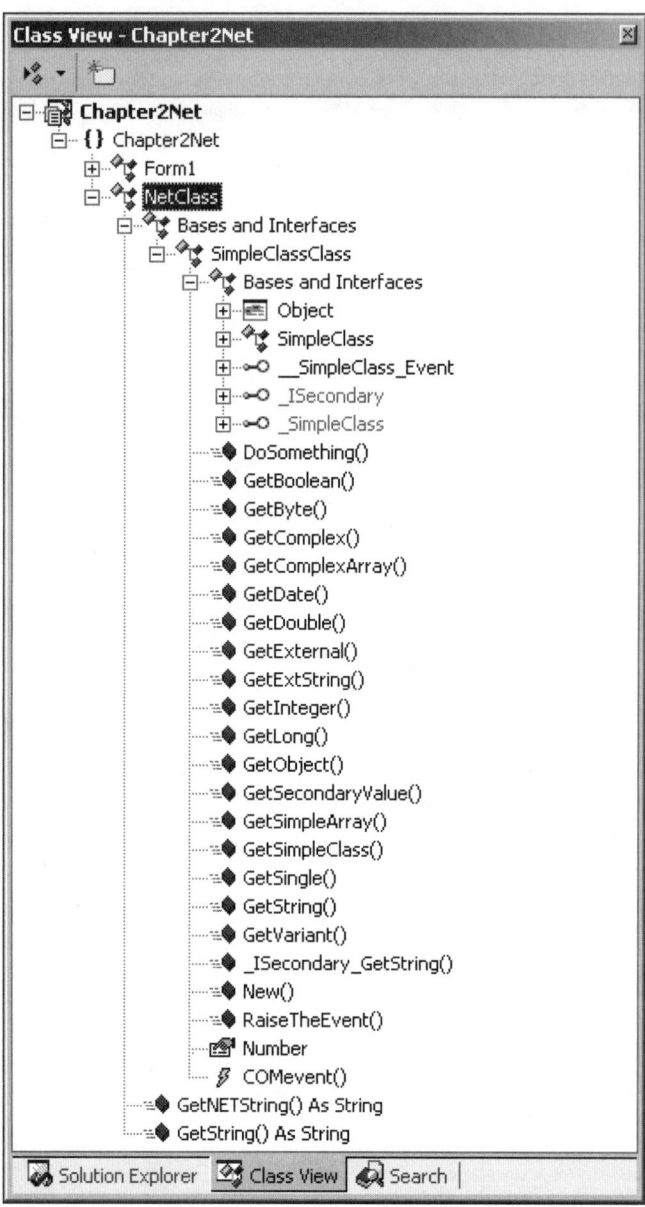

The display shows that NetClass directly implements GetNETString and GetString methods, and derives from SimpleClass and the hidden _SimpleClass interface.

Reflection/Type Object

So far, we've looked at tools that we can use to examine our COM component during design time – either from the command line or within Visual Studio .NET. We can also programmatically explore the nature of our COM component by using a technology called **reflection**.

.NET assemblies contain metadata that describes the data types in the assembly, including information about classes and methods. Reflection in .NET is implemented by a set of objects that allow us to explore and interact with this type information.

In fact, earlier in the chapter we discussed the dynamic creation of objects and then saw how we can dynamically call methods by name. Those techniques utilize the reflection technology built into the .NET Framework. We can use reflection to dynamically create an instance of a type, bind the type to an existing object, or get the type from an existing object. We can then invoke the type's methods or access its fields and properties.

To work with reflection, we will make use of the `System.Type` class and classes found in the `System.Reflection` namespaces. Add these `Imports` statements to the top of our form's code:

```
Imports System.Type
Imports System.Reflection
```

We can list the interfaces that our `SimpleClass` implements. To do this, add a `ListBox` control to the form and name it `lstDisplay`. We'll use this control to list our information.

Then update the code in the `Load` event as follows:

```
Private Sub Form1_Load(ByVal sender As System.Object, _
    ByVal e As System.EventArgs) Handles MyBase.Load

    Dim t As Type = GetType(ch2com.SimpleClass)

    Dim members() As System.Type = t.GetInterfaces()
    Dim idx As Integer

    For idx = LBound(members) To UBound(members)
      lstDisplay.Items.Add(members(idx).Name)
    Next
End Sub
```

First, we need to get a `Type` object that represents the type of our object. We do this by declaring a variable of type `System.Type` and initializing it by calling the `GetType` function on our data type:

```
Dim t As Type = GetType(ch2com.SimpleClass)
```

We can then use this `Type` object to retrieve various kinds of information about the type. In this case, we're retrieving a list of the interfaces for the type by using the `GetInterfaces` method. This method returns an array of `System.Type` objects, and we are then able to loop through that array to display the interface names.

When we run the application, our resulting display should appear something like this:

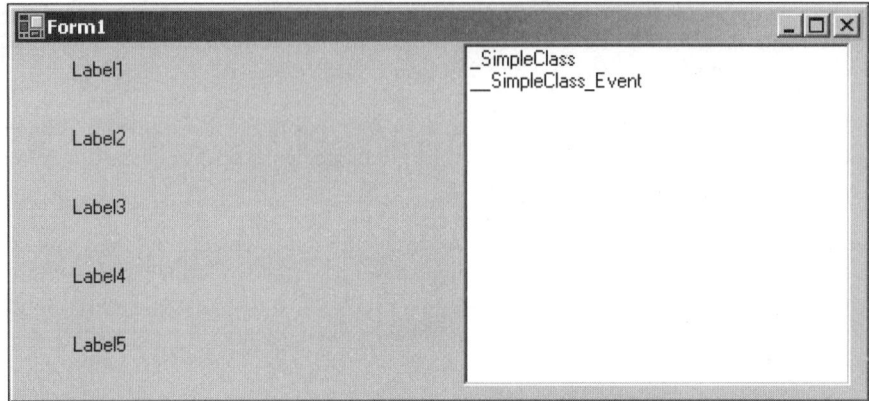

If we remember back to our experience with `ildasm`, this list will come as no surprise. The `SimpleClass` interface is merely a pointer to other interface data within the RCW – most importantly the `_SimpleClass` interface, which contains all of the methods available on our object. To see those methods listed, we need to enhance the code by calling the `GetMethods` method on that interface's `Type` object:

```
Dim t As Type = GetType(ch2com.SimpleClass)

Dim members() As System.Type = t.GetInterfaces()
Dim methods() As Reflection.MethodInfo = members(0).GetMethods(-1)
Dim idx As Integer

For idx = LBound(methods) To UBound(methods)
    lstDisplay.Items.Add(methods(idx).Name)
Next
```

Notice that we're now using the `System.Reflection` namespace, as well as the `System.Type` class. The `Reflection` namespace contains classes and data types that we can use to explore and interact with assemblies in very powerful ways.

Now, when we run the application, our display will show the list of methods available on the object:

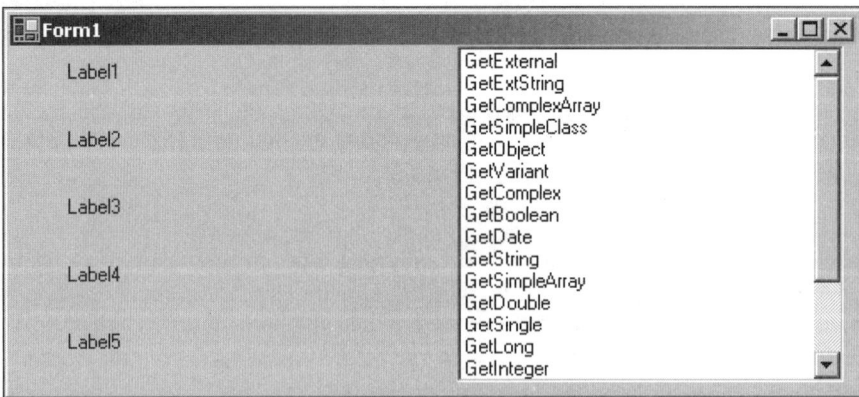

We can continue to dive deeper or examine other information about the classes, interfaces, methods, and other elements of our wrapper assembly. Full coverage on how to use the System.Reflection and System.Type capabilities is beyond the scope of this book, but here we've shown how to programmatically discover the interfaces and methods available on our objects. Combined with the ability to dynamically invoke methods, as we discussed earlier in the chapter, this can be used to construct very fluid and dynamic applications.

Summary

Most .NET applications for many years to come will probably make use of COM components. Fortunately, the .NET platform has strong support for integration of existing COM components into .NET applications.

In this chapter, we've explored the factors that need to go into the design of a VB6 ActiveX component to make it most compatible with .NET. We've also discussed various ways to reference or import those components so that they are available to our .NET applications – either through early or late binding.

We also covered how to interact with the COM objects – managing their lifetimes and even inheriting from them so as to derive new .NET subclasses based on the COM classes.

In the next chapter, we'll take a look at the reverse process – building COM applications that make use of .NET assemblies.

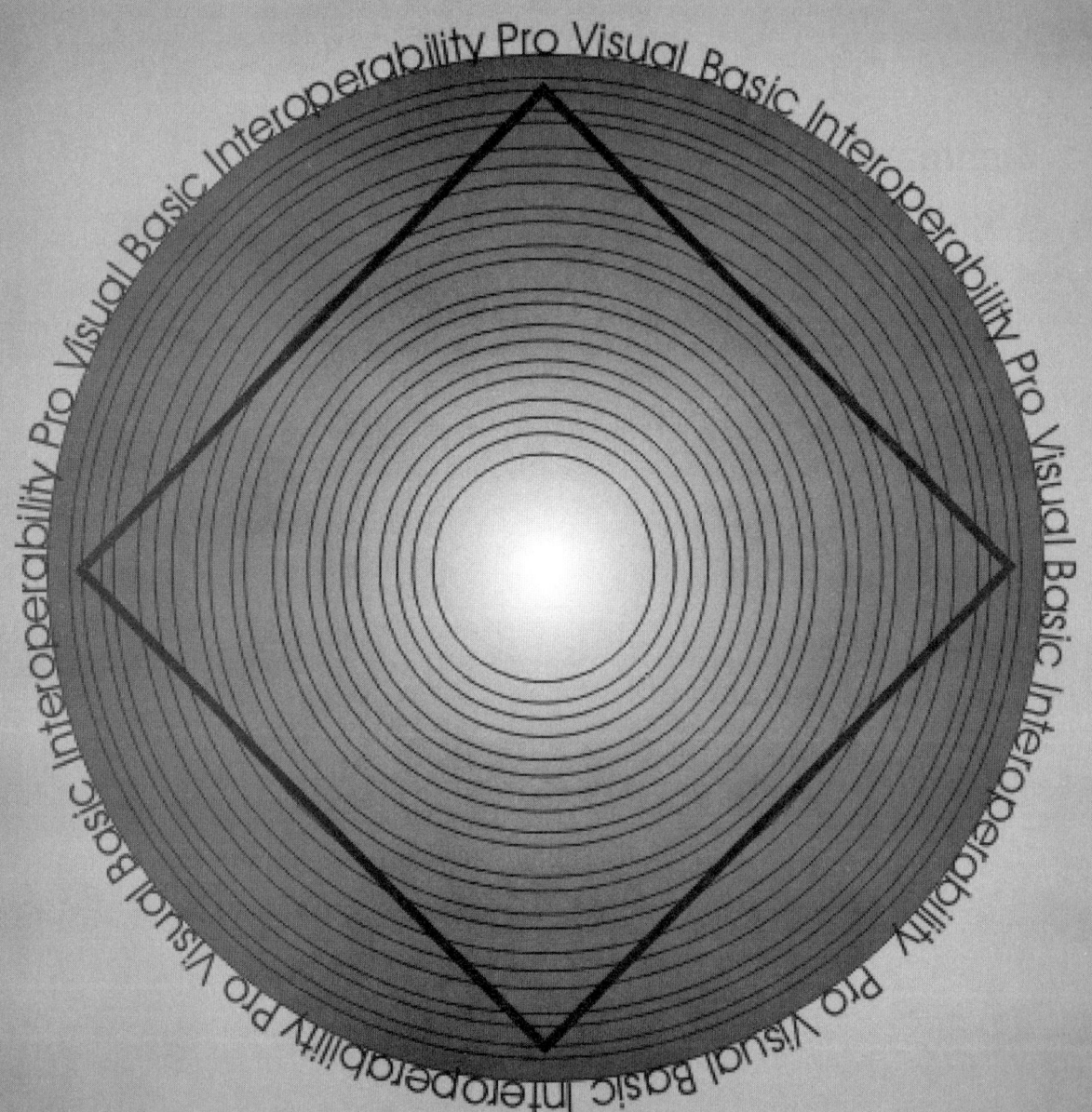

3

Using .NET Assemblies from COM

In Chapter 2 we discussed how to build .NET applications that can take advantage of existing COM components. .NET also provides support for the reverse – building COM or Windows applications that can take advantage of existing .NET assemblies. .NET assemblies are the .NET equivalent of components in COM, so what we're basically talking about here is how to call a .NET DLL from a COM-based VB6 application.

COM components are always registered and made available to all applications on the machine where they are installed. This is not true for .NET assemblies, which are only available to a single application by default. For our .NET assembly to be available to all COM and Windows applications on a machine we need to take extra steps in the creation and deployment of our assemblies.

Also, as we discussed in Chapter 2, the COM and .NET platforms have some different data types and different ways of handling data. As our COM applications call methods on .NET objects, this data must be transferred from one platform to the other – sometimes being converted along the way.

While the process of using a VB6 COM component from a .NET client is quite straightforward, the reverse process takes a bit more thought and effort on our part. The .NET assemblies and classes that we want to expose to COM need to contain a number of special elements – including extra .NET attributes and formal interfaces – in order to properly interact with the COM platform.

In Chapter 2 we explored the concept of a **runtime-callable wrapper** (RCW) assembly. In this chapter we'll see the reverse – a **COM-callable wrapper** (CCW) that wraps a .NET assembly such that it becomes available for use by COM-based client applications.

In this chapter we'll discuss the issues involved in creating a .NET assembly for use by COM and Windows applications. We will then discuss how to export the .NET assembly as a COM component – generating and registering a COM type library, and then we'll discuss how to effectively use the .NET assembly from our COM-based VB6 applications.

.NET Assembly Creation

Creating an assembly – or component – in .NET is as simple as creating a Class Library project and adding our code. This is comparable to the process of creating a COM component, in that we are writing code into our classes and then compiling the code to create a DLL.

Normally a .NET DLL is only usable by .NET applications. For it to be usable by COM applications, we need to include extra attributes and interfaces within our code. We also need to perform some extra steps to generate a type library and register the assembly as a COM component – topics we'll cover once we've walked through the process of writing our code.

Building a .NET Assembly

For our .NET DLL to be available for use by COM we need to take extra steps as we create our .NET project.

> *Though an EXE can also be a .NET assembly, classes in an EXE cannot be exported for use by COM through Visual Studio .NET. For that reason, in this chapter we'll be discussing how to use .NET DLLs from VB6.*

We need to be aware of the differences in data types between the COM and .NET platforms and the marshaling that occurs as we make each call from COM into .NET. These are the same basic issues that we discussed in Chapter 2, only this time from a different perspective.

Additionally, we need to provide .NET with extra information about our classes and interfaces so a proper COM type library can be generated when we expose our assembly to COM. This extra information is supplied in the form of attributes on our interfaces, classes, methods, and variables.

There are two techniques available for our use when adding attributes. One is easier, but offers less control, while the other requires more in-depth knowledge of COM and how VB6 uses components, but offers more flexibility. We'll discuss both, but first let's create our basic .NET project.

Creating the Project

To create a DLL within Visual Basic .NET, we need to create a Class Library project. Open Visual Studio .NET and add a new Class Library project named `Chapter3Net`.

We'll start with a project that contains a single class – `Class1`. As we did in Chapter 2, we'll build this project initially to contain a single class named `SimpleClass` – and in fact we'll mirror the code from Chapter 2 fairly closely as we build this new class.

In the Solution Explorer window, right-click on `Class1` and choose **Delete**. This will remove the class from our project.

> *It is also possible to simply rename the class, both in the Solution Explorer and in the code. For a simple class either way works, but for more complex classes such as a Form, a Component, or a Service, it is almost always easier to delete the old file and add a new one with the correct name.*

Then choose **Project | Add Class** to add a new class to the project. Name this new class `SimpleClass`.

This will start us with the following code:

```
Public Class SimpleClass

End Class
```

We'll build on this as we create our class for use by COM.

Controlling Object Creation

Visual Basic .NET classes have a special method called a **constructor**, which is always named New. This method is always called as each object is created, allowing us to initialize the object. The New method can accept parameters as well.

For our class to be creatable from COM, we must have a constructor method that accepts no parameters. If our class only has constructors that require parameters we will get an error when we attempt to instantiate an object from that class.

Though our COM-based clients have no concept of constructors or passing parameters as an object is created, they will interact with our .NET code via a wrapper class. That wrapper class will cause the constructor method to be called when the .NET object is created, but it will only be able to create objects that require no parameters for the constructor.

In VB6 we have the Instancing property on our classes that allows us to control how applications can create objects from our DLL. We can specify that objects can be created at will, or that they are private and can't be created or used outside our DLL at all. We can specify that an object can be created *within* our DLL, but can also be used by a client application if it gets a reference to the object.

The default Instancing property for a VB6 class is Multiuse, which means that objects can be created and used by a client as desired.

Visual Basic .NET doesn't have an Instancing property, instead relying on the scope of the class itself and the declaration and implementation of the constructor methods to control creation of the object. Of course, .NET classes can have several constructor methods, but when we're talking about COM interop, it is the scope of the constructor that accepts no parameters that counts, since that is the one that will be invoked when our object is created by the COM-callable wrapper.

The following table shows the VB6 Instancing property value and the corresponding Visual Basic .NET class scope and constructor implementation. On the left is the VB6 Instancing property value, and on the right is the corresponding Visual Basic .NET class declaration and constructor code for the equivalent functionality:

VB6 Instancing property	Visual Basic .NET class scope
| Private | ```
Friend Class TheClass
    Public Sub New()

    End Sub
End Class
```<br><br>Since the class is Friend, it cannot be created by any code outside our Visual Basic .NET project – meaning the class is private to our project or assembly. |
| PublicNot Creatable | ```
Public Class TheClass
    Friend Sub New()

    End Sub
End Class
```<br><br>Though the class is declared as Public – making it available to code outside our project – the constructor method is declared as Friend, meaning that only code *inside* our Visual Basic .NET project can actually create an instance of the class, though once created the object can be used by code *outside* our project or assembly. |
| Multiuse | ```
Public Class TheClass
    Public Sub New()

    End Sub
End Class
```<br>or<br>```
Public Class TheClass

End Class
```<br><br>Since both the class and constructor are Public, the class is available to code outside our project, and code outside our project can create objects based on the class. This is the equivalent to the default behavior of a VB6 class.<br><br>Alternately we can have *no constructor at all*, in which case the VB compiler will create an empty Public Sub New for us behind the scenes – which gets us the same basic functionality. |

VB6 `Instancing` property	Visual Basic .NET class scope

`GlobalMultiuse`	```Public Class TheClass``` `Private Sub New()`
	
	`End Sub`
	
	`Public Shared Sub MyMethod()`
	
	`End Sub`
	`End Class`
	
	In .NET this is a class with a `Private` constructor so no object can be created based on the class. All the methods in this class should be declared using the `Shared` keyword, so they are all callable directly from the class itself.

In the `SimpleClass` we'll create no constructor at all – allowing the VB compiler to automatically create an empty `Public Sub New` on our behalf behind the scenes. That is exactly what we want we want so our COM application can create objects based on our class.

Adding Methods to the Class

In our VB6 implementation of `SimpleClass` in Chapter 2 we implemented a set of methods that showed how we can pass blittable, non-blittable, and even some complex data types between COM and .NET. Let's create a similar set of methods in our .NET class to show that there is a high level of symmetry when going the other direction.

As with VB6 objects, Visual Basic .NET objects have a native interface that is composed of the `Public` methods contained within the class. This includes all `Sub`, `Function`, and `Property` methods declared with the `Public` keyword. In the case of Visual Basic .NET, the interface also includes all `Event` declarations that are `Public` as well.

Any methods we create in our class that are declared as `Public` in scope will define the native interface of our objects. For instance, as we did in the COM `SimpleClass` in Chapter 2, we can create a `GetString` method:

```
Public Class SimpleClass
   Public Function GetString() As String
     Return "A .NET string"
   End Function
End Class
```

This method will be available to all users of our object because it is declared as `Public`. Once we expose the .NET assembly to COM, we will be able to call this method from our COM-based client applications.

Implementing Methods

The same thing applies to any `Sub` or `Property` method as well. For instance, we could define another method in our interface such as:

```
Public Sub DoSomething(ByVal Index As Integer)
    Dim srtIndex As Short
    Dim intSum As Integer

    For srtIndex = 1 To Index
        intSum += srtIndex
    Next
End Sub
```

Which is roughly the equivalent of the `DoSomething` method we implemented in Chapter 2.

Because these methods are declared as `Public`, they are available for direct use by any clients.

Property Methods

We can implement properties that will be available from our COM clients. Properties in Visual Basic .NET are a bit different from in VB6 – a property method in Visual Basic .NET is a single block structure that is scoped as one unit. We can add a property to our class as follows:

```
Private msrtValue As Short

Public Property Number() As Short
    Get
        Return msrtValue
    End Get
    Set(ByVal Value As Short)
        msrtValue = Value
    End Set
End Property
```

Both the `Get` and `Let` portions of the property are scoped as `Public`, whereas in VB6 we can scope the `Get` as `Public` and the `Let` as `Friend` to create a property that can only be altered by other code within our project.

While we can't quite accomplish the same effect as declaring `Let` as `Friend` in VB6, we can also create read-only and write-only properties in Visual Basic .NET. For instance, we could alter the `Number` property to be read-only:

```
Public ReadOnly Property Number() As Short
    Get
        Return msrtValue
    End Get
End Property
```

In which case it will have the same effect as if we'd not implemented a `Property Let` in the equivalent VB6 code. Likewise, we can create a write only `Number` property:

```
Public WriteOnly Property Number() As Short
  Set(ByVal Value As Short)
    msrtValue = Value
  End Set
End Property
```

This is the equivalent of a VB6 property that has no `Property Get` routine, but only a `Property Let`.

For the purposes of our example assembly, however, let's restore the `Number` property to be a regular read/write property:

```
Public Property Number() As Short
  Get
    Return msrtValue
  End Get
  Set(ByVal Value As Short)
    msrtValue = Value
  End Set
End Property
```

This way we are exposing a read/write property that will be available for use from our COM application for retrieving and updating the value.

Events

In Chapter 2 we saw how events from our COM components are made available for use by .NET client applications. The same is basically true when we go the other direction – an event declared in our Visual Basic .NET code will be available to a VB6 client application.

Coding the Event

Events in Visual Basic .NET are coded using the same keywords – `Event` and `RaiseEvent` – as in VB6.

We'll define a new event named `NETevent` that can be raised by our code, along with a method to raise this event. First we need to add the method to our class:

```
Public Class SimpleClass
  Public Event NETevent()
```

Then we can add the method that will raise the event:

```
Public Sub RaiseTheEvent()
  RaiseEvent NETevent()
End Sub
```

At this point we have a fully functioning .NET event, which will be available to .NET and COM-based clients.

Passing Data

In Chapter 2 we discussed the concept of blittable and non-blittable data types. Blittable data types are isomorphic – meaning that they have the same representation in the .NET platform as they do in the COM platform. They can be easily and efficiently transferred between the two platforms. Non-blittable types may have different representations in the COM platform than in the .NET platform, and often must undergo some conversion as they are transferred from one to the other.

For a list of common blittable and non-blittable types please refer to Chapter 2.

Common Blittable Data Types

Let's add code to work with the common blittable types that are shared between VB6 and Visual Basic .NET:

```
' Blittable types
Public Function GetByte() As Byte
   Return 65
End Function

Public Function GetShort() As Short
   Return 42
End Function

Public Function GetInteger() As Integer
   Return 4242
End Function

Public Function GetSingle() As Single
   Return 42.42
End Function

Public Function GetDouble() As Double
   Return 4242.4242
End Function

Public Function GetSimpleArray() As Short()
   Dim ar(5) As Short

   ar(0) = 5
   ar(1) = 4
   ar(2) = 3
   ar(3) = 2
   ar(4) = 1
   ar(5) = 0
   Return ar
End Function
```

All of these methods return data that can be directly transferred to the COM client application without needing extra conversion. This is the same basic functionality that we implemented in the COM version of `SimpleClass`.

Common Non-Blittable Data Types

Next, let's add code to `SimpleClass` to work with the non-blittable data types commonly used in VB development. Again we'll add these methods to our class:

```
' Non-blittable types
Public Function GetString() As String
  Return "A .NET string"
End Function

    Public Function GetDate() As Date
      Return Now
    End Function

    Public Function GetBoolean() As Boolean
      Return False
    End Function

    Public Function GetVariant() As Object
      Return Now
    End Function

    Public Function GetObject() As Object
      Return New SimpleClass()
    End Function

    Public Function GetSimpleClass() As SimpleClass
      Return New SimpleClass()
    End Function

    Public Function GetComplexArray() As Short(,)
      Dim ar(1, 1) As Short

      ar(0, 0) = 5
      ar(1, 0) = 4
      ar(0, 1) = 3
      ar(1, 1) = 2
      Return ar
    End Function
```

The data returned by these methods will be usable in our COM application, but behind the scenes we know that the data is potentially being converted from the .NET representation into the COM representation as part of the marshaling process. We discussed this marshaling and conversion process in detail in Chapter 2, and it is the same here, only the data is moving in the reverse direction.

Structures

A Visual Basic .NET `Structure` corresponds to a VB6 user-defined type. In Chapter 2 we saw that a typical user-defined type is automatically made available as a `Structure` type in a Visual Basic .NET client application. As we've seen so far in this chapter, often the reverse process is a bit more complex. This is true as we expose a `Structure` from .NET for use by a COM client application.

We can declare a simple `Structure` in Visual Basic .NET by writing the following code outside of `SimpleClass`:

```
Public Structure ComplexData
   Public Name As String
   Public BirthDate As Date
End Structure

Public Class SimpleClass
```

This will work fine in .NET, and will *appear* to our COM client as a data type. Unfortunately our VB6 code won't be able to actually use the structure, since it won't translate to COM as a valid type without some extra work on our part.

Specifically, we need to specify how the Structure is stored in memory so it appears as a valid UDT in VB6, and we also need to provide some information to indicate the equivalent COM data types of some of our data.

Memory Layout

First off, we need to indicate the layout of the Structure in memory. .NET doesn't necessarily store this data in memory in the same way that COM does, but for interop they need to be handled the same. The <StructLayout()> attribute from the System.Runtime.InteropServices namespace allows us to specify this.

The <StructLayout()> attribute allows us to indicate that .NET should automatically decide on a layout for the data in memory, or that we need to manually specify where each field resides by using the <FieldOffset()> attribute. It also has a third option, where we specify that the structure must be stored sequentially in memory within fixed-size blocks, which turns out to be exactly the way VB6 expects a UDT to be stored in memory.

Using this sequential layout and specifying a 4 byte packing size our code appears as:

```
Imports System.Runtime.InteropServices

<StructLayout(LayoutKind.Sequential, Pack:=4)> _
Public Structure ComplexData
   Public Name As String
   Public BirthDate As Date
End Structure

Public Class SimpleClass
```

By using this attribute we are indicating that .NET should store this Structure in a sequential block of memory, and that it should be packed into 4 byte chunks. The default in .NET is to pack the data into 8 byte chunks, which will cause the data to be invalid when used by VB6, since it expects user-defined types to be packed into 4 byte chunks. Other languages in COM may expect their structures to be packed in other sizes, however this is the correct value for VB6.

We still can't use this data type in VB6 without getting a compile time error message telling us that the type uses a data type not supported by OLE Automation. This is because we need to define some more details about the variables in the type itself.

Data Type Marshaling

Earlier we discussed the difference between blittable and non-blittable data, and we've seen how both categories of data type are automatically marshaled between COM and .NET. Within a `Structure` we need to do a bit of extra work when dealing with `String` data, because the .NET runtime is unable to determine this information dynamically.

In particular, we need to tell .NET what type of COM representation should be used for our `String` variables. Typically we'll want to indicate that our `Strings` should be represented as a BSTR to COM, since that is the `String` data type used by VB6. To do this, we'll add an attribute to all `String` variables defined by our `Structure`:

```
<StructLayout(LayoutKind.Sequential, Pack:=4)> _
Public Structure ComplexData
  <MarshalAs(UnmanagedType.BStr)> _
  Public Name As String
  Public BirthDate As Date
End Structure
```

At this point we have a `Structure` that is fully usable by .NET code, and is also properly attributed so it will be exported for use by COM client applications.

Returning the Structure as a Result

We can add a method to `SimpleClass` that returns data based on our new `Structure`. Since the `Structure` defines a normal .NET data type, this code is quite straightforward. We can add a method to `SimpleClass`:

```
Public Function GetComplex() As ComplexData
  Dim var As ComplexData

  var.Name = "Fred"
  var.BirthDate = #1/1/1960#
  Return var
End Function
```

Later in the chapter we'll see how this data is used from within our VB6 client code. Even with these new attributes our `Structure` remains valid for use by .NET clients with no problem. The format of the data in memory is included as part of the metadata for our assembly and so .NET clients automatically adapt to this structure and work fine.

Enumerated Types

Enumerated types, or `Enum` types, are essentially the same in Visual Basic .NET as they are in VB6. Since they are based on an underlying blittable numeric data type, they marshal across platforms without any real problem.

We can declare an `Enum` type in our Visual Basic .NET class and it will be available for use within Visual Basic .NET. To do this, we can add the following code:

```
Public Enum Depth
  VeryDeep
  Deep
```

```
        Shallow
    End Enum

    Public Class SimpleClass
```

When our assembly is exported for use by COM, as we'll discuss later in the chapter, this new data type will also be made available for use within our VB6 client application.

ByVal and ByRef

So far we've been looking at data returned from functions. However, we can also accept data as parameters to our methods. The data *types* remain the same and are subject to the same conversion rules we discussed earlier for blittable and non-blittable data. Obviously they are faster if they are blittable than if they are non-blittable. However, with parameters we also need to take into account whether the data will be passed by value or by reference.

> *VB6 defaults to passing parameters by reference (*ByRef*), while Visual Basic .NET defaults to passing parameters by value (*ByVal*).*

The issues we face here are the same ones we faced in Chapter 2, as are the best practices. Blittable data types that are passed using the ByVal keyword cause the data to be *copied* across the platform boundary. The following Visual Basic .NET code illustrates this syntax:

```
    Public Sub BlittableByValue(ByVal Value As Long)

    End Sub
```

In this case the .NET code gets a copy of the original value and has no access to the memory containing the actual underlying data.

Blittable data types that are passed using the ByRef keyword provide the COM code with a pointer to the actual memory location of the underlying data, as illustrated by the following code:

```
    Public Sub BlittableByReference(ByRef Value As Long)

    End Sub
```

This means that any change to the data made by the .NET code will directly and immediately alter the value of the underlying data for both the .NET and COM code in our application.

In either case the COM code passes data to the .NET code – either the data itself or a pointer to the data, which is itself essentially an Integer value. This means that there is no significant performance difference between passing blittable data types by value as opposed to by reference.

The rules for non-blittable data are a bit different, and there can be a performance gain by using ByVal when possible.

When a non-blittable data value is passed using the ByVal keyword the data is copied across the platform boundary. The following code shows the syntax for such a method:

```
    Public Sub NonblittableByValue(ByVal Value As String)

    End Sub
```

The .NET code gets a copy of the original value – after any necessary conversions from COM format to .NET format have occurred. Since any changes to `ByVal` data are ignored, the data is *not* copied back from the .NET platform to the COM platform when the method call is complete – the copy process is one-way from COM to .NET.

Since the underlying data structure or format of non-blittable data is different between .NET and COM, it is not possible to pass a pointer to the memory containing the underlying data. This means that even when a non-blittable data value is passed by reference, the underlying data is copied – and possibly converted – before a pointer is created. We can pass a non-blittable data element with code such as:

```
Public Sub NonblittableByReference(ByRef Value As String)

End Sub
```

This copy process is essentially the same as when the data is passed by value – with the important difference that the data is *also copied back* to COM. When a non-blittable value is passed by reference it will be copied two times – a copy from COM to .NET and then another copy to get the potentially changed value back from .NET to COM.

None of these concepts are particularly new. This process of using pointers to some data and copying other data occurs in both COM and .NET during normal method calls. The primary difference here is that the non-blittable data types may require conversion during the process as we discussed in Chapter 2.

Setting up for Interop

At this point we have a functional .NET assembly that can be used by .NET applications. We are ready to move on to see how this assembly needs to be enhanced before it can be made available for use by COM client applications. In fact we've already started this process in a small way by adding some key attributes to the `ComplexData Structure`.

Now however, it is time to see how we expose `SimpleClass` and the assembly itself to COM. This can be done in a couple ways.

The easiest approach is to use the `<ComClass()>` attribute from the `Microsoft.VisualBasic` namespace. This attribute will take care of making our class work with a VB6 client.

Alternately, we may choose to use other attributes from the `System.Runtime.InteropServices` namespace to accomplish the same thing. This approach entails quite a lot more work on our part, but can offer greater flexibility if we need it.

There are attributes in `System.Runtime.InteropServices` that are useful in either case and we'll discuss those as well.

Once we've attributed our class as needed, we also need to export the .NET assembly to COM – creating a COM-callable wrapper, a COM type library and registering the component in the Windows registry. This can be done through Visual Studio .NET or at the command line and we'll walk through both techniques.

To start with, let's take a look at the easy solution, `<ComClass()>`, and some of the common attributes we may use along with it.

Using the <ComClass()> Attribute

The Microsoft.VisualBasic namespace includes a great many classes that help enhance the productivity of the VB developer. Among these is the <ComClass()> attribute, which can be applied to a Visual Basic .NET class to make that class available for use by VB6 code. The Microsoft.VisualBasic namespace, and thus the <ComClass()> attribute are available to Visual Basic .NET projects by default.

There are other attributes that we can use to augment <ComClass()> to control whether specific methods or data types are available for use by the COM client code. We'll explore these as well.

Applying the <ComClass()> Attribute

Using the attribute is very straightforward – we simply apply it to SimpleClass:

```
<ComClass()> _
Public Class SimpleClass
```

When we export the assembly for use with COM, a topic we'll cover later in the chapter, the appropriate class and interface data will automatically be generated to make SimpleClass appear just as though it were created by VB6. Since we've already applied attributes to the ComplexData structure, all our data types, our class, and our methods will be available for use by a COM client application.

Defining the CLSID

To be thorough, we may want to manually define the CLSID values that are used to define the class, its formal COM interface, and its events as SimpleClass is exported to COM. These are generated for us automatically during the export process, but if we supply them ourselves then we gain more control over the process and can ensure they don't change over time.

The ID values we need to supply are GUID values, and they can be generated by using guidgen.exe, which can be found in the following directory:

```
C:\Program Files\Microsoft Visual Studio .NET\Common7\Tools
```

Though it is a Windows application, it can be run from the Visual Studio .NET Command Prompt, which can be launched from Start | Programs | Microsoft Visual Studio .NET | Visual Studio .NET Tools.

Choose to create a Registry Format value and click New GUID to generate a value:

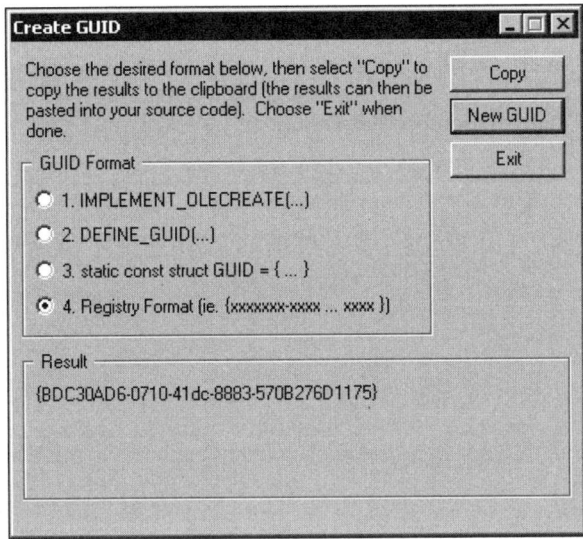

Then click Copy to copy the value to the clipboard. We'll do this once for each value we need to generate – copying the results into our code:

```
<ComClass(SimpleClass.ClassId, SimpleClass.InterfaceId, _
    SimpleClass.EventsId)> _
Public Class SimpleClass
```

```
    Friend Const ClassId As String = "BDC30AD6-0710-41dc-8883-570B276D1175"
    Friend Const InterfaceId As String = "699D706B-1272-4e8a-A643-EC2010C1E9CC"
    Friend Const EventsId As String = "42E35A08-2631-4f69-A6CE-CD3AF3617EC8"
```

Note that the brackets at the start and end of each GUID have been removed.

Also notice the additional parameters to the <ComClass()> attribute. These parameters link the class, interface, and event ID values to the constant values we've declared in our code. To be tidy, we might also choose to enclose these values in a Region block so they can be easily removed from sight:

```
<ComClass(SimpleClass.ClassId, SimpleClass.InterfaceId, _
    SimpleClass.EventsId)> _
Public Class SimpleClass
```

```
#Region "COM GUIDs"
    Friend Const ClassId As String = "BDC30AD6-0710-41dc-8883-570B276D1175"
    Friend Const InterfaceId As String = "699D706B-1272-4e8a-A643-EC2010C1E9CC"
    Friend Const EventsId As String = "42E35A08-2631-4f69-A6CE-CD3AF3617EC8"
#End Region
```

We now have control over the GUID values that define the key components of our class to the COM platform, so we can ensure that they don't change as we rebuild our assembly over time. To some degree this is not unlike setting binary compatibility in a VB6 project.

Hiding Elements

By default, all `Public` data types in an assembly are visible when exported to COM. This means that our `ComplexData` structure, `Depth` enumerated type, and `SimpleClass`, including all its `Public` methods, are visible and can be used by COM clients.

If we don't want a specific data type, class, or method to be available to COM clients we can make them unavailable by using the `<ComVisible()>` attribute from the `System.Runtime.InteropServices` namespace. This attribute will render any element in our interface invisible and unavailable for use by COM client code.

Before we use it, we should import the `InteropServices` namespace if we haven't already:

```
Imports System.Runtime.InteropServices
```

We can then add a method to `SimpleClass` that will be available to .NET clients, but *not* to COM clients:

```
<ComVisible(False)> _
Public Sub ForDotNetOnly()

End Sub
```

While all our other `Public` methods will be exported to COM, this one will not, and so it will not be available for use from VB6 or any other COM-based client.

We'll see how to register and use assemblies from COM later in the chapter. Before we go there however, let's take a look at some more advanced techniques. First we'll see how to manually implement the functionality provided by `<ComClass()>`.

Exposing the Class Manually

The `<ComClass()>` attribute is the quick and easy way to expose a class for use by COM. Sometimes, however, it may not offer us all the flexibility we might like. It always exposes a class in the manner expected by VB6 and doesn't allow us to do creative things like define an alternate native interface for our class. On the other hand, `<ComClass()>` does a lot of work for us, and if we don't use it then we are faced with the need to write a lot of extra code by hand.

To do this by hand, we need to understand how VB6 creates classes and interfaces within its COM components so we can simulate that process in our Visual Basic .NET code. This will involve the creation of a formal interface for our Visual Basic .NET class, implementing that interface within our class, and then attributing both the interface and class so they are exported appropriately for use by a COM client application.

> *Before we start you may want to make a copy of your existing `Chapter3Net` project, as the changes are relatively substantial and can be tedious to remove if you choose to revert to using `<ComClass()>`.*

To use this manual technique we need to eliminate the use of `<ComClass()>` and the associated GUID constants that we defined earlier – restoring `SimpleClass` to a simpler state:

```
Imports System.Runtime.InteropServices

<StructLayout(LayoutKind.Sequential, Pack:=4)> _
Public Structure ComplexData
  <MarshalAs(UnmanagedType.BStr)> _
    Public Name As String
  Public BirthDate As Date
End Structure

Public Enum Depth
  VeryDeep
  Deep
  Shallow
End Enum

Public Class SimpleClass
  Public Event NETevent()
```

We can now proceed to manually expose the appropriate data for use by COM.

Understanding Interfaces and Classes

VB6 objects have a native interface that is composed of the `Public` methods contained within the class. This includes all `Sub`, `Function`, and `Property` methods we include in the class itself. When we compile a VB6 class, the compiler creates a formal interface for the class behind the scenes. This interface has the same name as the class, but is prefixed with an underscore character.

> *Technically the* name *of the interface doesn't matter. The native, or default, interface is a special interface that is used by late-bound clients and is the default interface used by early bound clients. VB6 has the convention of naming it with by prefixing an underscore to the class name though, and so we'll follow suit here.*

So if we have a class in VB6 that is named `Customer`, VB6 will create an interface named `_Customer` on our behalf. This interface *is* the native interface for the `Customer` class – VB6 does all this work for us behind the scenes. It hides the actual `Customer` class and fools our VB code into believing that `_Customer` is actually `Customer`. All late-bound clients use this default native interface as well – unknowingly calling `_Customer` rather than `Customer` itself.

As with VB6 objects, Visual Basic .NET objects have a native interface that is composed of the `Public` methods contained within the class. This includes all `Sub`, `Function`, and `Property` methods, as well as all `Event` declarations that are `Public`. Unlike VB6, Visual Basic .NET does *not* create a separate native interface for the class. There is no need for such a thing in the .NET environment since .NET code can talk directly to an object without the need for an external formal interface.

> *When we applied the `<ComClass()>` attribute to a class earlier, it caused the creation of a formal interface named the same as our class, preceded by an underscore – `_SimpleClass`. This interface was then exported for use by COM, while the actual native interface of SimpleClass was not exported. Basically, `<ComClass()>` does for Visual Basic .NET exactly what VB6 does for its own classes.*

This is very important to understand, because for us to manually accomplish the same result as `<ComClass()>`, we too must create a `_SimpleClass` interface, expose it to COM, and prevent the normal native `SimpleClass` interface from being exported.

Defining a Formal Interface

If we want to expose a .NET class to VB6 in the most transparent manner possible, we can create an interface with the same name as our class, but prefixed with an underscore character. VB6 will automatically pick up on this, thinking that it is simply the definition of the native interface for our class.

> We don't *have* to do this. We can name our interface anything we want. However, if we name the interface something else, then our VB6 code will have to declare variables based on the interface type and create the *objects* based on the class type. In other words, we won't have tricked VB6 into thinking that our interface defines the native interface of the class, but rather we'll have simply defined a secondary interface for the class.

We can define an interface for `SimpleClass` by using the `Interface` keyword in Visual Basic .NET. Add the following interface definition to the `SimpleClass.vb` file:

```
Public Interface _SimpleClass
    Event NETevent()
    Property Number() As Short
    Sub RaiseTheEvent()
    ' Blittable types
    Function GetByte() As Byte
    Function GetShort() As Short
    Function GetInteger() As Integer
    Function GetSingle() As Single
    Function GetDouble() As Double
    Function GetSimpleArray() As Short()
    ' Non-blittable types
    Function GetString() As String
    Function GetDate() As Date
    Function GetBoolean() As Boolean
    Function GetVariant() As Object
    Function GetObject() As Object
    Function GetSimpleClass() As SimpleClass
    Function GetComplexArray() As Short(,)
    Function GetComplex() As ComplexData
End Interface

Public Class SimpleClass
```

This interface defines all the methods that we will be exposing to a COM client application. Note that the name is the same as our class, but with an underscore in front of the name – just what is expected by VB6.

In order for the interface to be made available to COM, we need to make use of the `<InterfaceType()>` attribute from the `System.Runtime.InteropServices` namespace:

```
<InterfaceType(ComInterfaceType.InterfaceIsDual)> _
Public Interface _SimpleClass
```

The `<InterfaceType()>` attribute allows us to control the type of COM interface that is generated for the interface. Our options are listed in the following table:

Interface Type	Description
`InterfaceIsDual`	Creates a dual interface that supports both early and late binding
`InterfaceIsIDispatch`	Creates an interface that can only be used via late binding
`InterfaceIsIUnknown`	Creates an interface that is derived from the `IUnknown` interface – the most basic of all COM interfaces

A dual interface is the most flexible and is the type of interface created by VB6. Typically, this is the option we'll want to choose when defining interfaces.

Since the interface has the same name as our class, but is prefixed with an underscore character, VB6 will assume that the interface defines the set of methods that comprises the native interface of our class.

Implementing the Interface

Defining an interface is only half the battle. We also need to provide an implementation of the interface. The `SimpleClass` class can provide that implementation, but we need to indicate that it implements the interface.

To do this, we use the `Implements` keyword within `SimpleClass`:

```
Public Class SimpleClass
   Implements _SimpleClass

   Public Event NETevent()
```

With that done, we now need to specify which method in our class will implement each of the methods defined on the interface. This is done by using the `Implements` clause on the end of each method and event declaration:

```
Public Class SimpleClass
   Implements _SimpleClass

   Public Event NETevent() Implements _SimpleClass.NETevent

   Private msrtValue As Short

   Public Property Number() As Short Implements _SimpleClass.Number
      Get
         Return msrtValue
      End Get
      Set(ByVal Value As Short)
         msrtValue = Value
      End Set
   End Property

   Public Sub RaiseTheEvent() Implements _SimpleClass.RaiseTheEvent
      RaiseEvent NETevent()
   End Sub
```

```vb
' Blittable types
Public Function GetByte() As Byte Implements _SimpleClass.GetByte
   Return 65
End Function

Public Function GetShort() As Short Implements _SimpleClass.GetShort
   Return 42
End Function

Public Function GetInteger() As Integer Implements _SimpleClass.GetInteger
   Return 4242
End Function

Public Function GetSingle() As Single Implements _SimpleClass.GetSingle
   Return 42.42
End Function

Public Function GetDouble() As Double Implements _SimpleClass.GetDouble
   Return 4242.4242
End Function

Public Function GetSimpleArray() As Short() _
    Implements _SimpleClass.GetSimpleArray
   Dim ar(5) As Short

   ar(0) = 5
   ar(1) = 4
   ar(2) = 3
   ar(3) = 2
   ar(4) = 1
   ar(5) = 0
   Return ar
End Function

' Non-blittable types
Public Function GetString() As String Implements _SimpleClass.GetString
   Return "A .NET string"
End Function

Public Function GetDate() As Date Implements _SimpleClass.GetDate
   Return Now
End Function

Public Function GetBoolean() As Boolean Implements _SimpleClass.GetBoolean
   Return False
End Function

Public Function GetVariant() As Object Implements _SimpleClass.GetVariant
   Return Now
End Function

Public Function GetObject() As Object Implements _SimpleClass.GetObject
   Return New SimpleClass()
End Function
```

```
   Public Function GetSimpleClass() As SimpleClass _
      Implements _SimpleClass.GetSimpleClass
    Return New SimpleClass()
 End Function

   Public Function GetComplexArray() As Short(,) _
      Implements _SimpleClass.GetComplexArray
    Dim ar(1, 1) As Short

    ar(0, 0) = 5
    ar(1, 0) = 4
    ar(0, 1) = 3
    ar(1, 1) = 2
    Return ar
 End Function

   Public Function GetComplex() As ComplexData _
      Implements _SimpleClass.GetComplex
    Dim var As ComplexData

    var.Name = "Fred"
    var.BirthDate = #1/1/1960#
    Return var
 End Function

   <ComVisible(False)> _
   Public Sub ForDotNetOnly()

   End Sub
 End Class
```

This is all very standard Visual Basic .NET coding – we've simply implemented an interface for our class that includes most of the methods our class contains.

Eliminating the Native Interface

Since we are providing a formal interface for our class, we don't want to continue to expose the native interface itself. This becomes confusing to the COM developer and interferes with the illusion that the native interface of our .NET class is defined by our formal interface.

Additionally, in .NET it is commonplace to change the native interface by adding or altering methods. If this interface is exported for use by COM, any time it changes we will cause versioning and compatibility problems with the COM client applications.

We can avoid these issues by making the native interface unavailable for use from COM clients. We can suppress the native interface through the use of the <ClassInterface()> attribute. The interface will remain available from .NET clients as normal, but will not be available for use by a COM client.

> It is recommended that this <ClassInterface()> attribute be used when exposing .NET classes to COM, in order to avoid any problems with COM clients as the interface of the .NET class changes over time.

We can add the attribute to `SimpleClass` with the following change:

```
<ClassInterface(ClassInterfaceType.None)> _
Public Class SimpleClass
```

The native interface – comprising all the `Public` methods – will no longer be exported for use by COM clients, so only our formal interface will be available.

The `<ClassInterface()>` attribute allows us to control the way a COM interface is generated for our class. The options available are listed in the following table:

Class Interface	Description
AutoDispatch	Creates an `IDispatch` interface that only supports late binding
AutoDual	Creates a dual interface that supports both early and late binding
None	Creates no interface – the class is not directly available for use from COM

Since we're manually providing an interface for the class via `_SimpleClass`, we've chosen to not expose the class itself directly.

Events

When we used the `<ComClass()>` attribute, our events were automatically handled and exposed to COM. Since we're doing the work manually, we'll need to go through some extra work to make the events work as well.

We already have `NETevent` declared in `SimpleClass` along with a `RaiseEvent` method to raise the event when we desire. The `_SimpleClass` interface also has a declaration for `NETevent` and `RaiseEvent`. This means that any .NET client can work with the event either directly through `SimpleClass` or through the `_SimpleClass` interface.

Before the event will be properly exposed to a COM client, however, we need to define a special interface through which COM will work with the event mechanism.

Under the covers, VB6 and COM use a callback mechanism to implement events. An event is raised in COM by having the object make a late-bound method call back into the client. The client method then triggers what we see as the event within our VB6 code.

> *The event mechanism in .NET is based on* delegates, *a more structured form of a callback that provides early binding and a clearer connection between raising and handling each event. This is quite different from COM, which is why we need to do this extra work to get our .NET events to come across to COM.*

We never see the details of this in VB6 because it is handled automatically behind the scenes. When we want to raise an event from a .NET class such that it can be handled by a VB6 client, we need to look under the covers just a bit. We still don't have to get too deep into the details, but we do have to write some code to help .NET properly link our events such that COM can receive them.

The first thing we need to do is declare a formal interface for our events. Though we already have a formal interface for our class, the COM event callback mechanism requires a special interface for use in handling events.

This interface must contain methods corresponding to all the events we'll be raising from our .NET class. In the case of `SimpleClass` we are raising a single event, so our interface should appear as:

```
Imports System.Runtime.InteropServices

<InterfaceType(ComInterfaceType.InterfaceIsIDispatch)> _
Public Interface SimpleClassEvents
    Sub NETevent()
End Interface
```

Notice that we're defining the interface at the top of the code module – before the code containing `SimpleClass` itself.

Also notice that we're using the `<InterfaceType()>` attribute – in this case to indicate that we want an `IDispatch` interface. Since COM event handling is late-bound, there is no reason to support the concept of an early bound or `Vtable` interface in COM.

The name of the interface doesn't really matter, though it is advisable to name it so that it is related to the class that is actually raising the events. It is critical, however, that the name of the event declared in the interface matches the name of the event in our actual class.

The final step in handling events is to link the event interface to our actual class. `SimpleClass` contains the code to raise our event, and `SimpleClassEvents` provides a formal interface that defines those events via an `IDispatch` interface to COM. To link all this together, we can add an attribute to the declaration of `SimpleClass`:

```
<ClassInterface(ClassInterfaceType.None), _
 ComSourceInterfaces("Chapter3Net.SimpleClassEvents")> _
Public Class SimpleClass
```

The `<ComSourceInterfaces()>` attribute links a list of event source interfaces to our class – thus allowing COM to realize that our class will be raising events via these interfaces. Basically, we're just indicating that our class may be raising events corresponding to the methods listed in the `SimpleClassEvents` interface.

When our .NET assembly is exported for use by COM, this attribute will trigger the creation of the necessary plumbing to link our .NET event to a COM event so our COM client code can handle the event just as though it were a normal COM event.

Removing <ComVisible()>

Now that no `Public` methods from `SimpleClass` are ever directly exposed to a COM client, the `ForDotNetOnly` method can also be changed by removing the `<ComVisible()>` attribute:

```
    Public Sub ForDotNetOnly()

    End Sub
End Class
```

When the COM interface was being automatically generated we needed this attribute to prevent the method from being exposed to COM. Now, however, we have total control over what methods are exposed. If they are in our _SimpleClass interface they are exposed, otherwise they are not. This illustrates how manually creating the interface gives us a great deal of flexibility and control over exactly which methods are or are not available for use by COM clients.

At this point we've duplicated the work that <ComClass()> does for us and have achieved exactly the same result – a formal interface exposed to COM and a class interface that is hidden from COM. Now we'll see how to register and use assemblies from COM.

Registering .NET Assemblies with COM

Every .NET application or DLL is self-describing, and its objects can be used by other .NET applications following the rules of .NET. Normally these .NET assemblies are only available to one application since they are installed in that application's directory. We can also place the assembly into the .NET Global Assembly Cache, thus making it available to all .NET applications on the machine – somewhat like a COM component.

Contrast this with a COM component, which is always registered in the Windows registry, and so is available to all applications on the machine. In fact, all applications on the machine use exactly the same COM component all the time.

> *Windows 2000 and higher have allowed some level of application-specific usage of COM components, but this is not widespread, nor is it particularly trivial to implement when compared to the way .NET works by default.*

When we want to make our .NET assembly available for use by a COM client, we need to somehow bridge the gap between the way the .NET platform and the COM platform work with components. This is true whether we've used the <ComClass()> technique, or manually implemented the interfaces and attributes for COM; either way the steps to export and register the assembly are the same.

Once we register our .NET assembly into the Windows registry, all COM applications will assume it is a COM component – thus being available to all applications on the machine. This process doesn't affect how the assembly is made available to .NET clients – they can still access the assembly as they normally would – we're simply adding new access for COM clients.

Keep in mind that there can be multiple versions of a .NET assembly on the same machine. .NET clients will continue to follow the .NET rules for locating and loading the version of the assembly they require. COM clients will always utilize the version of the assembly that is registered in the Windows registry on the system.

In general, the steps for making a .NET assembly available to COM clients are:

1. Create a COM-callable wrapper (CCW) for our .NET assembly

2. Create a COM type library for the wrapper

3. Register the type library in the Windows registry

> *Obviously any machine where we want to use the assembly must also have the .NET runtime installed.*

We can export our .NET assembly for use by COM clients in a couple different ways. We can allow Visual Studio .NET to automatically perform these steps for us, or we can do them by hand using command-line utilities. Let's take a look at both approaches – using Visual Studio .NET first.

Using Visual Studio .NET

Visual Studio .NET will automatically create a COM-callable wrapper – a COM component that delegates all calls into our .NET assembly. It will also create a COM type library for the wrapper and register it in the Windows registry. To make this happen we just need to set a property on our project and then build the .NET DLL.

In Visual Studio .NET, with our project open, right-click on the project in the Solution Explorer and choose **Properties**. This will bring up the project's properties dialog.

We need to tell Visual Studio .NET to automatically register our assembly for COM interop. The option for this is found under the **Configuration Properties** area in the menu to the left, so click on that item, then click on the **Build** option to bring up the appropriate window:

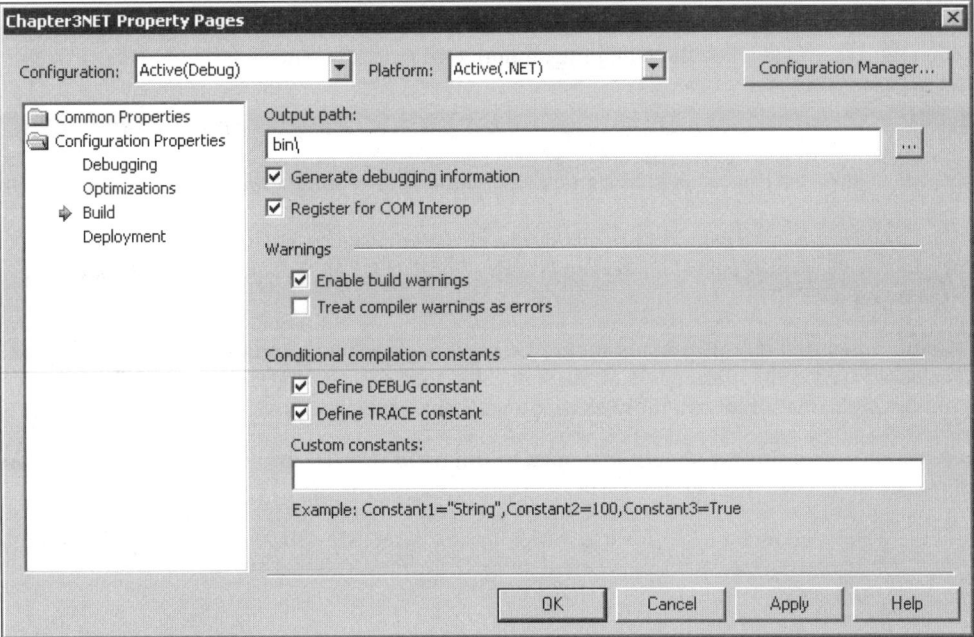

The option we're interested in is **Register for COM Interop**. Click this to select it as shown in the diagram, and we're all set. It is important to remember to do this for each type of configuration. In the diagram we're setting the property for the Debug configuration, and we'll need to set it also for the Release configuration when we go to build for release.

When we next compile the project, Visual Studio .NET will automatically create a COM type library and register that type library in the Windows registry.

Providing a Strong Name

In Chapter 2 we discussed how a runtime callable wrapper (RCW) should have a strong name – meaning it should be signed by the publisher of the COM component it wraps. The same is true for a COM-callable wrapper (CCW), which should also be signed by the publisher of the .NET assembly it wraps.

Creating a strong name for an assembly in Visual Studio .NET is as easy as adding an attribute to the `AssemblyInfo.vb` file that refers to the key file or key container that holds the publisher's key and then rebuilding the assembly.

Generating a Key File

In order to create a strong name during compilation, we need a key file that contains a public-private key pair. We can use the `sn.exe` command-line utility to generate this file, or we can use the key file we created in Chapter 2.

> **It is recommended that every organization generate a single public-private key pair and consistently use that private key to sign all its assemblies.**

The command to create a key file containing a public-private key pair is:

```
sn -k outfile
```

The key this generates can be used to sign our assemblies, providing a unique strong name for them.

> *The key itself is a long binary data stream composed of a private part and a public part. Anything signed with the private part of the key can be checked against the public part of the key to ensure the signature is valid.*

The key file generated by this process should be kept in a safe place and only used by the organization that generated it. It is the uniqueness of this key value that ensures that no other publisher can create the same strong name for an assembly as we do with our key.

To run the `sn.exe` utility we should first open a command window and navigate to the directory where we saved the `Chapter3Net.vb` file earlier.

In our case we can generate a key for use in signing our assembly with the following command:

```
sn -k mykey.snk
```

This will create a file named `mykey.snk`, which we can use to sign the assembly, or we can use the key file we created in Chapter 2.

Updating AssemblyInfo.vb

Now that we have a key file, we can use it within the `AssemblyInfo.vb` file in our Visual Basic .NET project. Open the code window for this file and add the following code:

```
Imports System.Reflection
Imports System.Runtime.InteropServices
```

```
' General Information about an assembly is controlled through the following
' set of attributes. Change these attribute values to modify the information
' associated with an assembly.

' Review the values of the assembly attributes

<Assembly: AssemblyTitle("")>
<Assembly: AssemblyDescription("")>
<Assembly: AssemblyCompany("")>
<Assembly: AssemblyProduct("")>
<Assembly: AssemblyCopyright("")>
<Assembly: AssemblyTrademark("")>
<Assembly: CLSCompliant(True)>

'The following GUID is for the ID of the typelib if this project is exposed to COM
<Assembly: Guid("3605D93E-CB49-42DD-9DEA-9017D33A8970")>

'Create a strong name for the assembly
<Assembly: AssemblyKeyFile("mykey.snk")>

' Version information for an assembly consists of the following four values:
'
'        Major Version
'        Minor Version
'        Build Number
'        Revision
'
' You can specify all the values or you can default the Build and Revision Numbers
' by using the '*' as shown below:

<Assembly: AssemblyVersion("1.0.*")>
```

Now rebuild the assembly. Not only will Visual Studio .NET create a CCW and the associated COM type library, but it will provide the assembly with a strong name that identifies the assembly as being different from any other assembly – even if they have the same name.

Using Command-Line Utilities

Sometimes we may be working with pre-existing assemblies, or developing without using Visual Studio .NET, using a text editor to create our code and command-line utilities to compile and work with our assemblies.

When we export and register an assembly manually we have a couple of options. We can choose to emulate exactly what Visual Studio .NET does, by creating and registering the type library, such that it utilizes the DLL we've created where it sits on disk. Alternately, we can choose to place the DLL into the .NET Global Assembly Cache (GAC) so it is available from a central location.

From an interoperability perspective it doesn't matter if we place the assembly in the GAC or not. The decision about whether to register it in the GAC will affect the ease with which the assembly can be deployed, since it is easier to deploy an assembly that is not in the GAC. However, we'll walk through both scenarios to be complete.

First though, let's recreate our assembly by using a text editor so we can walk through the process from the ground up.

Building the Assembly

To create an assembly without Visual Studio .NET we'll use a text editor. In this case we'll simply use Notepad, but any text editor should work fine.

Copy all the code we've created so far in our `SimpleClass.vb` file into the text editor. We'll need to add a bit of extra code as well, since we don't have Visual Studio .NET handling some things automatically.

Updating the Code

At the top of the file we'll need to add a couple of `Imports` statements:

```
Imports Microsoft.VisualBasic
Imports System.Reflection
Imports System.Runtime.InteropServices
```

The `Microsoft.VisualBasic` namespace is automatically imported by Visual Studio .NET for any Visual Basic .NET project but, since we're doing this by hand, we need to manually import the namespace. Also, we'll need the `System.Reflection` namespace for the attributes we're about to add to the project.

Visual Studio .NET always includes an `AssemblyInfo.vb` file in our Visual Basic .NET projects. This file contains some basic information about our assembly – some of which is very important for COM interop. Add the following lines to our file:

```
Imports Microsoft.VisualBasic
Imports System.Reflection
Imports System.Runtime.InteropServices

<Assembly: Guid("C62642E2-1549-4247-AE42-7C9BE12D825C")>
<Assembly: AssemblyVersion("1.0.*")>
```

Obviously this GUID value should be unique for this assembly, as it is used to identify the COM type library as we export it from .NET. A GUID value can be generated using the `guidgen.exe` utility as described earlier in the chapter. It is also always wise to indicate the version number of our assembly – especially when exporting it for use by COM.

Finally we need to specifically provide a namespace for our code. Visual Studio .NET automatically wraps our code with a namespace that is the same as our project name, but when we're coding by hand we need to use the `Namespace` keyword to specify this ourselves:

```
Imports Microsoft.VisualBasic
Imports System.Reflection
Imports System.Runtime.InteropServices

<Assembly: Guid("C62642E2-1549-4247-AE42-7C9BE12D825C")>
<Assembly: AssemblyVersion("1.0.*")>

Namespace Chapter3Net
```

Then at the bottom of the file make sure to add code to end the `Namespace` block:

```
End Class

End Namespace
```

Save this file into a directory on the hard drive as `Chapter3cmd.vb`.

Building the Assembly

We are now ready to compile our assembly into a DLL. We'll use the VB command line compiler to compile the assembly, including the key file we just created as part of the compilation. The command to do this is:

```
vbc /t:library Chapter3cmd.vb /keyfile:mykey.snk
```

The result will be a `Chapter3cmd.dll` file. Because we included the `/keyfile` switch the assembly includes our public key and thus is strongly named.

At this point we can either register the assembly for use by COM, so it is run from its current location on disk, or we can register it first in the .NET Global Assembly Cache (GAC), and then register it for use by COM from the GAC location.

Registering the Assembly Directly

Exporting our assembly will create a COM type library that is then registered in the Windows registry so it can be found by COM client applications. This is done in a single step by using the `regasm.exe` command-line utility. This utility is available from the Visual Studio .NET Command Prompt we used in Chapter 2 and earlier in this chapter.

From the command line, we can use `regasm.exe` to create the type library and register it with a command like this:

```
regasm /tlb:outfile.tlb /codebase assembly.dll
```

The `/tlb` switch is used to indicate the name of the type library file that will be generated. The `/codebase` switch indicates that the assembly should be registered in the Windows registry along with the path where the DLL resides. This allows COM to locate and load the DLL without having to place it in the GAC.

> If we intend to install the assembly in the GAC, the **/codebase** switch should not be used.

Alternately, we can use this utility to generate a registry script (`reg`) file that we can use to register the type. This can be useful for deployment, where a `reg` file is convenient. The command to do this is:

```
regasm /regfile:outfile.reg /codebase assembly.dll
```

In our case we'll use `regasm` to create a type library and register it in the Windows registry so we can use our assembly from a VB6 client application:

```
regasm /tlb:chapter3cmd.tlb /codebase chapter3cmd.dll
```

The result of this command is a new file, `chapter3net.tlb`, which is registered in the Windows registry. At this point our assembly is ready for use by COM client applications on this machine.

Inserting the Assembly into the GAC

An alternative to registering the assembly for use from its directory location is to install the assembly into the central .NET Global Assembly Cache (GAC), and then have COM invoke it from that location.

To put the assembly into the GAC we use a command-line utility named `gacutil.exe`. This utility allows us to add, remove, and list the contents of the GAC. To add an assembly to the GAC we use the following:

```
gacutil /i assembly.dll
```

To be placed in the GAC an assembly must have a strong name. We've already taken care of that by using the `/keyfile` switch when we compiled our assembly so we are set to go.

For our assembly the command line we'll need to type is:

```
gacutil /i chapter3cmd.dll
```

This will add the assembly into the Global Assembly Cache, making it available for use by all applications on this machine. We'll need to add the assembly to the GAC on any machine where our application will be installed, which adds a bit more complexity to the process of deploying our application to client workstations.

> **Adding an assembly to the GAC is comparable to registering a COM component in the registry – it becomes a machine-wide shared resource.**

We can now use the assembly from the GAC without having to have a local copy of the DLL in our application's directory. This makes a lot of sense, since it mirrors the behavior of a COM component – which would also be available machine-wide.

Registering the Assembly with COM

At this point we have a globally available assembly, so we are ready to use it to create the COM wrapper, and the corresponding COM type library, and register the type library in the Windows registry. This is done using the `regasm.exe` utility, just like we used without the GAC. The exception is that we won't make use of the `/codebase` switch on the command line:

```
regasm /tlb:chapter3net.tlb chapter3cmd.dll
```

The result of this command is a new file, `chapter3net.tlb`, which is registered in the Windows registry such that the assembly will be invoked from the GAC. At this point our assembly is ready for use by COM client applications on this machine.

Generating the Type Library Only

Sometimes we may need to perform more advanced work during the export of the type library. We'll discuss this further in Chapter 6 where we talk about custom marshaling. We may also want to generate a type library but not register it for development purposes, for example, to examine the type library output, or because we want to register it later on another machine. In such cases we can use the `tlbexp.exe` command-line utility.

The command line to export a type library based on an assembly is:

```
tlbexp assembly.dll /out:outfile.tlb
```

So we can use the following command line to export a type library for our `Chapter3Net.dll` assembly:

```
tlbexp chapter3net.dll /out:chapter3net.tlb
```

This will generate a new file named `chapter3net.tlb`, which is a COM type library that describes our assembly. This type library will not be automatically registered in the Windows registry, so the assembly will not be available for use by COM clients, but the type library can be used for development by referencing it from tools such as VB6.

Typically we'll use `regasm.exe` to generate the type library and register the assembly on a machine. We'll use `tlbexp.exe` when we only want to generate the type library.

Using .NET Objects from COM and Windows

At this point we have a .NET assembly containing a single class and a couple of interfaces. The assembly has been compiled, exported, and registered such that it is available for use by COM clients such as those we might create with VB6 or Active Server Pages (ASP).

Whether we used `<ComClass()>` or manually created a secondary interface for `SimpleClass` named `_SimpleClass`, we now have a class that will look to VB6 like a regular class it might find in an ActiveX DLL – which will simplify our use of the class within our VB6 code.

Also, if we took the manual approach remember that we declared our interface with a dual interface:

```
<InterfaceType(ComInterfaceType.InterfaceIsDual)> _
Public Interface _SimpleClass
```

This is the same when `<ComClass()>` is used, and it means that COM has access to this interface via both `vtable` binding (early binding) and `IDispatch` (late binding). Within VB6 we can use either early binding or late binding to interact with the class. If we were to create a scripting client using ASP we would only use the late binding approach.

Early Binding

When we use early binding, we are having our client application invoke a `vtable` interface exposed by the COM wrapper created for our .NET assembly. The COM wrapper can then make intelligent, early bound calls directly into our .NET assembly as needed. This is illustrated by the following diagram:

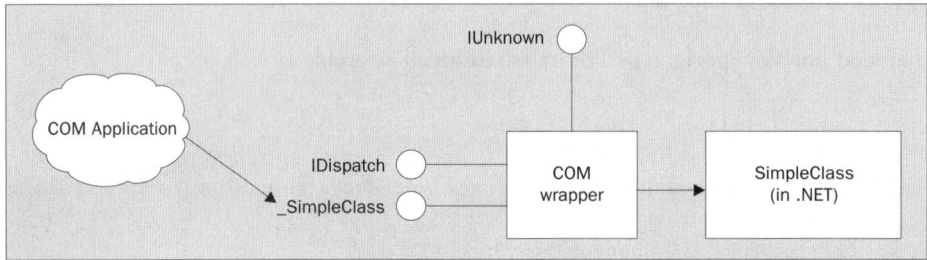

The COM client application makes early-bound calls through the `_SimpleClass` interface using `vtable` binding, just like we'd get using early binding to talk to a VB6 DLL. The CCW then makes the actual method calls to the underlying .NET assembly in a very efficient manner, providing the best possible performance.

Let's create a simple VB6 client application that uses early binding to interact with the .NET assembly. Open the VB6 IDE and create a new Standard EXE project.

Choose **Project | Properties** to bring up the project's properties dialog. Change the Project Name to `Chapter3COM` and click **OK**.

Since this is a simple client application we don't need to worry about issues such as Binary Compatibility as we do with ActiveX server components.

Now add four `TextBox` controls and a `CommandButton` to the form. Arrange them as shown in the following diagram:

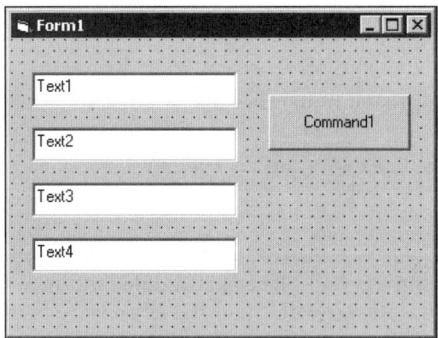

This will provide us with a basic application from which we can test interaction with our .NET assembly.

Referencing the Assembly

Since our .NET assembly is registered in the Windows registry like any other COM component, we can add a reference to it by using the Project | References menu option. Our Chapter3Net component should be listed in the dialog, along with all the other COM components on the machine.

Select the component in the dialog to add a reference:

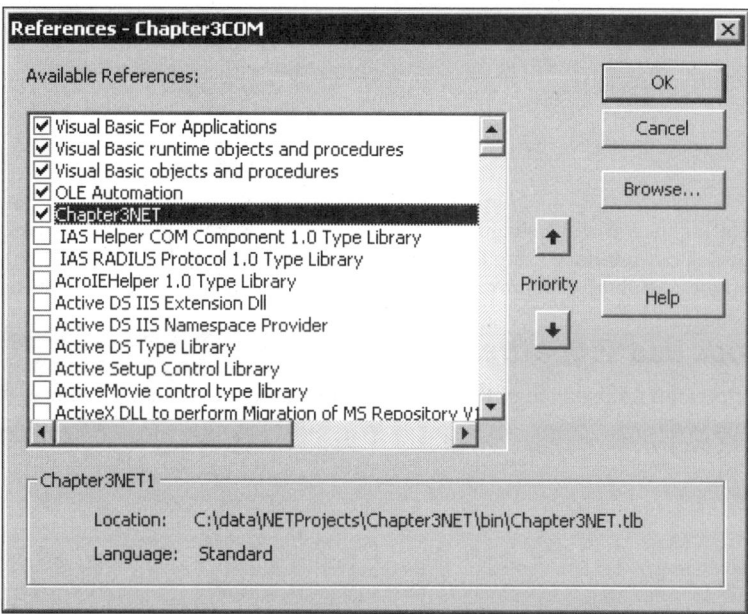

At this point the classes and data types from the Chapter3Net assembly are available for our use within the VB6 project.

Notice that the Location field in the dialog shows that we are referencing Chapter3net.tlb rather than the DLL directly. This is because the DLL itself is a .NET assembly and isn't directly available from COM, so instead we're using the type library we generated earlier in the chapter with Visual Studio .NET.

We could also reference the Chapter3cmd type library we created at the command line, as the functionality of that assembly is identical. Through the rest of the example we'll stick with the version we created through Visual Studio .NET, however.

Creating an Instance of the Class

To see how we can use the SimpleClass from our assembly in our code, double-click on the button to open the code window and enter the following:

```
Private Sub Command1_Click()
   Dim obj As SimpleClass

   Set obj = New SimpleClass
End Sub
```

In this code we're declaring a variable of type `SimpleClass` and then we're creating a new instance of the class. We now have a `SimpleClass` object with which we can interact just as we would with any VB6 class from an ActiveX DLL.

If we manually implemented the class, not using `<ComClass()>`, it is important to note that the reason this all works so smoothly is that we created the `_SimpleClass` interface – naming it the same as the class but prefixed with an underscore. If we had named the .NET secondary interface something else – such as `ISimpleClass` – our client code would appear differently (do not enter this code):

```
Private Sub Command1_Click()
   Dim obj As ISimpleClass

   Set obj = New SimpleClass
End Sub
```

Rather than declaring the variable using the class name, we would have to declare it using the interface name. However, by naming our interface using the same convention that VB6 does behind the scenes, we have convinced it to automatically use the formal interface definition when we interact with the class.

Calling Methods and Properties

Now that we've created an instance of the class, we can call its methods from our code. For instance, add the following code:

```
Option Explicit

Private Sub Command1_Click()
   Dim obj As SimpleClass
   Dim ar() As Integer

   Set obj = New SimpleClass

   obj.Number = 42

   Text1.Text = obj.GetString
   Text2.Text = obj.Number
   Text3.Text = obj.GetDate

   ar = obj.GetComplexArray
   Text4.Text = ar(0, 1)
End Sub
```

This code sets the value of the `Number` property, then displays `String`, `Integer`, and `Date` values on the form. We are also getting a multi-dimensional array and then displaying an element of that array on the form.

Notice that we have full IntelliSense while working with the object. Not only does that make for productive development, but it also means that we are using early binding to interact with the assembly, which provides the best possible performance.

When we run the application and click the button we should see a display similar to the following:

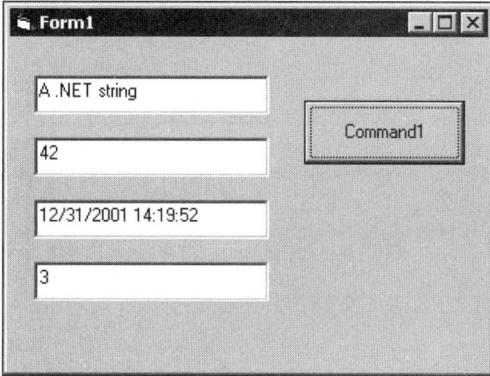

thus illustrating that our COM client application is calling the .NET assembly as though it were a simple ActiveX DLL.

Using the User-Defined Type

Our .NET assembly also defines a Structure named `ComplexData` – which translates into VB6 as a user-defined type (UDT). `SimpleClass` includes a method to return data of this type. We can write code to use this type by changing the code in our button's `Click` event:

```
Private Sub Command1_Click()
   Dim obj As SimpleClass
   Dim udt As ComplexData

   Set obj = New SimpleClass

   obj.Number = 42

   Text1.Text = obj.GetString
   Text2.Text = obj.Number

   udt = obj.GetComplex
   Text3.Text = Format$(udt.BirthDate, "Short date")
   Text4.Text = udt.Name
End Sub
```

As we can see, this code is the same as if we were working with a UDT defined within our VB6 project itself.

When we run the application and click the button we should see the values from the UDT displayed in the form as we expect:

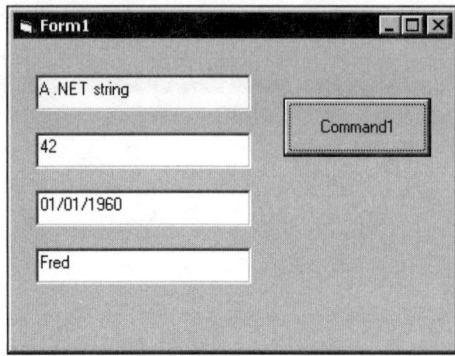

Handling Events

When we built our .NET class, we included an event named NETevent.

If we used <ComClass()> to expose the class to COM, it automatically provided support for events, and in our discussion of the manual approach we went through extra steps to make our event available for use by COM client applications.

Either way, from the perspective of a VB6 developer this is all transparent – we can handle these events just like we'd handle an event from any COM component.

First we need to declare a SimpleClass variable using the WithEvents keyword:

```
Option Explicit

Private WithEvents obj As SimpleClass
```

Then we can create an event handler for the NETevent event. We can enter this code directly, or we can select objEvent from the Object dropdown in the upper-left of the code window:

```
Private Sub obj_NETevent()
   MsgBox ".NET event raised"
End Sub
```

Finally we need to call the RaiseTheEvent method to trigger the event:

```
Private Sub Command1_Click()
   'Dim obj As SimpleClass
   Dim udt As ComplexData

   Set obj = New SimpleClass

   obj.Number = 42

   Text1.Text = obj.GetString
   Text2.Text = obj.Number

   udt = obj.GetComplex
```

```
    Text3.Text = Format$(udt.BirthDate, "Short date")
    Text4.Text = udt.Name

    obj.RaiseTheEvent
End Sub
```

Now when we run the application and click the button we'll not only see the values displayed in our form, but we'll get a message box indicating that the event fired:

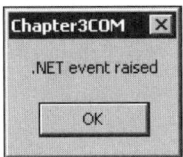

The extra work we put into the .NET code has made our .NET events appear like normal COM events to our VB6 client.

Late Binding

While early binding is preferable due to performance and ease of development, there are times when we may want to use late binding to reference our .NET assembly. This may be the case when we are creating a highly dynamic application that loads classes based on choices made at run time rather than at design time, or we may be using a scripting language in an environment such as ASP where late binding is our only option.

Late binding is slower than early binding, and we lose IntelliSense within the VB6 IDE (though Visual Interdev can provide IntelliSense regardless) – thus slowing development and making debugging more difficult. Additionally, we lose some other capabilities, such as the use of events and data types such as a UDT or Enum.

The following diagram illustrates how our client application uses the IDispatch interface on the COM wrapper to invoke the methods of our .NET object:

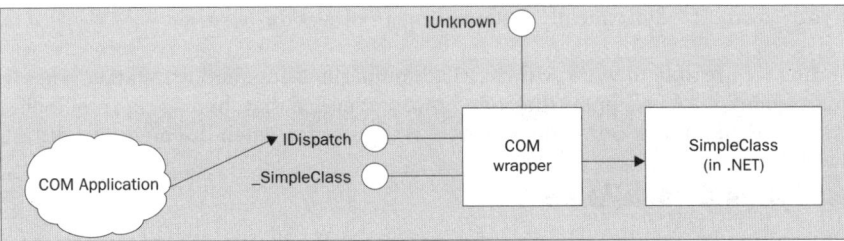

Since every call to IDispatch is a late bound call, this will have a substantial impact on performance.

Creating an Instance of the Class

Late binding in VB6 means using a variable of type Object or Variant rather than a variable of any specific data type such as SimpleClass. It also typically means that we are not specifically referencing the DLL containing our classes, but rather are creating those classes dynamically using the CreateObject function.

If we have the `Chapter3Net` component referenced in our project, we can use the **Project |
References** menu option to deselect the component from our references. This means our client project
no longer has any early-bound reference to the .NET assembly.

We can then update the code behind the button to dynamically create an instance of `SimpleClass` by
using its PROGID. A COM PROGID is composed of the COM server name – in our case
`Chapter3Net` – and the class name we want to create. This means that the PROGID for `SimpleClass`
is `Chapter3Net.SimpleClass`. To dynamically create an instance of this class, we can use
`CreateObject`:

```
Set obj = CreateObject("Chapter3Net.SimpleClass")
```

To put this into action, let's update our code. We'll rewrite the code to be quite similar to our earliest
experiment with early binding – removing the code that deals with events and UDTs. The highlighted
lines indicate key points of interest:

```
Private Sub Command1_Click()
    Dim obj As Object
    Dim ar() As Integer

    Set obj = CreateObject("Chapter3Net.SimpleClass")

    obj.Number = 42

    Text1.Text = obj.GetString
    Text2.Text = obj.Number
    Text3.Text = obj.GetDate
    ar = obj.GetComplexArray
    Text4.Text = ar(0, 1)
End Sub
```

As we can see, the variable we're using to access the `SimpleClass` object is of type `Object` – a generic
data type in VB6. Rather than using the `New` keyword to create an instance of the class, we are using the
`CreateObject` method – dynamically instantiating an object for our use.

Via late binding we are able to work with `String`, numeric, `Date`, and array data types – just as we
were with early binding. As we enter the code however, notice that there is no IntelliSense within the
IDE – the only way to know if our code is correct is at run time when the method calls are attempted.

Specialized Types Unavailable

Because we are using late binding, we don't have access to the data types exposed by the .NET
assembly. All we have access to are the `IDispatch` interfaces exposed by its classes.

This means that any `Structures` – which would translate as a VB6 user-defined type, or `Enum` data
types – will not be available via late binding. If we are relying on these types for our client application
we'll need to use early binding to gain access to them. This is not a new problem, as late-bound code
has never been unable to work with `Enum` or UDT values.

Events Unavailable

It is not possible to receive events from a late-bound COM object, whether they are coming from .NET, VB6 or any other technology. Even though the COM event mechanism uses late binding, the concept of events doesn't carry through to late-bound client technologies.

If we are invoking our .NET class using late-bound technologies either with VB6 or from a scripting client such as ASP then we will have to forgo the use of events in our code.

Dealing with Locked Files

.NET avoids virtually all issues around locked DLLs by not locking any DLL throughout the lifetime of a client application. However, it remains a serious issue in the COM platform. As we bridge our .NET assemblies into the COM platform, we are confronted with the issues that exist in the COM platform – including having to worry about locked DLLs.

COM clients open any DLLs they use, and keep them open throughout the life of the client application. This prevents that DLL from being updated while the client application is running, since the DLL is locked and can't be altered or replaced.

Once a COM client application opens our .NET assembly, the assembly will be locked until that client is closed. For example, if we use our .NET assembly from a VB6 client application, we won't be able to update the assembly with a new version until the VB6 application is closed.

> As developers, we will run into this if we attempt to have both the Visual Studio .NET and VB6 IDEs open at the same time to construct our client application and .NET assembly at the same time. The VB6 IDE will hold the DLL open after we first run the client application in debug mode – forcing us to close VB6 each time we want to update the .NET assembly.

This problem is even more acute if we are using an Active Server Pages (ASP) client, since the only way to release a DLL being used by ASP is to restart IIS. This is not a new problem – it is one we've faced on the COM platform for years, but it is a condition imposed on .NET only when we export our DLLs for use by COM clients.

Object Lifetimes

The COM and .NET platforms handle object termination quite differently. We discussed this in Chapter 2 in the section titled *Object Lifetimes*, so we won't rehash the concepts here. However, this is an issue that may take some consideration in our application design as we use .NET objects from our COM client applications.

When all references to a COM object are released, that object is immediately terminated. This is true of the COM wrapper for our .NET class as well – as soon as all references to the wrapper are released it is immediately terminated. However, the underlying .NET object is running within the managed .NET environment and it *is not* immediately destroyed. Instead, it becomes available for garbage-collection and will be destroyed at some time in the future based on the normal .NET object termination process.

Normally this is not a problem, but we do need to be aware of this behavior. It can become critically important if our .NET object maintains references to any expensive resources until it is destroyed. By *expensive resource* we mean large regions of memory, unique items like a lock on a file, or limited resources like a database connection. Most objects don't hold files or database connections open for their entire lifetime, but those that do must be handled with special care.

Within .NET the convention for dealing with objects that hold expensive resources is to have them implement the IDisposable interface, and then to have the client application call the Dispose method on that interface when the resources should be released.

Implementing a Dispose Method

We can follow the same basic flow in order to allow our COM client application to tell the .NET object to release its expensive resources. However, we won't have access to the IDisposable interface from within our COM client code, so we'll need to make the Dispose method available on our normal object interface.

To do this, we'll add a Dispose method to our _SimpleClass interface within the .NET code. If we're using the <ComClass()> attribute we can simply add the Dispose method to our class and we're done. If we've chosen to manually implement the interfaces then we need to add the method declaration to the _SimpleClass method and add the method itself to the SimpleClass class.

Since typically we'll use the <ComClass()> attribute, that's what we'll show here.

To add a Dispose method for use within .NET, we need to implement the IDisposable interface in our class. This is a standard within the .NET environment and is the expected approach:

```
<ComClass(SimpleClass.ClassId, SimpleClass.InterfaceId, _
  SimpleClass.EventsId)> _
Public Class SimpleClass
  Implements IDisposable
```

Then we need to provide an implementation of the Dispose method:

```
Public Sub Dispose() Implements IDisposable.Dispose

  ' release expensive resources here

End Sub
```

This code allows us to properly dispose of the object from .NET clients. Since we're using the <ComClass()> attribute on SimpleClass it is also automatically included as part of the interface used by COM clients, and so they too can call the Dispose method. Rebuild the project so the changes are available, and now both .NET and COM clients can call the Dispose method to cause our object to release any expensive resources.

Using the Dispose Method

To see how this works from our COM client, return to the `Chapter3COM` project in VB6 and change the code in our `Click` event as follows:

```
Private Sub Command1_Click()
    Dim obj As SimpleClass
    Dim ar() As Integer

    Set obj = New SimpleClass

    obj.Number = 42

    Text1.Text = obj.GetString
    Text2.Text = obj.Number
    Text3.Text = obj.GetDate
    ar = obj.GetComplexArray
    Text4.Text = ar(0, 1)

    obj.Dispose
End Sub
```

Since `Dispose` is just a regular method on our `SimpleClass` object, we can call it either early- or late-bound. In this case we've changed the declaration of the `obj` variable so it is early-bound. It now becomes the responsibility of the client application developer to always call this method to release the .NET object's resources when appropriate.

Calling `Dispose` doesn't change the fact that the .NET object remains in memory until it is garbage-collected; it merely allows us to release any expensive resources as soon as they are no longer needed. Also remember that the COM client will keep the .NET DLL locked, not only after `Dispose` is called but even after the .NET object is garbage-collected. The DLL won't be unlocked until the COM client application is closed.

Multiple and Default Interfaces

Both COM and .NET objects can implement multiple interfaces. If we implement secondary interfaces in our .NET code we can choose to expose those interfaces for use from within our VB6 code.

Additionally, if we *aren't* using `<ComClass()>`, but are manually implementing all the interfaces, we can also choose which interface should be the default, or native, interface for COM clients. This is an advanced concept, and use of it will be counter-intuitive to most developers, but it nonetheless remains an option at our disposal.

Any interface that we want exposed to COM must have the `<InterfaceType()>` attribute applied to specify the type of COM interface that is to be exposed. We discussed using `<InterfaceType()>` to create various types of interface earlier in the chapter. Typically we'll use a dual interface, as that is the most flexible, allowing for both early- and late- bound client types.

Implementing a Secondary Interface

If we return to our `Chapter3Net` project in Visual Studio .NET, we can add a new interface declaration to our `SimpleClass.vb` file:

```
Imports System.Runtime.InteropServices

<InterfaceType(ComInterfaceType.InterfaceIsDual)> _
Public Interface ISecondary
  Function SomeOtherMethod() As String
End Interface
```

The `<InterfaceType()>` attribute indicates that this interface should be exposed for both early and late binding when the assembly is exported to COM. The interface itself is normal in all other respects – simply defining a method that returns a `String` data value.

Implementing the Interface

We can then implement this interface within `SimpleClass`. If we are using the `<ComClass()>` attribute our code would appear as:

```
<ComClass(SimpleClass.ClassId, SimpleClass.InterfaceId, _
  SimpleClass.EventsId)> _
Public Class SimpleClass
  Implements IDisposable
  Implements ISecondary


  Public Function SomeOtherMethod() As String
    Return "Text from SomeOtherMethod"
  End Function
```

Alternately, if we've implemented the `_SimpleClass` interface by hand:

```
<ClassInterface(ClassInterfaceType.None), _
 ComSourceInterfaces("Chapter3Net.SimpleClassEvents")> _
Public Class SimpleClass
  Implements _SimpleClass
  Implements IDisposable
  Implements ISecondary


  Public Function SomeOtherMethod() As String _
    Implements ISecondary.SomeOtherMethod
    Return "Text from SomeOtherMethod"
  End Function
```

> Note that **_SimpleClass** is the *first* interface implemented here. That is critically important, as that makes it the default interface. We'll discuss this in more detail shortly when we see how to manipulate the default interface.

This is normal Visual Basic .NET coding – simply using the `Implements` keyword to indicate that we want to implement the `ISecondary` interface, and then implementing a method that is linked to the `SomeOtherMethod` by using the `Implements` clause.

When we recompile our project, the COM wrapper and type library will be updated so this new interface is available for use by our COM clients.

> *In fact, because the Windows registry and underlying type library are updated during this process, when we reload our VB6 client project it will automatically pick up the new type information without us having to re-reference the assembly.*

Using the Secondary Interface

We can only use multiple interfaces through early binding in VB6. Before we can try out this new interface we need to ensure that the `Chapter3Net` component is referenced by our `Chapter3COM` VB6 project. This can be done as we discussed earlier in the chapter – by using the **Project | References** menu option and the corresponding dialog.

With the component referenced, we can change the code in our button's `Click` event to make use of this new interface:

```
Private Sub Command1_Click()
    Dim obj As SimpleClass
    Dim objSecondary As ISecondary
    Dim ar() As Integer

    Set obj = New SimpleClass
    Set objSecondary = obj

    obj.Number = 42

    Text1.Text = objSecondary.SomeOtherMethod
    Text2.Text = obj.Number
    Text3.Text = obj.GetDate
    ar = obj.GetComplexArray
    Text4.Text = ar(0, 1)

    obj.Dispose
End Sub
```

In VB6 we use secondary interfaces by declaring a variable to use the interface as a type – which we've done here in declaring the `objSecondary` variable as type `ISecondary`.

We then assign our object to that variable – essentially casting it to the secondary interface data type. At this point we have two variables referencing the same object, but via different interfaces. This is illustrated by the following diagram:

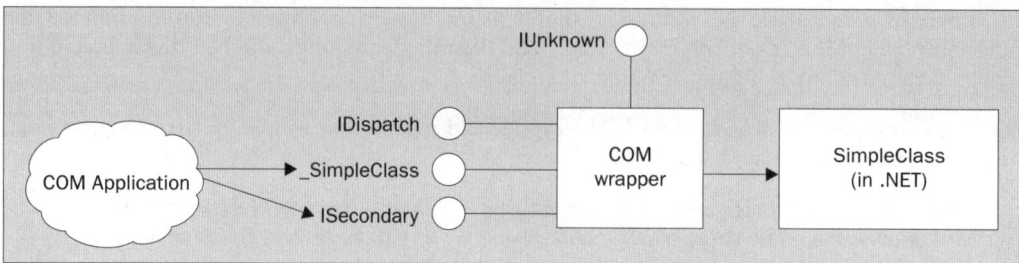

The obj variable continues to point to the _SimpleClass interface, since it is of type SimpleClass (a detail we can ignore due to the work VB6 does behind the scenes), while the objSecondary variable points to the ISecondary interface of the *same object*.

We can now call either interface just by using the appropriate variable. In this case we're setting the value of the Text1 control to SomeOtherMethod by calling through the ISecondary interface.

Changing the Default Interface

The native, or default, interface of a class is a special thing. It is this interface that is available for use through late binding (IDispatch).

It is this default interface that VB6 uses behind the scenes any time that we write code that directly interacts with a class. We've seen this already. When we write code to interact with SimpleClass:

```
Dim obj As SimpleClass

Set obj = New SimpleClass

MsgBox obj.GetString
```

Behind the scenes we know that VB6 is *really* talking to a formal interface named _SimpleClass and just gives us the illusion of talking directly to the object.

The specific name of this formal interface does not have to be the class name prefixed with an underscore. We have been using that convention since that is what VB6 does, but it is not required.

It is also not necessary for the default interface to contain all the Public methods of our .NET class. VB6 always creates the default interface based on the Public methods in a VB6 class, and if we use the <ComClass()> attribute we get the same behavior. However, if we manually create the default interface (as we discussed earlier) we can choose the specific methods that we do and do not wish to include as part of the COM interface.

Earlier in the chapter we manually implemented the _SimpleClass interface and included all the methods but one from SimpleClass. We left out the ForDotNetOnly method, and it was not made available for use by COM even though we'd removed the <ComVisible()> attribute from that method. This illustrates how we can selectively choose which methods to include as part of the default interface.

When we implement interfaces manually, we choose the order in which the interfaces are implemented. For instance, we implemented the _SimpleClass interface first:

```
<ClassInterface(ClassInterfaceType.None), _
 ComSourceInterfaces("Chapter3Net.SimpleClassEvents")> _
Public Class SimpleClass
   Implements _SimpleClass
   Implements IDisposable
   Implements ISecondary
```

Because it is the first interface listed, it is the default interface. If we had written our code such that ISecondary was the first interface:

```
<ClassInterface(ClassInterfaceType.None), _
 ComSourceInterfaces("Chapter3Net.SimpleClassEvents")> _
Public Class SimpleClass
   Implements ISecondary
   Implements _SimpleClass
   Implements IDisposable
```

things would be different. In fact, it would appear in VB6 and to any late-bound clients as though SimpleClass had only one method named SomeOtherMethod. With this code, ISecondary is the default interface and so only the methods listed on that interface are available to late-bound clients, and VB6 IntelliSense will list only those methods as being part of the native interface when we declare a variable of type SimpleClass.

To access all the other methods we've implemented, we would need to declare a variable of type _SimpleClass and use it as a secondary interface, as we were just discussing in the previous section.

This illustrates the importance of the order of the interfaces when we implement them manually rather than using <ComClass()>. It also demonstrates how manual implementation can provide us with a great deal of flexibility and control over exactly what is and is not exposed to COM clients for their use.

Inspecting a .NET Assembly from COM

We have access to various tools in the COM platform that we can use to examine COM components, including their interfaces, members, and other information. In VB6 development we typically use the built-in Object Browser to examine the data types available to our application. We can also dynamically interrogate components by using the TypeLib Information component within our project.

The Object Browser

Within the VB6 IDE we have access to a powerful Object Browser window. This window allows us to examine the details of the components included in our project – seeing the classes, interfaces and other data types exposed by each component. This includes .NET assemblies that have been exported for use by COM and referenced by our VB6 project.

With our Chapter3COM project open, we can bring up the Object Browser by pressing F2. In the upper-left corner is a drop-down list, where we can select the component we want to explore – in our case we can select Chapter3Net:

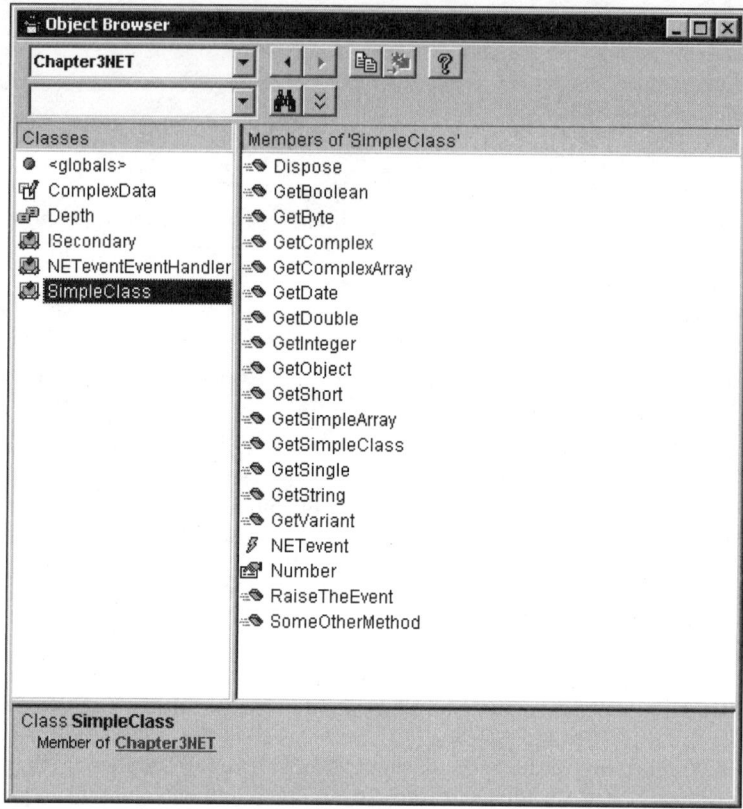

The screenshot shows the display where we've selected SimpleClass in the left-hand list. On the right we can see all the methods, properties, and events exposed by the class and available for our use in our application.

On the left we also see the ComplexData UDT, the Depth Enum and the ISecondary interface that we implemented in our .NET assembly. The NETeventEventHandler is a type automatically added by the .NET export process in order to enable the proper use of .NET events within COM.

Also note that the _SimpleClass interface is not visible, as VB6 always hides the default interface from sight since it is automatically using it to get a list of the methods on the actual class. Hiding the default interface is part of the way VB6 preserves the illusion that we are actually talking to SimpleClass itself.

Using the TypeLib Information Component

In Chapter 2 we discussed how to use the System.Type and System.Reflection classes to dynamically examine a COM component that is imported for use by .NET. COM applications can examine objects in a similar fashion by using the TypeLib Information component. Before we can use this component we need to reference it within our Chapter3COM VB6 project by using the Project | References menu option:

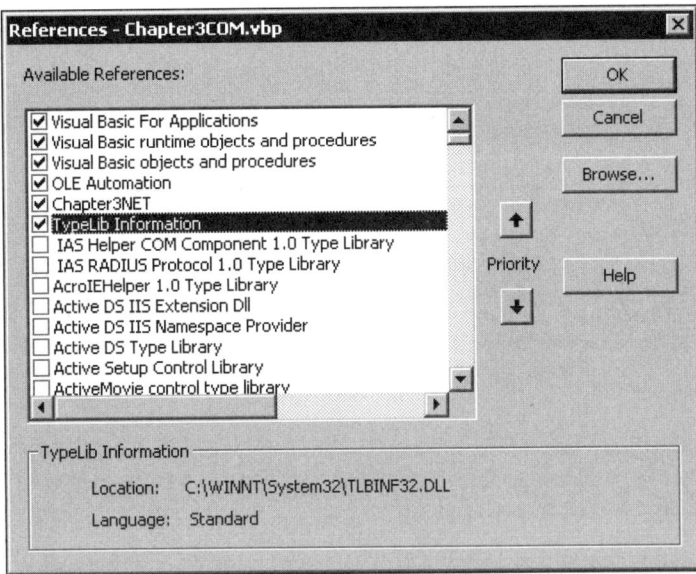

Select the TypeLib Information entry and click OK to add the reference to our project. This component allows us to dynamically interrogate COM components to find their interfaces, methods, and other information. Though not as powerful or complete as the capabilities provided by System.Type and System.Reflection in .NET, we can get at a lot of useful information.

Open the designer for our form and add a ListBox and CommandButton control – making the form appear similar to the following:

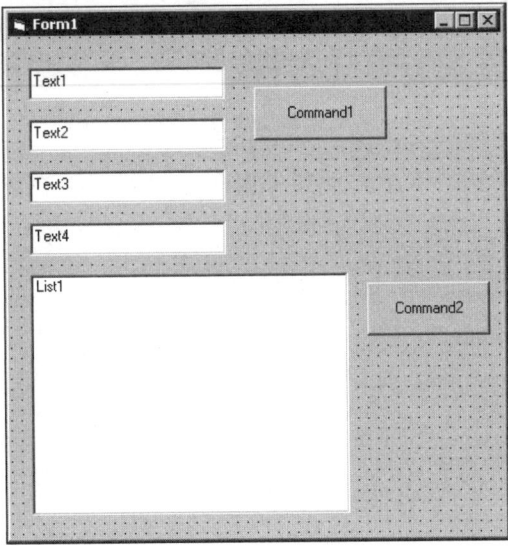

We'll use the ListBox control to display the information we retrieve about the Chapter3Net assembly. Double-click on Command2 to bring up the code window and enter the following:

```
Private Sub Command2_Click()
   Dim tli As TLIApplication
   Dim info As TypeInfo
   Dim member As MemberInfo

   Set tli = New TLIApplication
   Set info = tli.ClassInfoFromObject(CreateObject("Chapter3Net.SimpleClass"))

   For Each member In info.DefaultInterface.Members
      List1.AddItem member.Name
   Next
End Sub
```

We are creating an instance of a TLIApplication object, which allows us to get type information from a type library or from an existing object. We then use its ClassInfoFromObject method to get access to the type information for a SimpleClass object.

The type information is stored in a variable of type TypeInfo. We can use this variable to get a list of the interfaces, members, and other information about the SimpleClass object.

In this example we are looping through the list of members – methods and properties – exposed by the default interface of SimpleClass. Each member is represented by an object of type MemberInfo, and we're populating the ListBox control with the names of each method or property.

When we run the application and click on the second button we'll get a display something like this:

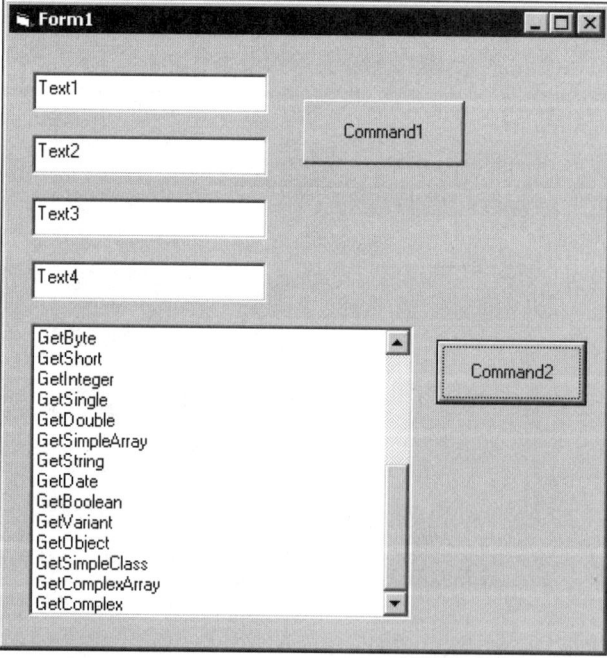

The list not only includes all the methods and properties we included on the interface, but also various elements that are normally hidden from our view – providing an interesting way to explore everything about our object's interfaces.

Summary

.NET provides us with the capability to export a .NET assembly for use by COM or Windows client applications, creating a COM type library that represents the assembly and registering it in the Windows registry so it is available like any other COM component.

In this chapter we've seen how we can use the <ComClass()> attribute and Visual Studio .NET to make this process virtually painless – easily exposing a class to COM in virtually the same way a VB6 class would be exposed. This is the approach we'll typically take due to its simplicity and the fact that it solves most needs.

We also explored the manual techniques we can use to emulate what <ComClass()> does for us behind the scenes. These techniques are not only valuable in helping us understand what <ComClass()> does for us, but they can also provide us with a great deal of flexibility and control over exactly what is and is not included in the interfaces exposed to COM by our assemblies.

Not only did we see how Visual Studio .NET can generate a COM type library and register it by checking a single box in the project's properties, but we also explored the use of the regasm.exe, gacutil.exe, and tlbexp.exe command-line utilities. Using these tools we can do the same thing as Visual Studio .NET, but we can also go further by choosing whether to run an assembly from its location on disk, or to place it in the GAC so it is run from a central location.

In Chapters 2 and 3 we have walked through the core concepts involved in calling COM components from .NET and in calling .NET assemblies from COM. As we go forward through the remainder of the book we'll apply these concepts and see how they apply to common technologies we use during development such as building a user interface and performing data access. We'll also dive deeper into details and explore the threading issues that can arise when we build multi-threaded applications with Visual Basic .NET, or when we need to work with data types not supported by the default marshaling in .NET interop services.

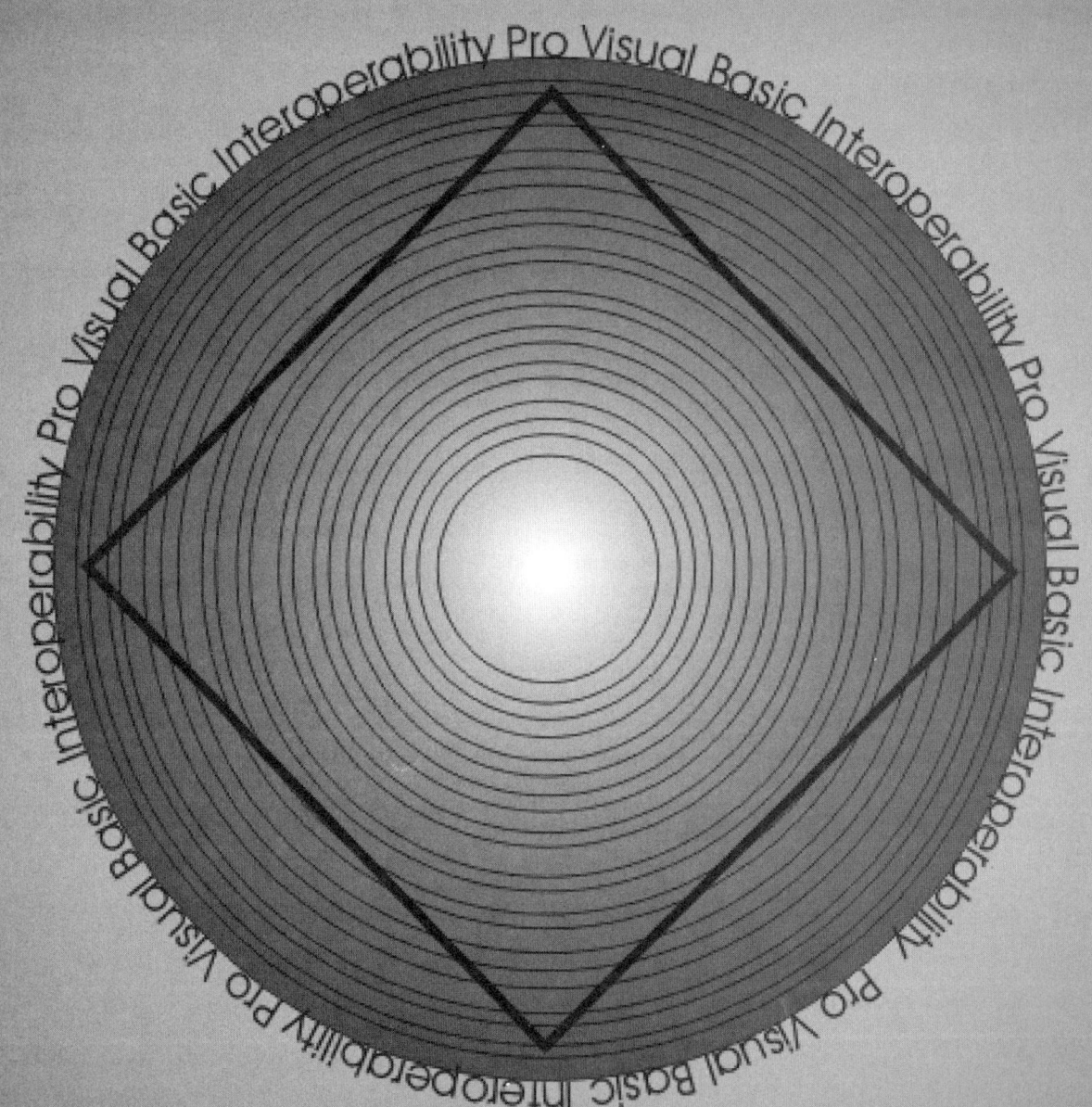

4

Calling COM Components in MTS and COM+ from .NET

In Chapter 2 we discussed how to call COM components from .NET applications. In many cases our COM components will be running in MTS or COM+, rather than being directly loaded by the client application. Microsoft Transaction Server (MTS), under Windows NT 4.0, provides extra services that we often wish to use, such as two-phase transactions, thread pooling, and so forth. COM+, under Windows 2000, offers even more advanced services; not only two-phase transactions, but also queued components, object synchronization, and others.

Both MTS and COM+ provide powerful features for administration, monitoring, and deployment of our server-based components. We can drag-and-drop a COM DLL into MTS or COM+ to have it automatically registered and ready for use. We can use an export tool to create a client setup program that configures client workstations to use the COM component by calling across the network to the server using DCOM (distributed COM).

> *For more information about MTS and COM+, and how to create COM components that exploit these features, please refer to* Professional VB6 MTS Programming *(ISBN 1-861002-44-0),* Professional Windows DNA *(ISBN 1-861004-45-1), or* Professional VB6 Distributed Objects *(ISBN 1-861002-07-6).*

.NET applications can make use of COM components that are running in MTS or COM+, either on the same machine as the client application, or across the network via DCOM. We can also create server-based Web Services or .NET Remoting services that are accessible to .NET client applications without using DCOM – and those .NET components can then call any MTS or COM+ components running on the server. In this case, the client code never directly interacts with the MTS/COM+ component, but rather relies on the intermediate Web Service or Remoting service to handle those details.

It is also possible to directly use the services provided by COM+, such as transactions, object pooling, queued components, and synchronization, directly from our .NET objects. This topic is covered in Chapter 5. In Chapter 5 we'll also discuss how .NET objects running in COM+ interoperate with other .NET objects running in COM+. As part of that process we'll see how .NET objects running in COM+ interact with COM components that are also running in COM+.

In this chapter however, we'll focus on the use of MTS or COM+ based COM components that are being called by Visual Basic .NET client applications.

Using COM+ Components

One of the key benefits of COM and DCOM is something called **location transparency**. This is the idea that there is no coding difference between calling a component or an object on the same machine as the application, or on another machine across the network. It simply doesn't matter to the coder *where* the component is physically running – the location is transparent.

This benefit is particularly true for VB6 developers. In VB6 there is no difference in code to call an object from a component that is running in process with the client application, out of process on the same machine, or on a totally separate machine across the network. In all cases we use either the New or CreateObject method to create an instance of the object from our client code and then call its methods. COM and DCOM transparently figure out where the component is and handle the details of getting our method calls from our client to the component and back again.

> *In MTS, location transparency breaks down when we are actually writing the components that run in MTS. In that case we need to use the* CreateInstance *method to create other MTS-hosted objects. COM+ resolves this issue, restoring complete location transparency to our code whether in or out of COM+.*

Consider this VB6 code:

```
Dim obj As Customer

Set obj = New Customer
MsgBox obj.Name
Set obj = Nothing
```

There is no way, looking at this code, to know whether the Customer class is in a component loaded directly into the client process or not. For all we know, the Customer class is in a component running on some remote server.

Likewise, just by looking at the code there is no way to know whether that component is running in MTS or COM+, or is simply being loaded directly by COM. COM itself handles those details transparently on our behalf.

This all works to our benefit when we want to use a COM component running in MTS or COM+ from a .NET client application. The location transparency provided by COM extends not only to COM-based client applications, but also to client applications created using .NET – meaning that there is no difference in our Visual Basic .NET code regardless of whether the COM component we're calling is running in our .NET client process or on a separate machine running in COM+ or MTS.

Creating a COM+ Component

For the most part, creating a COM+ component with VB6 is merely a matter of creating an ActiveX DLL project. However, if we know that our ActiveX DLL will be running within COM+, we can take advantage of the transactional support provided by COM+ within our code. This is also reflected by the `MTSTransactionMode` property in the VB6 IDE Property window for each of our classes.

> *The `MTSTransactionMode` property dates back to Microsoft Transaction Server under Windows NT 4.0, but remains valid for use in indicating our transactional behavior within COM+ under Windows 2000.*

To illustrate how to build and then use a COM+ component from Visual Basic .NET, let's build a simple DLL that allows us to retrieve and update some data in the `Pubs` database that is provided as a sample with Microsoft SQL Server. If this database is unavailable, the code can be easily adapted to work with any test database available in your environment.

Creating the Project

Open VB6 and create a new ActiveX DLL project. Use the Project | Properties menu to bring up the project's properties and set the component's name to `Chapter4COM`. Also click the Unattended Execution and Retained In Memory options as shown in the screenshot:

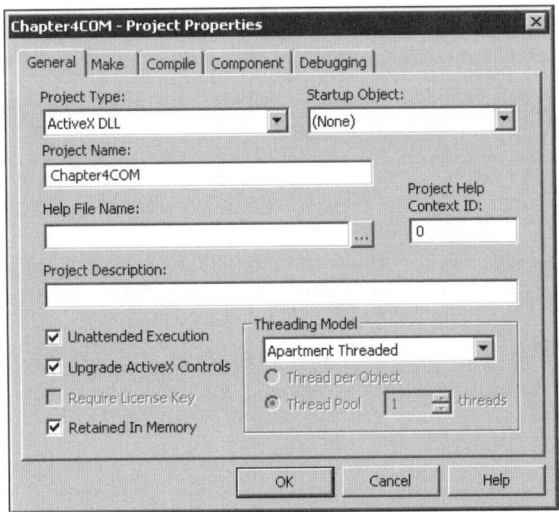

The Unattended Execution option prevents any accidental interaction with the user on the part of our DLL. This means our DLL cannot raise any message boxes – even in the case of an error. This is important for any component intended to run on a server, as there may be no user present to click the OK button on such a dialog – causing the entire process to halt.

The Retained In Memory option is a performance helper. This indicates that the DLL should be retained in memory even when no objects from the DLL are in use. By keeping the DLL loaded in memory, we improve the performance of any subsequent calls to objects in the DLL, since it won't need to be reloaded before that use. Of course this is a tradeoff, since it will consume memory until the process is terminated, so it should not be used for components that are rarely invoked.

Creating the Class

By default, we start with a class named `Class1` in our project. Using the `Properties` window, change its name to `PubsServices`. Since we intend this component to run in COM+ and use transactions, set the `MTSTransactionMode` property to 2-RequiresTransaction as shown in the diagram:

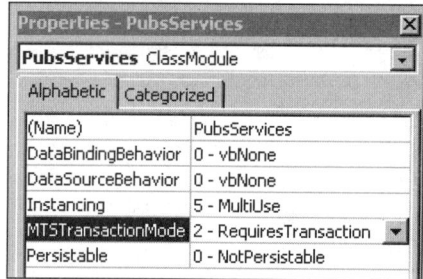

We can now move on to coding our class. We'll go through the basic code required first, then we'll go through and add the code that takes advantage of the COM+ features.

First, let's define a constant to contain the database connection string. In the following example we're using a SQL Server 2000 database, though at least the server name (`Source`) will need to change to match your environment:

```
Option Explicit

Private Const DB_CONN As String = "Provider=SQLOLEDB;Data Source=myserves;Initial
Catalog=pubs;User ID=sa;Password="
```

The two lines shown here that define the constant should be placed on one line within our code.

By using exactly the same database connection string for all connections to the database we are allowing the OLEDB database driver to provide database connection pooling. This is very important in n-tier applications.

Make sure that the option to allow pooling is turned on for the database driver if it supports it. We may also need to tweak the settings as to how long to retain the connection after inactivity for best performance.

If we used a different connection string for each user of the system we would defeat the purpose of connection pooling – thus eliminating one of the most powerful benefits offered by COM+ and middle-tier components. It doesn't matter whether or not we use a constant, hard-code the connection string, get it from a configuration file, or whatever. What counts is that the options specified in the connection string are identical for all data access – including both username and password settings.

Referencing ADO

Before we can write any data access code, we need to add a reference to the ADO library. The ADO version available on any machine may vary. The code shown in this chapter is written using ADO 2.7, but should work with earlier versions as well.

Use the Project | References menu option to bring up the references dialog. Select the box to reference the ADO library similar to that shown in the following screenshot:

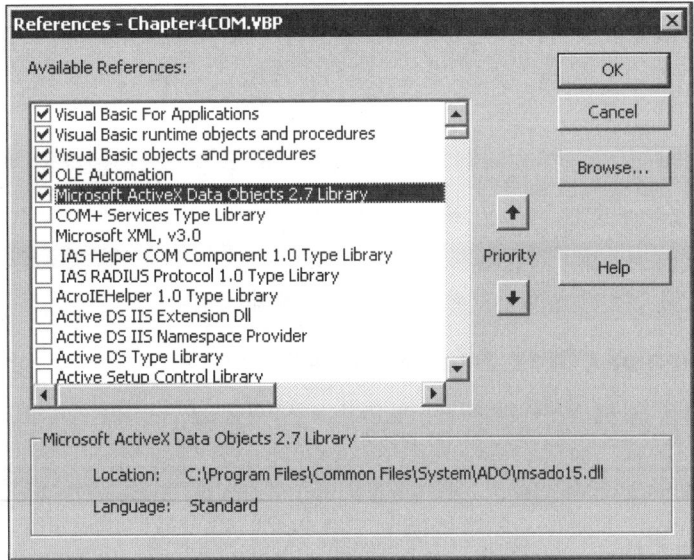

This will make the ADO library available for use within our code.

Retrieving Author Data

Next we can create a function to return the last name of an author from the Authors table:

```
Public Function GetAuthor(ByVal id As String) As String
   Dim rs As Recordset
   Dim strSQL As String

   Set rs = New Recordset
   strSQL = "SELECT au_lname FROM authors WHERE au_id='" & id & "'"
   rs.Open strSQL, DB_CONN, adOpenForwardOnly, adLockReadOnly
   If Not (rs.EOF And rs.BOF) Then
      GetAuthor = rs("au_lname")
   End If
   rs.Close
   Set rs = Nothing
End Function
```

This method simply opens a `Recordset` object and populates it based on the SQL `SELECT` statement to select a specific author based on the author's ID column. If we find a record then we return the last name, otherwise we return an empty `String` value.

Updating Author Data

Reading data is pretty boring from a transactional perspective. Transactions are more important when updating data, so let's also create a method to update an author's last name within the database:

```
Public Sub UpdateAuthor(ByVal id As String, ByVal lname As String)
   Dim cn As Connection
   Dim strSQL As String

   Set cn = New Connection
   strSQL = "UPDATE authors SET au_lname='" & lname & _
      "' WHERE au_id='" & id & "'"
   cn.Open DB_CONN
   cn.Execute strSQL
   cn.Close
   Set cn = Nothing
End Sub
```

This method simply executes a SQL `UPDATE` statement to update the author's last name within the table.

Notice that neither the read nor update methods contain any transactional code. This is because we're intending to have COM+ provide that service on our behalf.

Taking Advantage of COM+ Transactions

COM+ provides two types of transactional support – automatic and manual.

Automatic transactions are the easiest to implement, since they require no extra coding on our part. With an automatic transaction, the transaction is committed to the database as long as our method returns without raising an error. If our method raises an error, COM+ will realize that something went wrong and will roll back the database. This is true even when multiple components are involved in the transaction – any one of them raising an error will cause the entire transaction to be rolled back.

Manual transactions require some minor coding on our part, but provide us with a bit more control over the process. We specifically control whether or not our method will cause the transaction to roll back. In this case we need to manually call `SetComplete` to indicate that our method completed successfully, or `SetAbort` to indicate that we encountered some problem and that the database should be rolled back by COM+.

As it stands, our code will work with automatic transactions. Since we have no error handling code in our methods, any error that might occur will be automatically raised up through COM+, allowing COM+ to roll back the database.

However, we can enhance our code to implement manual transactions if we so desire. To do this we'll make use of the `ObjectContext` object provided by COM+ to call `SetComplete` and `SetAbort` as appropriate.

Referencing the COM+ Services Library

Before we can interact with any COM+ services from within our code we need to add a reference to the COM+ Services Type Library. Use the Project | References menu option to bring up the references dialog and then select the library as shown in the screenshot:

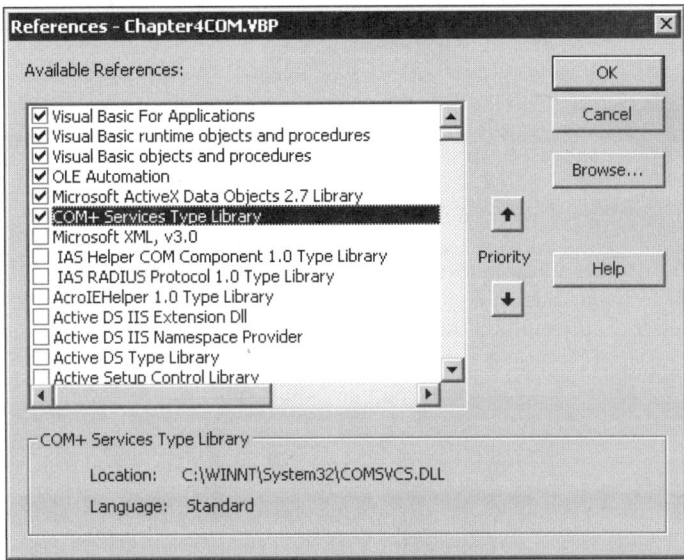

This library provides us with the references necessary to interact with COM+ from our code – including calling SetComplete and SetAbort.

Implementing ObjectControl

SetComplete and SetAbort are methods on the COM+ ObjectContext object. A reference to this object can be gained by calling the GetObjectContext method, which is now available to us since we've referenced the COM+ Services Type Library.

We can make this call at the top of every method in our class if we want, or we can centralize the process by implementing a simple interface within our object – ObjectControl. This is the approach we'll take here, because it allows us to centralize this common code – making the use of COM+ functionality simpler within each of our individual methods.

The ObjectControl interface defines three methods – Activate, Deactivate, and CanBePooled. Activate is called before each method is invoked on our object, while Deactivate is called before our object is destroyed by COM+ when the method call is complete.

The CanBePooled method allows our object to indicate whether it can participate as part of COM+ object pooling. Since VB6 objects are not capable of participating due to threading limitations, this method must always return False.

We can use the Activate method to get a reference to the ObjectContext object before any of our methods are called – thus always ensuring that the code in any method of our object will have access to that object reference.

To do this, we need to indicate that we want to implement the `ObjectControl` interface:

```
Option Explicit

Implements ObjectControl
```

We also need to declare an instance variable to hold the reference to the object:

```
Option Explicit

Implements ObjectControl

Private objContext As ObjectContext
```

Any time we use the `Implements` keyword to indicate we're implementing an interface, we are required to provide implementation code for all the methods defined on that interface. This means that we are now required to implement the `Activate`, `Deactivate`, and `CanBePooled` methods:

```
Private Sub ObjectControl_Activate()
   Set objContext = GetObjectContext
End Sub

Private Function ObjectControl_CanBePooled() As Boolean
   ObjectControl_CanBePooled = False
End Function

Private Sub ObjectControl_Deactivate()
   Set objContext = Nothing
End Sub
```

The `Activate` method simply contains code to get a reference to the `ObjectContext` object – initializing the instance variable with the reference. This means that the code in any of our methods can make use of the `objContext` variable to interact with COM+ as needed.

The `CanBePooled` method simply returns `False` – indicating that our object cannot be pooled. No VB6 objects can be pooled due to the way VB6 handles multi-threading and makes use of thread-specific memory.

The `Deactivate` method sets the `objContext` reference to `Nothing`. This is not strictly necessary since our object will typically be destroyed right after `Deactivate` is called, which would automatically dereference the object. However, by explicitly dereferencing the object we keep our code clearer and more readable.

Adding Code for Reading

Now that we have access to the `ObjectContext` object we can interact with COM+ as needed to implement manual transactions. We can update our read method to trap any errors – calling `SetAbort` if they occur. Otherwise we'll call `SetComplete` to indicate that the method was successful.

While transactional protection is not necessary for a read operation, we can't necessarily predict how our component may be used in the future. It could be used in conjunction with other methods that perform updates, and so the read operation may in fact require transactional protection such that a failure of the read should cause any updates to be rolled back.

Here are the code changes:

```
Public Function GetAuthor(ByVal id As String) As String
  Dim rs As Recordset
  Dim strSQL As String

  On Error GoTo ErrH
  Set rs = New Recordset
  strSQL = "SELECT au_lname FROM authors WHERE au_id='" & id & "'"
  rs.Open strSQL, DB_CONN, adOpenForwardOnly, adLockReadOnly
  If Not (rs.EOF And rs.BOF) Then
    GetAuthor = rs("au_lname")
  End If
  rs.Close
  Set rs = Nothing
  If Not objContext Is Nothing Then objContext.SetComplete
  Exit Function
ErrH:
  If Not rs Is Nothing Then
    If rs.State = adStateOpen Then rs.Close
    Set rs = Nothing
  End If
  If Not objContext Is Nothing Then objContext.SetAbort
  Err.Raise Err.Number, Err.Source, Err.Description
End Function
```

Notice that we're not simply calling `SetComplete` and `SetAbort` – we first check to see if the `objContext` variable contains an object reference. This is not necessary if our code is running in COM+, but is useful since it allows our code to seamlessly run *outside* of COM+, allowing us to test the code by running it within the VB6 IDE for instance. Of course outside of COM+ we won't enjoy the transactional protection, but at least our code will run for debugging purposes.

In the case of an error we are re-raising the error so our client application is aware that something went wrong. The call to `SetAbort` is enough for COM+ to roll back any transaction, but we do need the error returned to the client or it will never know that the method failed.

Adding Code for Updating

We can make the same basic changes to the update method as well:

```
Public Sub UpdateAuthor(ByVal id As String, ByVal lname As String)
  Dim cn As Connection
  Dim SQL As String
```

```
      On Error GoTo ErrH
      Set cn = New Connection
      SQL = "UPDATE authors SET au_lname='" & lname & "' WHERE au_id='" & id & "'"
      cn.Open DB_CONN
      cn.Execute SQL
      cn.Close
      Set cn = Nothing
      If Not objContext Is Nothing Then objContext.SetComplete
      Exit Sub
   ErrH:
      If Not cn Is Nothing Then
         If cn.State = adStateOpen Then cn.Close
         Set cn = Nothing
      End If
      If Not objContext Is Nothing Then objContext.SetAbort
      Err.Raise Err.Number, Err.Source, Err.Description
   End Sub
```

At this point our component is ready to go – fully transaction aware and ready for use within the COM+ environment.

Binary Compatibility

As with any COM component, we should always use Binary Compatibility to ensure that the GUID values, type library, and vtables representing our component remain consistent as we recompile over time.

As we discussed in Chapter 2, we should always set Binary Compatibility against a copy of the compiled DLL – thus ensuring that the component and its interfaces can't be changed without us manually updating that copy.

After compiling the project and making a copy of the DLL, we can use the Component tab of the Project Properties dialog to set Binary Compatibility against the copy:

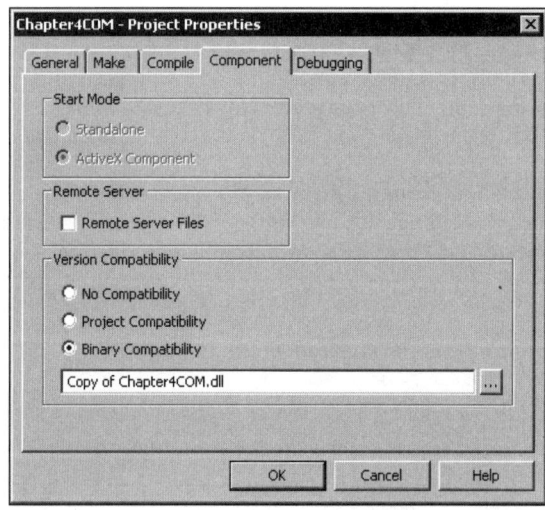

This will ensure continued consistency as we compile the component going forward.

Putting the DLL into COM+

At this point we have a DLL that is COM+ aware, and we can move on to actually place the DLL into the COM+ environment.

Server and Library Applications

Before we do this, we need to decide what type of COM+ application to use. In COM+, the term **application** has special meaning. It is a container into which components are placed. All the components in an application share a set of common properties that define how they run. These properties include defining the process in which the code will run, security options, and so forth.

In MTS this is called a **package** instead of an application, but the purpose and meaning are the same.

Our options are to run our code within a Server Application or a Library Application. Our code will remain the same either way – what we are choosing at this point is where the code will run within COM+.

Library Applications are loaded directly into the same process as the client application, while Server Applications run in a process separate from the client application.

Library Applications have less overhead on each method call, since there is no need to marshal the method call from one process into another and back again. On the other hand, they are less stable since if either the client application or COM+ component were to crash, it would bring down the entire client process.

Server Applications incur extra overhead on each method call, but are potentially more stable since our code is running in a separate process from the client code. Additionally, Server Applications allow us to take full advantage of the security options built into COM+.

If we intend to invoke our components so they run on an application server separate from the machine where the client application is running, then we need to select the Server Application option.

Either type of application will work fine when invoked by a .NET client application. A Library Application will be loaded into the .NET application's process to run, while a Server Application will run in a separate process and the .NET application will make all method calls across the process boundary.

For this example we'll create a Server Application to host our COM+ component.

Creating the COM+ Application

Before we can put our component into COM+, we need to define the COM+ Application where the component will reside. Each Application specifies many options for the components, including whether the component will run in the client application's process, the security options for all components, and so forth.

To administrate COM+, choose Start | Programs | Administrative Tools | Component Services to bring up the Component Services administration console. In the panel on the left, expand Component Services, My Computer, and COM+ Applications options to get a list of all the existing COM+ Applications on the system:

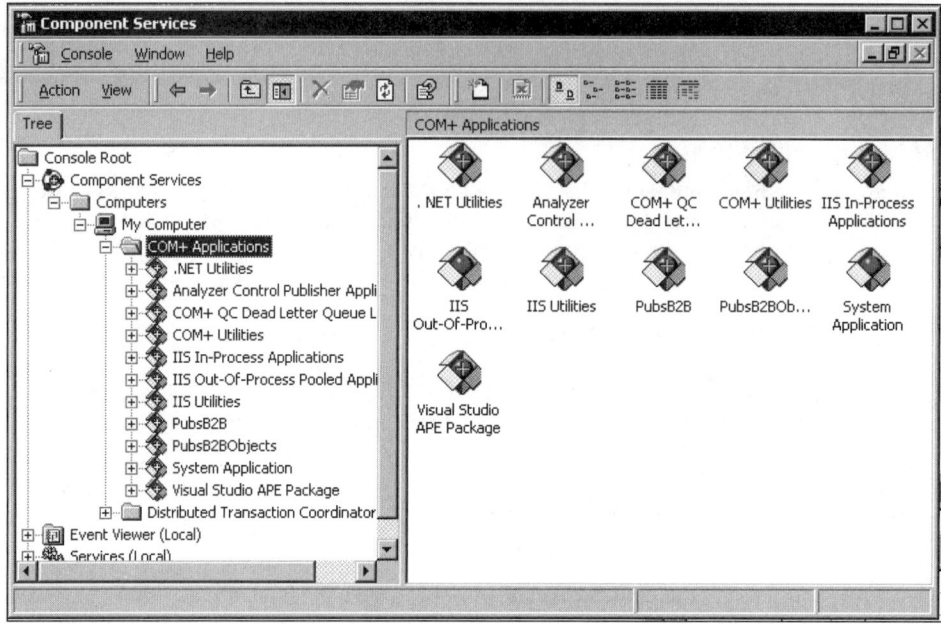

Where appropriate, we can add our component to an existing Application. In this case, however, we'll add a new Application to house our component. To do this, right-click on the COM+ Applications option in the left-hand pane and select New | Application from the menu. This will bring up the COM Application Installation Wizard.

Click Next to move to the first interactive panel of the wizard:

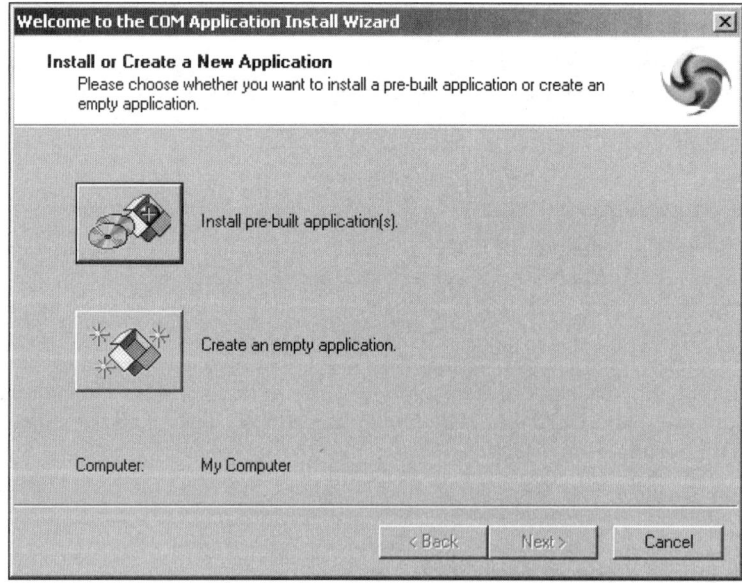

Since we are creating a new Application for our component we'll want to click on the **Create an empty application** option. The other option is used to install pre-existing COM+ Applications that have been created on another server.

The next panel is where we choose whether to create a Library or Server Application, and where we give our Application a name. The default is to create a Server Application, so we are all set there – all we need to do is enter a name:

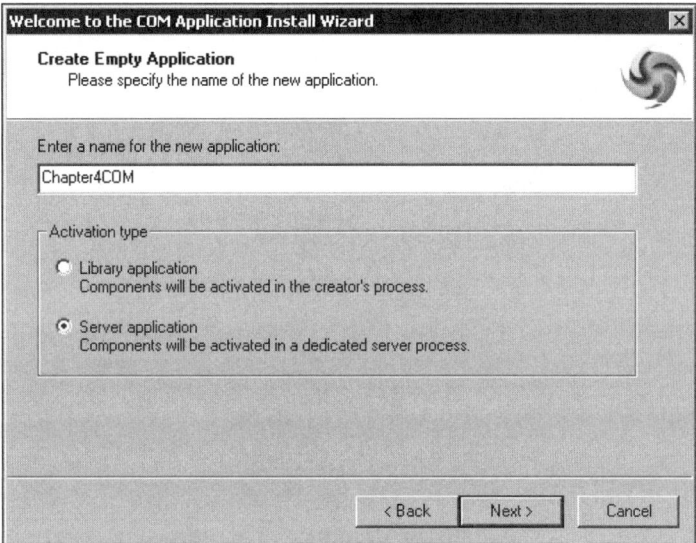

Enter `Chapter4COM` as the name and click **Next** to move to the next panel. This next panel allows us to specify the user name under which our component will run, and is an option available only to Server Applications since Library Applications just run in the client application's process.

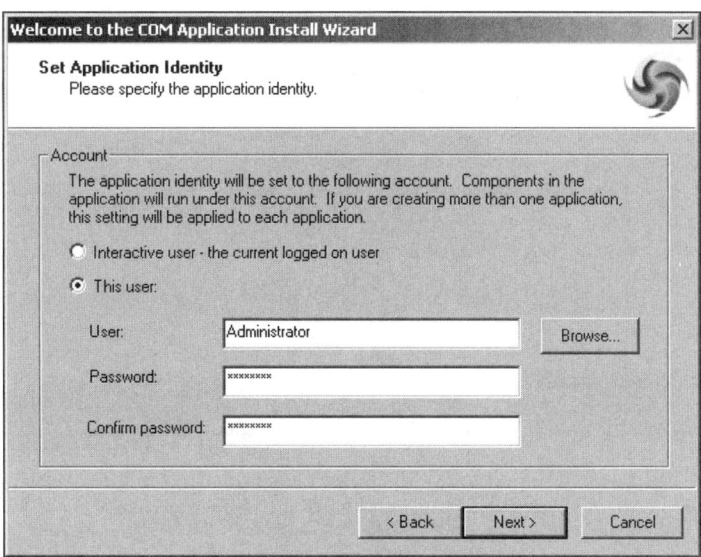

We should always specify a user and password here. If we accept the default – to run under the logged in user – then our application will be unavailable if no one is logged into the server. Additionally, we may run into problems if someone with very little security access logs into the server, since our component may not even have access to the database we're invoking.

Here we've specified that the application will run under the Administrator user regardless of who is logged into the server interactively.

> *Typically we'll want to create a special user account under which our applications should run so we can control the specific security access available to that user, but for the purposes of testing in this chapter the Administrator user will do fine.*

After we click Next here, and Finish on the final panel of the wizard, the wizard will add our new Application to the COM+ environment.

Adding the Component to the Application

Select the Chapter4COM application in the left pane and expand it so we can select the Components element:

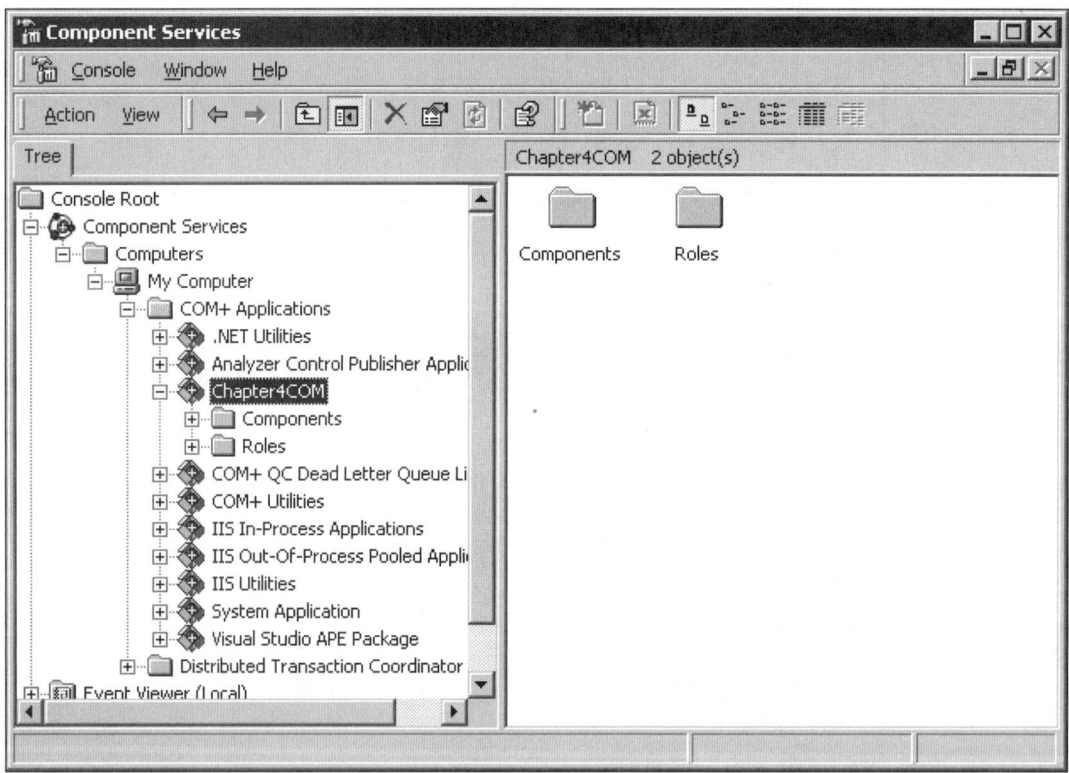

Now we are ready to add our DLL into COM+. We can do this by using a COM+ wizard, or more simply we can drag-and-drop our DLL into the right-hand pane shown above. If we run the wizard we'll need to make a series of choices.

After the introductory panel of the wizard, we need to indicate that we want to install new components:

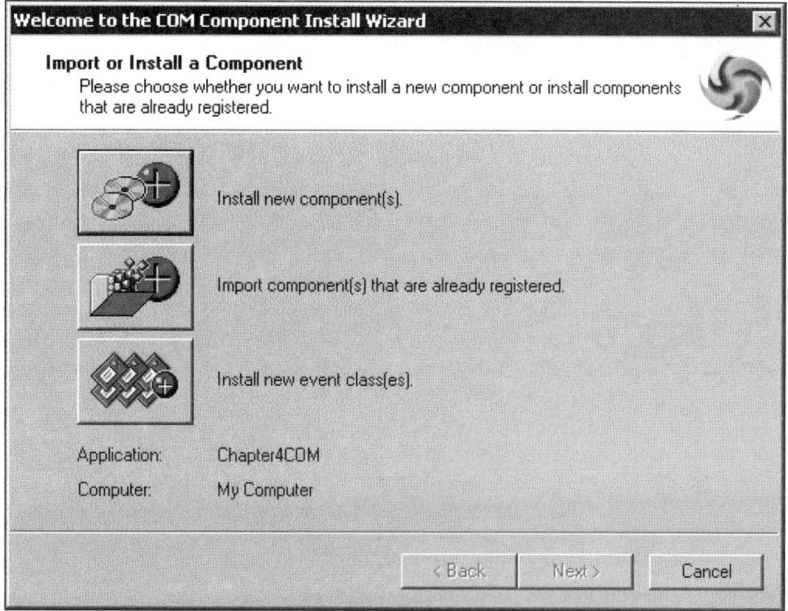

We will then be presented with a file dialog where we can select the component to be added. Navigate to the location of `Chapter4COM.dll` and select it. The wizard will then show us a panel with the component we've selected, along with an **Add** button in case we want to add more components.

If we click **Next** on this panel the wizard will register the component within COM+ and we're all set. In fact, if our component wasn't registered in the Windows registry on the server, that registration will be done for us automatically.

The result is that our DLL is listed as a component in COM+. In the following diagram we see the component listed with the Status View option selected in the toolbar:

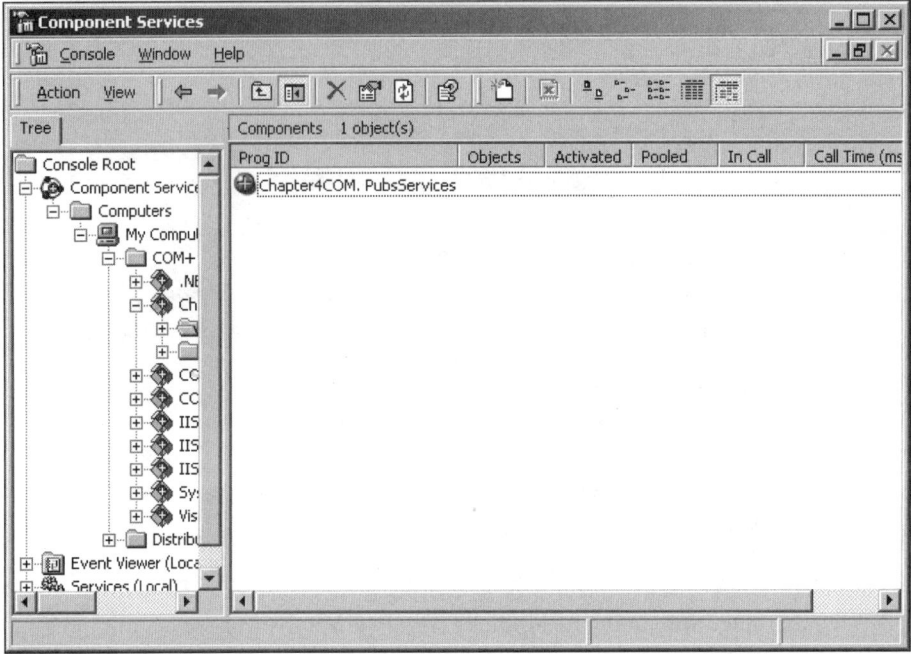

This view provides us with valuable information as we interact with the component – including the number of objects in existence at the moment, the number actually in use, and so forth. The information displayed can be very valuable when debugging and when monitoring a production system.

At this point we are ready to build a client application to make use of the COM+ component.

Calling COM+ Components from Visual Basic .NET

In Chapter 2 we discussed how COM components created by VB6 can be invoked by a Visual Basic .NET client application or assembly. Earlier in this chapter we discussed location transparency – a major feature of COM that shields the client application from having to know where the COM component is actually running.

When Visual Basic .NET code invokes a COM component running in COM+, it is no different from invoking a COM component *not* running in COM+. The same .NET wrapper object is created and the same marshaling of method calls and parameters occurs as discussed in Chapter 2. The one key difference is that when invoking a component running in COM+, it is very important to be aware of and to manage the object lifetime by calling `Marshal.ReleaseComObject` when we're done using the component.

> We should always call `Marshal.ReleaseComObject` when we're done using a component running in COM+.

The reason this is so important in COM+ is because we are dealing with shared server resources. If a .NET application on a client workstation keeps a small COM object in memory on the client machine for a few seconds or minutes, only that client workstation has its resources tied up. That was our scenario in Chapter 2, and so using `ReleaseComObject` wasn't all that important.

When working with COM+, however, we are almost always creating components that run on a shared server, where many clients are using the resources of this one machine. This changes things entirely, since holding a reference to an object for a few extra seconds or minutes causes us to consume resources that could be put to better use by all the other clients who are also using the server.

For completeness, let's run through the process of building a simple Visual Basic .NET application that makes use of the COM+ component we built earlier in the chapter.

Creating the Project

Open the Visual Studio .NET IDE and create a new Visual Basic .NET Windows Application project. Name it `Chapter4Net`. We'll start with a blank form to which we can add some controls that will allow us to enter an author ID, retrieve the last name, edit the last name, and update the data.

Setting Up the Form

Add two labels, two `TextBox` controls – named `txtID` and `txtName` – and two buttons named `btnGet` and `btnUpdate` as shown in the following diagram:

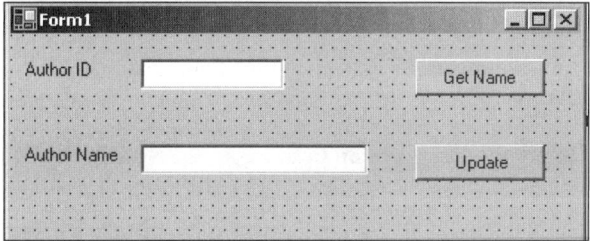

Set the `Enabled` property on `txtName` and `btnUpdate` to `False`. Until we've retrieved an author's data we don't want the user interacting with those controls.

We can also initialize the form with a valid author ID value – making it easier to test. Double-click on the form to bring up the code window. We should be in the form's `Load` event handler, so we can add the following code:

```
Private Sub Form1_Load(ByVal sender As System.Object, _
    ByVal e As System.EventArgs) Handles MyBase.Load
  txtID.Text = "172-32-1176"
  txtID.SelectAll()
End Sub
```

This initializes the `txtID` control with a value and selects all the text in that control so we can easily enter a different value if we choose.

Referencing the COM+ Component

Before we can get into writing any real code, we need to add a reference to the `Chapter4COM` component we authored earlier in the chapter.

> **Because this component references the COM+ Services type library, we will not be able to create a primary interop assembly for `Chapter4COM.dll`.**

Microsoft doesn't provide a primary interop assembly for `comsvcs.dll` – the DLL containing the COM+ Services type library we've referenced. Because of this, we can't create a primary type library for `Chapter4COM.dll`, since creation of a primary interop assembly requires that primary interop assemblies exist for any referenced components.

> *Technically it is possible to create a primary interop assembly for* `comsvcs.dll` *by using the steps outlined in Chapter 2. However, as we noted in Chapter 2, the publisher key for a primary interop assembly should be the key held by the publisher of the COM component itself – in this case Microsoft. This means that any primary interop assembly we might create would have our key instead of Microsoft's, and that could become very confusing in the future if Microsoft (or all the other readers of this book) start publishing primary interop assemblies for* `comsvcs.dll`.

This means that we can reference it directly from Visual Studio .NET or we can create a type library at the command prompt. These options are both covered in detail in Chapter 2.

In this chapter we'll go ahead and simply reference the component using Visual Studio .NET to reference the COM DLL directly.

Use the **Project | Add Reference** menu option to bring up the **Add Reference** dialog, then switch to the COM tab within that dialog. Select the `Chapter4COM` entry from the list:

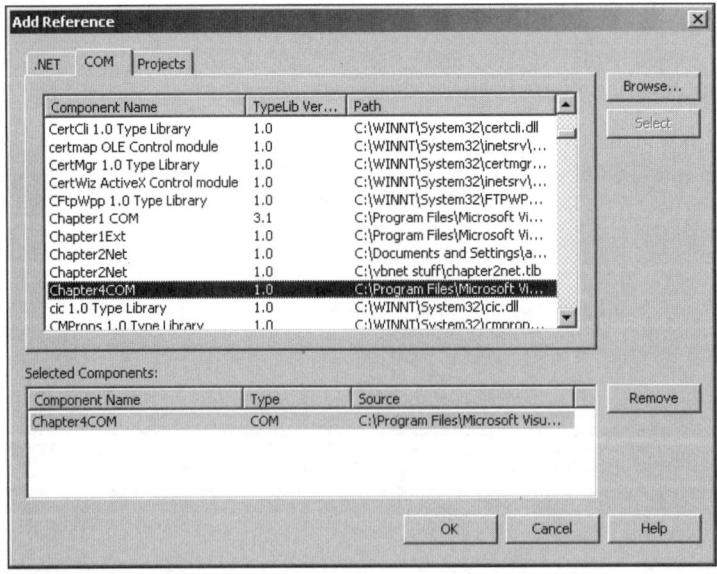

The location transparency capability of COM will automatically ensure that when we invoke the component it is invoked within the context of COM+, rather than directly within the context of our Visual Basic .NET client application.

Click **OK** to add the reference. Visual Studio .NET automatically creates an RCW assembly for `Chapter4COM.dll` and for `comsvcs.dll` and adds these references to our project. We can now move on to write the code behind our form.

Importing System.Runtime.InteropServices

Since we know that we'll be using the `Marshal` class to explicitly indicate when we're done using the COM component, we should add an `Imports` statement to the top of our code:

```
Imports System.Runtime.InteropServices
```

The `InteropServices` namespace includes the `Marshal` class as we discussed in Chapter 2. Importing this namespace simply makes our code clearer as we use the `Marshal` class.

Getting Author Data

Now we are ready to interact with the `Chapter4COM` component within our code. First let's add the code to retrieve the data for an author based on the ID value entered in the `txtID` control:

```
Private Sub btnGet_Click(ByVal sender As System.Object, _
    ByVal e As System.EventArgs) Handles btnGet.Click

  Dim objService As New Chapter4COM.PubsServices()

  txtName.Text = objService.GetAuthor(txtID.Text)

  Marshal.ReleaseComObject(objService)
  objService = Nothing

  If Len(txtName.Text) > 0 Then
    txtName.Enabled = True
    btnUpdate.Enabled = True
    txtID.Enabled = False
    btnGet.Enabled = False
    txtName.Focus()
  Else
    txtName.Enabled = False
    btnUpdate.Enabled = False
    txtID.Enabled = True
    btnGet.Enabled = True
    txtID.Focus()
    txtID.SelectAll()
  End If
End Sub
```

Much of this code deals with managing the UI – enabling and disabling the `TextBox` and `Button` controls as appropriate.

The code of interest to us is the creation, use, and release of the COM+ component. We first create the object as we declare the variable:

```
Dim objService As New Chapter4COM.PubsServices()
```

Notice that this is no different from creating a regular COM component as we did in Chapter 2, since we are relying on COM and COM+ to automatically figure out that the component is running in a COM+ Application and to invoke it from there. Not only can we not tell from the code that this class comes from a COM DLL, but the fact that it is running in COM+ is also transparent. This isn't terribly surprising, since in VB6 the code to create an object is the same, regardless of whether the object is in COM+ or not.

We then call the `GetAuthor` method to retrieve the author data:

```
txtName.Text = objService.GetAuthor(txtID.Text)
```

Though this appears to be a simple method call within our Visual Basic .NET code, we know that within the COM component itself we are calling `SetComplete` or `SetAbort` as appropriate to tell COM+ whether or not the operation succeeded. Because of this, COM+ automatically deactivates and destroys the object *immediately* upon completion of the method.

Even though our Visual Basic .NET code appears to have a valid reference to an object, the fact is that we have a reference to a 'placeholder' within COM+. Any subsequent method calls against our `objService` variable will cause COM+ to create a new object behind the scenes, run the method, and then deactivate and destroy that object. We are given the *illusion* of retaining a reference to an object, when in reality we get a new and different object for each method call.

This is normal COM+ behavior following the **Just-In-Time** (JIT) **activation** rules. For all non-pooled transactional COM+ objects, an object is created and destroyed each time a method is called – the object being created 'just in time' to process the method call. This behavior is consistent from whatever client application we are calling the COM+ component, including both VB6 and Visual Basic .NET.

> *As we noted earlier, VB6 objects cannot be pooled. Pooled objects remain in memory and are used quite differently. The client application still never gets a real reference to an object – instead getting a reference to a COM+ placeholder. Each time a method is called, a free object is grabbed from the pool and services the request. This means that each client method call may be handled by a different object from the pool, and that each object in the pool will be servicing method calls from any number of clients in any order.*

Once we're done interacting with the COM+ object, we must explicitly dereference it and set the variable to `Nothing`:

```
Marshal.ReleaseComObject(objService)
objService = Nothing
```

As we discussed in Chapter 2, .NET doesn't immediately destroy objects – they are destroyed when the garbage collection mechanism gets around to locating and cleaning up all dereferenced objects. This may not happen immediately. In the COM platform however, there is an expectation that an object is destroyed as soon as there are no references to that object from any client code.

When we invoke a COM object that is running directly within our Visual Basic .NET client application's process, it often doesn't matter whether that object is dereferenced and destroyed immediately or not. If the COM component holds expensive resources until destroyed, it is obviously important to manually force its destruction, but otherwise we can typically wait until the .NET garbage collection mechanism releases the component.

In the case of a COM+ component running in a Server Application, however, the rules are different. Such a component is running in a separate process or even on a separate server machine, and there is a cost to maintaining each reference to such an object. Ideally, we would only maintain a connection to that remote process or computer as long as we're actively using the remote object – releasing the object and any connection as soon as we're done.

This means that we should always explicitly dereference COM+ objects when we are done using them, rather than waiting for the .NET garbage collection process to eventually release the reference. Otherwise we will be holding that reference and tying up those server-side resources for seconds or even minutes after we are done using the component.

The call to `ReleaseComObject` provides this service by decrementing the reference count of the COM+ object immediately – thus allowing COM+ to free any associated resources and minimizing any resource costs on the server. To minimize the use of server-side resources, this should be done as soon as we are through using the COM component.

Updating Author Data

The process of updating the author's last name is very similar. We just need to create an instance of the COM+ object, call the `UpdateAuthor` method, and then release the reference. The rest of the code behind the `btnUpdate` control's `Click` event deals with updating the controls on the form as appropriate:

```
Private Sub btnUpdate_Click(ByVal sender As System.Object, _
    ByVal e As System.EventArgs) Handles btnUpdate.Click

  Dim objService As New Chapter4COM.PubsServices()

  objService.UpdateAuthor(txtID.Text, txtName.Text)

  Marshal.ReleaseComObject(objService)
  objService = Nothing

  txtName.Text = ""
  txtName.Enabled = False
  btnUpdate.Enabled = False
  txtID.Enabled = True
  btnGet.Enabled = True
  txtID.Focus()
  txtID.SelectAll()
End Sub
```

Again, the key lines of code here are the ones that deal with the object from the `Chapter4COM` component:

```
Dim objService As New Chapter4COM.PubsServices()

objService.UpdateAuthor(txtID.Text, txtName.Text)

Marshal.ReleaseComObject(objService)
objService = Nothing
```

As we did when retrieving the author data, we use the `New` keyword to instantiate the object and then we call the `UpdateAuthor` method.

Since our COM+ object is transactional and is not pooled, we know that it is invoked using the JIT semantics. This means that the object isn't actually created by COM+ until the method is called, and the object is deactivated and destroyed as soon as the method is complete.

> *As we discussed earlier, VB6 COM components cannot be pooled by COM+ due to threading issues inherent in VB6.*

We then call the `ReleaseComObject` method to allow COM+ to release any reference and resources associated with our client application and we're all done.

Running the Project

At this point we have a VB6 COM component installed in a COM+ Application and a working .NET client application ready to run. If we press *F5* to run the application we should see the form displayed, with a valid author ID already in place.

> *As with any component hosted in a COM+ Server application, it will take a bit of time to run the first time. COM+ needs to create a process for the component, load the DLL, and create the object before our first method can be completed. On subsequent calls speed should improve dramatically as the process is already started with the DLL loaded in memory.*

Click the **Get Name** button to retrieve the author's data:

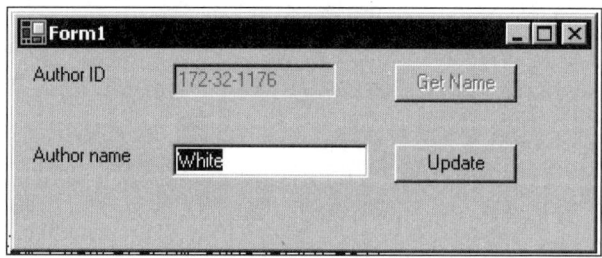

We can see that the component was invoked from within COM+ by looking at the Component Services management console:

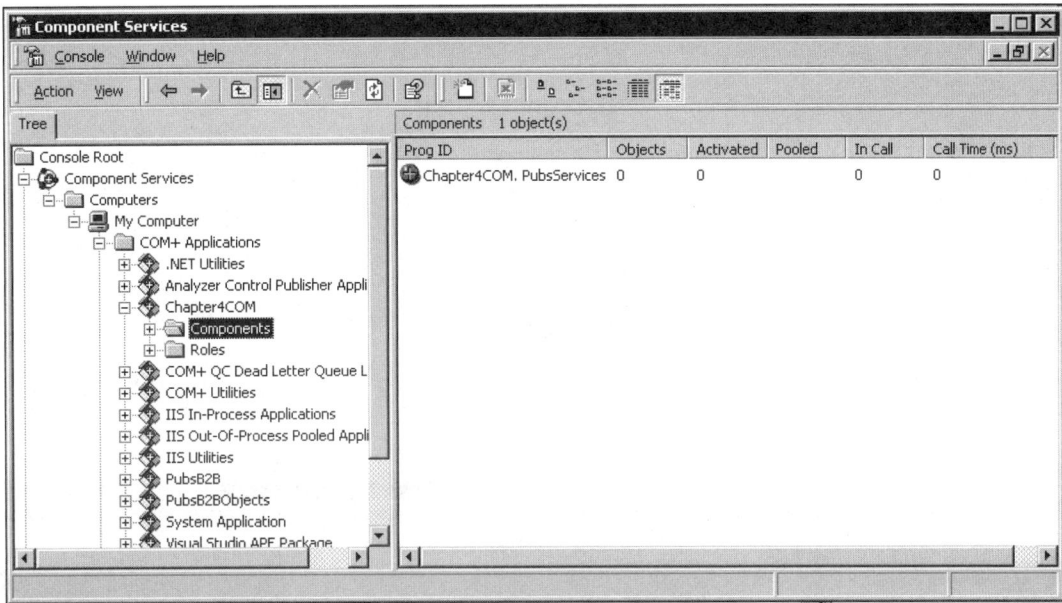

If we watch this window when we click on the **Get Name** or **Update** buttons we should be able to see the number of **Objects** and **Activated** objects go up and down as our client application invokes the component. In this screenshot we see that the component *has* been activated, but at present there are no existing objects or activated objects. If the component had never been activated then we'd see no numeric values in the display at all. The zeros indicate that it has been activated, but that there is no current activity.

We can also monitor the number of transactions that are active, and see how many have been committed or rolled back:

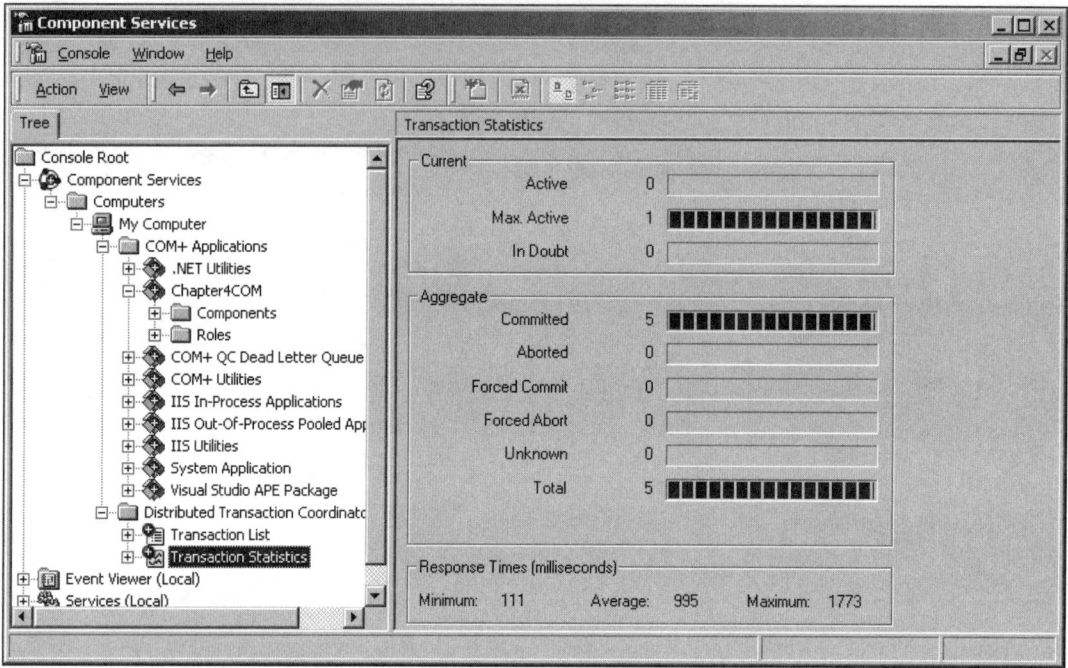

Again, if we have this display open as we click on the Get Name and Update buttons we'll see these values dynamically update to reflect the activities of our client application.

This illustrates that our Visual Basic .NET client application is invoking the VB6 COM component within the context of COM+, and that COM+ is providing the transactional protection we are looking for. Though this client application is a Windows Forms application, the same coding technique applies equally well to any other Visual Basic .NET application, including Web Forms, console applications, and so forth.

Queued Components

So far we've explored the creation and use of VB6 COM components running in COM+. Another feature of COM+ that is available to the VB6 developer is the use of **queued components**. This feature of COM+ allows us to indicate that any method call to our server-side component should be queued up rather than delivered directly to the object.

This is not a feature of MTS, only COM+. It also relies on MSMQ behind the scenes, and so if that option is not installed on the server, MSMQ will need to be installed before this code will work.

This is illustrated by the following diagram:

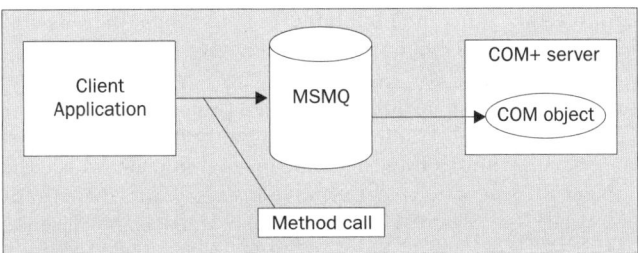

The client application makes a method call to the server-side object running in COM+. However, if the COM+ object is a queued component, the method call will actually be directed into an MSMQ queue and will be delivered to the actual server-side object at some point in the future.

> *For more information on queued components in COM+, please refer to* Professional Windows DNA *(ISBN 1-861004-45-1), or the* ASPToday *article at* http://www.asptoday.com/content/articles/20011119.asp.

Queued components can be useful in situations where the server may not always be available from the client, but where we want the client application to continue running anyway. When the server is available it will be processing the queued requests almost immediately, but when the server is unavailable the method calls will be queued up and processed later. This is all transparent to the client application, so it continues to operate normally.

They can also be useful in helping us control the load placed on the server. If we have many clients simultaneously calling methods on our server, the server may become overloaded. However, if the method calls are queued, then the server will process them only as fast as it can handle and is far less likely to become bogged down.

Queued components run **asynchronously**, meaning that the client doesn't wait for the method to complete before moving on. In fact, the method may not even execute right away – it may be queued up and processed later – all without the client being aware. This means that the client cannot be designed to expect a response from the method. Typically this means that queued components are not used to retrieve data, as it can become very complex to retrieve data asynchronously. Instead, queued components are usually used to start a background process like a batch update of data, or other relatively long-running processes where we may not want the client or the user to wait until the processing is complete.

Creating a Queued Component in VB6

We don't actually queue all method calls for a component in COM+ – it is a *COM interface* that is marked as queued within the COM+ management console. Sometimes this will be the native interface of our COM component; other times we'll create a secondary interface specifically for use in a queued setting.

Before an interface can be marked as queued, it must conform to one key rule – there can be no return values from any method call on the interface. This means that the interface can include no Property or Function type methods; only Sub methods are allowed. In addition, the parameters to the method must be passed by value – using the ByVal keyword – meaning that they are passed from the client to the object, but are not passed back to the client.

The reason for this rule is that the method call is queued. The client application does not wait for the method to be actually run on the server. In fact, the client application may not be running at all by the time the server gets around to running the method. Obviously then, there is no way to return any values to the client as a result of the method call or via its parameters.

Let's see how this works by modifying our Chapter4COM project to include an interface that we can mark as a queued interface. Our existing interface has a method that returns a value, and so it cannot be marked as a queued interface within COM+. This means that in order to use the queued component technology with our object we'll need to either remove the GetAuthor method, or add a secondary interface that has no methods that return values. Obviously it makes more sense to add a secondary interface in this case.

Open the Chapter4COM project in VB6.

Defining the Interface

Our PubsServices class has the GetAuthor method that returns a value, and so the native interface of the class cannot be marked as queued. Fortunately, VB6 allows us to implement multiple interfaces on a single class, and so we can add a secondary interface to the class that only contains methods that return no values.

To define the interface, add a new class module to the project and name it IQueued. We don't need to worry about any properties on this class other than the Instancing, which should be left at the default of Multiuse. In particular, the MTSTransactionMode property won't matter, as this class will never be directly invoked by any client – it is merely acting as an interface template for the PubsServices class.

Now add the following code to define a method that returns no values:

```
Option Explicit

Public Sub UpdateAuthor(ByVal id As String, ByVal lname As String)

End Sub
```

This defines an interface that contains a single method – UpdateAuthor. This method is not a Function, so it has no return value. Additionally, its parameters are declared using the ByVal keyword, and so they will not return any values either.

Notice that this code contains no implementation code – just the basic declaration of the method. That is fine, since we are merely trying to define an interface. The work will be done in the PubsServices class where we'll actually *implement* this interface.

Implementing the Interface

Now that the interface is defined, open up the code window for the PubsServices class. This class already has a native interface, which is composed of all the methods declared using the Public keyword. We'll now add a secondary interface to the class by implementing the IQueued interface.

To do this, add an `Implements` statement at the top of the class:

```
Option Explicit

Implements ObjectControl
Implements IQueued
```

With the interface declared, we can move on to provide an implementation for the `UpdateAuthor` method defined by that interface. Add the following code:

```
Private Sub IQueued_UpdateAuthor(ByVal id As String, ByVal lname As String)
  UpdateAuthor id, lname
End Sub
```

This implements the `UpdateAuthor` method as defined by the `IQueued` interface. The implementation merely invokes the existing `UpdateAuthor` method. By doing this there is no difference between calling the native `UpdateAuthor` method or the `UpdateAuthor` method from the `IQueued` interface – the functionality is identical.

However, since we'll be marking the `IQueued` interface as queued within COM+, there will be a substantial difference in how they actually work when called by our client. The native `UpdateAuthor` method will always be run immediately when it is called, while the `IQueued` version of the method will run some time in the future when the COM+ component retrieves the method call from the queue.

Compile the `Chapter4COM` project to create an updated version of the DLL. Then copy this new version of the DLL into the COM+ management console as we discussed earlier – making sure that COM+ is running the current version of our component. We should now see both the `PubsServices` and `IQueued` classes in the console:

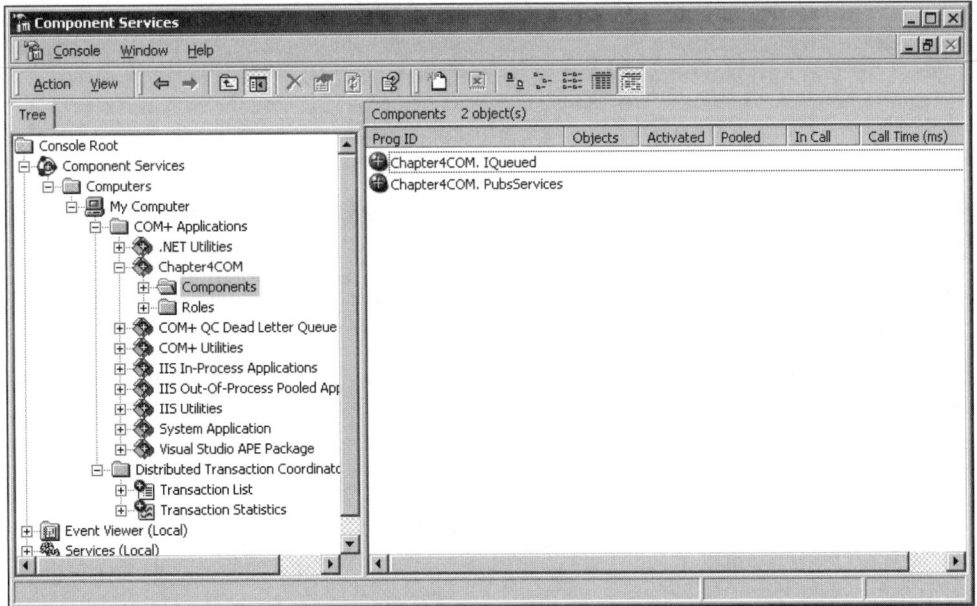

Make sure to update the copy of the DLL against which we have set binary compatibility. It is always important to do this any time we add a new class or method to our project.

Making the Component Queued in COM+

Now that our component has a write-only interface, we can mark the application and the interface as queued to enable the COM+ queued component functionality. First off, right-click on the Chapter4COM application entry in the left-hand pane and choose **Properties**. This will bring up the properties dialog for the COM+ Application that contains our component. Select the **Queuing** tab on the dialog:

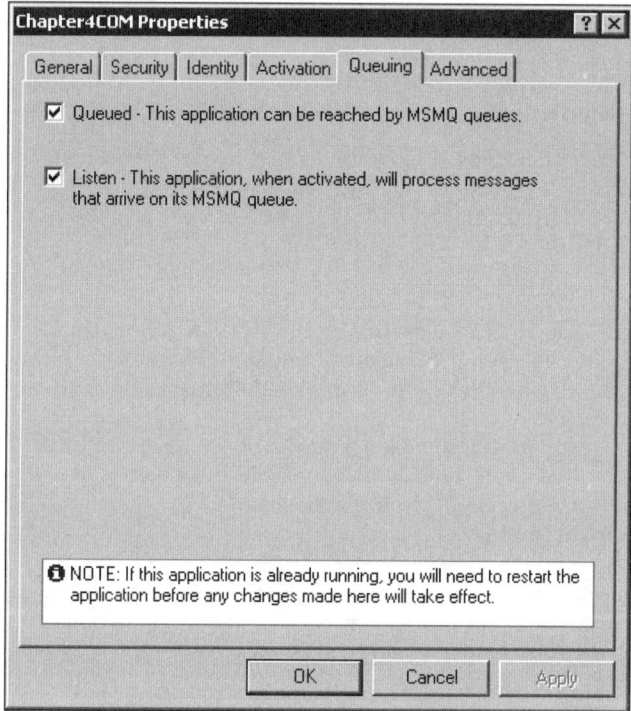

Check the **Queued** box to make this application support queued components. This will cause COM+ to create a set of private MSMQ queues on the server that will receive the queued method calls as they are made by client applications.

We can optionally click to check the **Listen** box as well. This is recommended, as it will cause COM+ to automatically be listening for incoming queued method calls. If we don't check this box, the method calls will queue up in MSMQ until we manually start the COM+ Application by right-clicking on the application in the console and choosing **Start**. By checking the listen box, we are telling COM+ to start a process for the application when the system is booted up and to have that process actively listen for incoming queued method calls. Without this process actively listening, the queued calls will just sit in MSMQ waiting for a listener to be started.

Check the **Listen** box and click **OK**. At this point the COM+ Application is all set up and will support any queued components we care to configure. We can now move on to mark the IQueued interface on the PubsServices class as queued.

Note that we are not changing the `IQueued` class to be queued – we are changing the `IQueued` interface on the `PubsServices` class. Remember that the `IQueued` class contains no code – it is merely a template. It is the `PubsServices` class that *implements* the interface, and so that is the class we want to mark as queued.

> *Ideally the `IQueued` class wouldn't even be visible here, since we don't ever directly use it. However, VB6 has no other way of creating an interface template that we can implement within `PubsServices`.*

To do this, in the left-hand pane of the COM+ console expand the entry for `PubsServices` and then its underlying **Interfaces** entry:

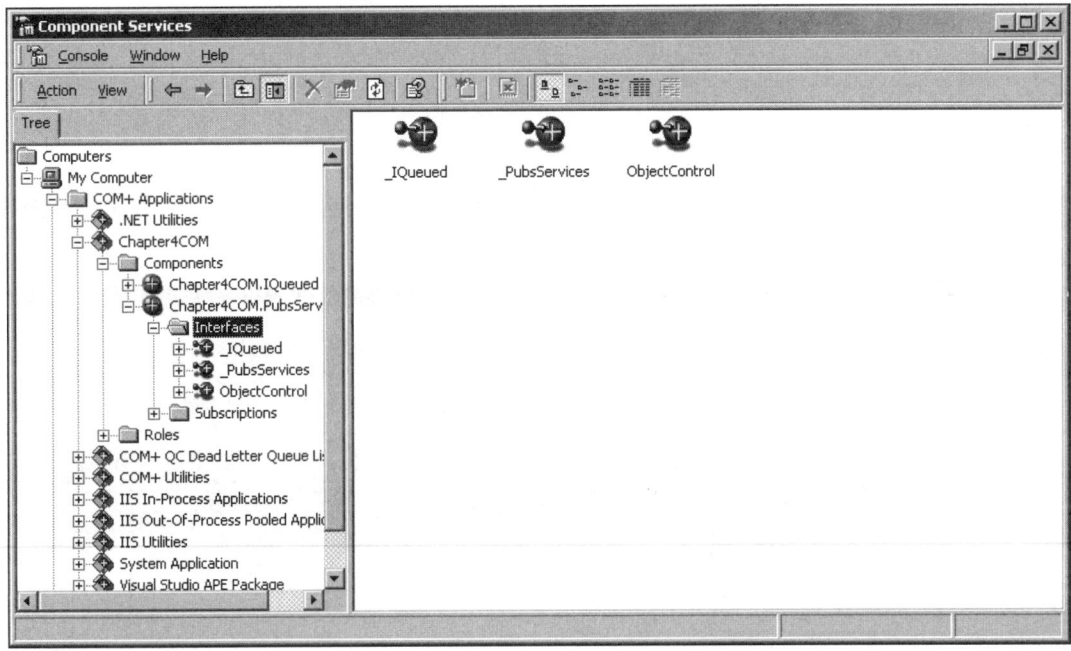

We can now see the list of interfaces implemented by the `PubsServices` class – including the `IQueued` interface. The interface has an underscore character in front of it due to the way VB6 implements interfaces, and it is this `_IQueued` interface that we need to mark as queued in order for the method calls to be queued as the client calls them.

Right-click on the `_IQueued` entry in the left-hand pane and select **Properties** to bring up the properties dialog for this interface. Select the **Queuing** tab in the dialog and click the **Queued** box to enable queuing for this interface:

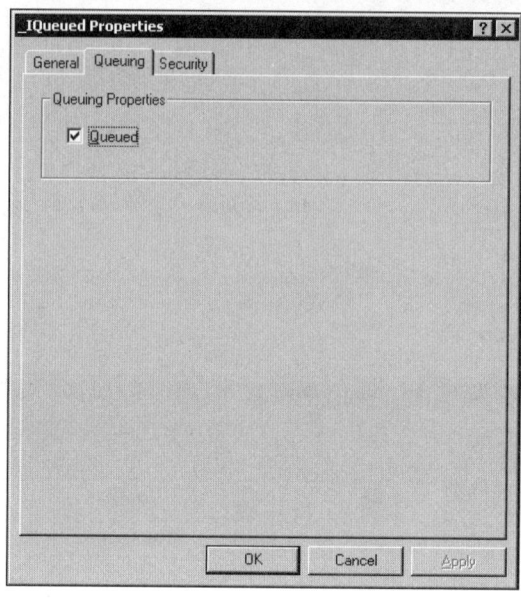

Click OK to complete the process. At this point our Chapter4COM component is a queued component and the PubsServices class can be invoked in a queued fashion via the IQueued interface.

The MSMQ queues themselves can be found on the COM+ server by using the Computer Management console. To start the console choose Start | Programs | Administrative Tools | Computer Management. Expand the Services and Applications item in the left-hand pane, then expand Message Queuing and Private Queues. Here we find a list of Chapter4COM queues:

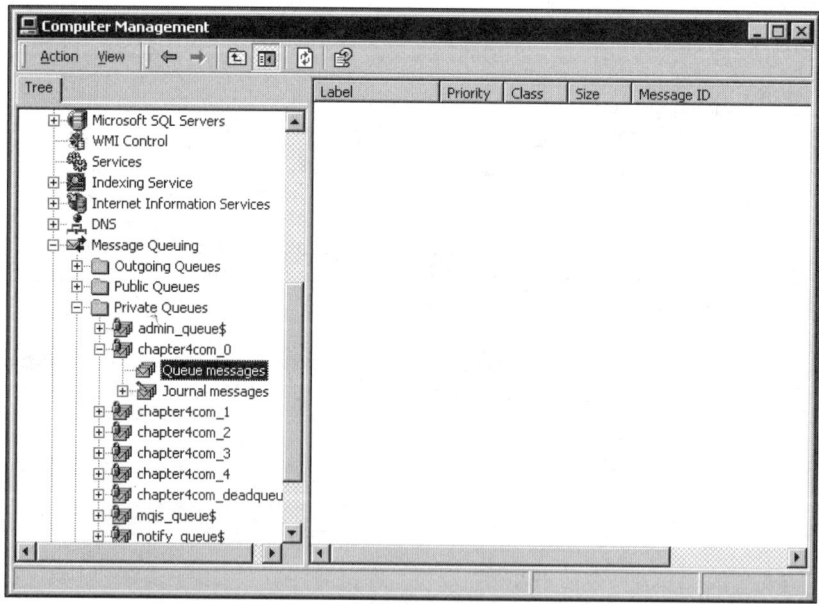

Since the queue will only be used by COM+ on the server, it is a private queue – available only to this server. There are a number of queues listed for our component numbered from zero to four and then a deadqueue. These are all part of an automatic retry mechanism built into queued components, so if a method fails for some reason, it will be retried up to four times before being placed in the deadqueue to indicate that it could not be processed. As shown, the display will list any pending method calls that are queued up for processing by our COM+ component.

We can now move on to see how to invoke a queued component from Visual Basic .NET.

Calling the Queued Component from Visual Basic .NET

A queued component's methods are called the same as any other component's methods – there is no coding difference in how the methods are called. There is a difference in how the object is *instantiated*, however – and that is true for client applications written in Visual Basic .NET as well as those written in VB6.

Open Visual Studio .NET and bring up the `Chapter4Net` client application.

Since we've changed the interface of the `Chapter4COM.dll`, we'll need to remove and re-add the reference to the component from within Visual Studio .NET. To do this, right-click on the **Chapter4COM** entry under **References** in the Solution Explorer and choose **Remove**. Then re-add the reference to the project as we did earlier in the chapter.

Open the designer for the form and add a new button named `btnUpdateQueued` as shown:

Set its `Enabled` property to `False` just like we did with `btnUpdate`. To make the button enable and disable appropriately with our existing code, update the `Click` events for `btnGet` and `btnUpdate` as shown:

```
Private Sub btnGet_Click(ByVal sender As System.Object, _
    ByVal e As System.EventArgs) Handles btnGet.Click
  Dim objService As New Chapter4COM.PubsServices()

  txtName.Text = objService.GetAuthor(txtID.Text)

  Marshal.ReleaseComObject(objService)
  objService = Nothing

  If Len(txtName.Text) > 0 Then
    txtName.Enabled = True
    btnUpdate.Enabled = True
    btnUpdateQueued.Enabled = True
    txtID.Enabled = False
    btnGet.Enabled = False
    txtName.Focus()
```

```
    Else
      txtName.Enabled = False
      btnUpdate.Enabled = False
      btnUpdateQueued.Enabled = False
      txtID.Enabled = True
      btnGet.Enabled = True
      txtID.Focus()
      txtID.SelectAll()
    End If

  End Sub

  Private Sub btnUpdate_Click(ByVal sender As System.Object, _
      ByVal e As System.EventArgs) Handles btnUpdate.Click
    Dim objService As New Chapter4COM.PubsServices()

    objService.UpdateAuthor(txtID.Text, txtName.Text)

    Marshal.ReleaseComObject(objService)
    objService = Nothing

    txtName.Text = ""
    txtName.Enabled = False
    btnUpdate.Enabled = False
    btnUpdateQueued.Enabled = False
    txtID.Enabled = True
    btnGet.Enabled = True
    txtID.Focus()
    txtID.SelectAll()
  End Sub
```

We can then move on to write the code to invoke our component by using the queuing capabilities in COM+.

Calling the Queued Component

The code to call the queued component is virtually identical to the code we have behind the btnUpdate control, with the exception that we need to instantiate the COM+ object in a different way, and we need to call it via the queued interface – IQueued.

Rather than creating the COM+ object by using the New keyword as we normally would, we need to create it through the use of a **moniker**. A moniker is a special type of identifier for a COM component – rather like a standard ProgID, but which also includes other information to control how the component is instantiated and used.

In our case, we're going to use a moniker that contains the ProgID, but also indicates that we want to communicate with the component via a queued interface. Rather than creating the object as:

```
    Dim objService As New Chapter4COM.PubsServices()
```

We will instead create it via this moniker as:

```
Dim objservice As Chapter4COM._IQueued

objservice = GetObject("queue:/new:Chapter4COM.PubsServices")
```

The variable is declared using the _IQueued interface – the same one we marked as queued in the COM+ management console. Then the queued moniker is used to identify the class we want to instantiate.

The GetObject function is part of the Microsoft.VisualBasic namespace. We can also opt to use the Marshal class from the InteropServices namespace with the following code to accomplish exactly the same thing:

```
Dim objservice As Chapter4COM._IQueued

objservice = Marshal.BindToMoniker("queue:/new:Chapter4COM.PubsServices")
```

The BindToMoniker method provides the same functionality as GetObject in this case and so either way we get a queued reference to the object we need.

Using GetObject, we can write code behind the btnUpdateQueued control as follows:

```
Private Sub btnUpdateQueued_Click(ByVal sender As System.Object, _
    ByVal e As System.EventArgs) Handles btnUpdateQueued.Click
Dim objservice As Chapter4COM._IQueued

objservice = GetObject("queue:/new:Chapter4COM.PubsServices")

objservice.UpdateAuthor(txtID.Text, txtName.Text)

Marshal.ReleaseComObject(objService)
objService = Nothing

txtName.Text = ""
txtName.Enabled = False
btnUpdate.Enabled = False
btnUpdateQueued.Enabled = False
txtID.Enabled = True
btnGet.Enabled = True
txtID.Focus()
txtID.SelectAll()
End Sub
```

Notice that most of the code is the same as we wrote behind btnUpdate; only the declaration and creation of the object is different.

When we run the application now, we have the option of invoking the UpdateAuthor method synchronously as we did before, or we can invoke it in a queued fashion by clicking on the new button. The end result is the same – the author's name is updated. However, the queued option will function even if the Chapter4COM COM+ Application is not running or available, since the method call will be queued and delivered later when the COM+ Application becomes available.

Transferring Data

Typically we use COM+ to host VB6 components that are providing data access services to our client application. In some cases these components run on a server separate from the client workstation. In other cases the components are running on the same machine as the client (such as a web server), but are out of process to increase stability and maintainability of the application.

Whether in a separate process or on another machine, there is a cost associated with each method call from a client to the server-side component. For each method call, COM must marshal the parameters and return values from the client to the server and back again – incurring substantial overhead to the method call.

Because of this, it is very important to minimize the number of method calls made between the client and the server-side component. In our example application, only the author's last name is returned as a result. However, in a typical application it is likely that several data fields would be returned as a result of the method call.

For instance, we might want to provide a `GetAuthorData` method that returns all the data about the author, not just the last name. The question we then face is how to return that set of data to the client application in an efficient manner.

When working with VB6 there are several techniques, two of which are the most commonly used:

❑   Returning a disconnected ADO `Recordset`

❑   Returning a `Variant` array

Certainly there are other techniques as well – `PropertyBag` objects and user-defined types for instance. Additionally, many people have also started returning data as an XML document.

When calling VB6 COM objects from Visual Basic .NET client applications we need to find not only an efficient way to move the data from the server back to the client application, but we need to find a technology that will work on both the COM and .NET platforms.

The techniques that have commonality between the two platforms include:

❑   Returning a disconnected ADO `Recordset`

❑   Returning a `Variant` array

❑   Returning an XML document

Each of these approaches has its strong and weak points. In most cases the choice of which to use will be largely dictated by the nature of our existing COM+ components, as they will probably already be returning data in one of these formats. It is difficult to point to one technique and definitively say it is the best.

ADO `Recordset`s incur the overhead of using ADO, and require that both the COM and .NET code have references to the ADO libraries. On the other hand, returning an ADO `Recordset` as a result is very easy to do, which can increase developer productivity. `Variant` arrays carry no metadata, so code we write against them is hard to read and hard to maintain. On the other hand, they consume less network bandwidth than a `Recordset` and are also very easy to return as a result. XML documents are not particularly fast when compared to the other two techniques, but they follow an open standard and are reasonably easy to work with.

We'll cover ADO and ADO.NET in detail in Chapter 11, but we'll briefly discuss them here as well. Let's walk through a quick example of using ADO `Recordsets`, `Variant` arrays, and XML documents so we have a complete solution for returning data from VB6 in COM+ back to a Visual Basic .NET client.

Using ADO Recordset Objects

From VB6 it is quite easy to return a disconnected ADO `Recordset` object for use by a client application. To do this within our `Chapter4COM` project's `PubsServices` class we can add the following method:

```
Public Function GetAuthorDataRS(id As String) As Recordset
   Dim rs As Recordset
   Dim strSQL As String

   On Error GoTo ErrH
   Set rs = New Recordset
   strSQL = "SELECT au_id,au_lname,au_fname,phone " & _
      "FROM authors WHERE au_id='" & id & "'"
   rs.CursorLocation = adUseClient
   rs.Open strSQL, DB_CONN, adOpenDynamic
   Set rs.DataSource = Nothing
   Set GetAuthorDataRS = rs
   Set rs = Nothing
   If Not objContext Is Nothing Then objContext.SetComplete
   Exit Function
ErrH:
   If Not rs Is Nothing Then
      If rs.State = adStateOpen Then rs.Close
      Set rs = Nothing
   End If
   If Not objContext Is Nothing Then objContext.SetAbort
   Err.Raise Err.Number, Err.Source, Err.Description
End Function
```

This code simply retrieves all the information about a specific author, puts it in a disconnected `Recordset` object and returns that object as the result of the function. The key is that the `CursorLocation` is set to `adUseClient` and that the `DataSource` property is set to `Nothing` once the data is retrieved. This causes the `Recordset` to be disconnected so it can be efficiently passed back as a result.

Compile the `Chapter4COM` project and update the COM+ Application with the new version as we've discussed earlier in the chapter. Don't forget to re-mark the `IQueued` interface as being queued as part of that process.

Using the Recordset

In our `Chapter4Net` Visual Basic .NET project we can make use of the returned `Recordset` object. We can do this in a couple different ways. One is to use the `Recordset` object directly via COM interop – a topic we'll discuss in depth in Chapter 11. Another is to use the .NET `OledbDataAdapter` object to load a `DataSet` object with the data from the `Recordset`, which is the approach we'll take here.

By loading a `DataSet` from the `Recordset` we minimize the interaction between our .NET code and the COM-based ADO object – thus minimizing our use of COM interop. This approach also allows us to use typical .NET data access techniques within our .NET code.

Even though our underlying database is SQL Server, the .NET code isn't talking to SQL Server directly at all, but rather is talking to an ADO `Recordset` created in VB6. This is why we use the `OledbDataAdapter` object, as it provides the support we need for interacting with ADO `Recordset` objects.

Setting Up the Form

Open the designer for the form and add a `ListView` control named `ListView1` and a `Button` control named `btnGetRS` as shown:

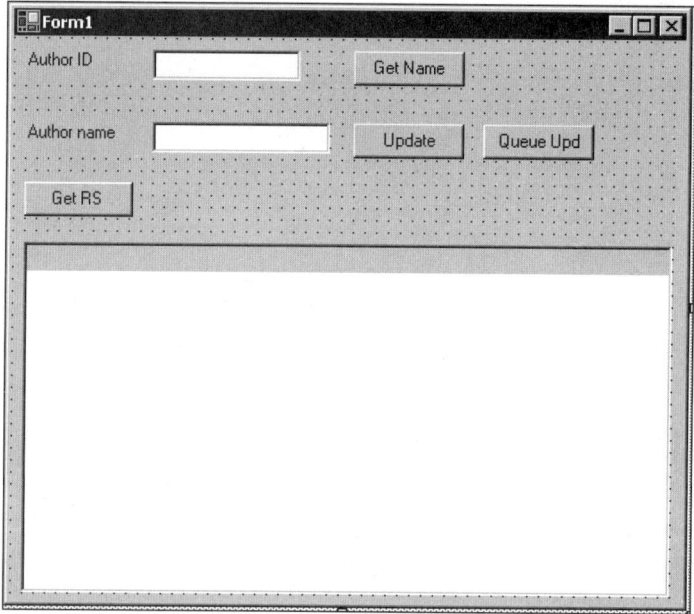

We'll use the `ListView` control to display our data, and the `Button` control to trigger the retrieval of the data. Bring up the code window for the form and add the following code to the form's `Load` event:

```
Private Sub Form1_Load(ByVal sender As System.Object, _
    ByVal e As System.EventArgs) Handles MyBase.Load
  With ListView1
    .View = View.Details
    .Columns.Add("ID", 100, HorizontalAlignment.Left)
    .Columns.Add("Last", 100, HorizontalAlignment.Left)
    .Columns.Add("First", 100, HorizontalAlignment.Left)
    .Columns.Add("Phone", 100, HorizontalAlignment.Right)
  End With
  txtID.Text = "172-32-1176"
  txtID.SelectAll()
End Sub
```

This sets up the columns in the `ListView` so we can display the author's ID, name, and phone number.

Referencing the ADO Library

Before we can accept a `Recordset` as a result within our Visual Basic .NET code, we need a reference to the ADO library within our .NET project. This will happen for us automatically when we remove and re-add the reference to `Chapter4COM.dll` so we have access to our new method.

Visual Studio .NET automatically notices that we now have a method that returns an ADO `Recordset` and it automatically adds a reference to the ADODB COM component that provides that data type. So by simply updating our `Chapter4COM.dll` reference we get access to ADO.

If we look in the references list in the solution explorer, we will see that Visual Studio .NET has created an RCW for the ADODB component and has added it to our project. Once this is done we can work with ADO objects, including the `Recordset`, from within our application.

Using the Recordset

Retrieving a `Recordset` from the COM+ component is now as simple as:

```
Dim objservice As New Chapter4COM.PubsServices()

Dim rs As ADODB.Recordset = objservice.GetAuthorDataRS(txtID.Text)
Marshal.ReleaseComObject(objservice)
```

We simply call the `GetAuthorDataRS` method on our `PubsServices` object, placing the resulting value into a variable of type `ADODB.Recordset`.

This value can then be placed into an ADO.NET `DataSet` object by using the ability of the `OleDbDataAdapter` object to load a `DataSet` from a `Recordset`:

```
Dim da As New OleDb.OleDbDataAdapter()
Dim ds As New DataSet()

da.Fill(ds, rs, "authors")
```

We create both `OleDbDataAdapter` and `DataSet` objects, then use the `OleDbDataAdapter` object's `Fill` method to fill the `DataSet` with the data from the `Recordset`.

Using these concepts, we can write the following code in the `Click` event of the button:

```
Private Sub btnGetRS_Click(ByVal sender As System.Object, _
    ByVal e As System.EventArgs) Handles btnGetRS.Click
  Dim objservice As New Chapter4COM.PubsServices()
  Dim da As New OleDb.OleDbDataAdapter()
  Dim ds As New DataSet()

  Dim rs As ADODB.Recordset = objservice.GetAuthorDataRS(txtID.Text)
  Marshal.ReleaseComObject(objservice)

  da.Fill(ds, rs, "authors")
  Marshal.ReleaseComObject(rs)
  Set rs = Nothing
End Sub
```

Once the `DataSet` object is fully populated we are releasing the reference to the `Recordset` object – thus minimizing the amount of time that it is kept in memory. This is always wise, since a `Recordset` object could consume a large amount of memory if it has a lot of data.

All that remains now is to add the code that populates the `ListView` control from the data in the `DataSet`, so let's add that:

```
Private Sub btnGetRS_Click(ByVal sender As System.Object, _
    ByVal e As System.EventArgs) Handles btnGetRS.Click
   Dim objservice As New Chapter4COM.PubsServices()
   Dim da As New OleDb.OleDbDataAdapter()
   Dim ds As New DataSet()

   Dim rs As ADODB.Recordset = objservice.GetAuthorDataRS(txtID.Text)
   Marshal.ReleaseComObject(objservice)

   da.Fill(ds, rs, "authors")
   Marshal.ReleaseComObject(rs)
   Set rs = Nothing

   Dim dr As DataRow = ds.Tables("authors").Rows(0)

   With ListView1
     .Items.Clear()
     Dim lvi As New ListViewItem(CStr(dr("au_id")))

     lvi.SubItems.Add(dr("au_lname"))
     lvi.SubItems.Add(dr("au_fname"))
     lvi.SubItems.Add(dr("phone"))

     .Items.Add(lvi)
   End With
End Sub
```

We can now run the application and click the button. The data will be retrieved from the COM+ component and displayed in the `ListView` control:

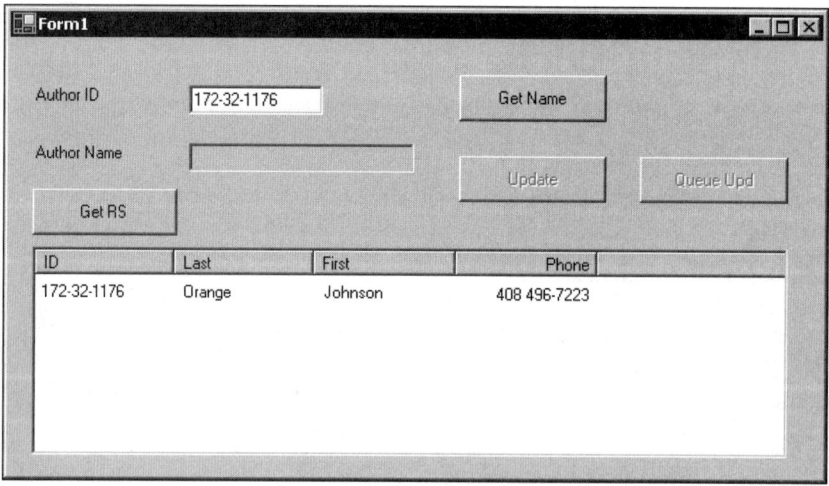

The interaction with the ADO `Recordset` object is minimized, and we are able to mostly work with standard .NET objects and concepts as we populate the display.

Using Variant Arrays

A drawback to returning an ADO `Recordset` object is that we must reference the ADO library within our .NET project – thus linking our .NET application to a COM component. This is often not ideal, as it eliminates many of the deployment benefits of .NET. It forces us to deploy and register ADO support to any machine as we deploy our application, and ADO support is relatively large and complex.

Instead we may choose to return an array of `Variant` values that contains our data. Such an array can be easily generated within our VB6 code by using the `GetRows` method of the ADO `Recordset`.

In our VB6 `Chapter4COM` project's `PubsServices` class we can add the following method that retrieves all the data for an author and returns it as a `Variant` array:

```
Public Function GetAuthorDataVA(id As String) As Variant
   Dim rs As Recordset
   Dim strSQL As String

   On Error GoTo ErrH
   Set rs = New Recordset
   strSQL = "SELECT au_id,au_lname,au_fname,phone " & _
     "FROM authors WHERE au_id='" & id & "'"
   rs.CursorLocation = adUseClient
   rs.Open strSQL, DB_CONN, adOpenForwardOnly, adLockReadOnly
   If Not rs.BOF And Not rs.EOF Then
      GetAuthorDataVA = rs.GetRows
   Else
      Set GetAuthorDataVA = Nothing
   End If
   rs.Close
   If Not objContext Is Nothing Then objContext.SetComplete
   Exit Function
ErrH:
   If Not rs Is Nothing Then
      If rs.State = adStateOpen Then rs.Close
      Set rs = Nothing
   End If
   If Not objContext Is Nothing Then objContext.SetAbort
   Err.Raise Err.Number, Err.Source, Err.Description
End Function
```

The key line here is the call to `GetRows`:

```
GetAuthorDataVA = rs.GetRows
```

Since this converts the data in the `Recordset` into a two dimensional `Variant` array, which we then return to the client. As before, compile the project and update the COM+ Application with the new functionality, including resetting the **Queued** property on the `IQueued` interface.

Using the Variant Array

Open the `Chapter4Net` Visual Basic .NET project and add another button to the form named `btnGetVA`:

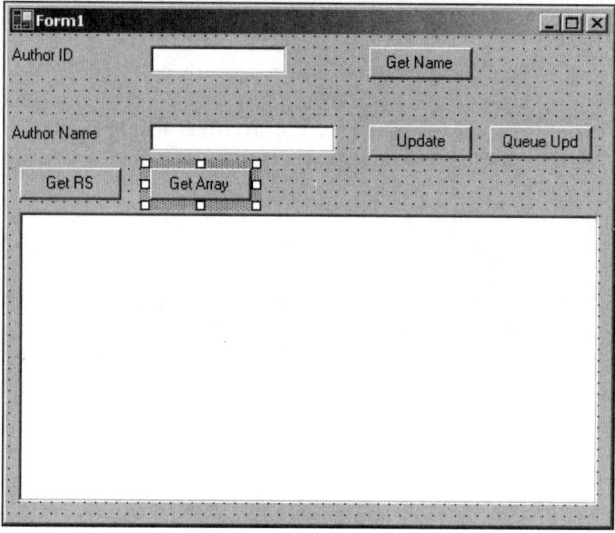

Double-click the button to open the code window for the `Click` event.

A `Variant` array translates into Visual Basic .NET as an array of type `Object` – a concept we discussed in Chapter 2. We don't need any special references to make this work, so a reference to the ADO library is not required.

The code to retrieve the array is shorter than the code we wrote for the `Recordset`:

```
Private Sub btnGetVA_Click(ByVal sender As System.Object, _
    ByVal e As System.EventArgs) Handles btnGetVA.Click
    Dim objservice As New Chapter4COM.PubsServices()

    Dim arData As Object = objservice.GetAuthorDataVA(txtID.Text)

    Marshal.ReleaseComObject(objservice)
    Set objservice = Nothing
End Sub
```

Again we are invoking a method on the COM+ component to retrieve its data – in this case a two dimensional array of type `Object`:

```
Dim arData As Object = objservice.GetAuthorDataVA(txtID.Text)
```

Once we have the array, we can use it to populate the `ListView` control:

```
Private Sub btnGetVA_Click(ByVal sender As System.Object, _
    ByVal e As System.EventArgs) Handles btnGetVA.Click
  Dim objservice As New Chapter4COM.PubsServices()
  Dim idx As Integer

  Dim arData As Object = objservice.GetAuthorDataVA(txtID.Text)

  Marshal.ReleaseComObject(objservice)
  Set objservice = Nothing

  With ListView1
    .Items.Clear()
    Dim lvi As New ListViewItem(CStr(arData(0, 0)))

    For idx = 1 To UBound(arData)
      lvi.SubItems.Add(arData(idx, 0))
    Next
    .Items.Add(lvi)
  End With
End Sub
```

The code to populate the `ListView` is not as readable with an array as it is with a `DataSet`, since we're just looping through the data by using numeric index values. We get no metadata about the data, just the raw data itself in a simple tabular form. This is one serious drawback to the use of a two dimensional array in representing our data.

The result, when we run the application, should be similar to the following screenshot:

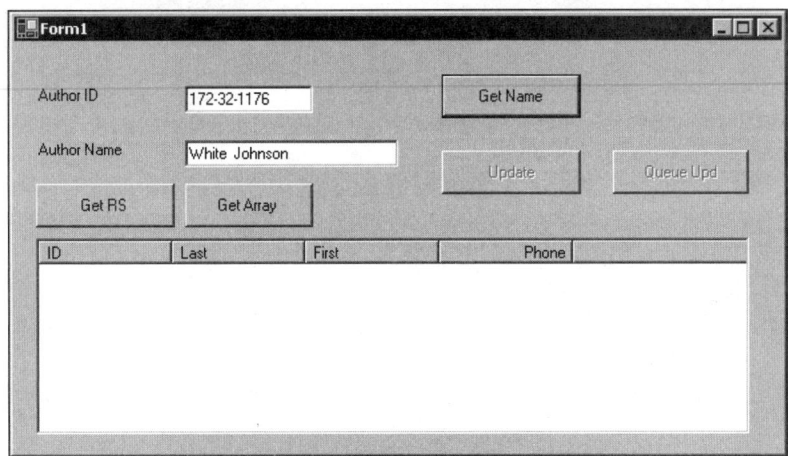

While the end result is the same as using an ADO `Recordset`, we have avoided the need to deploy ADO to all client workstations. At the same time, we've lost our metadata, so our code is harder to read and maintain.

Using XML Documents

If we want to avoid referencing the ADO library within our .NET application, and we want more readability than we can get by using a `Variant` array, we might instead opt to return an XML document from VB6 to the Visual Basic .NET client application.

XML is not the fastest technology at our disposal, so we can expect that our code will run slower using this technique than the previous two. However, XML provides us with a standards-based mechanism by which we can move our data between platforms – including moving the data from the COM platform to the .NET platform – and so there is value in this open approach.

To generate the XML document we can use the MSXML COM component within our VB6 code. Use the Project | References menu option within the `Chapter4COM` project to add a reference to this component:

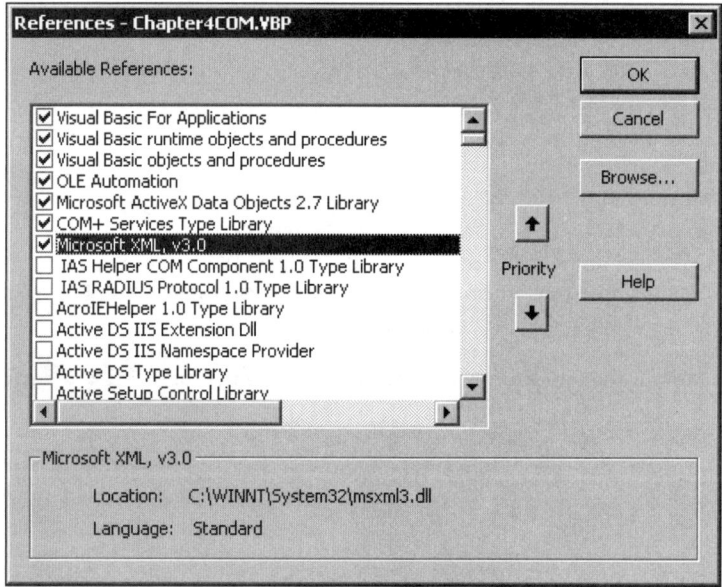

In this case we're referencing version 3.0 of the component. Other versions may work as well, since the functions we're using here are relatively basic.

We can then use the `DOMDocument` object within this component to build an XML document. The `DOMDocument` object represents a single XML document that contains data, so we'll create this object and populate it with our data in XML format.

The data itself is stored in the document within **elements**. An element is a tag such as:

```
<Author></Author>
```

or

```
<Author/>
```

Both are examples of a simple XML element that contains no data. The first syntax has a verbose closing tag, while the second uses a more compact form of indicating that the element tag is complete by including the slash right before the closing bracket.

The first syntax is used when our elements include data:

```
<Author>My author data</Author>
```

Including data in an element in this fashion allows our element to contain a single value. If we want the element to have multiple data values, we can use **attributes**. An attribute is included in the element using the second form of syntax:

```
<Author value1="my first attribute" value2="my second attribute"/>
```

Since we need to return multiple data values we'll be using the attribute approach in our example.

To create elements that we can add to our XML document we need to use an object of type IXMLDOMElement – which represents the element that is added to the document.

Add the following code to the PubsServices class to populate the Recordset object:

```
Public Function GetAuthorDataXML(id As String) As String
  Dim rs As Recordset
  Dim strSQL As String

  On Error GoTo ErrH
  Set rs = New Recordset
  strSQL = "SELECT au_id,au_lname,au_fname,phone " & _
    "FROM authors WHERE au_id='" & id & "'"
  rs.Open strSQL, DB_CONN, adOpenForwardOnly, adLockReadOnly

  If Not rs.BOF And Not rs.EOF Then
    ' place code here to generate XML
  Else
    GetAuthorDataXML = ""
  End If

  rs.Close
  If Not objContext Is Nothing Then objContext.SetComplete
  Exit Function
ErrH:
  If Not rs Is Nothing Then
    If rs.State = adStateOpen Then rs.Close
    Set rs = Nothing
  End If
  If Not objContext Is Nothing Then objContext.SetAbort
  Err.Raise Err.Number, Err.Source, Err.Description
End Function
```

Now we can move on to actually creating XML based on the `Recordset`.

> *It is worth noting that the `Recordset` object can save itself to a file in XML format. While this is sometimes useful, the XML that is generated is very large and is often not optimal. Additionally, it must be stored to a file – which we would then have to read in so we could return the data to the client. This is why we are generating the XML document by hand.*
>
> *It is also possible to directly return XML from SQL Server 2000, which may be an option as it avoids the conversion of data from a `Recordset` to an XML document.*

To create an XML document the first thing we need to do is declare variables for the XML document and the root element of the document:

```
Public Function GetAuthorDataXML(id As String) As String
   Dim rs As Recordset
   Dim SQL As String
   Dim xml As DOMDocument
   Dim root As IXMLDOMElement
```

We can then create the document and the root element, and append the root element to the document:

```
   On Error GoTo ErrH
   Set rs = New Recordset
   SQL = "SELECT * FROM authors WHERE au_id='" & id & "'"
   rs.Open SQL, DB_CONN, adOpenForwardOnly, adLockReadOnly
   If Not rs.BOF And Not rs.EOF Then

      ' place code here to generate XML
      Set xml = New DOMDocument
      Set root = xml.createElement("authors")
      xml.appendChild root
   Else
      GetAuthorDataXML = ""
   End If
```

At this point the document is created and contains a single root element. If we were to view the XML at this point we'd see:

```
<authors/>
```

We could place our data into the root element, since in this case we know we're returning only a single row of data. However, for the sake of completeness we'll create code to support the return of multiple rows of data. In this case we'll need a different element for each row – all of which will be contained within the root element.

We can simply loop through the `Recordset`, creating an XML element named `<author/>` for each of the records returned:

```
If Not rs.BOF And Not rs.EOF Then
  ' place code here to generate XML
  Set xml = New DOMDocument
  Set root = xml.createElement("authors")
  xml.appendChild root

  Do While Not rs.EOF
    Set element = xml.createElement("author")
    With element
      .setAttribute "au_id", rs("au_id")
      .setAttribute "au_lname", rs("au_lname")
      .setAttribute "au_fname", rs("au_fname")
      .setAttribute "phone", rs("phone")
    End With
    root.appendChild element
    rs.MoveNext
  Loop
Else
  GetAuthorDataXML = ""
End If
```

Each `<author/>` element gets assigned a set of attributes that hold our actual data. This means that for each row of data in our `Recordset` we'll have an element similar to:

```
<author au_id="id" au_lname="lastname" au_fname="firstname" phone="555-1234"/>
```

Each of these elements is appended to our document's root element with the following line of code:

```
root.appendChild element
```

The result is a document structured like this:

```
<authors>
  <author au_id="id" au_lname="name" au_fname="name" phone="555-1234"/>
  <author au_id="id" au_lname="name" au_fname="name" phone="555-1234"/>
  <author au_id="id" au_lname="name" au_fname="name" phone="555-1234"/>
</authors>
```

For each author in our `Recordset` we'll have an `<author/>` element in the document, all contained within a single root element named `<authors/>`.

The XML document now contains all the data for our author and we can return the XML document in `String` format as the result of our function:

```
    Loop
      GetAuthorDataXML = xml.xml
  Else
      GetAuthorDataXML = ""
  End If
  If Not objContext Is Nothing Then objContext.SetComplete
  Exit Function
ErrH:
  If Not rs Is Nothing Then
    If rs.State = adStateOpen Then rs.Close
    Set rs = Nothing
  End If
  If Not objContext Is Nothing Then objContext.SetAbort
  Err.Raise Err.Number, Err.Source, Err.Description
End Function
```

Now compile the `Chapter4COM` component and update the COM+ Application. We're ready to switch back to Visual Basic .NET and make use of this new XML document.

Using the XML Document

Within the Visual Basic .NET `Chapter4Net` project we can add a new button to the form named `btnGetXML`:

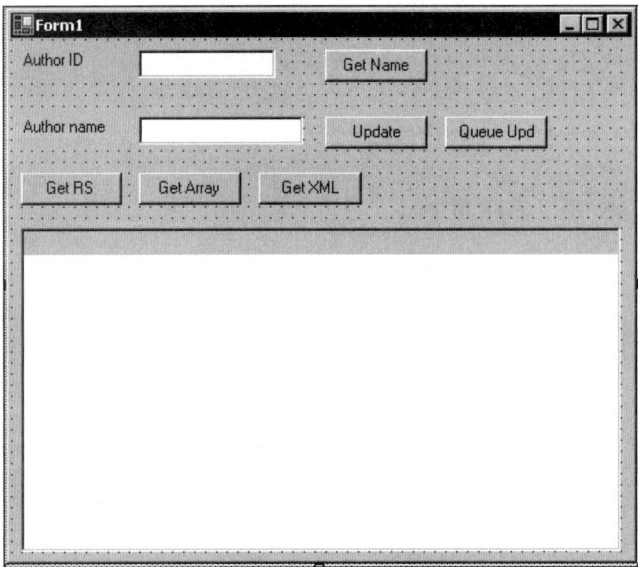

We'll use this button to cause the `ListView` control to be populated with author data retrieved via an XML document. Double-click on the button to bring up the code window.

The XML Assembly

Before we can use XML within our Visual Basic .NET code we need a reference to the
System.Xml.dll assembly. By default this assembly is referenced for us in a Windows Application
and so we don't have to do any work beyond adding an Imports statement to the top of our form code:

```
Imports System.Runtime.InteropServices
Imports System.Xml
```

The System.Xml namespace offers very comparable functionality to what we had in VB6 using the
MSXML component. It too has a class to represent an XML document, XmlDocument, and an object to
represent an element within a document, XmlElement. These fill the same roles, and have virtually the
same methods, as their counterparts in the MSXML COM component.

Using the XML Document

Now we can write code for the Click event of btnGetXML to retrieve the XML document from our
COM+ component:

```
Private Sub btnGetXML_Click(ByVal sender As System.Object, _
    ByVal e As System.EventArgs) Handles btnGetXML.Click
  Dim objservice As New Chapter4COM.PubsServices()

  Dim xmlDoc As New XmlDocument()
  xmlDoc.LoadXml(objservice.GetAuthorDataXML(txtID.Text))

  Marshal.ReleaseComObject(objservice)
  Set objservice = Nothing
End Sub
```

We are calling a method on the COM+ component as we have in the past, but in this case we're passing
the resulting text containing the XML directly into the LoadXml method of an XmlDocument object as
a parameter:

```
Dim xmlDoc As New XmlDocument()
xmlDoc.LoadXml(objservice.GetAuthorDataXML(txtID.Text))
```

This immediately populates the XmlDocument object with the data, making it available for our use. We
can then move on to use the XmlDocument object to populate the ListView control.

To do this, we'll first retrieve the root element, <authors/>, from the document by calling the
FirstChild method on the document object itself. Once we have the root element, we can loop
through all the elements it contains – each one being an <author/> element as we discussed when we
created the document in VB6:

```
Private Sub btnGetXML_Click(ByVal sender As System.Object, _
    ByVal e As System.EventArgs) Handles btnGetXML.Click
  Dim objservice As New Chapter4COM.PubsServices()

  Dim xmlDoc As New XmlDocument()
  xmlDoc.LoadXml(objservice.GetAuthorDataXML(txtID.Text))
```

```
    Marshal.ReleaseComObject(objservice)
    objservice = Nothing

    Dim objRoot As XmlElement = xmlDoc.FirstChild

    ListView1.Items.Clear()
    For Each objElement In objRoot
      With ListView1
        Dim lvi As New ListViewItem(objElement.GetAttribute("au_id"))

        lvi.SubItems.Add(objElement.GetAttribute("au_lname"))
        lvi.SubItems.Add(objElement.GetAttribute("au_fname"))
        lvi.SubItems.Add(objElement.GetAttribute("phone"))

        .Items.Add(lvi)
      End With
    Next
  End Sub
```

We first retrieve the root element from the document:

```
    Dim objRoot As XmlElement = xmlDoc.FirstChild
```

Knowing that the root element contains a list of all the <author/> elements, we can then loop through all those elements to get each set of data for an author:

```
    For Each objElement In objRoot
```

Each element contains all the data for an author, so we can then retrieve the individual fields of information from the properties of this root element by calling the GetAttribute method to populate the ListView control.

While XML may be a bit slower than returning a Variant array, the resulting code is much easier to read since we can use human-readable subscripts to get at the various fields of data. It also avoids the need to reference the COM ADO library from within our .NET code, helping us minimize our dependence on non-.NET code and simplifying our application's deployment. Better still, XML is an open standard, so this technique can be used not only between COM and .NET, but between other platforms as well.

Calling .NET Components in COM+ from VB6

We've now seen how we can invoke a COM component that is running in COM+ from a .NET application. It is also possible to do the reverse – invoking a .NET component that is hosted in COM+ from a VB6 application. This isn't as simple as it might seem, primarily because of the way .NET utilizes the services provided by COM+.

Unlike VB6 development with COM+, when we are working with Visual Basic .NET all the interaction with COM+ is typically handled for us automatically by the .NET runtime. This includes creating any required COM+ Applications, inserting our components into the application and so forth.

Our options remain the same – we can use automatic transactions or manual transactions. If we use automatic transactions, the transaction will be rolled back if our code raises an error, while if we use manual transactions then we'll specifically call `SetComplete` or `SetAbort` to indicate whether our method completed successfully.

The primary difference is in how our code gets configured and registered within the COM+ environment. With COM we had to manually place the DLL into a COM+ application, but with .NET this is an automatic process that is done for us by the .NET runtime. We can optionally also choose a manual approach to registering the assembly with COM+ – a topic we'll cover in detail in Chapter 5.

The automatic registration process is invoked any time we mark a class in our assembly with attributes that require the use of COM+ services. These attributes come from the `System.EnterpriseServices` namespace and include the following:

Attribute	Description
Transaction	Enables two-phase commit processing for this class
ObjectPooling	Enables COM+ object pooling for this class
Synchronization	Enables method call synchronization for this class, ensuring that the current method completes before another method call can be processed by the same object
InterfaceQueuing	Enables the COM+ queued component functionality for this class

While this is all very nice, the configuration only makes our .NET components available for use by .NET client applications – not for use by COM-based client applications such as we can create with VB6. Specifically this is because .NET does not export a type library with a meaningful interface for our .NET component.

This means that we need to do some extra work to make our COM+-hosted .NET assembly available for use by COM client applications. This is basically the same work we did in Chapter 3. The .NET class needs a COM interface, which we can create by using the `<ComClass()>` attribute or the other manual techniques discussed in Chapter 3. We can then mark the assembly in Visual Studio .NET so that a COM type library is created and registered for the assembly, so when it is loaded into COM+ it can be called by COM client applications.

Creating a COM+ Component in .NET

To see how this works, let's create a simple .NET project that makes use of COM+ services. This will be a simple .NET DLL, marked with attributes such that it will automatically cause the .NET runtime to invoke COM+ services on our behalf. In Chapter 5 we'll get into much more detail about how to create and work with COM+ components in Visual Basic .NET. Our example here will be fairly basic so we can see the steps necessary to make the assembly callable from a COM client.

Creating a .NET assembly that works within COM+ involves just a few steps:

1. Reference the `System.EnterpriseServices.dll` assembly

2. Build a class that inherits from `ServicedComponent` and thus has access to the COM+ services

3. Attribute the class to indicate which services to use (transactions, queuing, etc.)

4. Add attributes to the assembly to indicate the name of the COM+ application into which the assembly should be registered

With these steps complete, the first time a .NET client invokes the assembly the .NET runtime will automatically register it in COM+ so it can take advantage of the COM+ services.

To make this assembly also available for use by COM clients we must perform a few extra steps:

1. Create a COM interface for the class using `<ComClass()>` or by manually implementing the interface

2. Tell Visual Studio .NET to register the assembly for use by COM as we discussed in Chapter 3

3. After building the assembly, manually register it with COM+ by using the `regsvcs.exe` command-line utility

Steps one and two are the same as we did in Chapter 3 to expose an assembly for use by COM. Step 3 is required because the automatic registration of a .NET assembly with COM+ only works when the assembly is invoked by a .NET client – a COM client won't trigger the automatic registration process and so we must do it by hand.

Setting Up the Project

Open Visual Studio .NET and create a new Class Library project named `Chapter4COMplus`. The Class Library project type will create a DLL, which is exactly what we need for use within COM+.

In the Solution Explorer window right-click on the project and choose **Properties** to bring up the project properties dialog window.

Right-click on `Class1` in the Solution Explorer and delete it. Then add a new class to the project named `Transactions`.

Generating a Strong Name

Before the .NET runtime can invoke any COM+ services for our assembly, the assembly must have a strong name. We discussed strong named assemblies in Chapter 3 when we covered the use of a .NET assembly from a VB6 client application.

To create a strong name, we must have a key file or a key container that we can reference from within our project. We can use the one we used in Chapters 2 and 3, or use the instructions from Chapter 2 to create a new key file using `sn.exe`.

To reference the key from our project we need to add an attribute to the `AssemblyInfo.vb` file, so double-click on the file in Solution Explorer to bring up its code window and add the following attribute:

```
'Create a strong name
<Assembly: AssemblyKeyFile("mykey.snk")>
```

When the project is built it will now be given a strong name based on the information in this key file.

Referencing System.EnterpriseServices

Not only does our component require a strong name to use COM+ services, but we must also make use of some classes provided by the `System.EnterpriseServices` namespace. These are available in a .NET DLL that must be referenced by our project.

Choose the **Project | Add Reference** menu option to bring up the references dialog and add a reference to the `System.EnterpriseServices.dll`:

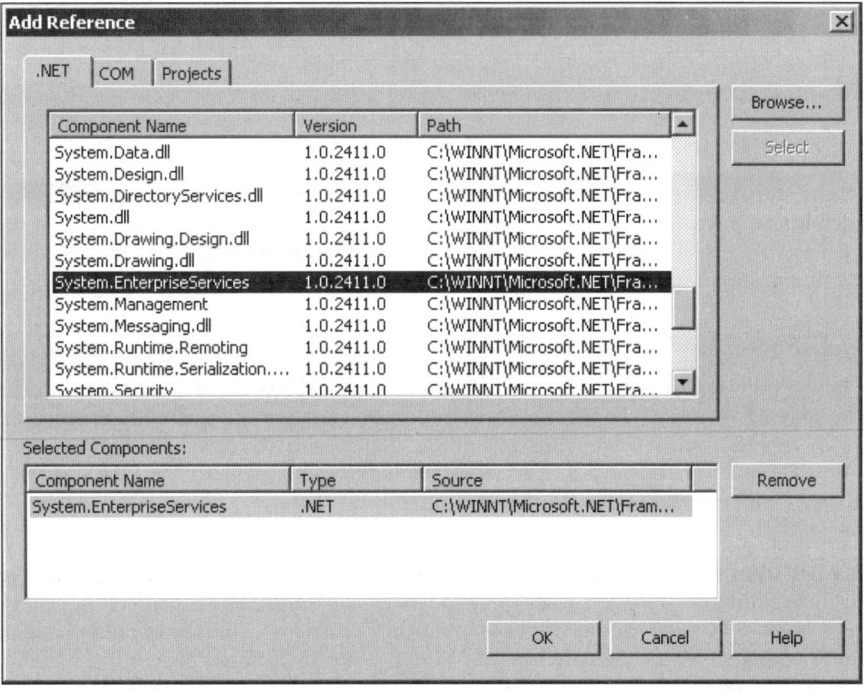

This DLL contains the classes and attributes we require to interact with the COM+ services within our code. To simplify the use of this DLL and its namespace, add an `Imports` statement to the top of any class in the project:

```
Imports System.EnterpriseServices
```

All the code that follows assumes we have added this `Imports` statement to the top of our class.

Importing System.Data

Since the assembly we're building will interact with data, we'll also want to add a couple `Imports` statements to the top of our class:

```
Imports System.Data
Imports System.Data.SqlClient
```

These will simplify the use of ADO.NET and the client for Microsoft SQL Server.

Specifying the COM+ Application

Since our assembly will be running within COM+, it will be running within a COM+ application. If we don't specify a name for the application, the .NET runtime will create one for us based on the name of our assembly. However, we can override this by adding a simple attribute to our project's `AssemblyInfo.vb` file.

Double-click that file in the Solution Explorer to bring up its code editor and add the following code:

```
Imports System.Reflection
Imports System.Runtime.InteropServices
Imports System.EnterpriseServices

<Assembly: ApplicationName("Chapter4COM")>
```

This will cause the .NET runtime to place the assembly into a COM+ application named `Chapter4COM` – the application we created earlier in the chapter. We could also specify an application that doesn't already exist and the .NET runtime would create it for us, but it is often easier to use an existing application that is all configured and ready for use.

Building a Class

So far we haven't done anything particularly special. Merely referencing `System.EnterpriseServices` from our project doesn't trigger any special behavior – it just makes the enterprise services features available for our use. Now we're about to use them.

Marking the Class as Transactional

When we attribute a class by using one of the enterprise services attributes, we are telling the .NET runtime that we want the service specified by the attribute. The `<Transaction()>` attribute, for instance, indicates that we want our class to have two-phase transactional protection. Typically we should use this when we are working with two or more databases, as it is invaluable in such a setting. If we are only working with a single database, the two-phase transactional processing will incur unnecessary overhead and should be avoided.

Even though our example will only work with a single database, we'll illustrate how to make our code protected by a two-phase commit transaction by adding an attribute to the class:

```
Imports System.EnterpriseServices
Imports System.Data
Imports System.Data.SqlClient

<Transaction(TransactionOption.Required)> _
Public Class Transactions
```

The `<Transaction()>` attribute accepts a parameter that indicates how the class works with transactions. In this case we're indicating that a transaction is required for the methods in this class.

The options available are shown in the following table, along with the corresponding `MTSTransactionMode` property values in VB6:

Visual Basic .NET	VB6	Description
Disabled	NotAnMTSObject	This class cannot participate in a COM+ transaction and should not be run within COM+.
NotSupported	NoTransactions	This class does not work with COM+ transactions and will run outside of any COM+ transaction that exists.
Required	RequiresTransaction	The methods of this class must run within a transaction and will use an existing transaction if it exists.
RequiresNew	RequiresNewTransaction	The methods of this class must run within a transaction newly created for the object, even if another transaction already exists.
Supported	UsesTransaction	This class supports transactions but does not require them. The methods can run either in a transaction or not.

By adding this attribute, we have indicated to .NET that the class should be transactionally protected by using the two-phase commit services provided by COM+. Just adding the attribute isn't enough to make enterprise services work, however. There are a couple more steps we must take.

Inheriting from ServicedComponent

Once we've marked a class with an attribute that triggers the use of enterprise services, such as `<Transactional()>`, the class must then inherit from `ServicedComponent`. This base class exists in the `System.EnterpriseServices` namespace, and any class that subclasses it will inherit the functionality required to operate within the COM+ environment.

```
<Transaction(TransactionOption.Required)> _
Public Class Transactions
   Inherits ServicedComponent
```

At this point our class is ready for use in the COM+ environment. When any method of the class is invoked, the .NET runtime will ensure that the appropriate COM+ services are enlisted on our behalf.

Coding the Class

Now we are ready to move on and write a method within the class. This method will simply update an author within the Pubs database:

```
Private Const DB_CONN As String = _
    "Data Source=myserver; Initial Catalog=pubs;User ID=sa;Password="

Public Sub UpdateName(ByVal id As String, ByVal lname As String)
    Dim cn As New SqlConnection(DB_CONN)
    cn.Open()
    Dim cm As New SqlCommand()

    Try
        cm.CommandType = CommandType.Text
        cm.Connection = cn
        cm.CommandText = "UPDATE authors SET au_lname='" & lname & _
            "' WHERE au_id='" & id & "'"
        cm.ExecuteNonQuery()
    Finally
        cm.Dispose()
        cn.Close()
        cn.Dispose()
    End Try
End Sub
```

This is fairly straightforward ADO.NET code that simply opens a connection to the database and executes a command to update the authors table.

At this point we can either use automatic or manual transactional protection for our method, just as we could in VB6. To use automatic protection, we could apply the <AutoComplete()> attribute:

```
<AutoComplete()> _
Public Sub UpdateName(ByVal id As String, ByVal lname As String)
```

With this attribute, our method will cause the transaction to roll back if it raises an error, otherwise it will allow the transaction to complete (assuming no other parts of the transaction failed).

For symmetry with our earlier VB6 code, however, we'll implement manual transactional protection by calling SetComplete and SetAbort as appropriate. These methods are found on the ContextUtil class from the System.EnterpriseServices namespace. This class corresponds to the ObjectContext object we used in our VB6 code, but is automatically available within any Visual Basic .NET class that inherits from ServicedComponent.

Using these methods we can manually implement transactions with the following changes:

```
Public Sub UpdateName(ByVal id As String, ByVal lname As String)
    Dim cn As New SqlConnection(DB_CONN)
    cn.Open()
    Dim cm As New SqlCommand()
```

```
   Try
      cm.CommandType = CommandType.Text
      cm.Connection = cn
      cm.CommandText = "UPDATE authors SET au_lname='" & lname & _
        "' WHERE au_id='" & id & "'"
      cm.ExecuteNonQuery()
      ContextUtil.SetComplete()
   Catch
      ContextUtil.SetAbort()
   Finally
      cm.Dispose()
      cn.Close()
      cn.Dispose()
   End Try
End Sub
```

The key lines of code here are where we call `SetComplete` and `SetAbort`. If our method succeeds we are calling `SetComplete`, while an error will result in a call to `SetAbort` to indicate to COM+ that there was a failure. In this case COM+ will cause any database changes to be rolled back.

Registering the Assembly with COM+

The first time our assembly is invoked by a .NET client application, the .NET runtime will automatically create a COM+ application and will register the assembly within the application so it can take advantage of the COM+ services. Unfortunately this won't occur if the client is a COM application, and so in that case we must manually register the assembly with COM+.

Manual registration is done using the `regsvcs.exe` command-line utility. We'll take this approach here.

First build the assembly to create the DLL, then open a Visual Studio .NET Command Prompt window and navigate to the `bin` directory beneath our project where the DLL is located. Then enter the following command:

```
regsvcs chapter4complus.dll
```

This will register the `Chapter4COMPlus` assembly within the `Chapter4COM` application in COM+.

We can now bring up the COM+ management console to examine our application and the `Chapter4COMPlus` component. In particular, let's expand the **Interfaces** option so we can see the interfaces exposed by our component:

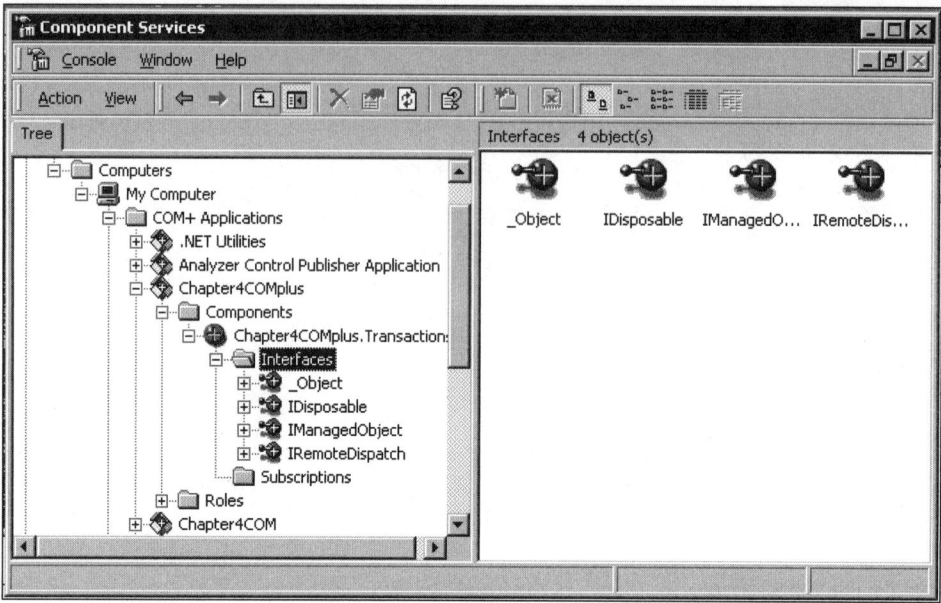

Notice that there is no Chapter4COMPlus interface. In fact, if we expand all these interfaces and look at all their methods we will not find any interface that has an UpdateName method. There would appear to be no way to invoke our component in any direct fashion.

The reason that a .NET client can invoke the assembly is that the .NET runtime is managing the call into our class and it uses these interfaces to do the work. This is the purpose behind the IManaged, IRemoteDispatch, and System_EnterpriseServices_IServicedComponentInfo interfaces – they contain various methods that are used by the .NET runtime to get information about the assembly and to invoke the methods available from its classes.

By default, no provision is made to allow a COM client application to invoke the class.

Since this implementation of the assembly is not useful to us, let's remove it from COM+. Select the Components entry in the left-hand tree view, then click on the Chapter4COMplus entry in the right-hand list and hit the *Delete* key. This will unregister the assembly from COM+.

Making the Class Available to COM Clients

As we discussed earlier, to make the class available from VB6 we'll need to take extra steps. In particular, we need to follow the steps we took in Chapter 3 to give our class a COM interface. We can either use the <ComClass()> attribute, or we can manually implement a formal interface. Typically we'll use the <ComClass()> attribute, as it is much easier and more straightforward, and so that is the approach we'll follow here.

Adding <ComClass()>

Open the code window for the `Transactions` class and add the `<ComClass()>` attribute:

```
<ComClass(), Transaction(TransactionOption.Required)> _
Public Class Transactions
```

This implements a COM interface for the class as we discussed in Chapter 3. Then we can check the Register for COM Interop option in the project's properties dialog as shown in the following screenshot:

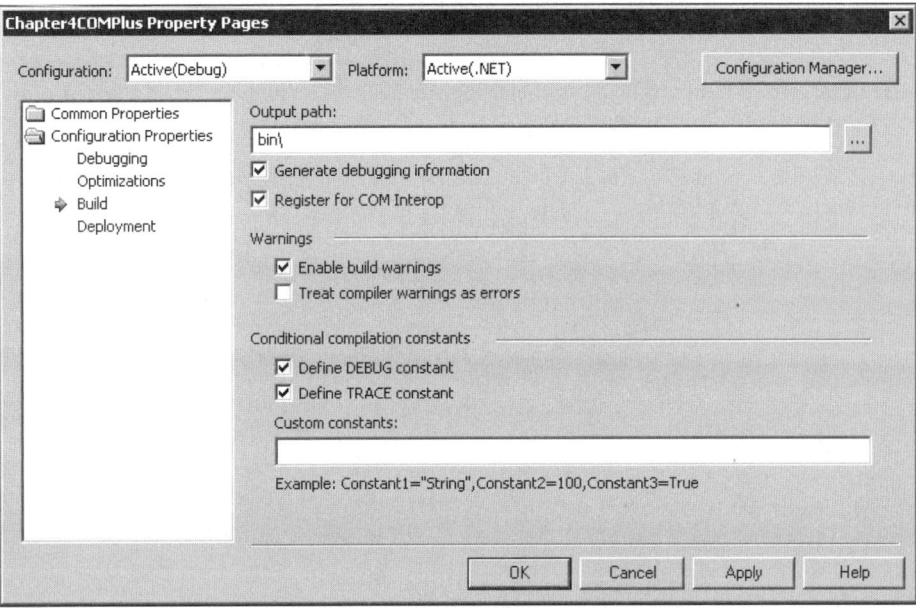

Rebuild the project to recreate the DLL. Visual Studio .NET will generate a COM type library for our class and will register it for use by COM clients.

We can then use the `regsvcs.exe` utility to update COM+ with the new version of the assembly:

```
regsvcs chapter4complus.dll
```

Now COM+ will have our new assembly – including its COM interface – ready for use.

Viewing the Interface

We can return to the COM+ management console and view our new interface.

We will see that the component now has a new interface named `_Transactions` that is available to COM clients such as a VB6 application. This interface includes the `UpdateName` method, meaning that we can invoke the method from a COM client. We won't cover those details here, as we can now interact with the assembly using normal COM/COM+ programming techniques within any VB6 client application.

Summary

COM and COM+ provide a great deal of location transparency – hiding the details of whether a COM component is running in the same process as a client application, or on another machine across the network. Because of this level of abstraction, interacting with a COM+ component from a Visual Basic .NET client is much the same as interacting with a COM component referenced locally.

In this chapter we explored the key differences – including the importance of releasing the reference to the COM+ component as early as possible in our code. We also examined how we can create and use a COM+ queued component through the use of a queued moniker and the GetObject method in Visual Basic .NET.

Finally we took a look at three ways we can return complex data from the COM+ component back to the Visual Basic .NET client application, including the use of disconnected ADO Recordset objects, Variant arrays and XML documents.

In Chapter 5 we'll move on to see how we can leverage the services provided by COM+ directly from our Visual Basic .NET application, focusing on how Visual Basic .NET COM+ components interact across COM+ Application boundaries and also how they interact with other VB6 components running in the COM+ environment.

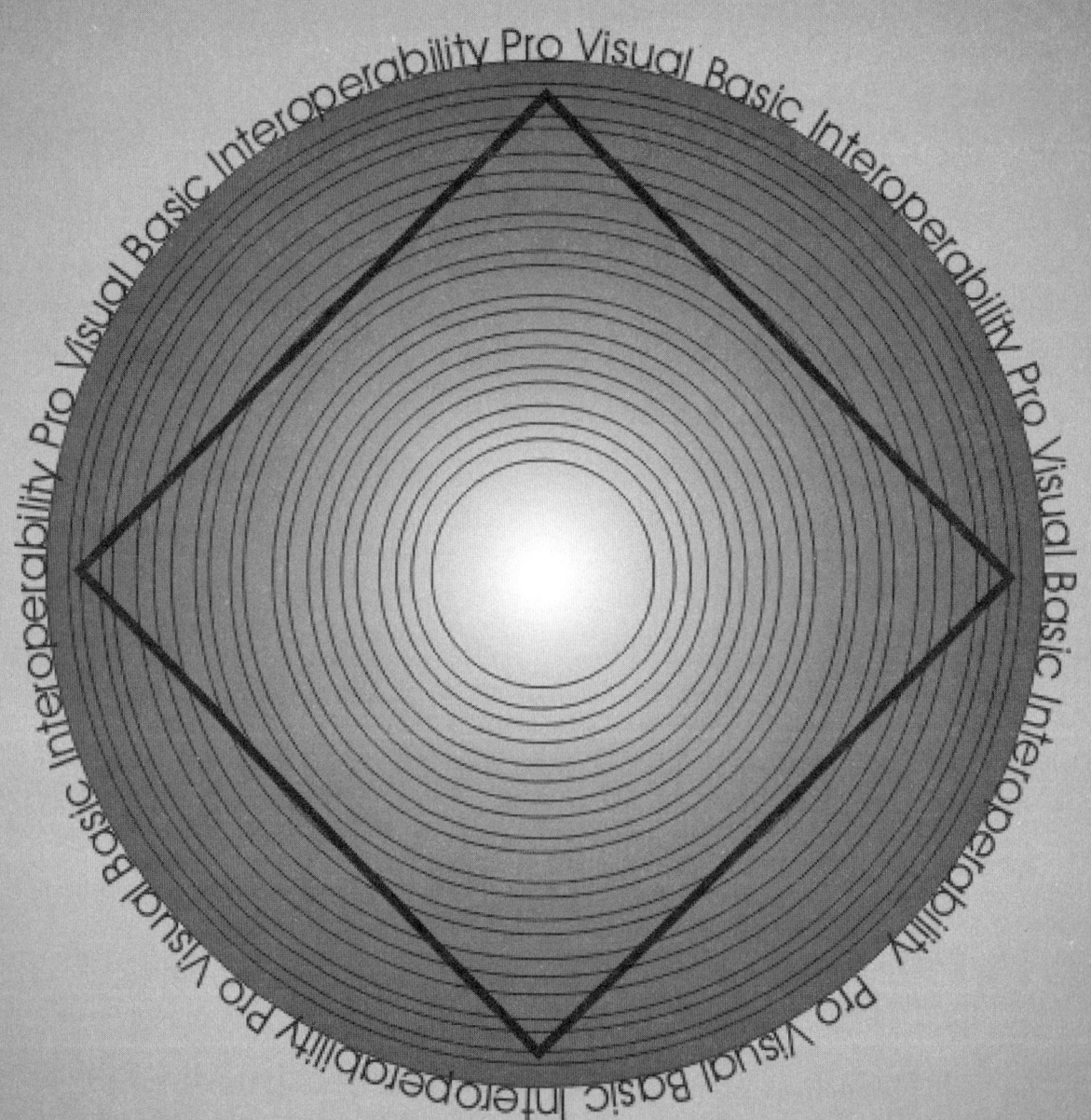

Pro Visual Basic Interoperability Pro Visual Basic Interoperability Pro Visual Basic Interoperability Pro Visual Basic Interoperability Pro Visual Basic Interoperability Pro Visual Basic Interoperability Pro Visual Basic Interoperability

5

Visual Basic .NET and COM in COM+

In Chapter 4 we discussed how to call a VB6 component hosted in COM+ from a Visual Basic .NET client application. We also discussed how to call a Visual Basic .NET assembly hosted in COM+ from a VB6 client application. In this chapter, we'll move beyond simple client-server interactions to discuss server-server interactions. Specifically we'll discuss how a Visual Basic .NET assembly running in COM+ interacts with VB6 components also running in COM+ and visa versa.

While we won't provide a complete discussion of the use of COM+ services from either VB6 or Visual Basic .NET in this chapter, it is worth some background discussion of how COM+ is used in both environments so we can fully understand how they interact with each other. In the process, we'll create some COM+ components that we can later use as we explore various forms of interaction between VB6 and Visual Basic .NET within COM+.

COM+ itself is the next step in the evolution of COM. COM provides a powerful framework on which to build component-based applications, but it doesn't provide services such as transactional protection, nor does it make it easy to manage or deploy applications. Microsoft created Microsoft Transaction Server (MTS) to help address these issues by layering a set of services on top of COM. These services included transactional support and enhanced management capabilities.

While MTS was a good move forward, it was an add-on to the Windows NT 4.0 operating system and to COM. It was not integrated into either; instead it was installed separately and sat on top of the existing technologies. With the advent of the Windows 2000 operating system, Microsoft took the opportunity to integrate the capabilities of MTS directly into the operating system and COM – creating COM+. COM+ includes the capabilities of MTS, but expands on them with new functionality. More importantly, it is directly integrated into the system so it provides far superior performance and reliability.

.NET provides access to a set of capabilities called **enterprise services**, including transactional protection, queued components, synchronization, and object pooling. Enterprise services, behind the scenes, rely on COM+ to do their work. The enterprise services do not support MTS under Windows NT 4.0, and so applications that use enterprise services will fail to run on that operating system. In fact, since they require COM+, applications that use enterprise services can only run on Windows 2000 and higher.

Let's take a more detailed look at how both VB6 and Visual Basic .NET interact with COM+ services – specifically transactional protection, since that is the most common scenario.

Transactional protection means two-phase commit transactional protection, which we should use when working with more than one database. If we are only working with one database, we should typically use the transactional support built into ADO in VB6 or ADO.NET in Visual Basic .NET, since two-phase commit offers us no benefit but does incur quite a bit of overhead in such a circumstance. In this chapter, although we'll only be using a single database in the examples, we'll accept the overhead so we can demonstrate how to work with transactional protection in a simple environment.

COM+ and VB6

When building COM-based applications such as those we create with VB6, we often use MTS or COM+ to provide transactional protection for our code as it interacts with databases. Sometimes MTS or COM+ are also used to help manage COM components, including simplified registration and configuration of Distributed COM (DCOM) so clients can interact with server-side components.

Creating an ActiveX DLL for COM+

To see how VB6 interacts with MTS/COM+, we'll create a simple VB6 ActiveX DLL. We'll use this DLL later as we explore the interaction between COM and .NET within COM+.

> Note that, since .NET only supports COM+, we will be creating this VB6 component for COM+ rather than MTS.

Setting Up the Project

Open the VB6 IDE and create a new ActiveX DLL project. Use the project's properties window to set the project name to comAuthor. Also check the Unattended Execution and Retained In Memory options so the DLL is properly configured for use on a server:

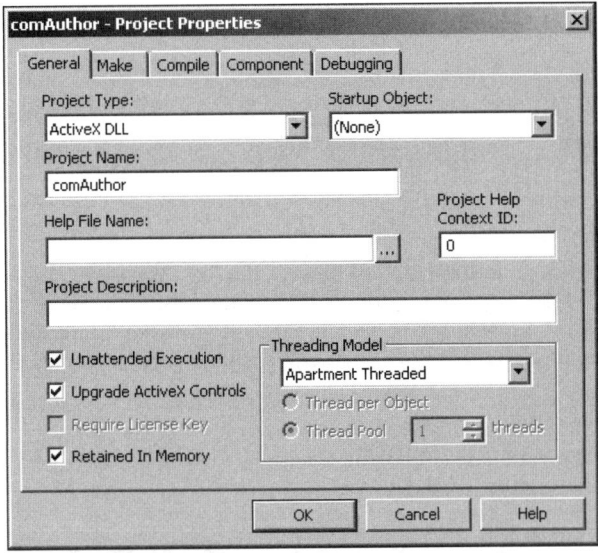

Writing the Code

Now change the name of Class1 to Author and write the following code (changing the connection string as necessary):

```
Option Explicit

Const DB_CONN As String = "Provider=sqloledb;" & _
    "server=myserver;uid=sa;password=;database=pubs"

Public Function UpdateAuthor(ByVal auName As String) As String
    Dim strOut As String
    Dim strSQL As String

    strOut = "Author updated"

    UpdateAuthor = strOut

    On Error GoTo COMERR
    strSQL = "UPDATE Authors SET au_lname = '" & auName & _
        "' WHERE au_id='172-32-1176'"

    Dim cn As Connection
    Dim cm As Command

    Set cn = New Connection
    cn.Open DB_CONN

    Set cm = New Command
    Set cm.ActiveConnection = cn
    cm.CommandType = adCmdText
    cm.CommandText = strSQL
    cm.Execute
```

```
   Set cm = Nothing
   cn.Close
   Set cn = Nothing
   Exit Function

COMERR:
   UpdateAuthor = Err.Description
End Function
```

This is standard ADO code to update the last name value of a single record in the `Authors` table of the `pubs` database, based on the new value provided as a parameter. The method does have a `String` return value, which is a bit unusual for an update method – but we'll be using this later to provide more details about transactional information within COM+ and so it is written as a function here.

Making the Class Transactional

VB6 provides some integration with MTS and COM+ by allowing us to set the `MTSTransactionMode` property on the class:

This property allows us to indicate whether our class should be marked as supporting or requiring transactions when it is imported into COM+. Note that it is simply a suggestion – the system administrator can always override the setting within the COM+ administrative console.

Note that this property setting doesn't *require* that our DLL run within MTS or COM+. The property is only used during the process of registering the DLL with COM+ so the appropriate transactional setting is provided to COM+. If we use the DLL outside of COM+, it will work the same regardless of the value of this property.

The available options here, along with their counterparts in the COM+ management console, are shown in the following table:

VB6	COM+ Property	Description
NotAnMTSObject	Disabled	This class cannot participate in a COM+ transaction and should not be run within COM+.
NoTransactions	Not Supported	This class does not work with COM+ transactions and will run outside of any COM+ transaction that exists.

VB6	COM+ Property	Description
Requires Transaction	Required	The methods of this class must run within a transaction and will use an existing transaction if it exists.
RequiresNew Transaction	Requires New	The methods of this class must run within a transaction newly created for the object, even if another transaction already exists.
UsesTransaction	Supported	This class supports transactions but does not require them. The methods can either run in a transaction or not.

In our case, let's mark the component as requiring a transaction so we can see how it works first in COM+ and then, later, how it interacts with .NET assemblies running in COM+.

Interacting with COM+

To interact with the features of COM+ within our code, we need to add a reference to the COM+ Services Type Library within our ActiveX DLL project. Reference the ADO 2.7 library at the same time:

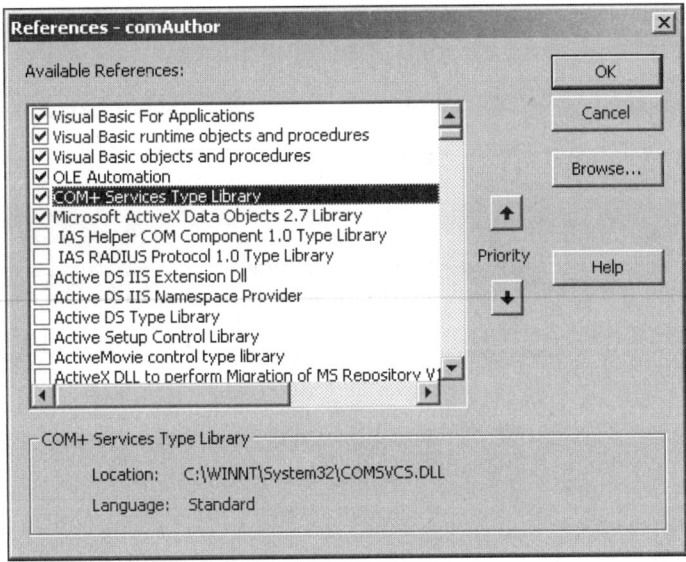

The COM+ Services Type Library reference makes the COM+ objects and interfaces available to our code. We can now add code to the class that utilizes the COM+ **context object** so we can indicate whether our database work was successful or not:

```
Public Function UpdateAuthor(ByVal auName As String) As String
    Dim strOut As String
    Dim strSQL As String
    Dim ctx As ObjectContext

    Set ctx = GetObjectContext
```

191

```
    strOut = "Author updated"

    UpdateAuthor = strOut

    On Error GoTo COMERR
    strSQL = "UPDATE Authors SET au_lname = '" & auName & _
      "' WHERE au_id='172-32-1176'"

    Dim cn As Connection
    Dim cm As Command

    Set cn = New Connection
    cn.Open DB_CONN

    Set cm = New Command
    Set cm.ActiveConnection = cn
    cm.CommandType = adCmdText
    cm.CommandText = strSQL
    cm.Execute

    Set cm = Nothing
    cn.Close
    Set cn = Nothing
    If Not ctx Is Nothing Then ctx.SetComplete
    Exit Function

  COMERR:
    UpdateAuthor = Err.Description
    If Not ctx Is Nothing Then ctx.SetAbort
  End Function
```

When a component runs within COM+, it is "wrapped" by a context object that is provided by COM+. This context object maintains information about any transaction our object is part of, along with various other information about the calling user, such as the user's ID, roles, and other security values.

The context object also contains methods that can allow the code in our component to interact with the COM+ environment. This means we can retrieve information about our current context, and it also means we can interact with COM+ to tell it whether our code completed successfully or not. We do this by calling SetComplete to indicate that we completed the transaction successfully or SetAbort to indicate that the transaction should be rolled back.

Returning the Transaction ID

At this point we've got a DLL ready for use. However, to make it easy to ensure that we know when we are and are not transactionally protected, let's make the value returned from the method a bit more descriptive. Replace the line:

```
    strOut = "Author updated"
```

with the following code:

```
strOut = "au "
If Not ctx Is Nothing Then
  If ctx.IsInTransaction Then
    strOut = strOut & ctx.ContextInfo.GetTransactionId
  Else
    strOut = strOut & "no transactional protection"
  End If
Else
  strOut = strOut & "not running in COM+"
End If
```

With this change, the return value from the method will include information about whether or not we are running in a transaction, or even within COM+ at all.

If we are unable to get a reference to the COM+ context object, we'll return text indicating that we are not running in COM+. This is quite possible, as our DLL will function just fine outside COM+, though obviously without any transactional protection.

Assuming we get a reference to the context object, we may still not be in a transaction. If the transaction support property in COM+ is set to Not Supported, it will not be part of a transaction since it doesn't support them. Even if the property is set to Supported, it may not be part of a transaction since it won't start one itself. In this case, we'll return text indicating that we are not transactionally protected – even though we are running in COM+.

If we are in a transaction, the transaction ID will be returned. The transaction ID is a GUID (globally unique identifier) value that identifies the current transaction. All components running within the context of a single transaction will share that same transaction ID.

Now build the DLL and we can move on to configure it within COM+.

Registering the DLL in COM+

There is no automatic way to put a VB6 DLL into a COM+ application. When we build our Visual Basic .NET assembly, we'll see that it does provide an automatic registration mechanism. Since this is a VB6 component, we'll need to create the COM+ application and install the DLL into it manually.

To do this, we will make use of the **Component Services** console on our server. This console can be found under **Administrative Tools** within the **Control Panel**. Once we bring up the console, we need to expand the **Component Services | Computers | My Computer | COM+ Applications** tree as shown in the screenshot:

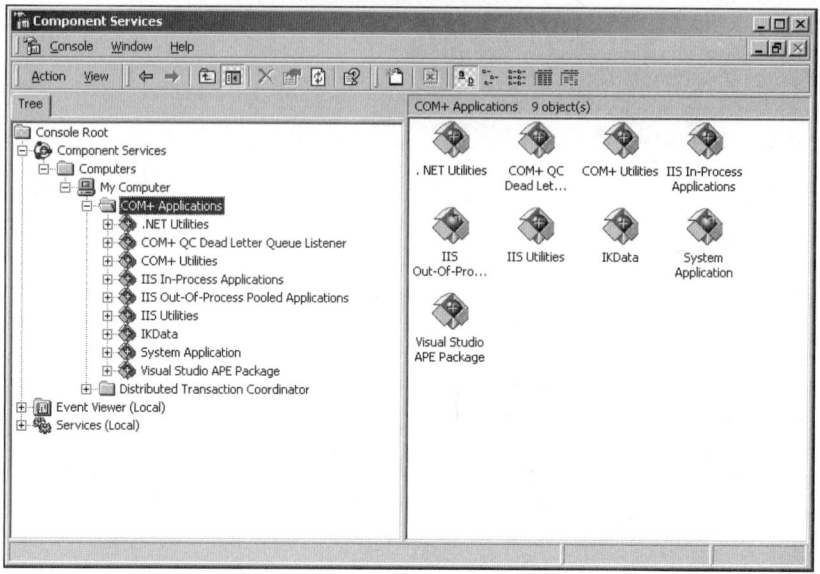

We now have a list of the applications that exist on our server. It is here that we'll add a new application to hold our VB6 DLL, as well as the .NET assembly we'll create later in the chapter.

Right-click on the COM+ Applications entry and choose the New | Application menu option to bring up the COM Application Install Wizard, as we did in Chapter 4.

Choose to Create an empty application on the second panel. On the third panel, name the application cpTest and make sure the Server application option is selected:

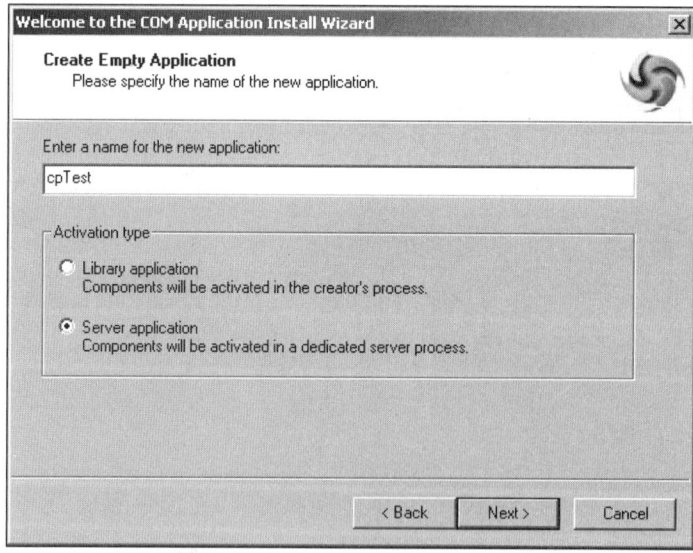

By being a server application, the DLL will be hosted in a process created by COM+ rather than in the same process as our client application. A library application would run within the client's process. Technically either option will work fine in this case but, by using a server application, we will be able to see when the component is active by using the management console.

On the next panel we get to choose which user account should run the application. The default is to run it under the current logged on user account – which is a poor practice. It is strongly recommended that a specific username be entered along with its password. Make sure that the user account chosen has sufficient security to run the code in our component – meaning that it needs access to both the DLL on disk and to the database server to which we'll be talking.

With that complete, the wizard will create the application. Expand that part of the tree and select the Components entry:

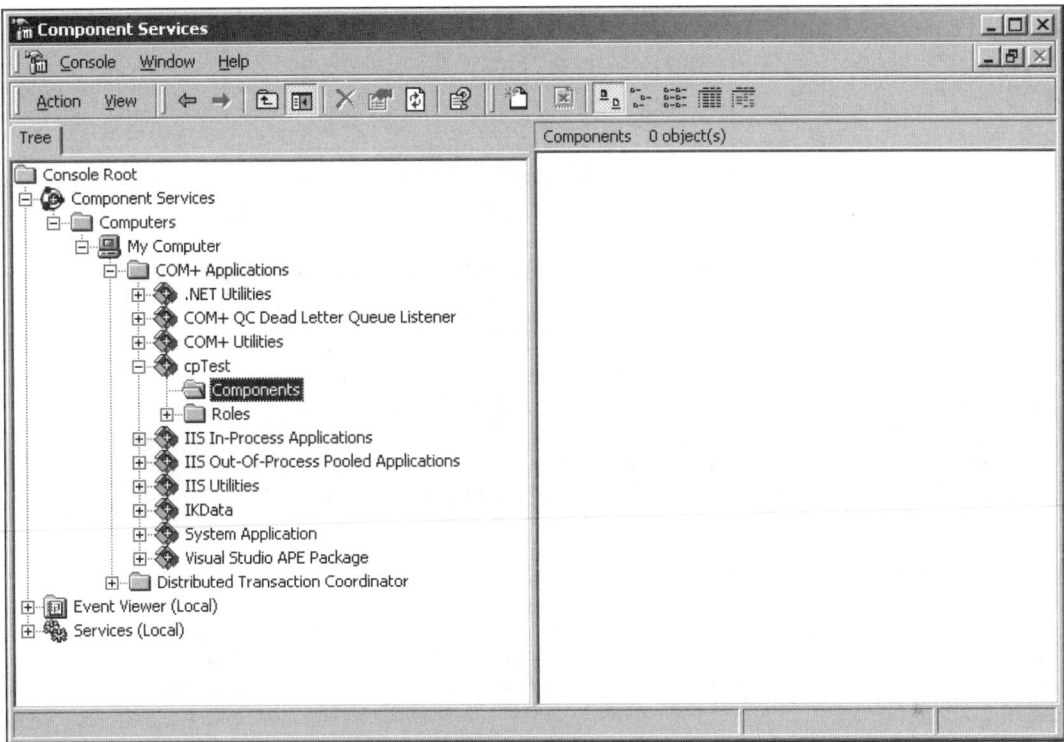

The window on the right lists all of the components that are currently installed in the application. It is here that we can add our VB6 DLL. This can be done by simply dragging and dropping the DLL from its location on disk into the right-hand pane of the window, or we can use a wizard by right-clicking on the Components entry in the left-hand pane and selecting New | Component.

In Chapter 4 we walked through the process of using the wizard to add the component. Typically, however, the drag-and-drop approach is used as it is simpler and more intuitive.

Right-click on the component, choose Properties, and then select the Transactions tab:

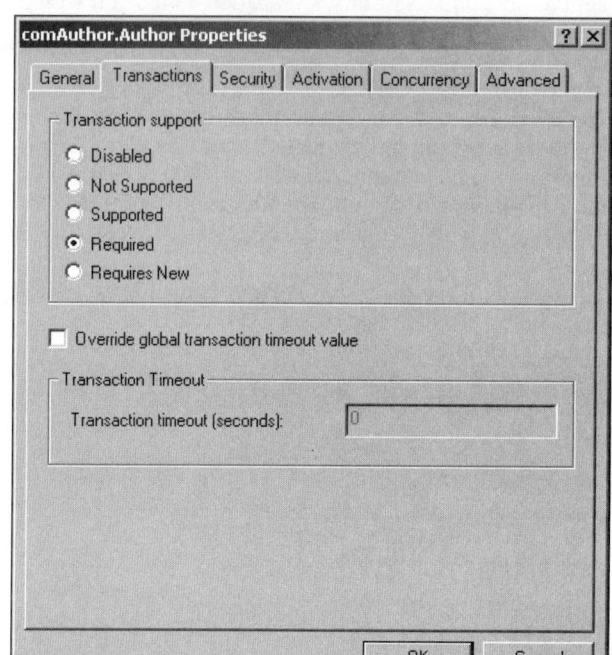

Because the Author class in the DLL is already marked as requiring a transaction, as confirmed by this screenshot, we need to do no further configuration once the DLL is copied into the application.

Once we've brought the DLL into the application we are ready to use it. The great thing is that the client application needs no extra or different code to use a component hosted in COM+; it is the same as talking to any other COM component.

Creating a VB6 Test Application

It is always wise to create a basic test application for COM+ components so we can run them in a simple environment and make sure they work properly. COM+ transactional components often require more security and more complete network access to the database server and possibly to other resources than would be required by our code normally.

For instance, with the DLL we just created, the code merely requires simple access to the database server. When running transactionally in COM+, however, the Distributed Transaction Coordinator (DTC) on our COM+ server needs to interact with the DTC on the database server machine in a bi-directional manner. This may require additional security or network configuration over and above that which might be required were we running our code outside of COM+.

To create a simple test application, create a new Standard EXE project in VB6 and add a command button to the form. Also use Project | References to add a reference to the comAuthor component.

he code window and enter the following:

:n")

uthor method, indicating that the person's last name should be
t will display the text returned from the method – text that
r which our code was running.

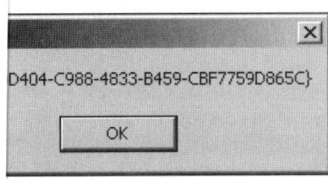

.NET

As we've seen so far in this book, .NET applications do not normally make use of COM. However, when our assemblies use .NET enterprise services, they *will* make use of the services provided by COM+. To a large degree this is transparent to our code, and .NET can even create and configure COM+ applications and install our components into them automatically, eliminating much of the extra effort that is required with VB6 DLLs.

> *It is important to keep in mind that any time we write .NET code that utilizes enterprise services, our code will only run where COM+ is present – on Windows 2000 or higher.*

Creating the Project and Class

To create a simple DLL that updates some data transactionally, we'll first create a simple class that interacts with the database using ADO.NET. This will be comparable to the VB6 component we created earlier in the chapter though we'll update a different table.

To get the transactional protection from .NET enterprise services we'll need to add a few lines of extra code to our class. The .NET runtime will then automatically invoke COM+ behind the scenes as needed to transactionally protect the database access.

> *Keep in mind that this is two-phase commit protection. Normal database access does not require two-phase commit but, rather, can be handled using the transactional capabilities built into ADO.NET. Two-phase commit is only needed when two or more databases are involved in the transaction. Enterprise services transactions should only be used when necessary, as they incur quite a lot of overhead and can slow down applications dramatically.*

Open Visual Studio .NET and create a **Class Library** project named **netEmployee**. Remove `Class1` and add a new class to the project named **Employee** with the following code (changing the connection string as necessary):

```
Imports System.Data
Imports System.Data.SqlClient

Public Class Employee
    Private Const DB_CONN As String = "server=myserver;" & _
      "uid=sa;password=;database=pubs"

    Public Function UpdateEmployee(ByVal emName As String) As String

        Dim tid As New Text.StringBuilder()
        tid.Append("Employee updated")

        Dim SQL As String = "UPDATE Employee SET lname = '" & emName & _
          "' WHERE emp_id='PMA42628M'"

        Dim cn As New SqlConnection(DB_CONN)
        cn.Open()

        Dim cm As New SqlCommand(SQL, cn)
        cm.ExecuteNonQuery()

        cm.Dispose()
        cn.Close()
        cn.Dispose()

        Return tid.ToString
    End Function
End Class
```

As with our VB6 example earlier, this is simple code that uses ADO.NET to update a single row in the `Employee` table of the `pubs` database with a new value provided as a parameter. This method also returns a `String` value as a result so we can return information for testing purposes. Normally an update method of this nature would not return such data.

Using COM+ Services

To make COM+ services available for use in our code, add a reference to
`System.EnterpriseServices`:

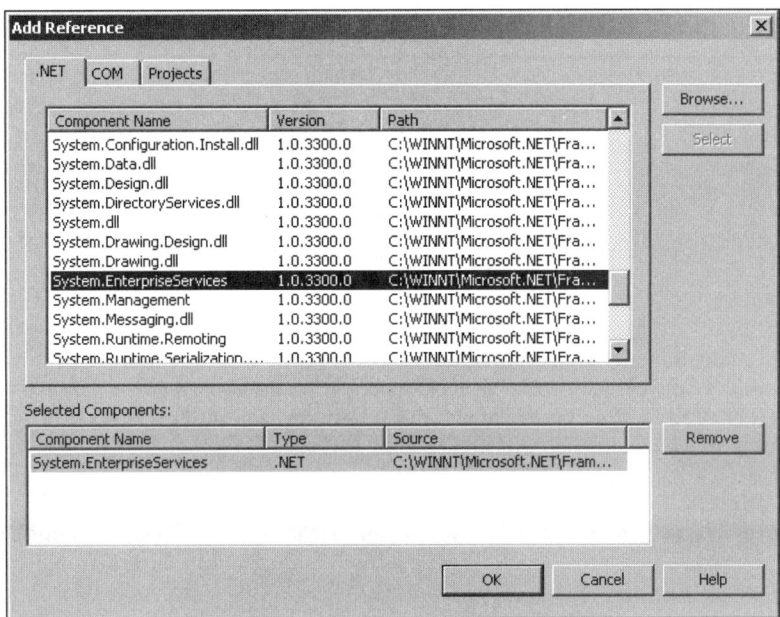

With this reference added, we can add code to make use of these services. Also note that we're replacing
the line:

```
        tid.Append("Employee updated")
```

with code to return the transaction ID value, just as we did in our VB6 code earlier:

```
Imports System.Data
Imports System.Data.SqlClient
Imports System.EnterpriseServices

<Transaction(TransactionOption.Required)> _
Public Class Employee
   Inherits ServicedComponent

   Private Const DB_CONN As String = "server=myserver;" & _
      "uid=sa;password=;database=pubs"

   <AutoComplete()> _
   Public Function UpdateEmployee(ByVal emName As String) As String

      Dim tid As New Text.StringBuilder()
      tid.Append("em {")
      tid.Append(UCase(ContextUtil.TransactionId.ToString))
      tid.Append("}")
```

```
        Dim SQL As String = "UPDATE Employee SET lname = '" & emName & _
          "' WHERE emp_id='PMA42628M'"

        Dim cn As New SqlConnection(DB_CONN)
        cn.Open()

        Dim cm As New SqlCommand(SQL, cn)
        cm.ExecuteNonQuery()

        cm.Dispose()
        cn.Close()
        cn.Dispose()

        Return tid.ToString
      End Function
    End Class
```

With these few changes, we've transformed our code such that it is now designed for transactional protection within COM+. In fact, with these changes, our code now *requires* COM+ on the machine where the assembly will be run. The code will not run on any operating system other than Windows 2000 or higher.

The <Transaction()> attribute on the class tells the .NET runtime that our class requires transactional protection. The options it accepts are similar to the values we set in the VB6 MTSTransactionMode property. The following table lists the options and their equivalents in the COM+ management console:

Visual Basic .NET	COM+ property	Description
Disabled	Disabled	This class cannot participate in a COM+ transaction and should not be run within COM+.
NotSupported	Not Supported	This class does not work with COM+ transactions and will run outside of any COM+ transaction that exists.
Required	Required	The methods of this class must run within a transaction and will use an existing transaction if it exists.
RequiresNew	Requires New	The methods of this class must run within a transaction newly created for the object, even if another transaction already exists.
Supported	Supported	This class supports transactions but does not require them. The methods can run either in a transaction or not.

The <AutoComplete()> attribute on the UpdateEmployee method indicates that COM+ should automatically commit the transaction unless our code raises an error. If any error or exception is raised, it is the same as if we called SetAbort on the transaction context. Notice that there is no error trapping code in the method – we are assuming that any error (database-related or not) will cause the transaction to fail due to this <AutoComplete()> attribute. If we *did* trap errors, then we would defeat the behavior of <AutoComplete()> and our component would always seem to work even when it failed.

Finally, the code that generates the text returned from the method has been enhanced to return the transaction ID. The `ContextUtil` is comparable to the `ObjectContext` object from our VB6 code, and it includes properties and methods that allow us to interact with our context – including retrieval of the transaction ID value. The brackets and `UCase()` statement are added to make the output appear the same as the display we get from the VB6 code we wrote earlier.

Adding Assembly Information

With the class ready to go, there's only one step left in building the component. We need to add some extra attributes to our assembly so the .NET runtime can properly interact with the COM+ environment. Open the `AssemblyInfo.vb` file and add the following code:

```
Imports System.Reflection
Imports System.Runtime.InteropServices
Imports System.EnterpriseServices

' General Information about an assembly is controlled through the following
' set of attributes. Change these attribute values to modify the information
' associated with an assembly.

' Review the values of the assembly attributes

<Assembly: AssemblyTitle("")>
<Assembly: AssemblyDescription("")>
<Assembly: AssemblyCompany("")>
<Assembly: AssemblyProduct("")>
<Assembly: AssemblyCopyright("")>
<Assembly: AssemblyTrademark("")>
<Assembly: CLSCompliant(True)>

' Attributes required for EnterpriseServices/COM+
<Assembly: AssemblyKeyFile("mykey.snk")>
<Assembly: ApplicationName("cpTest")>
<Assembly: ApplicationActivation(ActivationOption.Server)>

. . .
```

First off, to be loaded into COM+ our assembly requires a strong name, which means we need to have a key file or key container available as discussed in previous chapters. We need to reference it with an `AssemblyKeyFile` attribute so a strong name is generated for our assembly.

> *The `mykey.snk` file is a standard key file created using the `sn.exe` command line utility (see the* Creating a Strong Name *section in Chapter 2). Use a key file appropriate to your environment. If you have your keys in a key file container, use the* `/keycontainer` *option on the* `tlbimp` *utility.*

The `ApplicationName` attribute specifies the name of the COM+ application into which this DLL should be installed. If that application doesn't exist in COM+, the .NET runtime will create it for us.

The `ApplicationActivation` attribute specifies that, if the .NET runtime creates the application, it should be created as a server application.

There is no way to specify the user and password under which the COM+ application will run if it is designated as a server application. In this case, the application will be set up to run under the account of the currently logged in user. As we discussed earlier, this is typically not desirable – we should always specify a user account for any server application in COM+. Because of this, we need either to create and configure the application *before* first invoking the component, or to go into the COM+ console and configure the application with a user account *after* it is created by the .NET runtime. Either way, manual intervention is required.

> **COM+ server applications created by the .NET runtime run under the currently logged in user, and so must be reconfigured manually so that they run under a specified account.**

Note that, in our case, we are using the same application that we created and configured earlier for our VB6 component. This means that the .NET runtime will be installing our assembly into a pre-configured application that is already configured to run under a specific user account.

With these changes we can build the assembly. Then we're ready to have it registered with COM+.

Registering the DLL in COM+

.NET assemblies can be registered with COM+ either dynamically or manually, and we'll cover both options. First though, let's discuss what is going on with either process.

The COM+ environment is designed to work with COM components, not .NET assemblies. Installing the .NET runtime on a machine does not alter the behavior of COM+, meaning that, even with the .NET runtime installed, COM+ does not understand how to work with .NET assemblies.

To solve this problem, the .NET runtime includes a COM-based mechanism by which COM+ can interact with .NET assemblies. This mechanism is tied directly into COM interop as it involves adding a set of COM interfaces to any .NET assembly that is registered with COM+. These interfaces include `IManagedObject`, `IRemoteDispatch`, and `System_EnterpriseServices_IServicedComponentInfo`. We never deal with these interfaces directly; the .NET runtime uses these interfaces behind the scenes to get information about the assemblies and to make method calls to the objects in these assemblies.

Keep in mind that these COM interfaces are not meaningful or useful to the typical COM client. At this point, we have done nothing that makes our .NET assembly available to COM clients and so it will not be available to them. Nor will it be available to COM components hosted in COM+. We discussed making an assembly available to COM clients in Chapter 3, and we'll discuss making the assembly available for use by other COM components running in COM+ later in this chapter.

It is important to remember that different versions of the same .NET assembly can be registered with COM+ at the same time. This allows us to retain much of the version protection that is intrinsic to .NET even when our assemblies are running in the COM+ environment. Since all of the assemblies that are registered with COM+ have strong names, they can be uniquely identified through both version number and publisher by the .NET runtime – ensuring that it is able to invoke the correct assembly at our request.

Dynamic Registration

For dynamic registration we must have added attributes to our assembly that indicate the application name and the type of application to be created within COM+, which we did when we created the `netEmployee` assembly. With that information available, the .NET runtime will automatically install the assembly within the COM+ application the first time any .NET client attempts to use the assembly.

> *Note that it will not dynamically install the assembly in COM+ if a COM client application attempts to use the assembly. The dynamic installation feature only operates when a .NET client first uses the assembly.*

We'll make use of dynamic registration shortly, when we create a client application to test our assembly.

Manual Registration

.NET also supports manual registration of an assembly with COM+. Manual registration is important for COM interop since dynamic registration of a .NET assembly doesn't occur when the assembly is invoked by a COM client application.

This isn't as simple as the drag-and-drop approach we used for the COM component. Instead, manual registration of a .NET assembly involves the use of a command-line utility named `RegSvcs.exe`. This utility is located in a directory named:

```
C:\WINDOWS\Microsoft.NET\Framework\<build>
```

where `<build>` is the build number of the .NET runtime installed on the machine (and `WINDOWS` may be `WINNT`).

We can use this utility to add an assembly to COM+ with the following command:

```
regsvcs myassembly.dll
```

If we do this against our current project's DLL, `netEmployee.dll`, we'll get a warning that, "The class netEmployee.Employee has no class interface, which means that unmanaged late bound calls cannot take advantage of AutoComplete methods." This is warning us that we are not exposing a COM interface for our class, and so COM-based clients will not be able to use the assembly – something we already knew since we haven't implemented any interfaces for COM interop as yet.

Optionally, we can manually indicate the name of the COM+ application:

```
regsvcs /appname:myapp myassembly.dll
```

This is useful in the case that the author of the assembly didn't use the `ApplicationName` attribute to make the assembly contain the name of the desired COM+ application. If neither the command-line switch nor the attribute is available, the COM+ application will be named the same as the assembly itself.

The utility can also be used to unregister an assembly:

```
regsvcs /u myassembly.dll
```

We can also remove assemblies from COM+ by deleting them within the Component Services management console just as we would with any other COM+ component.

Creating a Visual Basic .NET Test Application

As with COM components hosted in COM+, it is always a good idea to create simple test applications to test .NET assemblies that will be running in COM+. This allows us to find and resolve any issues that may exist due to security or networking that prevent our code from working properly in the COM+ environment.

To create a simple test application, create a Windows Application in Visual Studio .NET named cpnetclient. Add a button to the form and add a reference to both `System.EnterpriseServices` and to the netEmployee project.

Obviously we'll be using the `netEmployee` assembly, so that makes sense, but why do we reference `EnterpriseServices`? Remember that our assembly is running in COM+, which is blissfully unaware of .NET. For our client to talk to any assembly hosted in COM+, we need to have access to the enterprise services library from the .NET runtime. Though there is no difference in our client's code in order to access the assembly in COM+, behind the scenes the .NET runtime will leverage enterprise services so it can properly invoke the assembly.

As we code, notice that we aren't doing anything special due to the fact that the `netEmployee` assembly is hosted by COM+. Add an `Imports` statement to import `netEmployee` within the form and then add the following code behind the button:

```
Imports netEmployee

Public Class Form1
    Inherits System.Windows.Forms.Form

Windows Form Designer generated code

    Private Sub Button1_Click(ByVal sender As System.Object, _
        ByVal e As System.EventArgs) Handles Button1.Click

        Dim em As New Employee()

        MsgBox(em.UpdateEmployee("Black"))

    End Sub

End Class
```

As with the VB6 test application, this one simply invokes the method on our COM+ component and displays the resulting text that is returned. The display should show the transaction ID of the transaction that protected our database update.

This code should work whether or not we've manually registered the `netEmployee` assembly with COM+. If we didn't manually register it, the .NET runtime will use dynamic registration to place it in the cpTest application as we specified in the `AssemblyInfo` file.

Manually registering the assembly will help avoid a longer delay the first time that the assembly is invoked. On subsequent calls to the assembly it doesn't matter whether we used manual or automatic registration.

If we now look at the application in the **Component Services** console (you may need to refresh it), we'll see both our VB6 and Visual Basic .NET components listed:

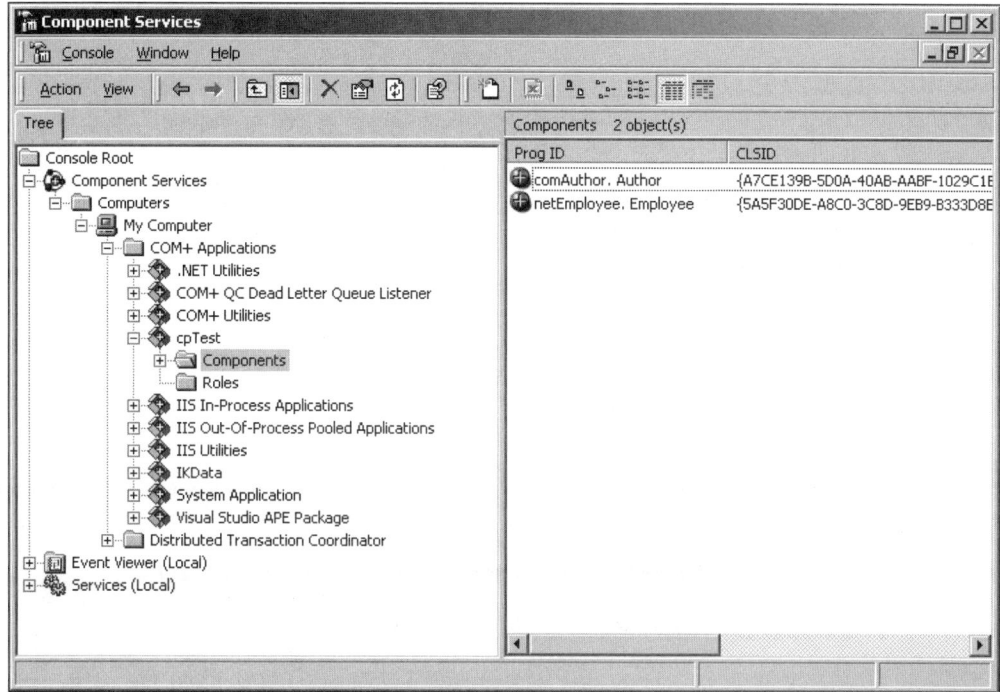

Running the test application gives something similar to this:

So far in this chapter we've focused on the basic concepts of building and installing COM+ components in both VB6 and Visual Basic .NET. Now that we have components built and working, we can move on to explore the ways in which they interact within the COM+ environment.

Calling VB6 Components from Visual Basic .NET in COM+

Many organizations have large numbers of existing COM components that are running in MTS or COM+. As we move to .NET, we'll begin to create .NET assemblies that will also run in COM+, and it is quite likely that some of these new .NET components will need to invoke methods on existing COM-based COM+ components.

> *Of course, existing MTS components will need to be upgraded to COM+ before this is practical – a move that is highly recommended anyway in order to gain the performance and reliability benefits of COM+ and Windows 2000.*

In Chapter 2 we explored the basic ways in which code written in .NET can make use of existing COM DLLs. Using a VB6 component from a Visual Basic .NET assembly running in COM+ is largely the same as using a COM component in any other case, with the important exception that the wrapper assembly created for the COM component must have a strong name.

Also, as we discussed in Chapter 4, we cannot create a primary interop assembly for a COM component that is hosted in COM+, since that would require us to have a primary interop assembly for the COM+ Services type library (`comsvcs.dll`). Microsoft has not provided a primary interop assembly for this DLL and so we cannot create a primary interop assembly for our COM component.

Unfortunately, Visual Studio .NET does not give a wrapper assembly a strong name when we simply reference a COM component from within the IDE.

> **We need to manually create the wrapper assembly by using the `tlbimp.exe` command-line utility and provide it with a strong name.**

We discussed this technique in Chapter 2, but we'll quickly review it here as well since it is the key to successfully utilizing a COM component from a .NET assembly within COM+.

To see how this works, we'll adapt our existing components so that the `netEmployee` assembly invokes the `comAuthor` component.

The first thing we need to do is create the wrapper assembly for the COM DLL. This needs to be done by hand so we can ensure that it has a strong name. Open a command window and navigate to the directory where `comAuthor.dll` resides. Create a `mykey.snk` file using `sn.exe` and then enter the following command:

```
tlbimp comAuthor.dll /out:comAuthorNet.dll /keyfile:mykey.snk
```

This will create a wrapper assembly based on the COM DLL that has a strong name. This wrapper assembly can now be used by any .NET code that needs to reference the COM DLL – including code that will also be running in COM+. For instance, open up the `netEmployee` project and use **Project | Add References** to add a reference to `comAuthorNet.dll`. Use the **Browse** button to locate it:

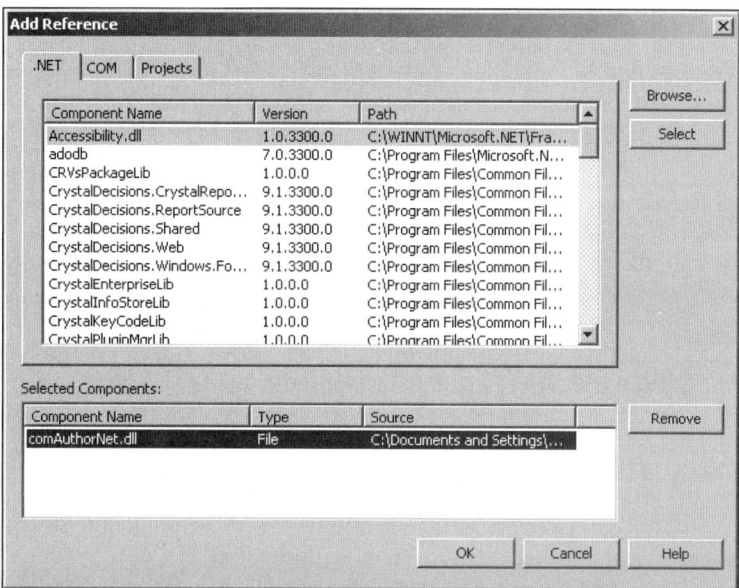

Now we can enhance our code in the Employee class to make use of the Author class. First add an Imports statement to the top of the code to import System.Runtime.InteropServices. Then edit the code as follows:

```
<AutoComplete()> _
Public Function UpdateEmployee(ByVal emName As String) As String
    Dim tid As New Text.StringBuilder()
    tid.Append("em {")
    tid.Append(UCase(ContextUtil.TransactionId.ToString))
    tid.Append("}")
    tid.Append(vbCrLf)

    Dim au As New comAuthorNet.Author()
    tid.Append(au.UpdateAuthor("Green"))
    Marshal.ReleaseComObject(au)
    au = Nothing

    Dim SQL As String = "UPDATE Employee SET lname = '" & emName & _
       "' WHERE emp_id='PMA42628M'"

    Dim cn As New SqlConnection(DB_CONN)
    cn.Open()

    Dim cm As New SqlCommand(SQL, cn)
    cm.ExecuteNonQuery()

    cm.Dispose()
    cn.Close()
    cn.Dispose()

    Return tid.ToString
End Function
```

Those familiar with VB6 programming in MTS will immediately notice that we are just creating the `Author` object as we normally would, rather than using any special `CreateInstance` method from the `ContextUtil` class. In typical VB6 code running in MTS, we would use the `CreateInstance` method on the MTS context object to create instances of other objects (thus ensuring that the context object can enlist the new object in any existing transaction), apply any security options, and so forth.

> *COM+ simplified this even for VB6 code, allowing us to simply use the standard* `CreateObject` *method built into VB6. COM+ is capable of intercepting the creation of the new object and transparently links the new object's context to our current object's context, so that transactions and other settings flow through properly.*

The .NET runtime and COM+ automatically take care of enlisting the COM component in any existing transaction and invoking it properly. In fact, the `ContextUtil` class in .NET doesn't even include a `CreateInstance` method as it has no meaning in the COM+ environment.

We are then able to add the text returned from `UpdateAuthor` to our existing text, meaning that the result of our method will now list both transaction ID values.

Finally we use the `Marshal.ReleaseComObject` method from `System.Runtime.InteropServices` to release the reference to the COM object. This is important as we want to make sure that the COM object is terminated as rapidly as possible to minimize the use of server-side resources. This requires us to import `System.Runtime.InteropServices`.

Build the `netEmployee` assembly and we're all set.

We may encounter an error at this point that causes the build to fail. Specifically, we may be told that the output file is locked and thus the new DLL can't be created. This is a holdover from COM. Since our assembly is running in the COM+ environment, we are bound by some COM-based behaviors – including the unfortunate tendency of COM hosts to keep DLLs open and locked. To solve this, return to the COM+ management console, right-click on the cpTest application, and choose Shut down. Keep in mind that any users actively using the components in this application will probably crash as their objects are destroyed.

When the .NET client application is run, it will invoke the `Employee` object, which in turn will invoke the `Author` object. The resulting message box should display two transaction ID values:

These values should be identical, as both the .NET assembly and the COM component should be enlisted in the same transaction within COM+.

As we discussed in Chapter 2, calling a COM component from within Visual Basic .NET is typically very straightforward, and the same holds true in COM+ with the exception that a strong name is required for the wrapper assembly.

Calling Visual Basic .NET Components from VB6 in COM+

When a .NET assembly is running within the context of COM+, it automatically gains some COM interoperability – including a special interface used by the COM+ environment and the .NET runtime to interact with the assembly properly. However, if we want to invoke the .NET assembly from a COM client application or from a COM component that is also running in COM+, we need to create the assembly as discussed in Chapter 3 – making it fully available for COM interop.

When a .NET assembly is invoked by a COM component in COM+, the automatic installation of the assembly into COM+ by the .NET runtime does not occur. In fact, by default, the .NET assembly is run without the knowledge of COM+ at all. This may interfere with proper transactional processing of our data.

> **To ensure the proper behavior of a .NET assembly when invoked by a COM component in COM+, we need to manually install and configure the .NET assembly within COM+ by using the `regsvcs.exe` command-line utility.**

Before we get too far, let's quickly return to the `netEmployee` project and restore it to its original condition. Remove the reference to `comAuthorNet.dll` from the project and remove or comment out the code that interacts with the `Author` object:

```
'tid.Append(vbCrLf)
'
'Dim au As New comAuthorNet.Author()
'tid.Append(au.UpdateAuthor("Green"))
'Marshal.ReleaseComObject(au)
'au = Nothing
```

We also need to create a COM interface for our .NET class as we discussed in Chapter 3. The assembly must have a strong name for this to work – but we've already got that covered since we added the `AssemblyKeyFile` attribute earlier.

To finish creation of the COM interface involves two steps. First we add the `<ComClass()>` attribute to the class:

```
<ComClass(), Transaction(TransactionOption.Required)> _
Public Class Employee
```

Second, we need to bring up the project's properties dialog and check the box in the Build panel so Visual Studio .NET registers our assembly for COM interop:

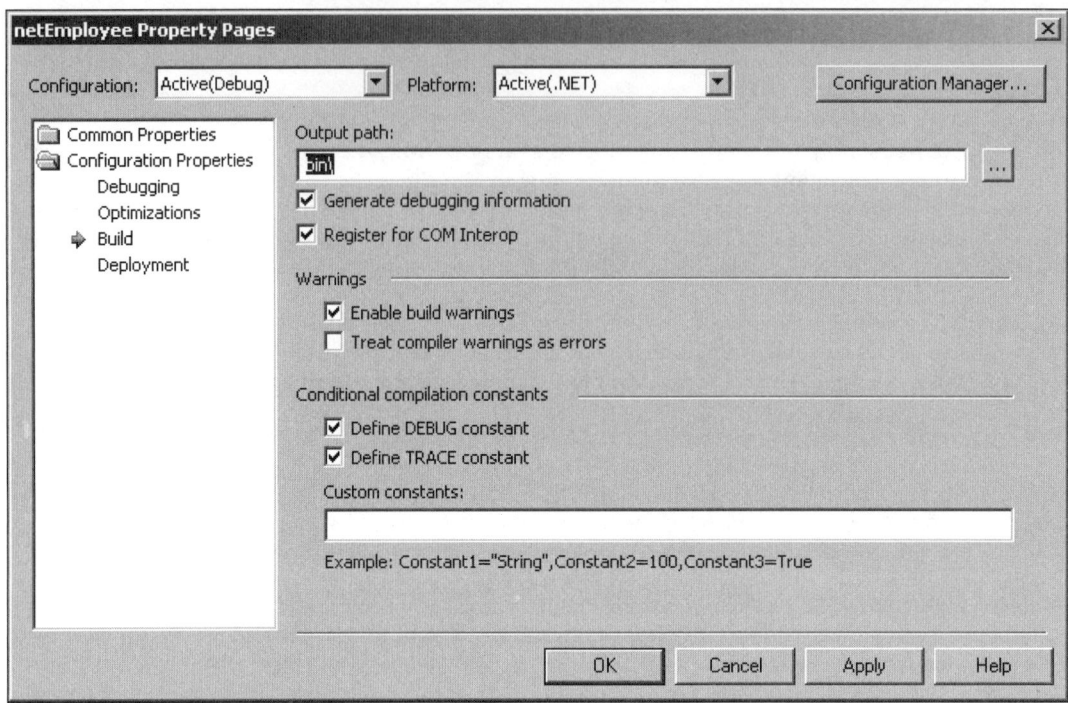

The assembly also must have a strong name, but we took care of that when we first built it, as that is a requirement for the assembly to run in COM+ in general.

Now we can rebuild the assembly and it is ready for use by COM clients.

Again, if we get an error due to the DLL being locked by COM+, we'll need to use the COM+ management console to shut down the cpTest application.

Of course, we need to remember that .NET will not dynamically register our assembly with COM+ when a COM client or COM component invokes it. This means that we need to update COM+ by hand using the regsvcs.exe command-line utility. Open a command window and navigate to the bin directory where netEmployee.dll resides and enter the following command:

```
regsvcs netEmployee.dll
```

Since the assembly contains the name of the COM+ application where it should reside, this is quite straightforward.

However, we still get the warning that Employee has no class interface and can't be used by late-bound unmanaged code. This is because <ComClass()> didn't create an interface *directly* on our class – instead it did what VB6 would have done by creating a formal _Employee interface for our class as we discussed in Chapter 3. This doesn't prevent our class from being used by VB6 or even late-bound scripting clients, but it may interfere with the way late-bound tools like Visual InterDev handle their IntelliSense displays.

The code in comAuthor should now be able to make use of the .NET assembly. Open the project in VB6 and add a reference to the netEmployee component. Then bring up the code for the Author class and make the following changes:

```
Public Function UpdateAuthor(ByVal auName As String) As String
    Dim strOut As String
    Dim strSQL As String
    Dim ctx As ObjectContext
    Dim em As Employee

    Set ctx = GetObjectContext

    strOut = "au "
    If Not ctx Is Nothing Then
      If ctx.IsInTransaction Then
        strOut = strOut & ctx.ContextInfo.GetTransactionId
      Else
        strOut = strOut & "no trans"
      End If
    Else
      strOut = strOut & "no context"
    End If

    strOut = strOut & vbCrLf
    On Error GoTo NETERR
    Set em = CreateObject("netEmployee.Employee")
    strOut = strOut & em.UpdateEmployee("Green")
    Set em = Nothing

    UpdateAuthor = strOut

    On Error GoTo COMERR
    strSQL = "UPDATE Authors SET au_lname = '" & _
      auName & "' WHERE au_id='172-32-1176'"

    Dim cn As Connection
    Dim cm As Command

    Set cn = New Connection
    cn.Open DB_CONN

    Set cm = New Command
    Set cm.ActiveConnection = cn
    cm.CommandType = adCmdText
    cm.CommandText = strSQL
    cm.Execute

    Set cm = Nothing
    cn.Close
    Set cn = Nothing
    If Not ctx Is Nothing Then ctx.SetComplete
    Exit Function
```

```
COMERR:
    UpdateAuthor = Err.Description
    If Not ctx Is Nothing Then ctx.SetAbort
    Exit Function

NETERR:
    UpdateAuthor = Err.Description
    If Not ctx Is Nothing Then ctx.SetAbort
    Exit Function
End Function
```

This is standard VB6 code to invoke another component within the context of COM+.

> *Notice the use of the standard* CreateObject *method rather than the* CreateInstance
> *method on the* ObjectContext *object. For a VB6 developer used to MTS this may seem odd.
> However, unlike MTS, COM+ is directly integrated into the operating system, is able to intercept
> any attempts to create objects, and automatically takes care of synchronizing their COM+ contexts
> to ensure that they are in the same transaction.*

Compile the component and we're all set. When we run the VB6 test application we created earlier in the chapter, we should get a message box that displays the transaction ID values from both the COM and .NET components:

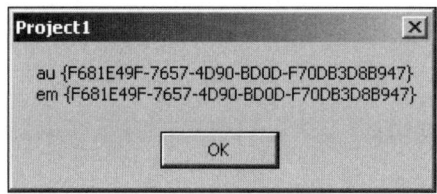

The two values should be identical, since both components should be running within the same transaction.

Calling a .NET component from a COM component when both are running in COM+ is effectively no different from that which we discussed in Chapter 3, with the exception that we need to use the regsvcs.exe command-line utility to first register the .NET assembly with COM+.

Summary

The interaction between COM components and .NET assemblies within the context of COM+ is very similar to the interactions between COM and .NET that we've discussed so far in the book, but there are important exceptions.

To put a .NET assembly into COM+, it must reference System.EnterpriseServices.dll and it must have a strong name. Any class that should be available through COM+ must inherit from ServicedComponent and must also be attributed to indicate which enterprise services are to be used. The options include transactional protection, object pooling, synchronization, and queued components. Specific methods can also be attributed to indicate how they will participate in transactions or otherwise work with the enterprise services.

For a .NET assembly in COM+ to invoke a COM component in COM+, the .NET assembly needs a reference to the Runtime-Callable Wrapper (RCW) for that COM component. Since that RCW must have a strong name, we need to create it using the `tlbimp.exe` command-line utility and provide a key file as part of the process. This will give the RCW assembly a strong name, allowing us to use it within COM+ to interact with the COM component.

For a COM component in COM+ to invoke a .NET assembly in COM+, the .NET assembly needs to expose a COM interface as we discussed in Chapter 3. We can then reference the assembly from the COM component just as we would with any other COM component, and we can then use it normally. The main exception here is that the .NET assembly will not be automatically registered with COM+ when invoked by a COM component, and so we need to use the `regsvcs.exe` command-line utility to register the assembly with COM+ before calling it from any COM component or COM client application.

In this chapter we've discussed all of these issues and walked through the ways that we must deal with the exceptions in our code, as well as the installation and configuration of the code into COM+. Combined with Chapter 4 – where we discussed calling components and assemblies in COM+ from both COM and .NET client applications – we are now ready to work with COM+-hosted components and assemblies.

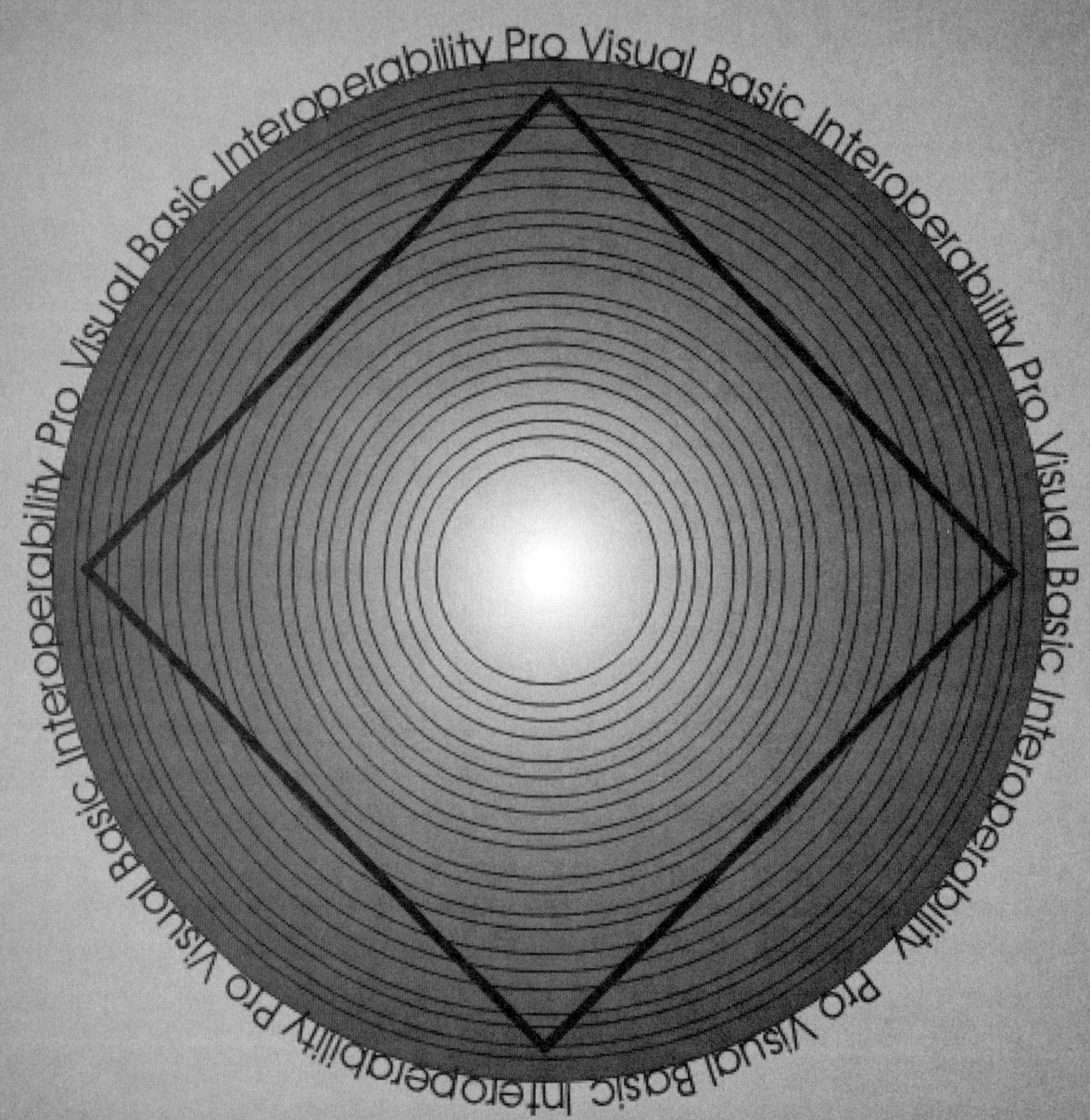

6

Custom Marshaling

Marshaling can have many different connotations. For the purposes of this chapter we are defining and using marshaling to mean moving information bi-directionally between unmanaged code and managed code. As we've seen, a wrapper can be created to call COM objects from managed code and to call managed assemblies from unmanaged code. Unfortunately not all communication will work automatically when imported using the default wrappers. There are several ways that a COM interface could be written that will preclude the use of Tlbimp.exe to create a Runtime-Callable Wrapper (RCW) that is usable by .NET. For many, passing a vt_Record (better known as user-defined type (UDT) or Structure), in a Variant is the most common example. This can be a serious problem if we are trying to seamlessly integrate our new .NET projects with existing COM components.

While Tlbimp.exe will handle most cases, Microsoft has given us the ability to override the default interfaces into ones that are more appropriate for use by .NET. Conversely this same mechanism allows us to override the interfaces so that our .NET objects are more usable by COM.

The ability to override is very powerful but also somewhat complex. What interface we need to override and how it needs to be done can make a big difference to the amount of understanding that you must have to successfully implement the overrides. Some of the more complex scenarios require us to understand how memory in unmanaged code is structured, for the Variant data type in particular.

In this chapter, we will give an overview of the several different mechanisms for using marshaling. We will look at some of the more complex mechanisms, including overriding the RCW, using structures stored in Variants, and even implementing our own ICustomMarshaler interface.

Unfortunately, there are several gotchas in this process that can sometimes be an artifact of Visual Basic .NET itself, and that are not a problem in many of the other .NET languages. We will go over what these are and give workarounds. While they are usually easily bypassed, they can be very aggravating if you are not aware of these issues.

With Visual Basic .NET, we finally get to do many of the cool things that our C++ counterparts could do in the past. The ability to play with the nitty-gritty of how information is marshaled, sent, and represented between objects is one of these things. But with this comes the need for a greater understanding of how memory is structured and marshaled between objects.

Any time we step away from the default processes we discussed in Chapters 2 and 3 to create an RCW or CCW through Visual Studio .NET, or through the `Tlbimp` and `Tlbexp` command-line utilities, we are performing **custom marshaling**. There are a number of scenarios where standard marshaling will not work and where we'll need to implement our own:

- ❑ Overriding the default type passed for another type

- ❑ Handling vt_Record type data in `Variant` returns, such as returning a structure (user defined type)

- ❑ Receiving pointers to memory that `Tlbimp.exe` cannot decipher

- ❑ Converting to and from custom types that may be exposed in languages such as Microsoft C++

- ❑ Overriding what type of object is returned/passed in a method

Of course there are other cases as well, but these are some of the most common. Essentially, if the automatic creation of a wrapper using Visual Studio .NET fails, then we are left with the prospect of using custom marshaling to overcome the limitation.

Custom marshaling is not for the faint of heart. In fact, it may not always be the best approach. Typically we will use custom marshaling because an existing COM component is exposing data in a way that can't be automatically used by .NET. When faced with such an issue, we can either utilize custom marshaling as described in this chapter, or we may choose to create another COM component with a simpler interface and have it *wrap* the existing COM component – delegating all method calls to the existing COM component, but offering a supported interface for use by .NET.

Of course creating such a wrapper component adds yet another layer to our communication between a .NET client application and the actual COM component and so it may not be ideal. This is where custom marshaling comes in – allowing us to alter the behavior of the RCW or CCW such that we can directly communicate with a COM component, even when its interface is not supported by default.

The Four Different Methods of Marshaling

There are four unique methods of Marshaling. Some of them have been shown in prior chapters. However, now that we are going to dive into the details of custom marshaling it is imperative that we understand what those methods are, what they are called and how to use each one.

Type I Marshaling: Using Tlbimp.exe

This is the default mechanism. It was examined in depth in Chapter 2. We can either use `Tlbimp.exe` or the Visual Basic .NET interface to create a "marshaler" of this type. If we create an RCW or a COM-Callable Wrapper (CCW) without overriding the default marshaling mechanism, we are using Type I marshaling. This is the type of marshaling we've mostly used in the book up to this point.

You can expect that Type I marshaling will cover most of your COM to .NET conversions. This is especially true of COM objects made in Visual Basic. But there are no guarantees; there are a few times when a VB COM object's RCW created with `Tlbimp.exe` will need to be overridden.

The following diagrams illustrate Type I marshaling, showing how it is used to call from .NET into COM and from COM into .NET:

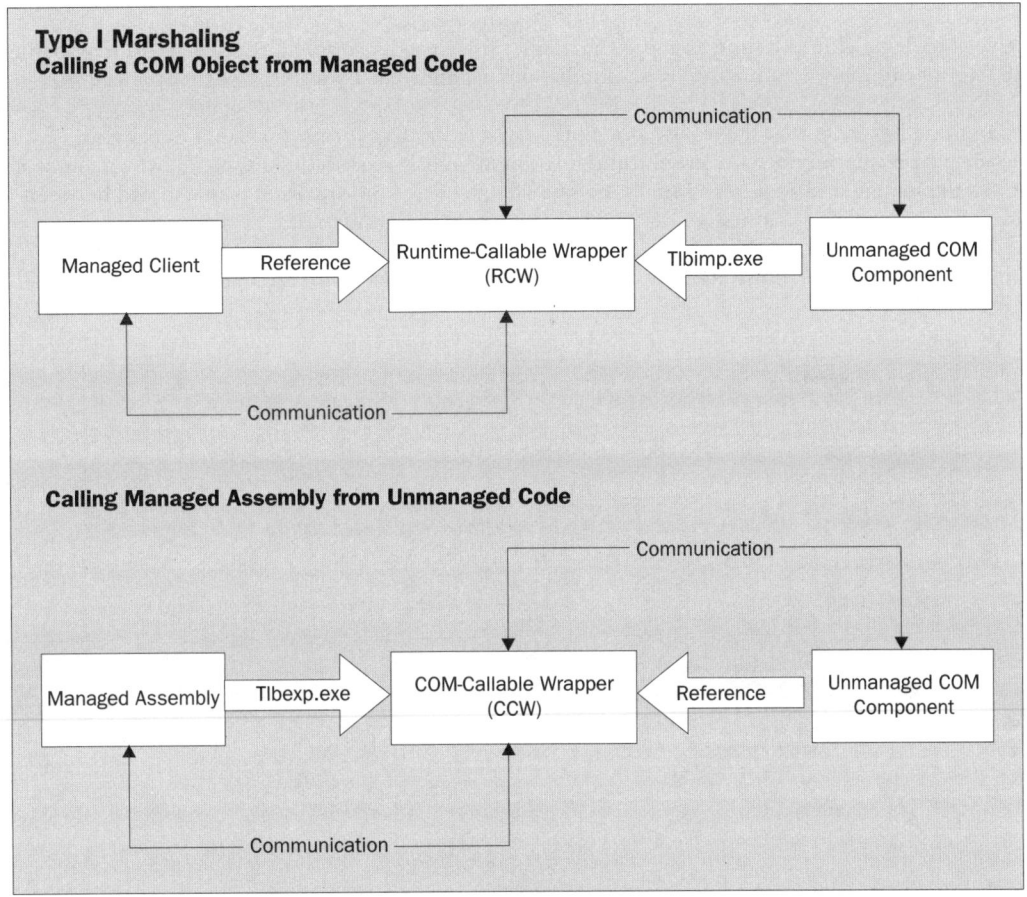

As we can see, there's a great deal of symmetry between the two approaches. Also, it is clear that all the work of Type I marshaling is handled automatically by the `Tlbimp` and `Tlbexp` utilities (or by Visual Studio .NET).

Type II Marshaling (Simple Data Type Marshaling): Adding Attributes to the Interface to Use a Standard Type

This is the easiest of the override mechanisms and is likely to be the most common. It allows us to change the passed or returned type of information that is automatically generated by `Tlbimp.exe`. This is a very powerful technique. It is also the easiest type of custom marshaling to implement.

We've seen Type II marshaling already. In Chapter 3 we used a simple form of Type II marshaling in .NET to specify the way our `String` should be exported for use by a COM client application.

It is important to note that this is also one of the most restrictive forms of custom marshaling. A value or reference type can only be converted from one type to another predefined type. However, since it is easy to implement and requires virtually no knowledge of how information is marshaled between COM and .NET, it should be our first choice since that is likely to be the easiest to maintain over time.

The following diagrams illustrate how Type II marshaling works from .NET to COM and from COM to .NET:

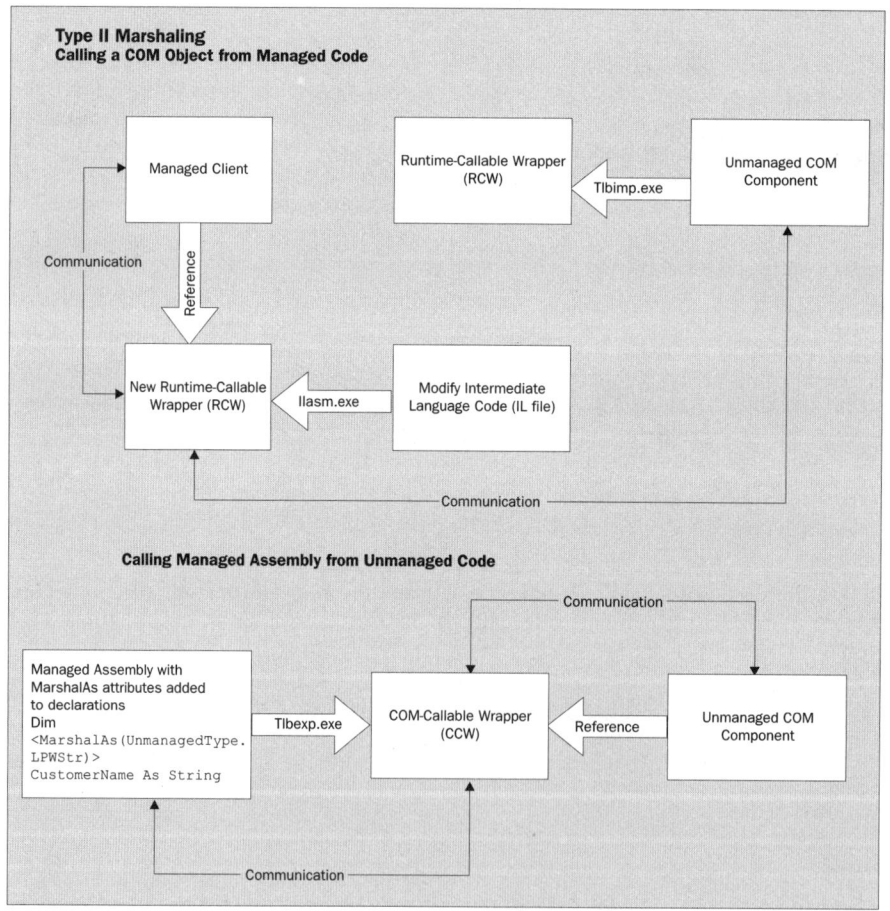

Notice that Type II marshaling is simpler in the second case, where a COM application is calling into a .NET assembly. All the extra work in this case is handled by attributes as we saw in Chapter 3.

The real complexity is introduced in the first example, where a .NET application is calling a COM component and we need to change the data type of a value during the process. This requires us to actually edit the code used to create the RCW itself. We'll explore this in detail later in the chapter.

Type III Marshaling: Marshaling into a Custom Data Structure to be Passed Between COM and .NET

This form of marshaling requires the programmer to override the marshaler to return a custom data type such as a Variant, so it can be read and marshaled in managed code.

To use this method of marshaling, the developer must know the memory structure of the data that is being passed to and from unmanaged code. The memory must then be parsed and converted to a type usable in managed code. Luckily, the .NET framework gives us the Marshal object that makes all of this possible.

The Marshal object is part of the System.Runtime.InteropServices namespace. It provides a variety of different methods to manage memory and convert information between managed and unmanaged code. This is essential to marshal memory between managed and unmanaged code by hand.

It should be noted that, since Type III marshaling is not always easy to understand for junior level programmers, it might be better to encapsulate this code in pre-built managed objects that can then be used by the developers who need to work with the components. In this way, our typical developers will not have to worry about the intricacies of Type III marshaling. For them, it will be just like speaking to any other managed object.

In terms of a common usage scenario, suppose we have a customer object that has a method that returns a UDT in a variant. The RCW that is produced will not be immediately usable. However, as a lead developer you can create a Managed Customer class that encapsulates all calls to a modified RCW and does the marshaling within the class. This will shield other developers from being exposed to the intricacies of Type III marshaling. From their perspective, they are just using the customer class.

Though the end programmer doesn't see anything special, the following diagrams show that there is some serious complexity involved for the developer who actually implements the Type III marshaling wrappers:

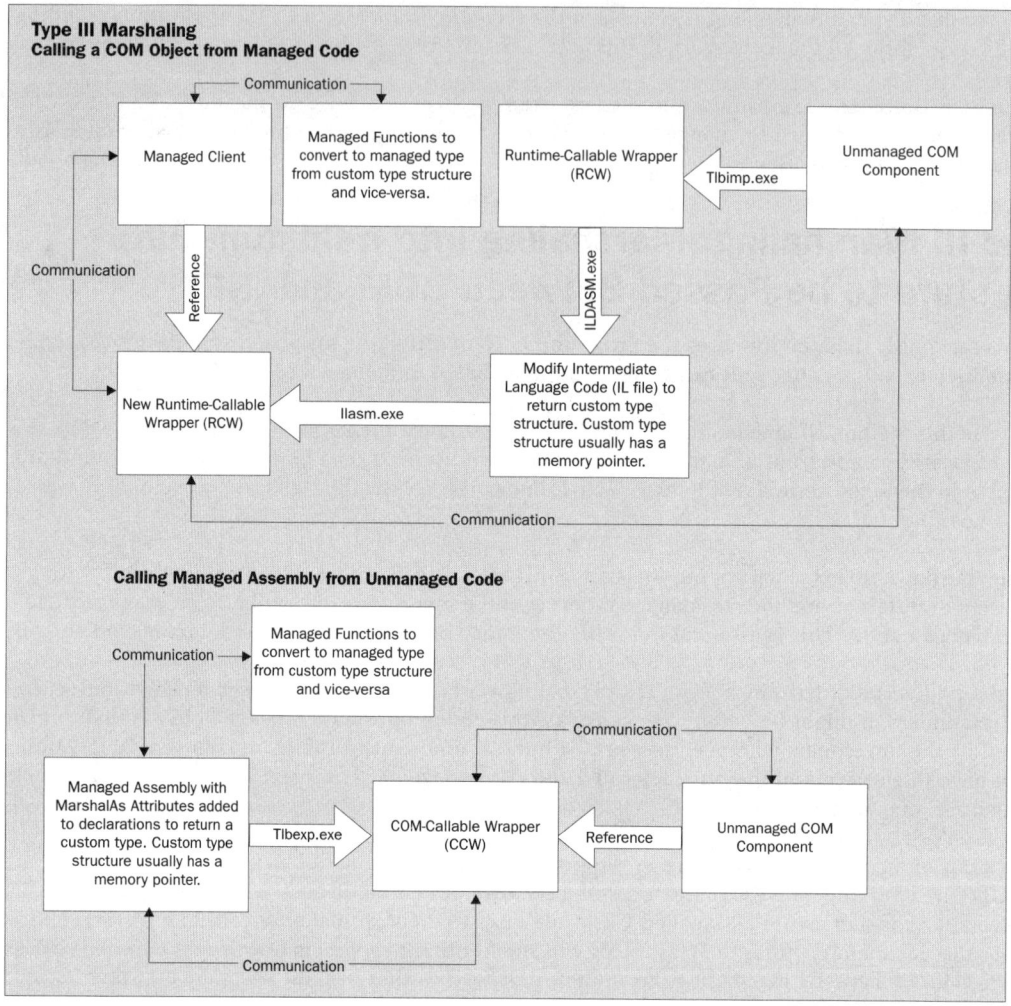

As we can see in the diagrams, Type III marshaling is much more complex than Types I or II, requiring the manual creation and editing of the wrapper class code and the direct manipulation of memory to manage the various data type transformations.

Type IV Marshaling: Implementing the ICustomMarshaler Interface

.NET services also provides an interface to roll your own marshaler. The ICustomMarshaler can be easily implemented to override the default mechanism provided by Interop services. The ICustomMarshaler does have one limitation in that it cannot be used to marshal value types, only reference types. This is due to the fact that the ICustomMarshaler interface is designed to convert between a reference to a managed object and an IntPtr reference to an unmanaged object. When we are implementing the ICustomerMarshaler interface, we are using Type IV marshaling.

Type IV marshaling is illustrated by the following diagrams:

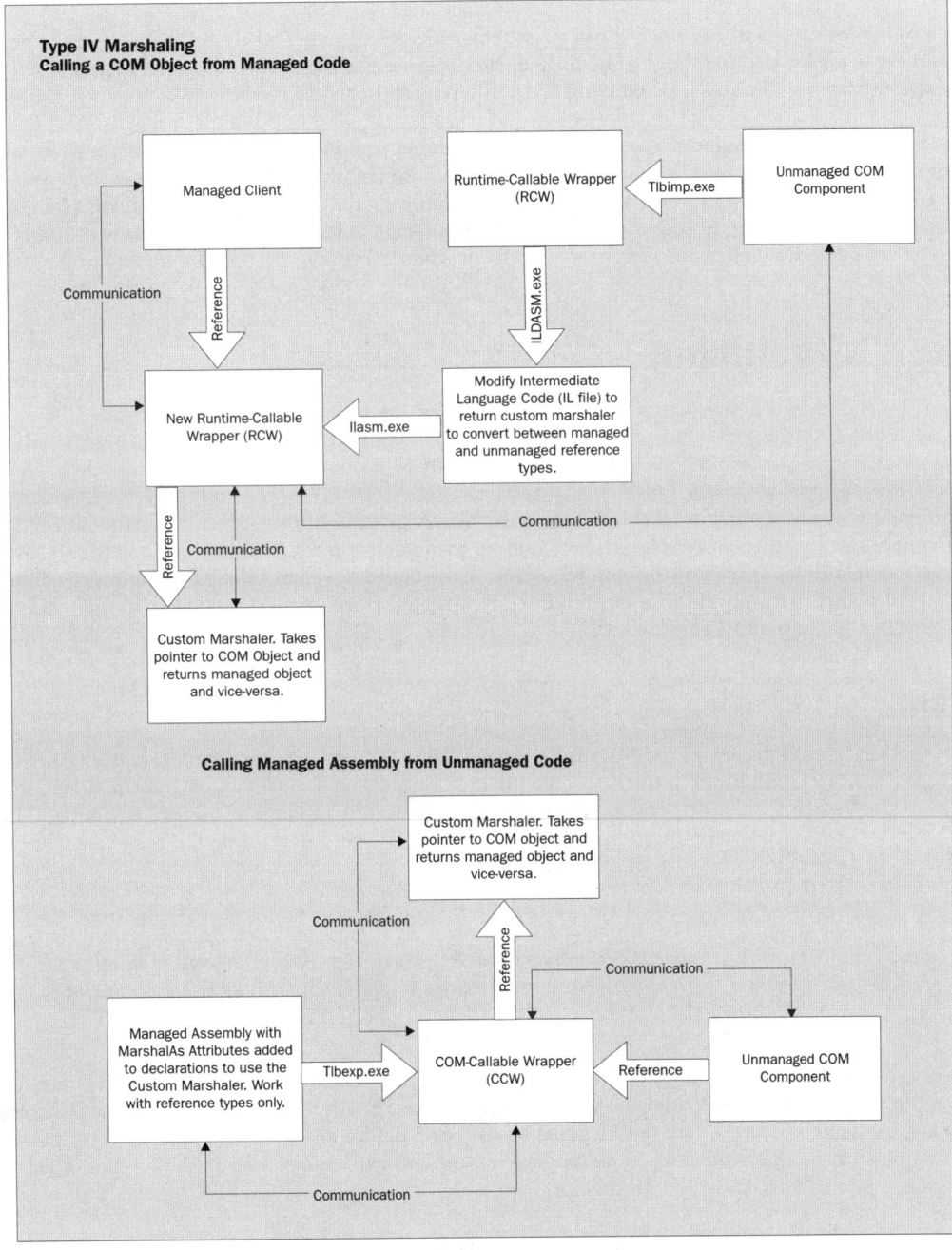

Type IV marshaling is simpler than Type III, but is still a relatively complex concept.

Let's now look further into how to implement Type II, III, and IV marshaling.

Performance Issues

Each of the four types of marshaling has a particular place and time that it should be used. As you would expect, I have found there to be little or no difference in the performance of Type I and Type II marshaling. Types III and IV marshaling are a different matter, however.

Since most of the conversion between managed and unmanaged types is done in code, it is impossible to measure in any generic and meaningful way. Due to the fact that the performance is largely dependent on the efficiency of the marshaling code that we write, it is important to always be cognizant of how the marshaling code will affect the overall performance of the system. The more efficient our marshaling code, the better our system will perform when using Types III or IV marshaling.

Type II Marshaling

Type II marshaling was previously discussed in Chapter 3, where we looked at overriding the data type returned to a COM object by using the `MarshalAsAttribute` class. However, that is only half of the story. Marshaling can also be overridden going from a COM object to managed code.

Adding custom marshaling to COM objects is not nearly as straightforward as it was in managed code. We cannot simply add the `MarshalAs` attribute to the code for our COM object since the COM compilers would not know how to handle it. Even if we could, we might not have the source code for the COM object that we want to override. Luckily, we have been given two utilities to make this much easier, `Ildasm.exe` and `Ilasm.exe`

Ildasm

The `Ildasm.exe` is known as the **Microsoft Intermediate Language Disassembler**. It is a utility that can take a **Portable Executable** (PE) file created with `Tlbimp.exe` and create a text Intermediate Language (IL) file that represents the PE. This text file can then be modified to add or modify attributes. This is the primary method we have for adding attributes to an RCW and overriding the interface that managed code uses to speak to a COM object.

> *A Portable Executable (PE) file is simple a file generated by a .NET compiler. PE files contain the compiled MSIL code and metadata describing the data types implemented in the code. Typically, PE files are generated by a .NET compiler such as Visual Basic .NET, but they can also be generated by utilities such as `Tlbimp` and `Tlbexp`.*

There are some gotchas that you must be aware of to implement this successfully. The first and foremost has to do with the way that Visual Basic .NET reads in the PE. Any custom types, such as structures, that are declared in and used by the PE must be declared before any interfaces take or return those custom types as a parameter. This is particularly a problem with public user-defined types (UDTs) that are passed to and from code as a parameter.

In Chapter 2 we discussed the `Ildasm.exe` interface and how to bring it up on the command line. But this can also be used completely as a command-line utility to generate an IL file. To do this against the Visual Basic RCW in Chapter 2, we would use the command:

```
Ildasm ch1com.dll /out:ch2com.il
```

This will create a new file called `ch2com.il`. It will also give a warning that it created a resource file `ch2com.res`. This file can then be opened and used to modify the interface of the RCW. Also notice that, when the `/out:` parameter is added, the Intermediate Language Disassembler's user interface is no longer brought up.

The more important command-line options that can be used are included here with a brief description:

Option	Description
/Output:filename	Allows the specification of an output file name for the IL file.
/PubOnly	Only includes public types in the IL file. This will give an uncluttered view of what actually is exposed to the users of the assembly.
/Item:class	Only exports the specified item. This can be used to make very targeted PE files that only expose part of a COM interface since the RCW produced with the new IL will only contain the definitions that were exported.
/ObjectFile:objectfile	Only exports the members of a particular object file of a given library.
/ALL	Exports all types of information from the source PE file. This seems to be the default and exports all header information, gives comments with the actual decimal values of the hex parameters as comments and all metadata.

Each of the command-line options listed above can be abbreviated by using only the first three characters. For example, `/Obj:` instead of `/ObjectFile:`

Ilasm

The is the **Microsoft Intermediate Language Assembler**. It takes the text that is produced by the Intermediate Language Disassembler and creates a new Portable. The IL text produced by the Intermediate Language Disassembler can be modified and, as long as it is in the correct format, recompiled with the Microsoft Intermediate Language Assembler. In fact, if you are familiar enough with the format of the text files, you could create your own PE files without the benefit of the `Tlbimp.exe` utility.

This is similar to making an Interface Definition File (IDL) in COM. Like IDL, if you know the syntax of the definition language you can create the entire interface for your COM object to be imported using . Unfortunately, unlike IDL, the structure of the IL files is not yet well documented, making writing one by hand very difficult. For the present time I would recommend that you use to create the IL files.

While Ildasm.exe lies with Tlbimp.exe in the
"C:\Program Files\Microsoft Visual Studio .NET\FrameworkSDK\Bin"
folder by default, Ilasm.exe can be found in
"C:\WINNT\Microsoft.NET\Framework\v1.0.3328". As we noted earlier in the book,
the easiest way to use these utilities is to start a Visual Studio .NET Command Prompt from the
Start menu.

To recreate the PE for our Chapter 2 example, we would use the following syntax:

```
Ilasm ch2com.il /dll /out=ch2com.dll /res=ch2com.res
```

produces an executable file by default. However, we can use the `/dll` parameter to override this functionality and produce an in-process RCW. The following common parameters can be used with `Ilasm.exe`.

`/DLL`	Creates a `DLL` file
`/EXE`	Creates an `EXE` file, the default behavior
`/Output=filename`	Specifies the name of the PE file that is created
`/key=keyfilename`	Specifies the name of the file that contains the key information to produce a file with a strong signature
`/resource=filename`	Specifies the resource file to be used, created with `Ildasm`

Using Ildasm or Ilasm with Type II Marshaling

For this example, we are going to do some simple Type II marshaling. Instead of overriding the interface of the .NET class as we did in Chapter 2, we are going to override a return type in a COM class' RCW.

A common occurrence is returning truly Boolean operators as integers. Since a Boolean data type is actually just the integer value of 0 or 1 (sometimes 0 and non-zero, but 0 and 1 will suffice for this example), this conversion should make a simple example. We are going to make a VB6 COM class that returns integers in a variety of ways. Then we are going to modify the interface to return and take a Boolean instead. To do this, we first need to create a new project in VB6.

Create the VB6 COM Component

Open a new ActiveX DLL project in VB6 and name the project VB6Type2:

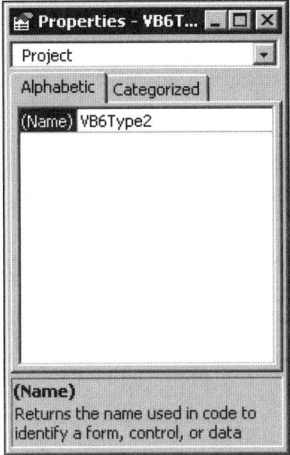

Change the class name from class1 to VB6TestClass. The class should have its Instancing property set to Multiuse.

Now we will declare three module-level variables that will hold our values. While this is not common practice for a business object, I want to show that the underlying value that we are passing in to the COM object and retrieving from the COM object is actually being changed. Place this code in the declarations section of our class module:

```
Private mintBoolProp As Integer
```

That will do it for our internal attribute. But we also want to expose a variety of different properties and methods. For a full example we will create one property that sets and returns our integer, one subroutine that will set our integer value, and one function to return our integer value. Add the following code to the class module:

```
Public Property Get BoolAsIntProp() As Integer
  BoolAsIntProp = mintBoolProp
End Property

Public Property Let BoolAsIntProp(NewValue As Integer)
  mintBoolProp = NewValue
End Property

Public Function BoolAsIntFunc() As Integer
  BoolAsIntFunc = mintBoolProp
End Function

Public Sub BoolAsIntSub(NewValue As Integer)
  mintBoolProp = NewValue
End Sub
```

Now compile the project and make the VB6Type2.dll. Before closing the project, you may want to save it for future reference.

Use Tlbimp to Create the Runtime-Callable Wrapper

Now that we have a COM DLL, we can use the `Tlbimp.exe` utility to create our RCW. Go to the command prompt and change directories to the one containing our newly compiled VB6 COM component. Type in the following line to create your RCW (use a Visual Studio .NET Command Prompt to ensure the command is available):

```
Tlbimp vb6type2.dll /out=vb6t2.dll
```

We now have an RCW for use from within .NET. Unfortunately `Tlbimp` didn't create it quite the way we'd like, so we need to do some more work before we can use it.

Use Ildasm to Create the Intermediate Language Code

We've created a new DLL file called `vb6t2.dll`, against which we can now run the Intermediate Language Disassembler. Stay at the command prompt and enter the following line:

```
Ildasm vb6t2.dll /out=vb6t2.il
```

When completed, a message will be produced warning that a resource file, `vb6t2.res`, was also created. More importantly, it created an IL file containing the code for the RCW in text form.

Modify the IL to use Booleans Instead of Integers

Now we have an IL file that we can edit. This should be called `vb6t2.il`. Open it up in your favorite text editor. Right at the beginning we'll find a set of assembly references marked as external. For our simple example there is only one specified, the `Mscorlib.dll`. Among other things, this contains the `System` namespace. We can use similar code to create as many external references to .NET assemblies as we need. However, to do this you will need to know the assembly's public key. This can be obtained by using the Strong Name Tool (`SN.exe`) with the `-Tp` switch. See the Microsoft documentation on `SN.exe`.

```
.assembly extern mscorlib
{
  .publickeytoken = (B7 7A 5C 56 19 34 E0 89 )          // .z\V.4..
  .ver 1:0:3300:0
}
```

Following this we should find information on our own assembly name (notice that it is not marked as external) and the COM component that we are wrapping. Your example may have a different public key token or version number but should still be essentially the same. Normally these will not need to change unless we want to change the name of the assembly itself. For the most part we will not need or want to change the assembly name. However, it is conceivable that we may want to have one RCW that uses custom marshaling and another that uses the default marshaling (or another type of marshaling), each having a different assembly name.

```
.assembly vb6t2
{
  .custom instance void
[mscorlib]System.Runtime.InteropServices.GuidAttribute::.ctor(string) =
( 01 00 24 63 31 33 33 32 39 36 35 2D 35 34 37 39   // ..$c1332965-5479
                                                                          2D
34 31 36 62 2D 39 35 33 66 2D 32 62 37 64 62   // -416b-953f-2b7db
                                                                          66
38 30 33 30 34 30 00 00 )                        // f803040..
  .custom instance void
[mscorlib]System.Runtime.InteropServices.ImportedFromTypeLibAttribute::.ctor
(string) = ( 01 00 08 56 42 36 54 79 70 65 32 00 00 )        // ...VB6Type2..
  .hash algorithm 0x00008004
  .ver 1:0:0:0
}
.module VB6Type2.dll
// MVID: {BA46F44C-3200-4EC7-8A06-6C88011128F4}
.imagebase 0x00400000
.subsystem 0x00000003
.file alignment 512
.corflags 0x00000001
```

Please note that any information given in hexadecimal format has a comment after it (denoted by the //) that shows what the actual values are. The Ildasm.exe inserts the comments automatically, which is a nice little detail included by Microsoft that makes the IL somewhat easier to read.

That is the end of the header information and after that begins the actual assembly mapping (please note, not all of the IL header information was covered in depth as it is not germane to this discussion of marshaling). For our simple assembly there are only two class interfaces that we need to modify. These are the abstract interface of VB6TestClass (recorded as _VB6TestClass) and the actual class mappings that our interface will use, VB6TestClassClass. There is also a third item defined, an interface VB6TestClass. It implements the original _VB6TestClass interface and contains the pointers used to create the actual COM object. The class structure declaration lists all three definitions:

```
//
// ============== CLASS STRUCTURE DECLARATION ==================
//
.namespace vb6t2
{
  .class interface public abstract auto ansi import _VB6TestClass
  {
  } // end of class _VB6TestClass

  .class public auto ansi import VB6TestClassClass
         extends [mscorlib]System.Object
         implements vb6t2._VB6TestClass,
                    vb6t2.VB6TestClass
  {
  } // end of class VB6TestClassClass

  .class interface public abstract auto ansi import VB6TestClass
         implements vb6t2._VB6TestClass
  {
  } // end of class VB6TestClass

} // end of namespace vb6t2
```

If you open up COM components that have been changed and recompiled several times, you may notice several different versions of your interface that were created by Tlbimp.exe. This is due to how VB6 and earlier versions handle creating interfaces with VB6 compatible server. We only need to change the abstract and managed interface for our most recent version. The current version is easily identifiable by the fact that its name does not contain any version information. In this case, we should only have one version in our file, as it is the first time we have compiled it.

Each earlier version would be displayed as a separate class interface with the version number as part of its name. The version number will be preceded by three underscores and begin with a v. For example, Customer___v0 would be the name for version 0 of the customer class. Since we do not have any older version in this case, and the old versions are rarely used, we should not have to worry about modifying the old versions of the interfaces.

Locate the abstract (interface) class heading for our VB6TestClass. It should look like this:

```
.class interface public abstract auto ansi import _VB6TestClass
```

In this section are the properties that we want to change first. In the interface definition we can find information on each of our properties and methods. Locate the get portion of our property. It should look like this:

```
.method public hidebysig newslot specialname virtual abstract
        instance int16  get_BoolAsIntProp() runtime managed internalcall
{
    .custom instance void
[mscorlib]System.Runtime.InteropServices.DispIdAttribute::.ctor(int32) =
( 01 00 00 00 03 68 00 00 )                          // .....h..
    } // end of method _VB6TestClass::get_BoolAsIntProp
```

Before making any changes, it might be worth saving a copy of the IL file first – just in case.

Change the return of the get portion of our method from an int16 to a bool.

> **Keep in mind that these values are case-sensitive.**

When complete, our new code should look like this:

```
.method public hidebysig newslot specialname virtual abstract
        instance bool  get_BoolAsIntProp() runtime managed internalcall
{
    .custom instance void
[mscorlib]System.Runtime.InteropServices.DispIdAttribute::.ctor(int32) =
( 01 00 00 00 03 68 00 00 )                          // .....h..
    } // end of method _VB6TestClass::get_BoolAsIntProp
```

Notice that all we needed to do was change the return type from int16 to bool. It was that easy. Be careful though. We must change to return types that are actually compatible with the original COM interface declaration. If we use an inappropriate type, like a string for an integer, we might get unexpected returns, but not always an error – but either way the result is not what we are after.

What is compatible, you ask? Well to make a long story short, it depends... In this case we can map a Boolean to an int16 because we know the value is supposed to represent Boolean information. If it were actually an integer value representing more than two states, a Boolean would not work here. If the original COM value was a string, we may be able to convert it to a numeric value. If it is an integer, we may want to use a double, if not, an Int16 may work better...

The following link provides information on converting the different data types from COM to managed code (*enter on one line*):

http://msdn.microsoft.com/library/default.asp?url=/library/en-us/cpguidnf/html/cpconmarshalingcomtypestonetframework.asp

From this, we can do the same with the set portion of the property. For the set, we do not change the return value, since it has none (it is marked as void), but the parameter that is passed to it, int16&. It is important to note that the & after the int16 parameter denotes that the parameter is being called by reference. Our new code should be in the format:

```
    .method public hidebysig newslot specialname virtual abstract
            instance void  set_BoolAsIntProp([in][out] bool& A_1) runtime
managed internalcall
    {
       .custom instance void
[mscorlib]System.Runtime.InteropServices.DispIdAttribute::.ctor(int32) =
( 01 00 00 00 03 68 00 00 )                      // .....h..
    } // end of method _VB6TestClass::set_BoolAsIntProp
```

Finally, we can do the same to our function and subroutine. I'm sure by now that this is getting somewhat repetitious. But, in this case, repetitious is good. It means that, if we understand one case, we understand them all.

```
    .method public hidebysig newslot virtual abstract
            instance bool  BoolAsIntFunc() runtime managed internalcall
    {
       .custom instance void
[mscorlib]System.Runtime.InteropServices.DispIdAttribute::.ctor(int32) =
( 01 00 01 00 03 60 00 00 )                      // .....`..
    } // end of method _VB6TestClass::BoolAsIntFunc

    .method public hidebysig newslot virtual abstract
            instance void  BoolAsIntSub([in][out] bool& NewValue) runtime
managed internalcall
    {
       .custom instance void
[mscorlib]System.Runtime.InteropServices.DispIdAttribute::.ctor(int32) =
( 01 00 02 00 03 60 00 00 )                      // .....`..
    } // end of method _VB6TestClass::BoolAsIntSub
```

There is one more thing that we need to do before our interface is complete. The property set and get methods are tied together to make a single property. Change the portion of the IL code that ties these together. Without changing this part of the property declaration, the public interface to the property will not work correctly. There are three places that we need to change the code on the property declaration: on the property's return value and the in/out parameters on the calls into the let and set (get). Here is the resulting piece of code:

```
    .property bool BoolAsIntProp()
    {
      .custom instance void
[mscorlib]System.Runtime.InteropServices.DispIdAttribute::.ctor(int32) =
( 01 00 00 00 03 68 00 00 )                          // .....h..
      .get instance bool vb6t2._VB6TestClass::get_BoolAsIntProp()
      .set instance void vb6t2._VB6TestClass::set_BoolAsIntProp(bool&)
    } // end of property _VB6TestClass::BoolAsIntProp
```

That is it for the abstract interface. Below that we will find the runtime's interface. It is headed by the following line:

```
    .class public auto ansi import VB6TestClassClass
```

If we look closely, we'll see that the internals of this class are pretty much the same as the _VB6TestClass interface. The changes that need to be made are exactly the same. Change the return type for the property get, set, method, function, and property declaration to bool. Now save the resulting IL file.

For the reassembled RCW to work you must change both the interface _VB6TestClass and the underlying VB6TestClassClass.

Finally the third class is listed, VB6TestClass. This class does not need to change to implement marshaling. This class points to the underlying COM object and gives its GUID so that the RCW wrapper knows which COM object to call.

```
.class interface public abstract auto ansi import VB6TestClass
       implements vb6t2._VB6TestClass
{
    .custom instance void
[mscorlib]System.Runtime.InteropServices.GuidAttribute::.ctor(string) =
( 01 00 24 36 32 44 38 35 37 39 44 2D 36 43 43 41   // ..$62D8579D-6CCA

2D 34 41 35 34 2D 42 34 32 42 2D 38 35 31 42 42    // -4A54-B42B-851BB

45 46 39 38 38 46 43 00 00 )                       // EF988FC..
    .custom instance void
[mscorlib]System.Runtime.InteropServices.CoClassAttribute::.ctor(class
[mscorlib]System.Type) = ( 01 00 17 76 62 36 74 32 2E 56 42 36 54 65 73 74   //
...vb6t2.VB6Test

43 6C 61 73 73 43 6C 61 73 73 00 00 )              // ClassClass..
  } // end of class VB6TestClass
```

Create the New Runtime-Callable Wrapper

We now have the changed IL code. Now we need to create the new RCW that uses it. For this we are going to use the complementary utility to `Ildasm.exe`, the Intermediate Language Assembler `Ilasm.exe`. Enter the command prompt and move to the directory that contains the IL code. From it we can run the following line:

```
Ilasm vb6t2.il /dll /res=vb6t2.res /out=vb6t2.dll
```

This command will give a quick summary of what was created in the new RCW. The command window will give the following information:

We can see here that the utility has successfully created a PE file.

Make a New Managed Project to Use Our Modified RCW

To make sure that all of this works, we want to create a new project in managed code to use our new wrapper. Open up a copy of Visual Studio .Net and create a new Visual Basic .NET console application entitled ManagedInterface.

To talk to our new RCW, we need to add a reference to it. On the References section of the Solution Explorer, right-click and choose Add Reference. On the window that pops up, stay on the .NET tab and browse to our newly created vb6t2.dll. Select the component, press Open, and then OK.

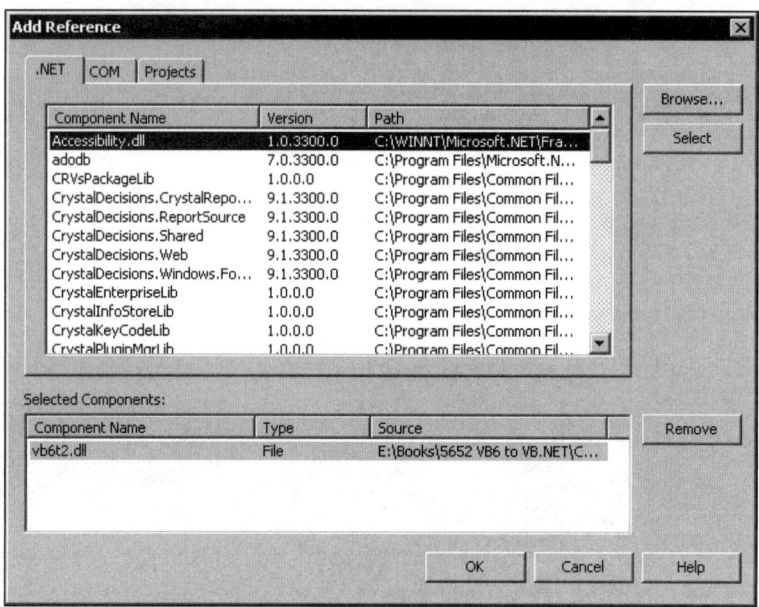

Go to the code module, Module1. In this module we will want to directly access the classes and structures of the console and VB6t2 namespaces. Add Imports statements to the beginning of the module to facilitate this:

```
Imports System.Console
Imports vb6t2
```

Add a new subroutine to display the results of our test. This subroutine will take a string (that is the message that we want to display in the console), display it, and then ask the user to press *Return* to continue. Add the following code to the module:

```
Private Sub WriteTest(ByVal strMsg As String)
    WriteLine(strMsg)
    Write("Press Return")
    ReadLine()
End Sub
```

Now that we can display any messages we have, we can create an instance of our VB6 class from our RCW. Call this instance objTest and declare it in the Main subroutine.

You might notice that what we are creating is marked as an interface. There is a similar declaration entitled VB6TestClassClass. In Chapter 2 we discussed the way in which Tlbimp creates the interface and its related class based on the underlying COM component – here we see the inner workings of the code it generates.

Ignore VB6TestClassClass and only create an instance of the matching interface VB6TestClass.

```
Dim objTest As New VB6TestClass()
```

Try setting the value of the `BoolAsIntProp` property to `True`. Also notice that the IntelliSense shows that the property takes a `Boolean` instead of an integer:

```
objTest.BoolAsIntProp = True
```

```
objTest.BoolAsIntProp = True
Public Overridable Overloads Property BoolAsIntProp() As Boolean
```

The fact that this returns a `Boolean` value shows us, at least superficially, that our override of the default return of `Integer` seems to have worked. But let's make sure that we have what we think we have. Try setting the property to `True` and then display the value. After this, set the property back to `False` and display the resulting value. To do this, add the following code:

```
WriteTest("Set to True in Property: " & CType(objTest.BoolAsIntProp, String))

objTest.BoolAsIntProp = False

WriteTest("Set to False in Property: " & CType(objTest.BoolAsIntProp, String))
```

We also want to try testing our method and function. Use the `BoolAsIntSub` subroutine to set the value to `True` and then display it using the `BoolAsIntFunc` function:

```
objTest.BoolAsIntSub(True)

WriteTest("Set to True in Sub and returned as True in Function: " & _
CType(objTest.BoolAsIntFunc, String))
```

Run the Example

Now code has been added to handle all cases: setting a property, reading a property, setting a value as a parameter of a subroutine, and pulling the property out as a return from a function. Press the Start button on Visual Studio .NET and see the results.

From this example, we can see that it is relatively easy to override the default return value from an object in COM. While this is somewhat more complex than going from managed code to unmanaged code, as exemplified in Chapter 2, it is still doable with only a precursory understanding of the intricacies of the data types.

As we'll see, the relative ease of Type II marshaling contrasts with the difficulties of Type III Marshaling.

Type III Marshaling

Type III marshaling is for values that can't be directly mapped between managed and unmanaged code. The most obvious example of a type that would require Type III marshaling is the Variant exposed as a parameter in COM. This cannot be easily imported by the Tlbimp.exe utility due to the fact that a Variant can easily return any number of things, including a public user-defined type (UDT). What is being returned? Well, Tlbimp.exe just does not know. While Tlbimp.exe will be able to compile the assembly, an Interop error will occur when trying to reference the variable if it contains a UDT. The error states that Interop cannot marshal vt_Record types from a variant.

However, if *we* know that a UDT is being returned out of the Variant (possibly as part of a proprietary state-passing mechanism), then we can use Type III marshaling to move it in and out of managed code.

The secret to Type III marshaling is knowing the structure of the Variant and what is being returned by the data property. To make an all-inclusive generic Variant handler that can handle any manner of return structures, arrays, and values would be extremely difficult and will not be handled in the context of this chapter. However, perhaps Microsoft or a third party will produce such a generic handler in the near future.

A quick look at the variant structure itself shows some of the difficulties in producing a generic marshaler. Since the variant structure uses the union operator, it can have many different forms. However, this is not to say making a more generic handler is impossible, only difficult. What follows is the variant structure:

```
struct tagVARIANT {
    union {
        struct __tagVARIANT {
            VARTYPE vt;
            WORD        wReserved1;
            WORD        wReserved2;
            WORD        wReserved3;
            union {
                LONG          lVal;        /* VT_I4               */
                BYTE          bVal;        /* VT_UI1              */
                SHORT         iVal;        /* VT_I2               */
                FLOAT         fltVal;      /* VT_R4               */
                DOUBLE        dblVal;      /* VT_R8               */
                VARIANT_BOOL  boolVal;     /* VT_BOOL             */
                _VARIANT_BOOL bool;        /* (obsolete)          */
                SCODE         scode;       /* VT_ERROR            */
                CY            cyVal;       /* VT_CY               */
                DATE          date;        /* VT_DATE             */
                BSTR          bstrVal;     /* VT_BSTR             */
                IUnknown *    punkVal;     /* VT_UNKNOWN          */
                IDispatch *   pdispVal;    /* VT_DISPATCH         */
                SAFEARRAY *   parray;      /* VT_ARRAY            */
                BYTE *        pbVal;       /* VT_BYREF|VT_UI1     */
                SHORT *       piVal;       /* VT_BYREF|VT_I2      */
                LONG *        plVal;       /* VT_BYREF|VT_I4      */
                FLOAT *       pfltVal;     /* VT_BYREF|VT_R4      */
                DOUBLE *      pdblVal;     /* VT_BYREF|VT_R8      */
```

```
              VARIANT_BOOL *pboolVal;        /* VT_BYREF|VT_BOOL      */
              _VARIANT_BOOL *pbool;          /* (obsolete)            */
              SCODE *       pscode;          /* VT_BYREF|VT_ERROR     */
              CY *          pcyVal;          /* VT_BYREF|VT_CY        */
              DATE *        pdate;           /* VT_BYREF|VT_DATE      */
              BSTR *        pbstrVal;        /* VT_BYREF|VT_BSTR      */
              IUnknown **   ppunkVal;        /* VT_BYREF|VT_UNKNOWN   */
              IDispatch **  ppdispVal;       /* VT_BYREF|VT_DISPATCH  */
              SAFEARRAY **  pparray;         /* VT_BYREF|VT_ARRAY     */
              VARIANT *     pvarVal;         /* VT_BYREF|VT_VARIANT   */
              PVOID         byref;           /* Generic ByRef         */
              CHAR          cVal;            /* VT_I1                 */
              USHORT        uiVal;           /* VT_UI2                */
              ULONG         ulVal;           /* VT_UI4                */
              INT           intVal;          /* VT_INT                */
              UINT          uintVal;         /* VT_UINT               */
              DECIMAL *     pdecVal;         /* VT_BYREF|VT_DECIMAL   */
              CHAR *        pcVal;           /* VT_BYREF|VT_I1        */
              USHORT *      puiVal;          /* VT_BYREF|VT_UI2       */
              ULONG *       pulVal;          /* VT_BYREF|VT_UI4       */
              INT *         pintVal;         /* VT_BYREF|VT_INT       */
              UINT *        puintVal;        /* VT_BYREF|VT_UINT      */
            } __VARIANT_NAME_3;
        } __VARIANT_NAME_2;

        DECIMAL decVal;
    } __VARIANT_NAME_1;
};
```

For more information on what the different members are used for, this link contains complete details:

http://msdn.microsoft.com/library/default.asp?url=/library/en-us/dnguion/html/drgui032999.asp

Unfortunately, Type III marshaling requires much more substantial modification and understanding of the IL. This understanding comes from information not yet documented by Microsoft. All information on the IL presented in this chapter was gained through a trial and error understanding.

A Type III Example

It is possible that you will have a class that returns a public UDT as a `Variant` return value on a variety of functions and subroutines in your legacy COM systems. You may want to access these properties in managed code but find that `Tlbimp.exe` produces an RCW that is not usable for these methods. Type III marshaling will fix your problem.

> *It should be noted that this example, as with all examples in this chapter, is for converting values to and from unmanaged code (in this case COM objects). However, these methods can just as easily be used to move information to and from managed code so that unknown managed types are readable by unmanaged code.*

Make the COM Object

We will start by making an example COM object by using VB6.

Create the New Project

Create a new ActiveX DLL project in VB6 named `VB6Type3.vbp`. Go to the predefined class, rename it `VB6TestClass`, and make sure that its `Instancing` property is set to `MultiUse`.

Add a New Public User-Defined Type

In our legacy COM object, we want to return a UDT through a `Variant`. We are going to make a simple UDT to represent a customer. This object will contain information on the customer's name, date entered, credit limit, and total orders. Add the following public UDT to the declarations section of the `VB6TestClass` module.

```
Public Type Customer
    CustomerName As String
    EnteredDate As Date
    CreditLimit As Double
    TotalOrders As Long
End Type
```

We also want our class to be able to use the same cached customer structure for all of its internal attributes, so declare a variable to hold our private structure. This should be done in the declarations section as well; name the variable `mudtCustomer`.

```
Private mudtCustomer As Customer
```

Create the Public Properties for the Unmanaged Class

The unmanaged class will need a series of public methods to test moving the structure in and out of the class through a `Variant`. Create one property to return the UDT directly as the UDT – as a control to make sure that structures work normally when used in an RCW. Remember, a user-defined type in VB6 is equivalent and marshaled to a structure in Visual Basic .NET

```
Public Property Get CustomerAsCustomer() As Customer
    CustomerAsCustomer = mudtCustomer
End Property

Public Property Let CustomerAsCustomer(NewValue As Customer)
    mudtCustomer = NewValue
End Property
```

For the rest, create a property that returns the UDT, a function that returns it, and a method that takes it as a parameter and sets the new value. Name them `CustomerAsVariant`, `GetCustomerFunction`, and `SetCustomerSub` respectively. Type all of these as `Variants`.

```
Public Property Get CustomerAsVariant() As Variant
  CustomerAsVariant = mudtCustomer
End Property

Public Property Let CustomerAsVariant(NewValue As Variant)
  mudtCustomer = NewValue
End Property

Public Function GetCustomerFunction() As Variant
  GetCustomerFunction = mudtCustomer
End Function

Public Sub SetCustomerSub(NewValue As Variant)
  mudtCustomer = NewValue
End Sub
```

To make sure that the UDT that is created in the function is retrieved, we are going to initialize its values in the `Class_Initialize` function. Add the following code to the `VB6TestClass` class module.

```
Private Sub Class_Initialize()
  mudtCustomer.EnteredDate = Now
  mudtCustomer.CreditLimit = 500
  mudtCustomer.CustomerName = "Kevin"
  mudtCustomer.TotalOrders = 5
End Sub
```

The test case in unmanaged code is almost complete. Compile the new DLL by going to the File menu and selecting Make VB6Type3.dll. Then save the project and close it. Alternately, you could simply use `RegSvr32` against the VB6 DLL in the books example.

Create the Runtime Callable Wrapper

Enter a command prompt and switch to the directory that contains the unmanaged DLL that was just created. `Tlbimp.exe` can now be used to create an RCW for our COM component. Use the following command in the command prompt.

```
Tlbimp vb6type3.dll /out=vb6t3.dll
```

This should yield the message that the type library was imported. We will now try to use our RCW "as is" in a managed project to illustrate the problem that we face with the RCW that was created.

Make a New Managed Project

Open up Visual Studio .NET and create a new Console Application titled ManagedInterface. As before, we want to add a reference to the RCW for our unmanaged VB6 project. Right-click on References and add a .NET reference to `VB6t3.dll`.

Create an Output Method to Display the Results

Once again, we need to add some `Imports` statements for the assemblies that will need to be accessed in this example. Add `System`, `Console`, `vb6t3`, `Reflection`, and `InteropServices` to the declarations section of `Module1`. Each of these namespaces we import allows us to automatically use its members. The `System.Reflection` namespace and `System.Runtime.InteropServices` namespace have methods essential to doing custom marshaling. Since we have need of both namespaces' members, we will import them.

```
Imports System
Imports System.Console
Imports vb6t3
Imports System.Reflection
Imports System.Runtime.InteropServices
```

Now add the `WriteTest` method from the last example into the module, to write output to the console and wait for the user to press the *Return* key.

```
Module Module1

    Private Sub WriteTest(ByVal strMsg As String)
        WriteLine(strMsg)
        Write("Press Return")
        ReadLine()
    End Sub
```

Return to `Sub Main` and declare an instance of the `VB6TestClass` and the imported `Customer` structure. Name these `objCustomers` and `objCustomer` respectively.

```
Dim objCustomers As New VB6TestClass()
Dim objCustomer As Customer
```

Set `objCustomer` equal to the return of the `CustomerAsCustomer` property and display the resulting values using the `WriteTest` method. Then do the same with the `CustomerAsVariant` property.

```
objCustomer = objCustomers.CustomerAsCustomer

WriteTest(objCustomer.CustomerName & ":" & objCustomer.EnteredDate & ":" &
objCustomer.CreditLimit & ":" & objCustomer.TotalOrders)

objCustomer = objCustomers.CustomerAsVariant
WriteTest(objCustomer.CustomerName & ":" & objCustomer.EnteredDate & ":" &
objCustomer.CreditLimit & ":" & objCustomer.TotalOrders)
```

Certainly, similar code would have worked in VB6, but what will happen here? If you run the project, it will quickly become apparent that returning the UDT as a `Customer` type works just fine.

However, when the *Return* key is pressed and the `CustomerAsVariant` property is accessed, an error message is produced. It tells us that we returned a `VT_RECORD Variant` type, which is not handled by the custom marshaler. This error reflects the current default marshaler's inability to handle a UDT, or more specifically `VT_RECORD` information, in a variant.

If our variant had returned an integer we would have gotten a valid return with no error because that is a simple type and the default marshaler can handle it, but since our return type is a complex UDT that is not supported by the default marshaler we get the following:

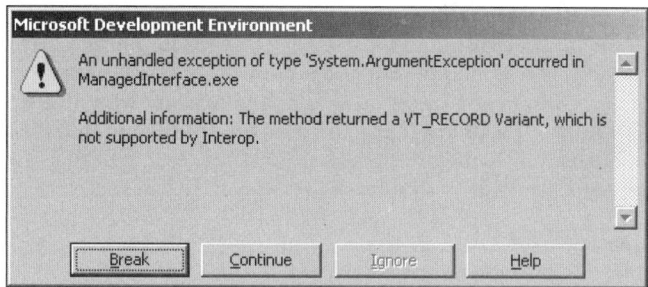

Obviously it is not uncommon to return a UDT via a `Variant` – so it would be nice to have a solution to this issue.

Modify the Runtime-Callable Wrapper to Return a Usable Type

This is where we need Type III marshaling.

Disassemble the Runtime-Callable Wrapper

Go back to the command prompt, make sure that we are in the directory with our RCW (`VB6t3.dll`), and use the `Ildasm.exe` utility to product the IL file for our RCW.

```
Ildasm vb6t3.dll /out=vb6t3.il
```

We now have a file named `vb6t3.il` that contains the disassembled intermediate language code for the RCW. The IL code itself is just text and so we can easily edit and work with it.

Locate Referenced Classes

Open `vb6t3.il` and find the structure for the `Customer` class. The `Ildasm` usually places this code at the end of the namespace. Keep track of where this is located since we will be adding a new `Variant` class right after this code. It should look similar to the following:

```
.class public sequential ansi sealed beforefieldinit Customer
       extends [mscorlib]System.ValueType
{
  .pack 4
  .size 0
  .custom instance void
[mscorlib]System.Runtime.InteropServices.GuidAttribute::.ctor(string) = ( 01 00 24
34 38 38 36 33 41 39 31 2D 44 35 33 31   // ..$48863A91-D531

2D 34 33 45 41 2D 42 35 42 42 2D 41 35 30 30 35   // -43EA-B5BB-A5005
```

```
41 42 36 30 46 35 35 00 00 )                    // AB60F55..
    .field public  marshal( bstr) string CustomerName
    .field public valuetype [mscorlib]System.DateTime EnteredDate
    .field public float64 CreditLimit
    .field public int32 TotalOrders
} // end of class Customer
```

Add a Variant Structure to the Namespace

We know that our IL for the methods that use `Variants` needs to return a `Variant` that managed code can understand. From our error about interop not supporting a `Variant` type of `VT_RECORD`, it apparently has a structure. While you could do research to find out what this structure is, we have already done this. As you may recall, the `Variant` structure uses a union and can have many different structures. If we look back at this structure provided in the beginning of this section we can see that the first four items of the structure are the same for all versions. They are:

```
VARTYPE vt;
WORD     wReserved1;
WORD     wReserved2;
WORD     wReserved3;
```

The following portion is a large union statement. If we follow it down we find the one that we care about when returning a UDT (structure) in a variant:

```
struct __tagBRECORD {
    PVOID          pvRecord;
    IRecordInfo * pRecInfo;
} __VARIANT_NAME_4;          /* VT_RECORD             */
```

We can now put these together to make our variant structure. Open the produced IL file from the example we have been making (`vb6t3.il`). Add a new class titled `Variant` to the IL code under the `Customer` class definition in `vb6t3.il`. You should use the following declaration derived from our analysis of the variant structure and knowing that we will receive a record type of `vt_Variant`. Please note, this particular example is not generic. It will only work with a parameter type of `vt_Variant`.

```
.class public sequential ansi sealed beforefieldinit Variant
       extends [mscorlib]System.ValueType
{
    .field public unsigned int16 vt
    .field public unsigned int16 wReserved1
    .field public unsigned int16 wReserved2
    .field public unsigned int16 wReserved3
    .field public native int pvRecord
    .field public native int pRecInfo
} // end of class Variant
```

The example does, however, illustrate the technique used to marshal a complex type through a `Variant`, and so can be adapted to other data types as needed.

Change Marshal Values to Return the Variant Structure Instead of an Object Type

When we've completed this task, overriding the default marshaler to use our new structure is as easy to do as it was with Type II marshaling. Locate the beginning of the _VB6TestClass. Looking under that, we will quickly find an entry for get_CustomerAsVariant. The current declaration returns an object marshaled as an unknown structure.

```
.method public hidebysig newslot specialname virtual abstract
        instance object
        marshal( struct)
        get_CustomerAsVariant() runtime managed internalcall
```

Change this code to return the value type of the new structure. By doing this, we will be able to access the contents of the Variant as our Variant structure type. The new code should look like this:

```
.method public hidebysig newslot specialname virtual abstract
        instance valuetype vb6t3.Variant
        get_CustomerAsVariant() runtime managed internalcall
```

Notice that the only changes that we made here were to use a value type of vb6t3.Variant instead of an object marshaled as an unknown structure. Do the same for the set_CustomerAsVariant:

```
.method public hidebysig newslot specialname virtual abstract
        instance void  set_CustomerAsVariant([in][out] valuetype
  vb6t3.Variant& A_1)  runtime managed internalcall
```

and the GetCustomerFunction:

```
.method public hidebysig newslot virtual abstract
        instance valuetype vb6t3.Variant
        GetCustomerFunction() runtime managed internalcall
```

and the SetCustomerSub:

```
.method public hidebysig newslot virtual abstract
        instance void  SetCustomerSub([in][out] valuetype vb6t3.Variant&
  NewValue) runtime managed internalcall
```

Finally, change the property declaration for CustomerAsVariant. Remember, we must change the declared type of the property and the mapped types for the set and get methods. So this:

```
.property object CustomerAsVariant()
{
  .custom instance void
[mscorlib]System.Runtime.InteropServices.DispIdAttribute::.ctor(int32) =
( 01 00 00 00 03 68 00
00 )                        // .....h..
  .set instance void vb6t3._VB6TestClass::set_CustomerAsVariant(object&)
  .get instance object vb6t3._VB6TestClass::get_CustomerAsVariant()
} // end of property _VB6TestClass::CustomerAsVariant
```

needs to become:

```
.property valuetype vb6t3.Variant CustomerAsVariant()
```

```
        {
          .custom instance void
[mscorlib]System.Runtime.InteropServices.DispIdAttribute::.ctor(int32) =
( 01 00 00 00 03 68
00 00 )                              // .....h..
          .set instance void vb6t3._VB6TestClass::set_CustomerAsVariant(valuetype
vb6t3.Variant&)
          .get instance valuetype vb6t3.Variant
vb6t3._VB6TestClass::get_CustomerAsVariant()
        } // end of property _VB6TestClass::CustomerAsVariant
```

Once this is complete, as with Type II marshaling, the same must be done for the
VB6TestClassClass. Make the same changes to this class and save the IL file. You may now close
your text editor.

Reassemble the Runtime-Callable Wrapper

Enter the command prompt and make sure that you are in the same directory as your IL for the vb6t3
project. Use Ilasm.exe to recreate the RCW to be used in the managed interface. This can be done in
the same format as our previous calls.

```
Ilasm vb6t3.il /dll /res=vb6t3.res /out=vb6t3.dll
```

This produces a new version of our RCW – but one that properly marshals the UDT through a Variant.

Finish the Managed Interface

Back to managed code now.

Re-reference the New Runtime-Callable Wrapper in Managed Code

Open the ManagedInterface project that we created earlier in the Type III marshaling example in
Visual Studio .NET. Remove the reference to the vb6t3.dll library and re-add the one that we just
created. This will ensure that our interface is looking at the RCW that we just created.

Import the IRecordInfo Interface

The last parameter in our variant structure is pRecInfo. This member is a pointer to the IRecordInfo
interface. This interface is a common COM interface that is used to manipulate structures stored in a
Variant. While using this interface is most likely familiar to many C++ programmers, it is likely new
to most VB programmers. More information about the IRecordInfo interface can be found on MSDN
at the following link:

http://msdn.microsoft.com/library/default.asp?url=/library/en-us/automat/htm_hh2/chap12_69wl.asp

COM interfaces like IRecordInfo can be imported and used in managed code by the COMImport
attribute. To use this attribute to import an interface, we need to know the public method declarations and its
GUID. The following code block lists this information, which you can find in Microsoft's documentation.
Add the following code to the declarations section of Module1 to import and use this COM interface.

```
<ComImport(), Guid("0000002F-0000-0000-C000-000000000046"),
InterfaceType(ComInterfaceType.InterfaceIsIUnknown)> Public Interface IRecordInfo
    Sub RecordInit(ByVal pvNewas As IntPtr)
    Sub RecordClear(ByVal pvExisting As IntPtr)
    Sub RecordCopy(ByVal pvExisting As IntPtr, ByVal pvNew As IntPtr)
```

```
     Sub GetGuid(ByRef pguid As Guid)
     Sub GetName(ByRef pbstrName As String)
     Sub GetSize(ByVal pcbSize As Long)
     Sub GetTypeInfo(ByRef ppTypeInfo As UCOMITypeInfo)
     Sub GetField(ByVal pvData As IntPtr, <MarshalAs(UnmanagedType.LPWStr)> _
        ByVal szFieldName As String, ByRef pvarField As Object)
     Sub GetFieldNoCopy(ByVal pvData As IntPtr, _
        <MarshalAs(UnmanagedType.LPWStr)> ByVal szFieldName As String, _
        ByRef pvarField As Object, ByRef ppvDataCArray As IntPtr)
     Sub PutField(ByVal wFlags As Int32, ByVal pvData As IntPtr, _
        <MarshalAs(UnmanagedType.LPWStr)> ByVal szFieldName As String, _
        ByRef pvarField As Object)
     Sub PutFieldNoCopy(ByVal wFlags As Int32, ByVal pvData As IntPtr, _
        <MarshalAs(UnmanagedType.LPWStr)> ByVal szFieldName As String, _
        ByRef pvarField As Object)
     Sub GetFieldNames(ByRef pcNames As Int32) _
        ', [out,size_is(*pcNames),length_is(*pcNames)] ref String rgBstrNames)
     <PreserveSig()> _
     Function IsMatchingType(ByVal pRecordInfo As IRecordInfo) As Boolean
     <PreserveSig()> _
     Function RecordCreate() As IntPtr
     Sub RecordCreateCopy(ByVal pvSource As IntPtr, ByRef ppvDest As IntPtr)
     Sub RecordDestroy(ByVal pvRecord As IntPtr)
  End Interface
```

Obviously there is a lot of research involved in determining the exact nature of these COM interfaces and determining how to implement them in our code. This is one example, but similar code would need to be researched and created for other complex COM data types.

Add a Method to Copy from the Variant Structure to the Managed Structure

Now that there is an interface to manipulate the information inside our Variant that is returned from unmanaged code, we need a method to copy this information into a managed structure. Add a new method to Module1 to do this. Call the method VariantToObject and make it have two parameters. One parameter will be a reference to our Variant structure and the other a reference to the managed structure to which we want to copy the information.

```
  Sub VariantToObject(ByRef v As vb6t3.Variant, ByRef o As System.ValueType)
```

The first thing that we are going to want to do is check to see if the Variant structure that we are passing in actually contains a UDT. We can do this by checking the vt attribute of the Variant structure. A return value of VarEnum.VT_RECORD or 36 indicates a record type. If the Variant does not contain what we expect, throw an exception. Add the following code to test for this.

```
  If Val(v.vt.ToString) <> VarEnum.VT_RECORD Then
     Throw New ArgumentException()
  End If
```

After it has been determined that there is a UDT in the Variant, we should check to see if it is of the same type. The following code compares the type name of the unmanaged UDT to that of the managed structure passed to the subroutine as o.

Please note, this only compares type names and does not validate that they are indeed the same structure. Dimension a variable as the type of the `IRecordInfo` interface that was imported earlier and set the `Variant` structure's `pRecInfo` value to it. The `pRecInfo` value contains a pointer to the `Variant`'s record info.

```
Dim ri As IRecordInfo
ri = CType(Marshal.GetObjectForIUnknown(v.pRecInfo), IRecordInfo)
```

Notice that we used the `Marshal` object's `GetObjectForIUnknown` method. This method takes a pointer to a COM object and returns back a usable reference in managed code. In this case, we have also made sure that it was typed as `IRecordInfo` using the `CType` function.

Continue with our comparison by getting the typename of our structure (o) passed to the routine and comparing it to the type stored in the `IRecordInfo` object. If they don't match, throw an exception. This code assumes that the name of the structure is the *same* as the name of the UDT used in the COM object. If they are *not* the same, this code should not be used. In this case, since they both come from the same COM DLL, we don't have a problem.

```
Dim UDTName As String
Dim t As System.Type
t = o.GetType()
ri.GetName(UDTName)

If UDTName <> t.Name Then
   Throw New ArgumentException()
End If
```

Once it has been determined that the reference to a structure passed to this method matches the name of the structure being stored in the `Variant`, we can copy the contents. This can be done using two methods. The `IRecordInfo` object contains a method called `GetField` that can be used to retrieve one of the values stored in the COM UDT. The second method is `SetValue`, which takes a field name and a value and sets it into a field of a `Type` structure. Let's take a look at the code and discuss it more in depth:

```
Dim fld As Object
Dim fi As FieldInfo

For Each fi In t.GetFields()
   ri.GetField(v.pvRecord, fi.Name, fld)
   fi.SetValue(CType(o, system.ValueType), fld)
Next
```

The first line enumerates through each field record in our type `t`. From our previous code, we know that `t` was defined as a `System.Type` and set to the structure type that we passed to the method. We can then use that field to pull out information about the stored UDT in the `Variant`.

`GetField` is called from the `IRecordInfo` object that we pulled out of the `Variant`. It takes three parameters. The first is the type of record, the second the name of the field we want the value for, and the third is a by-reference variable to hold the returned value for that particular name.

The value contained in the `fld` variable is then set into our managed structure using the `SetValue` method of the field information object. It is very important to note that the `SetValue` must be passed as a *value* type in Visual Basic .NET. If it is passed in as a *reference* type, it will make a copy of the object and set the value into it. The copy will be thrown away and the `SetValue` method will seem to do nothing. We make sure that our structure is a value type by typing it as one in the procedure declaration.

> **Always pass a value type to the `SetValue` method in Visual Basic .NET.**

End the sub-routine with the `End Sub` statement.

Add a Method to Copy from the Managed Structure to the Variant Structure

We will also need to have a method to copy information from a managed type back into a `Variant` structure. To do this, we will create a method called `ObjectToVariant`. This method will be very similar to the previous `VariantToObject` method except that it uses the `GetValue` method of the `FieldInfo` object and the `PutField` method of the record information object. We also don't check for the type of the value, since we are in control of this in managed code. These are the complementary methods to the `GetField` and `SetValue` methods from the `VariantToObject` method.

This subroutine should look like this:

```
Sub ObjectToVariant(ByRef o As System.ValueType, ByRef v As [Variant])
  Dim ri As IRecordInfo
  ri = CType(Marshal.GetObjectForIUnknown(v.pRecInfo), IRecordInfo)

  Dim UDTName As String
  Dim t As System.Type
  t = o.GetType()
  ri.GetName(UDTName)

  If UDTName <> t.Name Then
    Throw New ArgumentException()
  End If
  Dim fld As Object
  Dim fi As FieldInfo

  For Each fi In t.GetFields()
    fld = fi.GetValue(o)
    ri.PutField(INVOKEKIND.INVOKE_PROPERTYPUT, v.pvRecord, fi.Name, fld)
  Next
End Sub
```

Complete Our Test Interface for Type III Marshaling

Now we have the methods that we need to convert back and forth between our `Variant` structure, which contains a COM UDT, and the new managed structure. Return to the `Main` subroutine and clear its current contents. Add the following variable declarations to the top of the subroutine:

```
Dim objCustomers As New VB6TestClass()
Dim objCustomer As Customer
Dim vb6Variant As vb6t3.Variant
Dim vb6Variant1 As vb6t3.Variant
Dim objCustomer1 As Customer
```

Take the instance of the `VB6TestClass` and pull out the `objCustomer` structure from the `CustomerAsCustomer` method. Since this is being returned as a `Customer` structure and as such is Type I marshaling, we expect this to work. We do this test only to ensure that the simple case is working properly:

```
objCustomer = objCustomers.CustomerAsCustomer
```

```
WriteTest("Customer as Customer:" & objCustomer.CustomerName & ":" & _
    objCustomer.EnteredDate & ":" & objCustomer.CreditLimit & ":" & _
    objCustomer.TotalOrders)
```

Clear out the objCustomer by setting it equal to a new instance and get the value of the CustomerAsVariant method. Also notice that the IntelliSense now has this property typed as our custom Variant structure:

```
objCustomer = New Customer()
vb6Variant = objCustomers.CustomerAsVariant
            Public Overridable Overloads Property CustomerAsVariant() As vb6t3.Variant
```

Call the VariantToObject method, passing in our Variant object and the structure to copy to. After this has been completed, we can use the WriteTest method to print the results in the console.

```
objCustomer = New Customer()
vb6Variant = objCustomers.CustomerAsVariant

VariantToObject(vb6Variant, objCustomer)

WriteTest("Pulled in as variant:" & objCustomer.CustomerName & ":" & _
    objCustomer.EnteredDate & ":" & objCustomer.CreditLimit & ":" & _
    objCustomer.TotalOrders)
```

As a final test, change the values of the structure that we just retrieved and put it back into the COM object. We can then retrieve it to see if the COM object was able to handle our values correctly. Use the following lines to change the values:

```
With objCustomer
    .CustomerName = "Fred"
    .CreditLimit = 600
    .EnteredDate = Now
    .TotalOrders = 10
End With
```

With the values changed, we can call the ObjectToVariant method to convert back into the Variant structure. SetCustomerSub will then be called to send the new Variant back to the COM object.

```
ObjectToVariant(objCustomer, vb6Variant)
objCustomers.SetCustomerSub(vb6Variant)
```

The structure is now theoretically back in the COM object. Use the GetCustomerFunction to pull the current values into a new Variant variable, call VariantToObject, and display the results:

```
vb6Variant1 = objCustomers.GetCustomerFunction
VariantToObject(vb6Variant, objCustomer1)

WriteTest("written back to unmanaged code then re-read:" & _
    objCustomer.CustomerName & ":" & objCustomer.EnteredDate & ":" & _
    objCustomer.CreditLimit & ":" & objCustomer.TotalOrders)
```

We are now done with our test UI. Press the **Start** button and see what happens. After pressing *Return* when prompted, we see that information is pulled from and set back into the COM Variant as expected:

```
C:\Projects\Interop Chapter\TypeIII\ManagedInterface\ManagedInterface\bin\ManagedInterface.e...  _ □ X
Customer as Customer:Kevin:19/11/2001 17:10:11:500:5
Press Return
Pulled in as variant:Kevin:19/11/2001 17:10:11:500:5
Press Return
Written back to unmanaged code then re-read:Fred:19/11/2001 17:10:12:600:10
Press Return_
```

Type III marshaling can be used to pull out virtually any data from unmanaged code – as long as we have information about how it is represented in memory ahead of time. However, it is not for the casual coder. For an architect who is trying to make the communication between managed and unmanaged code as easy as possible, it might be more effective to encapsulate the details of the `VariantToObject` and `ObjectToVariant` methods in a managed class. The class would contain the calls to the unmanaged code and do the conversions back and forth automatically.

Type IV Marshaling

Type IV marshaling involves the creation of a class that implements the `ICustomMarshaler` interface. Objects of this type convert one reference type to another in a manner that we specify. What that means when we marshal back and forth to and from COM objects is that we can create our own *managed* class with a different interface from that of our legacy objects.

This can be very important if you have a need for managed classes with different interfaces from those of your older COM systems. You can also use one managed class that maps back to many different COM classes, assuming you have a custom marshaler for each. For example, we may have a new managed customer class that maps back to several different COM customer classes in different legacy systems, each with differing interfaces. Of course, an argument could be made that an XML serialization method may be better in this instance.

How it Works

The `ICustomMarshaler` interface has methods to map a managed object to an unmanaged object and vice versa. While the `ICustomerMarshaler` interface can be used to map reference types, value types cannot use it. For value types we will need to use Type II or Type III marshaling as we discussed earlier in the chapter.

The interface takes a reference to an unmanaged type and returns a managed type. It can also take a managed type and return an unmanaged type. In the IL code, the `Marshal` attribute can be used to state that a particular reference uses the custom marshaler that we have created to return a different type from that which was originally declared.

For example, you might have an unmanaged `People` class that returns `Person` objects. You have created and now use a new managed version of a `Person` object. You can create your own custom marshaler to convert between the managed and unmanaged `Person` classes. The IL interface code of the `People` class could be modified to return the managed `Person` class using your custom marshaler.

> One thing to keep in mind with Type IV marshaling is that we are getting a *copy* of the marshaled object, not a reference to the original.

The ICustomMarshaler Interface

Let's take a look at the methods that must be implemented to create our own custom marshaler.

Method	Description
MarshalNativeToManaged	Receives a pointer to an unmanaged object. Returns a reference to a managed object.
MarshalManagedToNative	Receives a reference to a managed object. Returns a pointer to an unmanaged object.
CleanUpNativeData	Receives a pointer to the unmanaged object. Useful if this needs to be released after the marshaling has occurred and if memory needs to be manually cleared.
CleanUpManagedData	Receives a reference to the managed object. Useful if this needs to be released after the marshaling has occurred and if memory needs to be manually cleared.
GetNativeDataSize	Returns the size in bytes of the native data to be marshaled. This is usually not needed and can be set to –1.
GetInstance	Returns a reference to the custom marshaler. If the marshaler does not retain state between calls, the same shared instance can be used.

These methods are defined by the `ICustomerMarshaler` interface and must all be implemented by our code.

Create an Unmanaged COM Component

To see how this works we will need to create an unmanaged COM project. This will contain a `People` class that retains a collection of `Person` objects, as described above. The `People` class will have two methods: `FetchPerson` and `SavePerson`. This will simulate a container that pulls and saves information from a persistence source.

Open up a new ActiveX DLL project in Visual Basic 6 and name it **VB6Type4**.

Create the Person Class

Go to the automatically created `Class1` and rename it to `Person`. Make sure that its `Instancing` property is set to `MultiUse`. Add attributes for age, birth month, birth day of month, and name to the declarations section.

```
Private mlngAge As Long
Private mlngBirthMonth As Long
Private mlngBirthDayofMonth As Long
Private mstrName As String
```

Also add public properties to return and set these values:

```
Public Property Get Age() As Long
   Age = mlngAge
End Property

Public Property Let Age(NewValue As Long)
   mlngAge = NewValue
End Property

Public Property Get BirthMonth() As Long
   BirthMonth = mlngBirthMonth
End Property

Public Property Let BirthMonth(NewValue As Long)
   mlngBirthMonth = NewValue
End Property

Public Property Get BirthDayofMonth() As Long
   BirthDayofMonth = mlngBirthDayofMonth
End Property

Public Property Let BirthDayofMonth(NewValue As Long)
   mlngBirthDayofMonth = NewValue
End Property

Public Property Get Name() As String
   Name = mstrName
End Property

Public Property Let Name(NewValue As String)
   mstrName = NewValue
End Property
```

The design of this class seems somewhat archaic in the fact that there are separate properties for age, birth month, and birth day of month. It would be much easier to maintain if there was a birth date property and an age method. However, there might be several existing systems that talk to this object under its current interface, we might not have the sourcecode to change it, or it might be a third-party product. We will use Type IV marshaling to create our own managed Person class that uses a custom marshaler to convert between the two.

Create the People Class

Add a new class module to the project and name it People. Make sure that its Instancing property is set to MultiUse. Add a private member to hold a collection of Person objects in the declarations section.

```
'Pretend that our collection is our persistence provider
Private mcolPeople As Collection
```

Actually retrieving and saving information is not required for this example so it is being simulated.

In the class initialize section we will create an instance of the `Collection` object and add a sample `Person` object. This will simulate a person existing in some persistence source such as a database.

```
Private Sub Class_Initialize()
   Dim objPerson As Person

   Set mcolPeople = New Collection

   'Add one person to collection to test
   Set objPerson = New Person
   With objPerson
      .Age = 33
      .BirthDayofMonth = 18
      .BirthMonth = 9
      .Name = "Dan"
   End With
   mcolPeople.Add objPerson

End Sub
```

Since we need to retrieve and save our `Person` object, add two public methods to do this. The `Fetch` method will return the `Person` object, and the `Save` method will take a reference to the `Person` object and re-add it to the collection as if it had been saved. Normally, our `Fetch` method might take a key value to determine which `Person` to retrieve but, for the sake of simplicity, our `Fetch` and `Save` methods will only handle one `Person`.

```
Public Function FetchPerson() As Person
   Set FetchPerson = mcolPeople.Item(1)
End Function

Public Sub SavePerson(NewValue As Person)
   Set mcolPeople = New Collection
   mcolPeople.Add NewValue
End Sub
```

As part of the final test, add a method to take and return a `Person` object by reference. This will show that Type IV marshaling can work bi-directionally on the same parameter. Name this method `PersonByRef`.

```
Public Sub PersonByRef(ByRef RefPerson As Person)
   Set RefPerson = mcolPeople.Item(1)
End Sub
```

Create the COM Component

The COM component is now done for this test. We can now save and compile it. To compile, select Make VB6Type4.dll from the File menu.

Generate the Runtime-Callable Wrapper

Go to the command prompt and switch to the directory where we compiled `vb6type4.dll`. Use `Tlbimp.exe` to create a new RCW specifying the output file as `vb6t4.dll`. The command should look like this:

```
Tlbimp vb6type4.dll /out=vb6t4.dll
```

The result is an RCW that allows our code to interact with the COM component.

Create the Managed Person Class and the Custom Marshaler

Now that there is a "legacy" COM component, we can create a managed version of the `Person` class and add a custom marshaler to convert between the unmanaged and managed versions. Open up Visual Studio .NET and create a new Visual Basic .NET class library project. Name the project PersonCustomMarshaler and add a reference to the `vb6t4.dll` by right-clicking on References in the Solution Explorer and selecting Add Reference.

Add the Managed Person Class

To convert between the unmanaged `Person` class and a managed version, we must first create the managed class. The interface of this class will be slightly different from its unmanaged counterpart. The managed `Person` class will have properties for name and birth date, and a method that returns the person's age based on the current date.

Open up the `Class1` module and add the following `Imports` statements so that we can use these namespaces directly in our code.

```
Imports System
Imports System.Reflection
Imports System.Runtime.InteropServices
Imports vb6t4
```

Replace the default `Class1` declaration with a public declaration for a `ManagedPerson` class:

```
Public Class ManagedPerson
End Class
```

We have two private attributes that our `ManagedPerson` class needs to keep track of: the person's name and birth date. Add two private members to hold this information:

```
Private mstrName As String
Private mdteBirthDate As Date
```

The customer marshaler that we will create can put information into our new class in one of two ways: through public property/method declarations or through a constructor. For this example, we will choose to use a constructor. We will also leave the original constructor in place in case this information is not known when the object is created outside of our custom marshaler. Add the two constructors: one to set the attributes automatically, and one to create a new blank instance of the object.

```
Public Sub New(ByVal Name As String, ByVal BirthDate As Date)
  mstrName = Name
  mdteBirthDate = BirthDate
End Sub

Public Sub New()

End Sub
```

Now that we are able to create an instance of our class in the manner we choose, we need to add a public interface. Add two properties: one for the person's name, the other for the person's birth date.

```
Public Property Name() As String
  Get
    Name = mstrName
  End Get
  Set(ByVal Value As String)
    mstrName = Value
  End Set
End Property

Public Property BirthDate() As Date
  Get
    BirthDate = mdteBirthDate
  End Get
  Set(ByVal Value As Date)
    mdteBirthDate = Value
  End Set
End Property
```

Finally, to fully simulate our original COM object, there needs to be a method that returns the person's age. This will be a calculated member based on the birth date and the current system date using the `DateDiff` function. To keep things uncomplicated, this property will simply be called `Age`.

```
Public Function Age() As Long
  Age = DateDiff(DateInterval.Year, mdteBirthDate, Now)
End Function
```

At this point we have essentially created a Visual Basic .NET version of our COM `Person` class.

Create a Custom Marshaler Class

With the managed person class in place, we can now create a custom marshaler to move information between the managed and unmanaged classes. Add a new class to the project by adding these lines to `Class1.vb`:

```
Public Class PersonMarshaler
End Class
```

This class needs to implement the `ICustomMarshaler` interface. Add a line to the class with the `Implements` keyword to do this:

```
Implements ICustomMarshaler
```

Now an important decision needs to be made. Does the custom marshaler class that we are making need to preserve the state of information between calls?

For most applications, you will not need to preserve state between calls to the custom marshaler object. In these cases, you can use one shared instance of the marshaler. However, there may be times, such as when you need to write to a specific memory location, that you need a custom instance of the marshaler for each client that is using it. This is not the case for us here and we can use a shared instance. Define a shared variable to hold our instance of the custom marshaler.

```
Private Shared objMarshaler As ICustomMarshaler
```

If we need a custom instance of the marshaler, we would simply remove the shared parameter from the variable declaration. This will insure that each time the marshaler is called, a new instance will be used.

Now create a function to return a reference to our custom marshaler. This must be called `GetInstance`. This function is also passed a string parameter, `cookie`, to identify which client is calling the method. If we were not using a shared marshaler, we might use the cookie to identify which instance of the marshaler object to return.

This method will check `objMarshaler` to see if it contains a valid instance of this marshaler. If it does not, it will create it. This instance is then passed back to the caller.

```
Public Shared Function GetInstance(ByVal cookie As String) As ICustomMarshaler

    If (objMarshaler Is Nothing) Then objMarshaler = New PersonMarshaler()
    Return objMarshaler

End Function
```

All we need to do now is implement the remaining five methods of the `ICustomMarshaler` class. The first method is `GetNativeDataSize`. This method returns the size in bytes of the native data to be marshaled. Since we are returning object references, this is not important and we can return −1.

```
Public Function GetNativeDataSize() As Integer _
    Implements ICustomMarshaler.GetNativeDataSize

    Return -1

End Function
```

The next method is `MarshalNativeToManaged`. This method takes an `IntPtr` to an unmanaged interface and returns a reference to a managed object. For this, we will take the easy way out and declare a variable as type `Person` from our RCW instead of declaring its COM interface in our code using `COMImport` like we did with `IRecordInfo`. We can then use the framework `Marshal` object's `GetObjectForIUnknown` to marshal the pointer into the managed `Person` class created with `Tlbimp`. With this, an instance of the `ManagedPerson` object can be created using the values from the `Person` object to initialize it on the constructor. Let's take a look at this method one piece at a time.

Declare the function declaration, the managed `Person` object from `Tlbimp` that created `vb6t4`, and a declaration for the `ManagedPerson` object from this project. Notice that we automatically create an instance of the `Person` object using the `GetObjectForIUnknown` method.

```
Public Function MarshalNativeToManaged(ByVal pNativeData As IntPtr) _
    As Object Implements ICustomMarshaler.MarshalNativeToManaged

Dim objPerson As Person = _
    CType(Marshal.GetObjectForIUnknown(pNativeData), Person)
Dim objManagedPerson As ManagedPerson
```

Now create a new instance of the `ManagedPerson` object, using the values from the `Person` object in the constructor. This new object can be returned from the function and the function ended.

```
With objPerson
    objManagedPerson = _
        New ManagedPerson(.Name, CDate(Trim(.BirthMonth) & "/" & _
        Trim(.BirthDayofMonth) & "/" & _
        Trim(Year(DateAdd(DateInterval.Year, (-1 * .Age), Now)))))
End With
Return objManagedPerson

End Function
```

The `MarshalManagedToNative` method is very similar except that it performs the complementary function. We are passed an instance of a `ManagedPerson` object and need to return an `IntPtr` to an unmanaged interface. To do this, we will once again create an instance of a `Person` class and copy the current values to it. We can then use the `Marshal` object's `GetComInterfaceForObject` to return an `IntPtr` to the COM interface. To do this, add the following code to the project:

```
Public Function MarshalManagedToNative(ByVal ManagedObj As Object) _
    As IntPtr Implements ICustomMarshaler.MarshalManagedToNative

Dim objManagedPerson As ManagedPerson = ManagedObj
Dim objPerson As New Person()

With objPerson
    .Name = objManagedPerson.Name
    .BirthMonth = Month(objManagedPerson.BirthDate)
    .Age = objManagedPerson.Age
    .BirthDayofMonth = Day(objManagedPerson.BirthDate)
End With

Return _
    Marshal.GetComInterfaceForObject(objPerson, System.Type.GetType("Person"))

End Function
```

The final two methods are to clean up any managed/unmanaged information, such as memory we may have allocated to copy information or object instances that have not been cleaned up. Since we do not allocate any memory that is not being automatically cleaned up, or retain state between method calls, we do not need to do this. However, we do need to simply declare the methods to comply with the `ICustomMarshaler` interface. Add the following lines of code:

```
Public Sub CleanUpNativeData(ByVal pNativeData As IntPtr) _
    Implements ICustomMarshaler.CleanUpNativeData

End Sub

Public Sub CleanUpManagedData(ByVal ManagedObj As Object) _
    Implements ICustomMarshaler.CleanUpManagedData

End Sub
```

When this is done, save the project and build it. Select **Build PersonCustomMarshaler** from the **Build** menu. We have now created our first custom marshaler.

Modify the Marshal Attributes on the Runtime-Callable Wrapper

Of course, we are not quite ready to use the custom marshaler yet. We have not told the Runtime-Callable Wrapper to use the custom marshaler object. This is done in exactly the same way as it was for Type II and Type III marshaling. Our first step is to deconstruct the RCW using `Ildasm.exe`. Exit to a Visual Studio .NET Command Prompt and switch to the directory containing `vb6t4.dll`. Then enter:

```
Ildasm vb6t4.dll /out=vb6t4.il
```

The code for our wrapper class is now accessible in text format in the IL file.

Add a Reference to the PersonCustomMarshaler Assembly

One of the first things that you will notice is that the RCW needs a reference to the `PersonCustomMarshaler` assembly, and the `PersonCustomMarshaler` assembly holds an instance of the RCW. This could have been avoided had the custom marshaler not imported the RCW's `Person` object. However, this is not important in this context and a circular reference is easier to use in the example. Add a reference to `PersonCustomMarshaler` in the IL file for the RCW. This can be inserted after the reference to the `mscorlib` assembly.

```
.assembly extern PersonCustomMarshaler
{
  .ver 1:0:718:28348
}
```

Your version number will most likely be different from the one used here. The version of an assembly can be retrieved in a number of ways. The easiest method is to find the assembly in the Windows Explorer, right-click on it, and select **Properties**. The assembly version information will be on the **Version** tab:

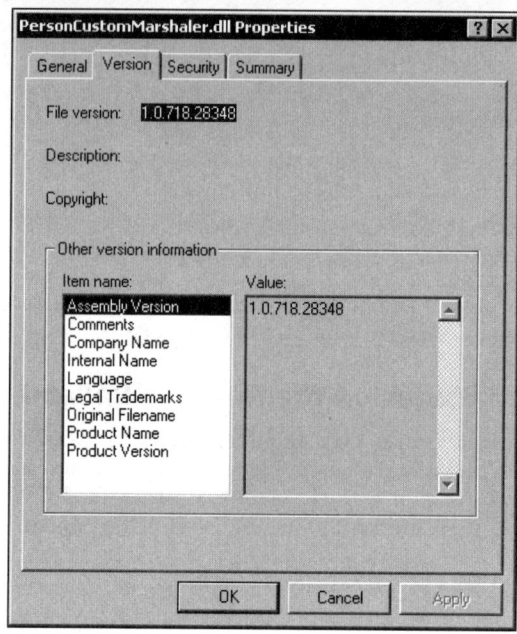

Set the Marshal Attributes in the IL Code

To use Type IV Marshaling, we are going to override the default RCW so that the `People` object returns the new `ManagedPerson` object instead of the imported `Person` object, using our custom marshaler. Locate the definition of the `_People` class in the IL. The first method defined is `FetchPerson`. This interface currently returns a reference to the imported `Person` class, as exemplified by this code:

```
.method public hidebysig newslot virtual abstract
        instance class vb6t4.Person
        marshal( interface)
        FetchPerson() runtime managed internalcall
```

Now replace the return type with `ManagedPerson` and change the marshal call to be custom and use our custom marshaler. The resulting code should look like this:

```
.method public hidebysig newslot virtual abstract
        instance class
[PersonCustomMarshaler]PersonCustomMarshaler.ManagedPerson          marshal(
custom ("PersonCustomMarshaler.PersonMarshaler,PersonCustomMarshaler",""))
        FetchPerson() runtime managed internalcall
```

Now do the same for the `SavePerson` method:

```
.method public hidebysig newslot virtual abstract
        instance void  SavePerson([in][out] class
[PersonCustomMarshaler]PersonCustomMarshaler.ManagedPerson&  marshal( custom
("PersonCustomMarshaler.PersonMarshaler,PersonCustomMarshaler","")) NewValue)
runtime managed internalcall
```

and then for the `PersonByRef` class:

```
    .method public hidebysig newslot virtual abstract
            instance void  PersonByRef([in][out] class
[PersonCustomMarshaler]PersonCustomMarshaler.ManagedPerson&  marshal( custom
("PersonCustomMarshaler.PersonMarshaler,PersonCustomMarshaler","")) RefPerson)
runtime managed internalcall
```

Do the same for the public `PeopleClass` definition and save the IL file. We are now ready to recreate the RCW using `Ilasm.exe`. Open a Visual Studio .NET Command Prompt window and switch to the directory that contains our IL file, `Vb6T4.il`. Run the following command:

```
Ilasm vb6T4.il /dll /res=vb6t4.res /out=vb6t4.dll
```

It is likely that you will have to re-reference the RCW in the custom marshaler application. To make sure you don't have problems, open the custom marshaler project, remove the reference to vb6t4.dll, and add it back in. Build the resulting assembly.

Create an Interface to Test the Marshaler

Open Visual Studio .NET if it is not already open and create a new Console Application. Name the application **ManagedInterface**. Add references to `PersonCustomMarshaler.dll` and vb6t4.dll. Reference both files from the custom marshaler's `Bin` directory.

Open the `Module1` file and add `Imports` statements for `System.Console`, `PersonCustomMarshaler`, and vb6t4.

```
Imports System.Console
Imports vb6t4
Imports PersonCustomMarshaler
```

Like the prior two examples, add in the `WriteTest` subroutine to write our results to the command line and wait for a response. It should look like this.

```
Private Sub WriteTest(ByVal strMsg As String)
   WriteLine(strMsg)
   Write("Press Return,")
   ReadLine()
End Sub
```

Now modify `Sub Main` to declare an instance of the `People` object and two managed `Person` objects.

```
Dim objPeople As New People()
Dim objPerson1 As ManagedPerson
Dim objPerson2 As ManagedPerson
```

Set the `objPerson1` equal to the return for the `People` object's `FetchPerson` method. Display the results and see that the new managed class is returned, filled with the data initialized in the COM object.

```
objPerson1 = objPeople.FetchPerson
WriteTest("Fetched Person:" & objPerson1.Name & _
    ":" & objPerson1.BirthDate & ":" & objPerson1.Age)
```

While we are using the `People` object, use the IntelliSense to check the return value of the `FetchPerson` method. As one would expect, it returns the custom `ManagedPerson` object, instead of the `Person` object that is imported by `Tlbimp.exe` by default.

```
objPerson1 = objPeople.FetchPerson
WriteTest("Fetched Perso
```
Public Overridable Function FetchPerson() As PersonCustomMarshaler.ManagedPerson

Clear out the `Person` object and try the same with the `PersonByReference` method. Interestingly enough, the `ManagedPerson` object as an in/out parameter is marshaled into a COM `Person` object, pointed to the existing `Person` object, and marshaled back to managed code.

Round-trip marshaling like this should be considered when designing your interfaces. Be careful that you only define your parameters as in/out when you need to set them as well as retrieve them. If we have no reason to set the values in the object, we should consider using an out-only parameter like the return of a function.

```
'Try it by reference
objPerson1 = Nothing
objPeople.PersonByRef(objPerson1)
WriteTest("Person by Reference:" & objPerson1.Name & ":" & _
    objPerson1.BirthDate & ":" & objPerson1.Age)
```

The final test will be to change the properties on the `ManagedPerson` object and use the `SavePerson` method to put the changes back into the COM object. Then the `FetchPerson` method can again be used to pull the new values from the COM object and display them. This will prove conclusively that our custom marshaler works bi-directionally between managed and unmanaged code.

```
objPerson1.Name = "Fred"
objPerson1.BirthDate = CDate("12/31/66")
objPeople.SavePerson(objPerson1)
objPerson2 = objPeople.FetchPerson
WriteTest("Saved and Retrieved Person:" & objPerson2.Name & ":" & _
    objPerson2.BirthDate & ":" & objPerson2.Age)
```

Before we run the project, you should erase all of the current references and re-add them to reflect any changes. This is particularly important if we are running the examples from code provided with this chapter. Now the project can be run. The values come up from the COM object and can then be set back into it. If this was done correctly, we should see the following results:

```
■ C:\Projects\Interop Chapter\TypeIV\ManagedInterface\bin\ManagedInterface.exe    _ □ ×
Fetched Person:Dan:9/18/1968:33
Press Return
Person by Reference:Dan:9/18/1968:33
Press Return
Saved and Retrieved Person:Fred:12/31/1966:35
Press Return_
```

To see how the custom marshaling actually works, you can add the `PersonCustomMarshaler` project solution. When the project is added, breakpoints can be set in the code and then used to see the interaction between the `ManagedInterface` project and the `PersonCustomMarshaler` project. This can be quite educational and should be used to experiment with what can and can't be marshaled back and forth in Type IV marshaling.

Managed Code to Unmanaged Code

All of the marshaling techniques discussed in this chapter can be used to go from managed code to unmanaged code as well. In fact, this is much easier as the attributes can be added to the code itself without having to go through the intermediate step of modifying the IL code. Examples of using Type II marshaling to go from managed code to unmanaged code can be found in Chapter 3 under *Data Type Marshaling*.

Summary

This chapter has discussed the four different types of marshaling and when each should be employed. Each different type of marshaling has its proper place and usage.

❑ Type I: The default marshaling mechanism and the easiest. This type should be used most often because it will handle most cases and be the easiest to maintain.

❑ Type II: This type of marshaling can override one data type with another when moving from managed to unmanaged code. It is also very easy to use, but can be somewhat complex when dealing with COM objects whose RCWs need to be disassembled.

❑ Type III: It can be argued that Type III marshaling is the most difficult to use. It can map undefined memory and data types between managed and unmanaged code. The catch is that we need to know what to expect. The most common use for this is to pull record information out of Variants or any other undefined memory structure.

❑ Type IV: With Type IV marshaling, we can override one reference type with another. An unmanaged object can be mapped into a managed structure with an entirely different structure. This may be useful when using predefined types in the .NET Framework that have similar but not identical interfaces.

While custom marshaling can be somewhat tricky, it is possible to move just about any type of information to and from unmanaged code. The trick is knowing the structure of what you are trying to marshal, the type of marshaling you need, and how to use it. Once this has been determined, the actual coding is not that difficult.

For further reading, consult the help section of the Marshal object to see all of the options available for Type III and Type IV marshaling:

http://msdn.microsoft.com/library/default.asp?url=/library/en-us/cpref/html/frlrfsystemruntimeinteropservicesmarshalclasstopic.asp

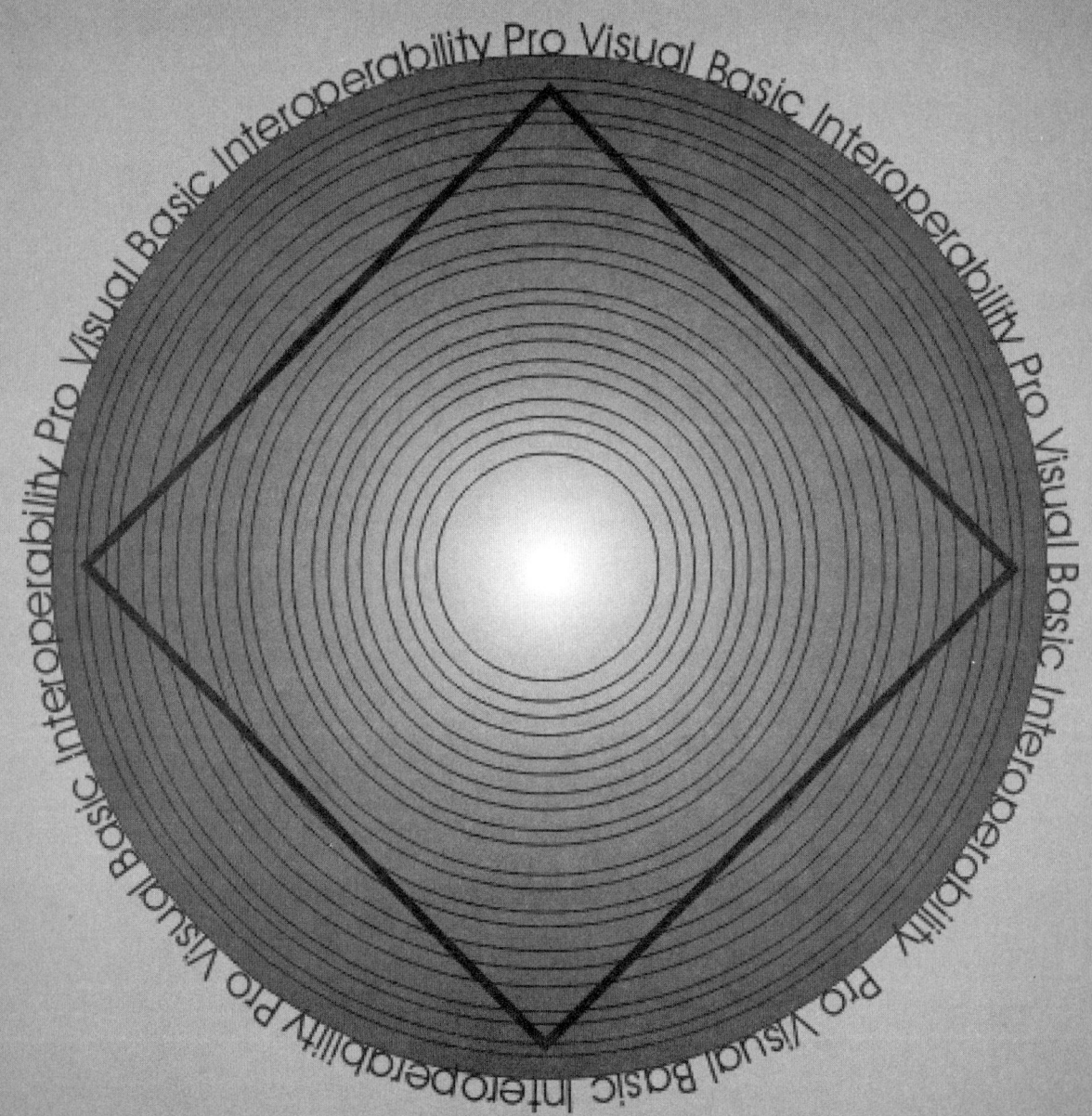

7

Threading Issues

So far we've been building applications in Visual Basic .NET and using VB6 components that run within the same process and thread. Likewise, those VB6 applications that have made use of Visual Basic .NET assemblies have had the most basic of threading models. Consequently, we have not had to worry about issues related to threading such as deadlocks, concurrency, and so forth.

Real-world applications are not likely to be this simple, and we will probably run into threading issues when interoperating between Visual Basic .NET and VB6. To make this as painless as possible, it is important to understand how both VB6 and Visual Basic .NET use threads.

Before we get into that, however, we should discuss threading and a few important terms. First, we'll cover some basic terms and concepts, then we'll discuss how threading works in VB6 with COM, and then how it works in Visual Basic .NET on the .NET platform.

The descriptions here are very high level. For a more detailed discussion of .NET threading, please refer to *Professional VB.NET* (ISBN 1-861004-97-4).

Threading Basics

In most modern operating systems such as Windows, our applications run within a **process**. A process is a region of memory that holds the code and variables used by our application. Typically, a process is isolated from all other processes so that code in one process cannot directly read or change code or variables in any other process.

It is important to realize that a process doesn't actually *do* anything. It merely defines a region of memory that contains our application's code and data. Any actual work occurs because each process contains at least one **thread of execution**. We can think of a thread as somewhat like a cursor within our code. The thread points to the bit of code that is currently being executed. As the CPU processes our code, the thread moves to the next instruction to be processed, and so forth.

The following diagram illustrates a process, which contains our code and data, and a thread of execution running through the code within the process:

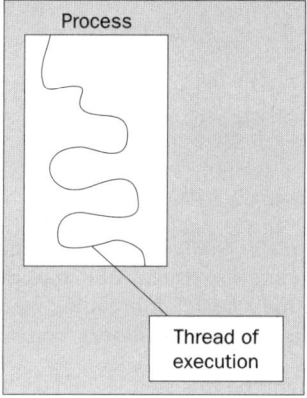

Another way to look at it is to view the process as a block of memory addresses – some containing instructions for the computer. It is this series of instructions that the thread performs – one at a time.

A process can have more than one thread simultaneously. This means that more than one bit of code can run at the same time, *if we have more than one CPU*. Remember that it is the CPU that does the actual processing, so one CPU means that only one thing can happen at a time. If we have two CPUs in our computer, then we really can do two things at once.

Many people find this confusing, since most Windows computers only have one CPU and it appears as though the computer is doing several things at the same time. If we have a process with two or more threads, it certainly *seems* like the computer is doing more than one thing within our process. This is because the operating system is employing a technique known as **time slicing**, or time sharing. Time slicing means that any given thread is only allowed to use the CPU for a very short period of time before having to allow another thread to take a turn. This "very short" period of time is typically a few milliseconds and so, to the human eye, it gives the illusion that more than one thing is happening simultaneously.

When we build **multi-threaded applications** – processes with two or more threads – we need to assume that multiple things really will happen at the same time. However, we cannot necessarily predict whether our application will be run on a computer with multiple CPUs.

Obviously, you may require that multiple CPUs be present – but it is more useful to consider what happens when you build and test your system on a single-CPU machine, and then to consider what might happen when it is run on a multi-CPU system in the future.

This is important, since multi-threading can cause a host of very complicated issues and bugs to occur in our code – things that simply would never occur in a single-threaded application. Multi-threading is *very* complex and hard to do well.

Let's take a quick look at some of this complexity, since we've been entirely shielded from it in the VB6 world.

Threading Complexity

When we only have a single thread in our process, we are guaranteed that only one thing will occur at a time. However, when we have more than one thread running concurrently in our process, we *can* have more than one thing going on simultaneously – and sometimes they can conflict.

Collectively these are **concurrency** issues, since they arise from trying to do multiple activities concurrently.

To understand the nature of the problem, it is important to realize just how fine-grained the processing of our code really is. Consider the following code:

```
If x < 5 Then
   x += 1
End If
```

Any VB6 developer looking at this code would swear that this would never increment x beyond the value 5.

Multi-threading developers (including Visual Basic .NET developers) need to realize that this code *can* increment x beyond the value of 5. When such a thing happens it is a concurrency bug.

How can this simple code cause x to increment beyond 5? To understand what's going on, we need to break the process down into simple steps. The following series of steps may or may not exactly equate to the code generated by the Visual Basic .NET compiler, but you'll get the idea:

1. Retrieve the value of x from memory

2. Check if x < 5

3. Jump to Step 7 if Step 2 returned `False`

4. Place x in a CPU register

5. Increment x by 1

6. Update the value of x in memory

7. Code complete

Each thread runs through this procedure from top to bottom. If there is just one thread following these steps, things are simple. However, if we have two threads, say, then things get interesting.

Let's assume x starts out with the value 4. Suppose the first thread runs from Step 1 to Step 3; the result of Step 2 was True and the first thread is about to place x in a CPU register and increment it by 1. Before the first thread reaches Step 4, the second thread also makes it from Step 1 to Step 3; it has also found the result of Step 2 to be True and so is about to increment x by 1 as well.

If they both increment x by 1, we'll get a result of 6, not 5 – and so our code will have incremented the value beyond that which the code *should* allow.

> *Even on a single-CPU system, the operating system simulates having multiple CPUs by allowing a thread to only run for a short time (about 20 milliseconds) before running another thread on the system. This gives us the illusion that all the threads are running concurrently even though they really aren't. It also means that concurrency issues exist on single-CPU machines just like they do on multi-CPU machines – though the problems are often compounded on real multi-CPU machines.*

But that isn't the half of it. It gets worse. Notice that incrementing a numeric value takes multiple steps in this model (just like it does in real life). This means that we might get a value of either 5 or 6 depending on the specific order in which the threads run the remaining steps. Sometimes we'll get 5 and sometimes we'll get 6. It all depends on millisecond timing as to which thread runs which step when.

This is a race problem, since the threads are racing against each other. It is also a shared storage problem, since both threads are updating the same memory – x – and they may overwrite each other's values.

To solve these issues we can use special system constructs that help us control our threads and ensure they don't conflict with each other. These include:

❑ Mutex

❑ Semaphore

❑ Critical section

❑ Safe increment/decrement functions

The Visual Basic .NET language even includes the SyncLock statement, which can be used to create a **monitor** to control threads to help make our job easier.

Using Single versus Multi-Threading

Multi-threading is one of the more eagerly awaited features of Visual Basic .NET. Finally, we VB developers can create multi-threaded applications!

Of course, over the past few years Microsoft has developed sophisticated systems, namely MTS (Microsoft Transaction Server) and COM+, to help programmers *avoid* having to create multi-threaded applications. They didn't do this just for VB developers, but also for C++ developers who found the creation of multi-threaded applications to be too difficult.

A common misperception is that a multi-threaded application will run faster than a single threaded application. This is almost never true. The requirement that we use various locking mechanisms to protect shared memory and to avoid having our threads conflict with each other almost always causes a multi-threaded application to run *slower* than a single-threaded implementation.

There are exceptions to this. One of the most notable is where we can break our problem into small, discrete segments – each with its own data. Then we can have several threads running, each working on a part of the problem and none of them needing to share data or otherwise conflict with the others. Then, on a multi-CPU machine, we *can* gain performance improvements.

Another case where multiple threads can be useful is in a very IO-bound application. Threads get stalled all the time in such applications, waiting for the user, database, or file system to respond. Architecting an application to have a worker thread that is "fed" data by IO threads can improve performance by allowing one thread to stay very busy while other threads are constantly starting and stopping due to various blocking factors.

The point of all this is that, while multi-threading is useful, it is not a panacea and it would be a poor decision to just make all applications multi-threaded without first understanding the related issues and making an educated decision.

That said – the fact is that we *will* create multi-threaded Visual Basic .NET applications, hopefully when it makes sense. When we do build such applications, they may need to interact with COM components. The .NET threading model and the COM threading model are different, and so this interaction can be somewhat complex and can have a substantial impact on how our applications perform. The purpose of this chapter is not to explain when to use multi-threading but, rather, to walk through the various issues that arise when the .NET threading model and the COM threading model come into contact.

Threading in VB6

Because multi-threading is so complex and hard to deal with, the COM environment is designed to provide many of the benefits of multi-threading to our applications, while providing us with an environment where we typically don't need to worry about multi-threading issues within our application code.

COM divides a process into **apartments**. An apartment is very much like a process, since it gives any code within the apartment the illusion that it is totally isolated from any other apartment or process on the computer. Also, each apartment has at least one thread of execution – just like a process. A good way to think about COM apartments is that they are a process within a process.

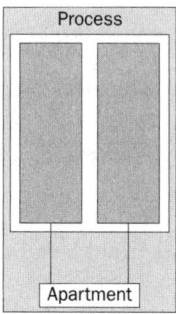

Having multiple apartments in a process is a common occurrence. MTS and COM+ both host our DLLs within a single process that has many apartments. The same is true with many ActiveX EXE projects in VB6 – one process with many apartments.

Unlike regular processes, COM apartments come in different flavors. The primary flavors are the Single-Threaded Apartment (STA) and the Multi-Threaded Apartment (MTA). There are other flavors, such as the Both-Threaded and Thread-Neutral models, but STA and MTA are the oldest and most common and so they are the ones we'll consider here; they are the ones we need to understand when interoperating between VB6 and Visual Basic .NET.

An STA is an apartment that has only one thread. Only one thing can be happening at a time within an STA. This is the type of apartment used by all VB6 code, which is why VB6 has no real multi-threading capability.

> *It is technically possible to do multi-threading with VB6. This involves calling a series of Win32*
> *API and COM API functions to properly create the thread, configure it for COM, and then manage*
> *it so it can be closed appropriately when our application is closed. Microsoft supports none of this*
> *and it is not for the faint-hearted so, while technically possible, it is almost never done.*

This may seem counter-intuitive to many VB6 developers. After all, aren't events an example of multi-threading? If we put a `Timer` control on a form, our application not only does the work in the `Timer`, but also the work in the rest of the application, such as in a `Button`'s `Click` event. The thing to keep in mind is that a single thread is handling all of this. If our application is busy doing work when the Timer control fires its event, the work is suspended while the `Timer` event code is run. It *has* to be suspended because the application's thread is needed to run the `Timer` event. When the `Timer` event is complete, the thread returns to its original work. VB6 often gives us the *illusion* of multi-threading, but it is always running in a single-threaded environment.

An MTA is an apartment that more closely simulates a real process, since it can have more than one thread at a time – meaning that more than one thing can be happening within the apartment at the same time. When writing multi-threaded code in an MTA, all of the complexity and issues that exist in writing workable and good multi-threaded code are present. In other words, it is hard to write good and well-performing multi-threaded code in COM just like it is in any other platform or environment. Most applications or components that make use of an MTA are written in C++.

Components can also be designated as supporting *both* models. This type of component will load and run in either an STA or MTA. Obviously, it will only enjoy the benefits of multi-threading when running in an MTA, but it will work correctly when running in an STA. This type of component cannot be created with VB6 and is typically created using C++.

The primary reason why VB6 only uses the STA model is to keep things simple. We almost never have to worry about synchronization or other complex threading issues when writing VB6 code. If we *want* multi-threading, we can use a tool such as MTS or COM+, which provides us with a type of multi-threading by creating a new STA each time a client requests some work. Since each STA has a thread, and we can have many STAs in existence at a time, our application can do more than one thing at a time – all without having to worry about threading issues, since each STA is totally isolated.

This technique is also used when we create an ActiveX EXE in VB6. We have the option to allow more than one thread to run within our ActiveX EXE if we so desire. This is defined through the project's properties – something we'll discuss in more detail later in the chapter. The way VB6 handles this, however, is by creating a new STA for each thread – meaning that none of our code ever encounters real multi-threading issues, since each thread is contained within its own isolated STA.

Since apartments are isolated, when code in one apartment calls code in another apartment, it is just like calling code in another process. Since apartments and processes are isolated and can share no memory, making a call from one to another requires that the method call and any parameter or result data be **marshaled** from one memory-space into the other. Marshaling is an expensive operation with serious performance ramifications, which is why it is important to minimize calls between apartments.

Threading in Visual Basic .NET

The .NET platform is quite different from the COM platform in terms of threading. In particular, the concept of an apartment is gone, and all code is always running in an environment where multi-threading is possible. Note that it is possible, but not *required*. Most .NET applications only use a single thread – including all typical Visual Basic .NET applications. To get multi-threaded behavior, we need to use specific features of the .NET Framework that cause the creation of secondary threads within our application.

The closest thing to an apartment in .NET is an **AppDomain**. All .NET code runs within an AppDomain, and an AppDomain is contained within a process. A process running .NET code will have one or more AppDomains – each of which is isolated from all other AppDomains and processes.

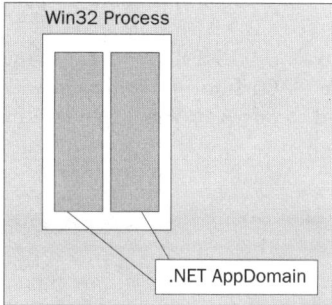

This sounds very similar to a COM apartment, but AppDomains always allow multiple threads, and have nothing to do with COM apartments.

As with apartments, no memory or data is shared between AppDomains. This means that any call from one AppDomain to another requires that the method call and any parameter or result data be marshaled from one memory-space to the other (typically using .NET Remoting). As in COM, this is a fairly expensive operation and so it is something that should be avoided or minimized in application design whenever possible.

Threading Interop

Pure .NET code has nothing to do with COM and, thus, nothing to do with apartments – STA, MTA, or otherwise. Likewise, pure COM code has nothing to do with .NET and, thus, nothing to do with AppDomains. However, as soon as we have .NET code calling COM components, or COM code calling .NET assemblies, these models come in to contact and they will affect each other.

The way Microsoft has implemented the .NET/COM Interop services will cause almost any type of interaction to work, but the interaction may not be fast. The single biggest reason for understanding the interaction between these two threading models is to ensure that our applications perform reasonably well when interoperating across platforms.

We already know that any call from .NET to COM or from COM to .NET requires that the method call and any parameter or result data be marshaled from one platform to the other, as discussed in Chapters 2 and 3. However, due to the differences in threading models and the way that the COM Interop subsystem works with COM components, it is quite possible to accidentally incur *extra* marshaling overhead if we don't pay attention.

Calling COM from .NET

In Chapter 2 we discussed how to invoke a VB6 COM component from within a .NET application. In that example, the .NET application was a single-threaded application and the COM component was a simple VB6 ActiveX DLL. Behind the scenes, it turns out that .NET's COM Interop mechanism automatically created an STA within which our VB6 code could run. This STA was created within the same *process* as our .NET application, and it shared the same thread. The original thread that was running our .NET application was also used to run the COM code.

> *.NET has no concept of COM. It is the COM Interop mechanism within .NET that understands COM apartments, including how to create and talk to them. If our code never uses COM Interop, then our .NET application will not create or interact with any apartments.*

The following diagram illustrates how our .NET code was running in an AppDomain before our thread created a COM STA apartment (via COM Interop), and switched over to the COM STA to run our VB6 code. The thread then returned to our AppDomain to continue running our .NET application:

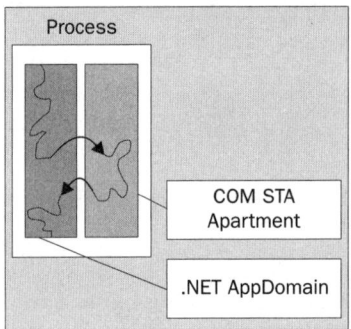

The STA is created when we first attempt to interact with a COM component. This triggers .NET's COM Interop to create and initialize the STA before it invokes the COM component itself. Once created, the STA remains until our application is closed – meaning that subsequent calls to a COM component do not require creation of an STA, since they can use the one that already exists. In fact, the way COM Interop works is that all components that need an STA will be loaded into this one apartment for our use from within .NET.

This is the simplest case. Things get more complex from here as we either call multiple COM components from our .NET code, or our .NET code starts to have multiple threads that want to invoke COM components.

Calling Multiple COM Components from .NET

Visual Basic .NET Windows Applications default to creating an STA when the application's primary thread invokes a COM object. This is not true for ASP.NET applications – a topic we'll cover later in this chapter.

The default of an STA typically works very nicely when we are interacting with a VB6 component from a simple Visual Basic .NET application. However, if we will be calling a multi-threaded COM component, or a mix of single and multi-threaded components, this may not be ideal. Many COM components created with C++ are multi-threaded and require an MTA to operate properly. Others may be created to work in either an STA or an MTA.

Suppose we *are* calling multiple COM components from our .NET application – some designed for multi-threading, others designed for single-threading. The multi-threaded components will require an MTA to run, while the single-threaded components will require an STA. If the correct type of apartment doesn't exist in our process, COM will automatically create the appropriate type of apartment.

> **Interop services always funnel any requests to COM components through the apartment it first creates on our thread.**

This can be complex, so let's walk through an example.

If we have a .NET application that first invokes a VB6 component, it will create an STA to run that code. If the .NET code subsequently calls a multi-threaded component, the interop services will funnel the call through the STA. The COM interop code running in the STA will attempt to use the component, and COM will automatically create an MTA in which it can run; the call will be serviced in this MTA.

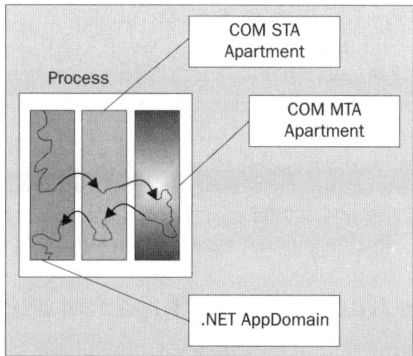

The result is that we've now marshaled the method call, including its parameters and return data, *twice* – once from .NET to COM, and then again from the STA to the MTA. Everything works just fine, but the double marshaling does have a negative impact upon performance.

Each .NET thread in our application can have exactly one primary COM apartment through which COM interop is handled. Being aware of which type of apartment – whether MTA or STA – is being used by our thread is key to getting good performance.

Visual Basic .NET always creates an STA by default. Other .NET languages may follow different rules – creating an MTA, an STA, or creating the appropriate type of apartment for the *first* COM component invoked. When using any .NET language, it is important to read through the help for that language to understand how it approaches this problem – or, better yet, read on to understand how we can take control of this process within our code.

Controlling the Primary Apartment Type

If we know that we'll be mostly calling a component of a specific threading model, we can achieve the best performance by ensuring that interop services creates that type of apartment first. That way, *most* of our method calls will be handled without double marshaling.

If we will be interacting with various COM components that have different threading models, we should make sure that we explicitly set our thread's `ApartmentState` property to the type of apartment that will be most commonly used by our specific components. To interact with our thread we'll use the `System.Threading` namespace, so we may want to add an `Imports` statement to simplify our code:

```
Imports System.Threading
```

We can then use the following call to set our `ApartmentState` property:

```
Thread.CurrentThread.ApartmentState = ApartmentState.STA
```

The state can be set to `MTA`, `STA`, or `Unknown`. As long as this call occurs before any COM component is invoked on our current thread, this setting will dictate the type of apartment that will be created to handle all COM calls by our thread. If we set the state to `Unknown`, interop services will create an apartment based on the type of component we first invoke.

> To manually control the apartment type used by Interop, this line of code should be placed in the constructor of our first object, the **Load** event of our first form, or any other location such that it is called before any COM components are invoked.

The `ApartmentState` property can also be read as our application executes, allowing us to discover the threading model that is being employed within our application. Typically, we'd want to check this value after making at least one call to a COM component when debugging the application in order to ensure that we do have the appropriate threading model in place.

Calling VB6 Components from a Multi-Threaded .NET Application

Our discussions so far have assumed a single-threaded .NET application calling into COM components requiring an STA or MTA model. Things get even more complex when our .NET application is itself multi-threaded.

Any .NET application can be multi-threaded, but most are not. Unless we specifically use features of the .NET system class library that create extra threads, our application will be single-threaded (even events do not create multiple threads). This is important to keep in mind because, in those cases where we do create extra threads, we need to be aware of the consequences for COM interop. For most .NET applications, this is not an issue.

When building a multi-threaded application, the first thread in our process is known as the **primary** thread. This is the thread we get automatically from the operating system through the creation of our process. Any other threads that we create are known as **background** threads.

Each .NET thread manages its own COM interop. This means that each thread has its own `ApartmentState` property, separate from that of any other threads in our application. Consequently, COM components used by any .NET thread will be running in separate apartments from COM components used by other .NET threads within our application. Each .NET thread has its own set of COM components that run in an apartment associated with that particular thread.

The following diagram illustrates this by showing a process with two .NET threads – a primary thread that then launches a background thread. Both the primary and background threads interact with COM components, causing the creation of two COM apartments – one for each .NET thread:

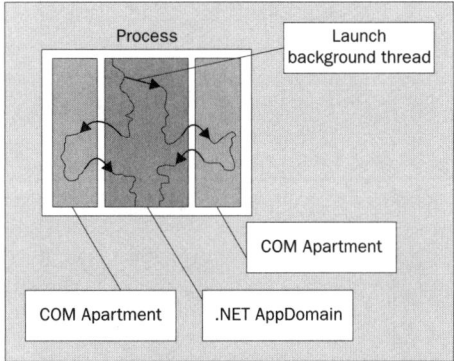

We already know that Visual Basic .NET defaults to using an STA on the application's primary thread. It defaults to using an *MTA* on any background threads that we create within our application. This means that, in the diagram, only the apartment created by the primary thread (on the left) is an STA by default. The other apartment will be created as an MTA, unless we manually change the ApartmentState property on our background thread before invoking the COM component – in which case we can make that second apartment an STA.

Now things get interesting, as there are various combinations of threading interaction we need to consider when working with VB6 components.

Creating a Test COM Component

Perhaps the best way to explore the threading interaction is to create a simple test application that illustrates how the process works.

First create a VB6 ActiveX DLL project named Chapter7COM. Rename Class1 to Worker and add the following code:

```
Option Explicit

Public Function Value() As Long
   Value = App.ThreadID
End Function
```

This Worker object's Value method will now return the ID of the thread on which the COM code is running. Compile the project to create the DLL. We're done with VB6 now, so close the IDE.

Creating a Test Visual Basic .NET Application

Now open Visual Studio .NET and create a new Windows Application project in Visual Basic .NET. Name it Chapter7Net.

Using **Project | Add Reference**, add a reference to the Chapter7COM.dll on the **COM** tab. This will make our VB6 component available for use within our Visual Basic .NET code.

Add ListBox and Button controls to the form as shown in the diagram, naming the Button btnStart:

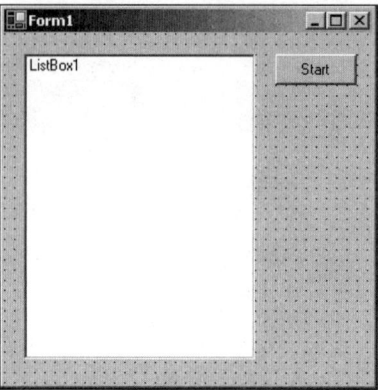

Because we'll be working with multiple threads, let's set up a mechanism by which any thread can safely display data in the ListBox control. This takes a bit of extra work since all UI updates must be handled by the thread that owns the form – the primary thread of our application in this case.

In the form's code window, we'll add an Imports statement for System.Threading and we'll declare a delegate:

```
Imports System.Threading

Public Delegate Sub StatusInvoker(ByVal id As Integer, ByVal t As String)

Public Class Form1
```

Then, within the code for Form1, we can add a method to update the display. Notice that the method signature of this method matches the delegate signature:

```
Public Sub Display(ByVal id As Integer, ByVal [Text] As String)
  ListBox1.Items.Add(id & ": " & [Text])
End Sub
```

Now any thread can invoke this method via the delegate in a thread-safe manner, by using the form's Invoke method to invoke this Display method with the StatusInvoker delegate we've declared. This will become clearer in a moment when we actually write this code.

The easiest way to work with threads in Visual Basic .NET is to create an object for each thread. Add a new class to the project using Project | Add Class and name it NetWorker. This class will contain the code to work with our COM Worker object. For now let's stub out a couple of methods:

```
Imports Chapter7COM

Public Class NetWorker
  Private mobjWorker As Worker
  Private mobjForm As Form1
  Private mintID As Integer

  Public Sub New(ByVal Form As Form1, ByVal id As Integer)
    mobjForm = Form
    mintID = id
```

```
        End Sub

    Public Sub DoWork()

    End Sub
End Class
```

The constructor, New, requires that we provide a reference to the application's form so we can update the display, as well as a numeric ID value so we can differentiate this worker from any other worker. The DoWork method is where we'll actually invoke the COM DLL – we'll return to this shortly.

Now go back to the code in Form1 and we'll create the code that starts up some threads:

```
Public Class Form1
    Inherits System.Windows.Forms.Form

    Private arThreads(2) As Thread

    Private Sub btnStart_Click(ByVal sender As System.Object, _
        ByVal e As System.EventArgs) Handles btnStart.Click
      ListBox1.Items.Clear()

      Display(0, ".NET thread     " & CStr(AppDomain.GetCurrentThreadId))
      Display(0, ".NET apt state " & _
        Threading.Thread.CurrentThread.ApartmentState.ToString)

      ' note that the New NetWorker() statements run on the main application
      ' thread - meaning that the constructor methods of the new objects
      ' also run on the main application thread
      arThreads(0) = New Thread(AddressOf New NetWorker(Me, 1).DoWork)
      arThreads(1) = New Thread(AddressOf New NetWorker(Me, 2).DoWork)
      arThreads(2) = New Thread(AddressOf New NetWorker(Me, 3).DoWork)

      ' here we actually start the secondary threads, which causes the
      ' DoWork method on each of them to be invoked
      arThreads(0).Start()
      arThreads(1).Start()
      arThreads(2).Start()
    End Sub
```

This code is behind the Start button and is not particularly complex. It first displays the thread ID and apartment state of our main application's thread in the list box. Then we create three threads, providing each thread with its own unique NetWorker object. The fact that each thread gets its own unique NetWorker object is very important, as this is how we are able to pass information to each thread.

This technique also helps to isolate each thread from the others. Each thread has its own set of data contained within its own object and so no thread shares data with any of the other threads. Notice that the ID values for each worker are different, allowing us to differentiate between them. Finally, we start each of the threads, meaning that each DoWork method is invoked on a different thread.

The final bit of work that we need to complete is writing the code in the NetWorker's DoWork method. Remember that *this* code will always be running on a background thread and so it cannot interact directly with any controls on the form. Instead, we are calling the Invoke method of the form, using the delegate we declared earlier, to update the form's display safely.

Enter this code, keeping in mind that we haven't yet created an instance of the COM object and so it won't run just yet:

```
Public Sub DoWork()
   Dim arData(1) As Object
   Dim delDisplay As StatusInvoker = AddressOf mobjForm.Display

   arData(0) = mintID

   arData(1) = ".NET thread     " & CStr(AppDomain.GetCurrentThreadId)
   mobjForm.Invoke(delDisplay, arData)

   arData(1) = ".NET apt state " & _
      Threading.Thread.CurrentThread.ApartmentState.ToString
   mobjForm.Invoke(delDisplay, arData)

   arData(1) = "COM thread      " & CStr(mobjWorker.Value)
   mobjForm.Invoke(delDisplay, arData)
End Sub
```

This worker method is largely concerned with displaying data back on the form's ListBox. When we created each instance of the NetWorker object, we provided each with a reference to the form – this is what we have in the mobjForm variable. Form objects have an Invoke method that specifically exists to allow background threads to call methods on the form, and this is what we are using here to call the form's Display method.

The Invoke method doesn't allow us to simply pass the address of the Display method, however. Instead, it requires a delegate – a formal variable that points to the method we want to call. We declared this delegate earlier, when we created the code for our form, and we're just using it here.

Using this technique, we display our current thread ID, our apartment state, and the thread ID retrieved from the COM object.

Notice that nowhere in our code are we yet *instantiating* the VB6 Worker object. Where we do this – and whether we manually set the apartment state on our threads – will have a big impact on how this code runs. Let's try some combinations.

COM Object on Primary Thread

The most obvious approach may be to create the COM components on the application's primary thread – after all, we know that it will use an STA by default.

By creating all of the VB6 objects on the primary thread, we avoid having any extra threads created in our process, but we also cause all COM processing to occur on the primary thread. This can tie it up, making the primary thread unavailable for things like servicing the UI to keep it responsive to the user. Also, in this example we'll leave the background threads alone so that they each create their own MTA through which they interact with the COM component. This will result in double marshaling as each call goes from .NET to the MTA, and then to the STA.

We can do this by creating the Worker objects in the constructor of NetWorker:

```
' all code in the constructor is run on the main application thread
Public Sub New(ByVal Form As Form1, ByVal id As Integer)
  mobjForm = Form
  mintID = id
  ' create worker here to have it invoked from main application thread
  mobjWorker = New Worker()
End Sub
```

Even though the DoWork method will be invoked on a background thread, the NetWorker objects themselves are being *created* by the application's primary thread. This means that all of the code in the constructor is running on the primary thread, so that thread is used to actually instantiate the Worker objects.

Run the application and click the Start button. The result should be something like this:

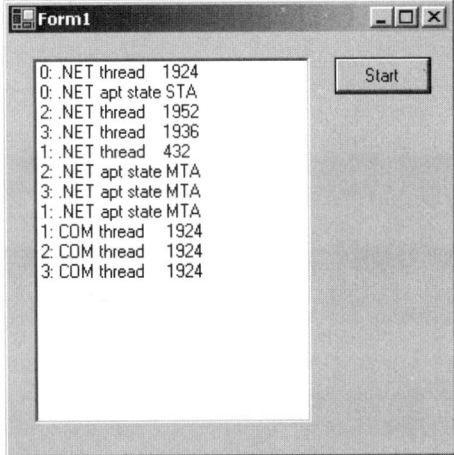

The specific thread ID values will change each time, but the important thing to note is that the application's main thread ID is the same as that used by each of the VB6 COM objects. The primary .NET thread created all of those COM objects, and so they are all running in the STA associated with that thread.

Each individual background .NET thread has a different thread ID because we explicitly created a different thread for each. Also notice that each of them defaults to using an MTA to interact with COM as we discussed earlier.

> **Each background thread goes through its MTA and then to the STA to call the COM component – meaning that each call incurs double marshaling.**

Since all of the VB6 objects are running within the same STA on the same thread, they all share access to any global variables within the VB6 DLL – the objects are not totally isolated from each other. This may be beneficial or not depending on our requirements, but it is an important point to keep in mind.

COM Object on Background Threads, STA on its Own Thread

We can change our code to create the COM objects directly on the background threads.

In this case, we'll leave the background threads with their default setting, meaning that they'll still create MTA apartments. Since our primary .NET thread won't be creating the COM objects, they'll be created in an STA that is automatically initialized by COM – and it will have its own thread. This avoids tying up the primary thread to do all of the COM processing, but will still keep all of the COM objects within the same STA so that they can share global variables if desired. It also means that each method call from a background thread will incur double marshaling from .NET to the MTA to the STA, as before.

To do this, we need to stop creating the objects in the constructor of the `NetWorker` class:

```
' all code in the constructor is run on the main application thread
Public Sub New(ByVal Form As Form1, ByVal id As Integer)
  mobjForm = Form
  mintID = id
  ' create worker here to have it invoked from main application thread
  'mobjWorker = New Worker()
End Sub
```

and, instead, create the object within the `DoWork` method itself:

```
' all code in DoWork is run on a background thread
Public Sub DoWork()
  Dim arData(1) As Object
  Dim delDisplay As StatusInvoker = AddressOf mobjForm.Display

  ' create worker here to have it invoked directly by secondary thread
  mobjWorker = New Worker()
```

Since `DoWork` is always running on a background thread, we are now making that background thread create the COM object. Start the application now:

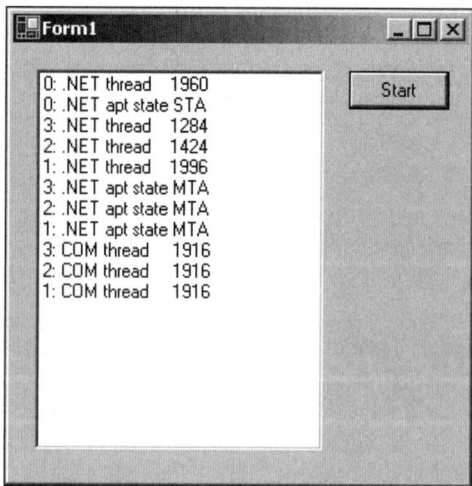

This is almost the same as our first experiment, with the important exception that the COM objects are running on a different thread from our application's main thread. Each COM object was created by a separate worker thread, but those worker threads are all still set (by default) to use MTA apartments – a type of apartment that is incompatible with our VB6 component.

Essentially, our VB6 component is "homeless" – it can't run in the MTA of the worker threads. To resolve this, COM itself automatically creates an STA within our process, with a proxy in the MTA that relays any calls from .NET through the MTA to the STA where the object resides. We discussed this mechanism earlier in the chapter.

This automatically generated STA is not directly associated with any .NET thread – it is independent. All of the homeless single-threaded COM objects in our process are then created and run in that STA. In other words, any subsequent single-threaded objects created by threads that only have an MTA will be created in this central STA.

Since this central STA is single-threaded, all of the objects that it contains will run on that same thread. Our background threads each have their own MTA that they use to invoke the COM object – so we get the same double marshaling behavior as before.

The potential benefit to this approach is that our application's main thread is not tied up with servicing calls to the COM component, meaning it can remain focused on making the UI responsive or other work. All of our STA COM components are effectively running on their own dedicated background thread, where they can share global variables and interact as they normally would under VB6.

Forcing the Use of STA on Background Threads

So far we've allowed the background threads to use the default apartment state of MTA, which causes all of the COM objects to share the same STA and also causes double marshaling for each method call from a background thread to a COM object.

We can override the apartment state of a background thread to STA, which will change the behavior quite a lot.

In this case, each background thread will be set to use an STA thread, and so, each of the COM worker objects will be created within an STA that belongs to a specific .NET thread. This avoids all of the double marshaling we've seen so far, but isolates each COM object from the others since they'll be running in totally separate apartments. The primary thread remains unaware of any of this activity and is not tied up with processing all of the COM components.

To do this, set the `ApartmentState` property before creating the COM object:

```
' all code in DoWork is run on a background thread
Public Sub DoWork()
  Dim arData(1) As Object
  Dim delDisplay As StatusInvoker = AddressOf mobjForm.Display

    ' before talking to COM, but on our new thread
    ' we can set the ApartmentState as appropriate
    Threading.Thread.CurrentThread.ApartmentState = _
      Threading.ApartmentState.STA

    ' create worker here to have it invoked directly by secondary thread
    mobjWorker = New Worker()
```

279

This change will cause each of our background threads to use an STA to create any COM objects, rather than the default MTA we've seen so far. In fact, it will cause each background thread to use *its own* STA (each thread gets its own STA).

We could also set the property to MTA – but that would have no impact since MTA is the default for background threads.

The following diagram shows the type of results we should see:

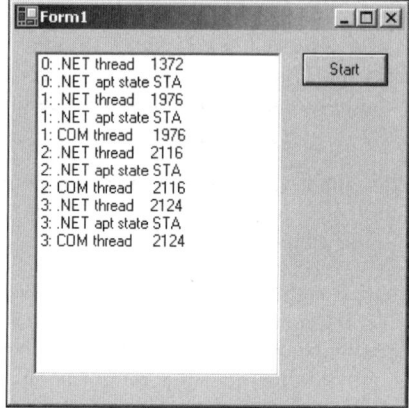

Notice that the thread ID of each worker thread matches the thread ID of its COM object. In this case, each COM object is running on the same thread as its caller and within an STA owned by that caller.

> **This avoids any double marshaling as our background threads call their COM objects.**

It is also important to note that each COM object is now running in a separate STA, so our objects are now totally isolated from each other and cannot share global data within the VB6 component.

The following table summarizes our findings:

STA on primary thread	Create COM objects on primary thread, then call from background threads	Incurs double marshaling, COM objects not isolated from each other, primary thread used for COM processing
STA on its own thread	Create COM objects on background threads with apartment state of MTA, then call from background threads; or set primary thread apartment state to MTA and create COM objects from primary thread	Incurs double marshaling, COM objects not isolated from each other, COM objects don't tie up primary thread
STA on worker threads	Create COM objects on background threads with apartment state of STA and then call the COM objects from those background threads	Avoids double marshaling, COM objects isolated from each other, COM objects don't tie up primary thread

Calling ActiveX EXE Components from Visual Basic .NET

While the most commonly used VB6 COM components are in DLL form, VB6 does allow us to create COM components that run in their own process in the form of an ActiveX EXE. Because an ActiveX EXE runs in its own process, our Visual Basic .NET code will have much less control over the way STAs are created to house the COM objects.

In fact, control over the creation of any STAs that house COM objects in an ActiveX EXE rests entirely within the Project Properties window for our VB6 ActiveX EXE project:

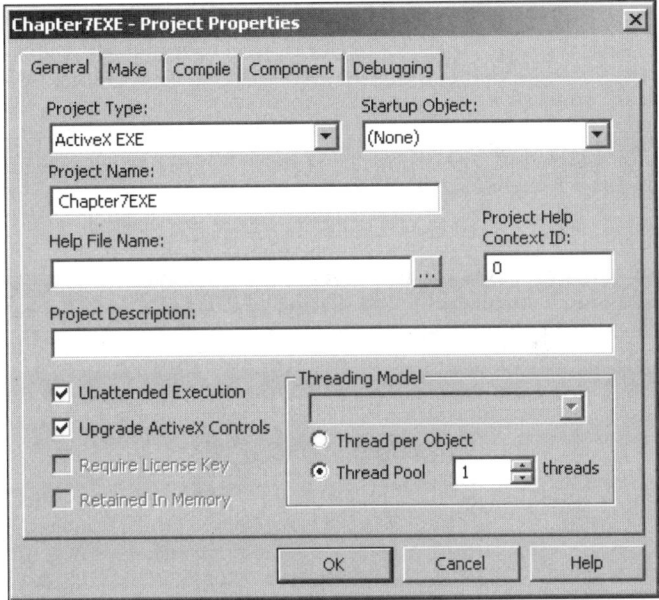

The Threading Model frame contains options that allow our EXE to host a thread pool or to create a separate thread for each object. In either case, each thread that is created will have its own STA and the objects running in that STA will be isolated from objects running in any other STAs.

By default, ActiveX EXE applications use a thread pool with 1 thread – meaning that there is one thread and one STA to house all of the objects created within the component.

We can raise the number of threads, and thus STAs, in the pool by altering the Thread Pool threads value. Objects are created on those threads using a simple round-robin scheme. For instance, with a pool size of 2, object 1 is created on thread 1, object 2 on thread 2, object 3 on thread 1, object 4 on thread 2, and so on.

We can also opt to create a thread and STA for each object that is created. This ensures that each object will be isolated within its own apartment and will have its own thread on which to run.

Regardless of which threading option we utilize, our Visual Basic .NET application will be running in a separate process and will rely on COM to marshal our method calls from the .NET process to the VB6 process. The .NET interop services will handle the details of making the call, so we can invoke the objects directly without worrying about their threads, since that is handled by the ActiveX EXE itself.

281

This is the case when a .NET application invokes something like Excel or Word. Excel runs in its own process, entirely separate from the client .NET application. Nothing that the .NET application does will affect how Excel manages its own threads within its own process, and so the .NET application really doesn't have to worry about Excel's internal threading issues.

Calling VB6 Components from ASP.NET

While all of our discussions so far are great for Windows applications, it turns out that there is an odd bit of behavior in ASP.NET that causes some complexity in that environment. ASP.NET always initializes an MTA for our use in invoking COM components. This occurs *before* any of our code gets to run, and so we are stuck with the MTA even if we want to invoke VB6 components that require an STA.

Obviously, this means that ASP.NET Web Forms will always incur double marshaling when invoking VB6 COM components, which is a serious performance issue.

Technically, this is a bug in ASP.NET. Microsoft is aware of the bug and has indicated that it will probably be resolved in a future release of .NET.

To avoid this issue, any Web Forms that will be invoking COM components that require the STA model should use the ASPcompat tag to cause ASP.NET to operate in **ASP compatibility mode** for that page. ASP compatibility mode changes the way that ASP.NET processes the page in several ways – including changing the default COM apartment to an STA.

To use the ASPcompat tag, we can use the Properties window to alter our Web Form DOCUMENT:

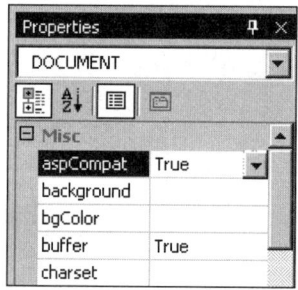

Alternately, we can manually change the @Page tag at the top of our Web Form to include the setting. For example:

```
<%@ Page ASPcompat="true" Language="vb" %>
```

Either way, we have enabled ASP compatibility mode, which will cause the primary COM apartment created by ASP.NET to be an STA, so we will get the best performance when interacting with VB6 COM components or any other COM components that require the STA model. Of course, ASP compatibility mode does more than simply change the way COM components are invoked, and some of the side effects may not be desirable for our application. For more details, please refer to *ASP.NET Programmer's Reference* (ISBN 1-861005-30-x) published by Wrox Press.

Calling .NET from COM

Typically, calling a COM component from Visual Basic .NET is not complex, though we've seen how things can get tricky if the Visual Basic .NET application is multi-threaded.

The reverse process, having a VB6 COM application call a .NET application, is even more straightforward. Since VB6 is inherently single-threaded, it will always be invoking .NET assemblies using that single thread. This is illustrated by the following diagram:

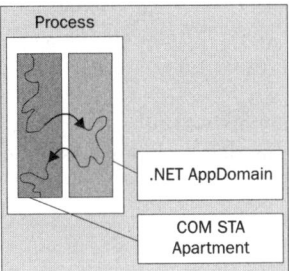

We can see that the COM thread is running in an STA. When it calls a .NET object, the thread transfers into a .NET AppDomain that is created within the same process to run the .NET code. When the thread is done with the .NET code, it returns to the STA and continues running the VB6 code.

This does not preclude the Visual Basic .NET code from starting its own background threads. That is perfectly acceptable since they are not running in the context of the STA but, rather, are running within the .NET AppDomain. Even if we do start background threads, the primary thread for our assembly will be the client application's thread, as shown in the previous diagram.

This is as complex as it gets. Even if we are using an ActiveX EXE to create multiple STAs (and thus multiple threads) within our VB6 application, the thread from each STA will be used to invoke the .NET code as we've discussed. Obviously, it is much simpler to call into a multi-threaded environment from a single-threaded environment such as VB6.

Summary

The advanced threading capabilities provided by Visual Basic .NET are a very powerful feature. They can complicate matters when interoperating with COM components, however, and so it is very important to make note of the interaction between the .NET AppDomain threads and the COM apartments where our code is running.

Always try to minimize double marshaling, while at the same time balancing the requirements of the application code in terms of tying up an application's primary thread and achieving the desired isolation between COM objects.

Remember that none of these threading issues exist in a simple, single-threaded Visual Basic .NET or VB6 application. It is only when we start creating multiple threads in a Visual Basic .NET client application that makes use of COM components that these issues become important.

If our COM objects will be doing a lot of processing, we should avoid creating them on the primary thread. The primary thread typically manages the UI and having it tied up doing a lot of background processing will make the UI appear unresponsive. In such a case, we should create the COM objects from our background threads.

If our VB6 COM objects require shared memory, then they must all run in the same STA and so we need to run them on the primary thread, or in a central STA by making all the .NET threads use MTAs.

If our VB6 COM objects don't require shared memory, then we can simply use the `ApartmentState` property to ensure that our background threads all create their own STAs, in which each background thread can create and use its own set of COM objects. This offers the best performance, but does isolate the COM objects on one thread from those on any other thread.

In most applications, the default behaviors will provide optimal performance. In this chapter, we've walked through the scenarios where the default behaviors may not be optimal and have shown the threading options available for our use.

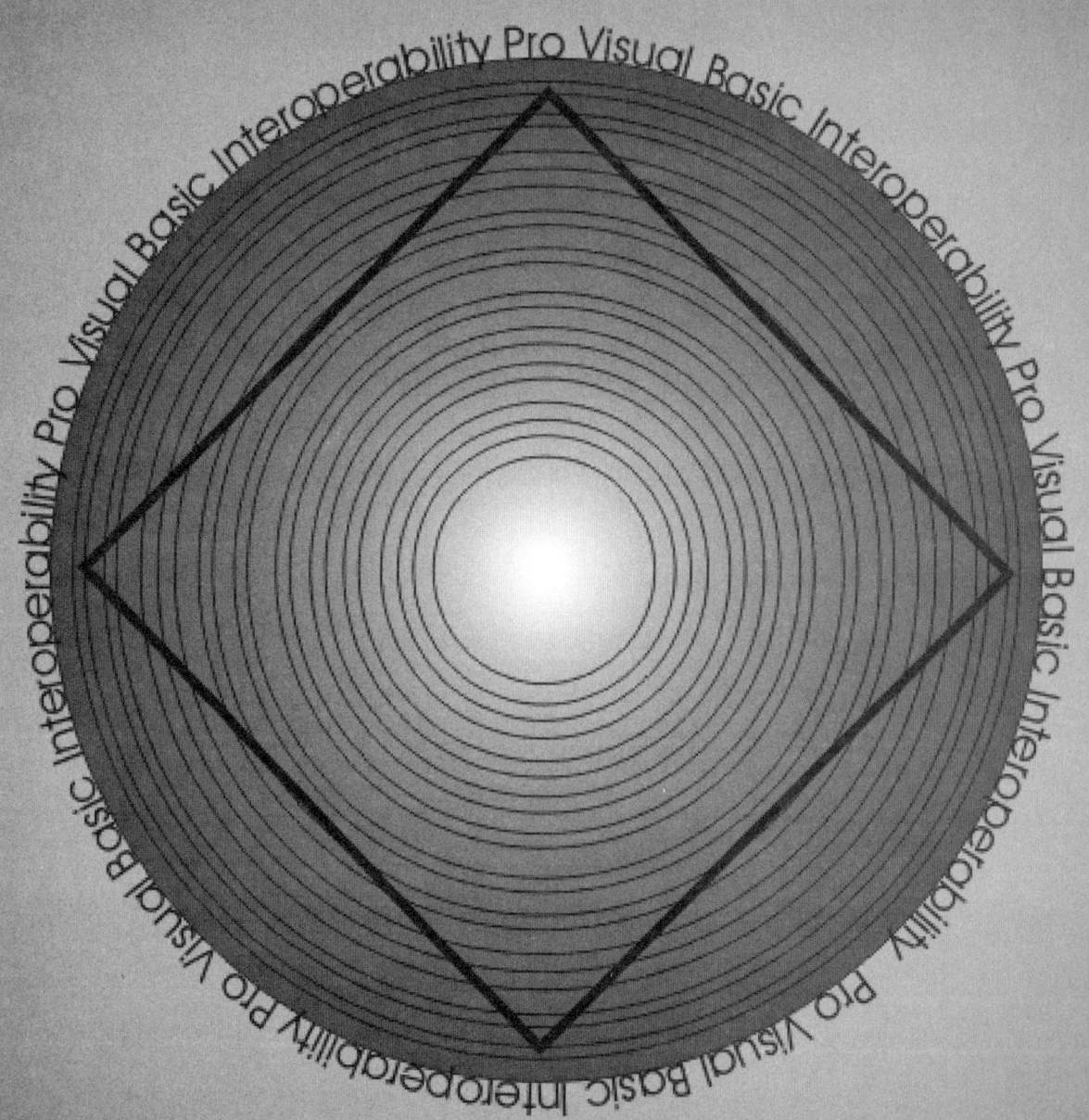

8

DCOM, Remoting, and Web Services

The .NET platform does not directly incorporate COM although, as we've seen, it does provide solid interoperability with the COM platform. Since .NET doesn't incorporate COM, it should come as no surprise that it does not incorporate Distributed COM (DCOM) either.

DCOM has often been described as "COM with a longer wire". This is because the code we use to invoke a COM component that is running on the same machine as our client application is identical to the code we use to invoke a COM component that is running on another physical machine. Even though DCOM is used to invoke that remote component, it makes no difference to our code.

The .NET Framework provides alternatives to DCOM in the form of XML Web Services and .NET Remoting. We also have access to DCOM through the COM interoperability services provided by the .NET Framework. Let's discuss each of these options in a bit more detail, and then we'll walk through examples of using each approach.

XML Web Services

XML Web Services allow applications to communicate with each other across a network by sending and receiving data formatted into a specific XML structure. This structure is described by the Simple Object Access Protocol (SOAP) standard, which is governed by the World Wide Web Consortium (W3C; see http://www.w3.org). The XML Web Service technology built into .NET is merely a formal implementation of this SOAP specification, integrated tightly within .NET.

SOAP is also known as the **XML Protocol**. From the W3C web site:

"The goal of XML Protocol is to develop technologies which allow two or more peers to communicate in a distributed environment, using XML as its encapsulation language. Solutions developed by this activity allow a layered architecture on top of an extensible and simple messaging format, which provides robustness, simplicity, reusability and interoperability."

The XML Protocol, or SOAP, defines a high-level mechanism by which two applications can communicate by using simple text-based XML. The specification includes a general description of how a message is sent and received, the format of the XML *envelope* that describes the message and the way in which most common data types are to be represented by XML within the message itself.

Collectively this all adds up to a definition of how one application can call procedures or methods of another application across most networks. Most notably, this protocol works fine over the Internet, going across port 80 just like other web traffic, and thus bypassing most firewall security.

Since SOAP is a standard that is being implemented on most major platforms and technologies, it is an ideal technology for interoperability between applications running on different platforms. The only requirement is that all of the platforms support XML and that the implementations conform to the SOAP specification. Virtually any platform we can imagine would be able to work with the simple text of XML, so SOAP is essentially a universal transport protocol.

SOAP (and thus Web Services) is not specifically designed to be a replacement for DCOM. The design goals for SOAP revolve around providing an open and standard mechanism by which applications can invoke services on remote machines, regardless of the operating system, programming language, or other details of that remote machine. XML Web Services don't directly support a number of concepts we find in DCOM, such as working with server-side objects that maintain state, or making multiple method calls to the same remote object.

However, .NET and COM are effectively two different platforms, and so it makes a lot of sense to look at XML Web Services as a tool for communicating between these two platforms.

Within .NET, we have integrated support for SOAP in the form of XML Web Services. On the COM platform Microsoft provides us with the SOAP Toolkit, which we can download from MSDN and install on our machine. This toolkit extends VB6 so it can create and call SOAP services across the network.

.NET Remoting

While XML Web Services is a great technology for interoperability, .NET Remoting is a much more obvious replacement technology for DCOM. Remoting provides the same capabilities as Web Services in terms of invoking a service on a remote computer, but also supports the concepts of making multiple method calls to the same remote object and having server-side objects that maintain state. Remoting is also much more tightly integrated into the .NET Framework, providing complete support for delegates, events, and passing objects by value across the network.

When compared to DCOM, Remoting is a much simpler and more streamlined technology. DCOM is tightly integrated into the Windows security environment, which can be nice because it allows us to use existing Windows security administrative tools, but it has the drawback of being overly complex in many cases. Remoting on the other hand, is not integrated into Windows security. In fact, Remoting uses HTTP or simple TCP sockets for communication, and so is secured using simple firewall or router configurations. This makes Remoting much easier to implement than DCOM in many cases – especially over the Internet or an intranet where firewalls have historically made DCOM implementations very difficult.

With all its capabilities, however, Remoting is essentially proprietary to .NET. Its design goals revolve around features and performance rather than around broad interoperability. There is no COM equivalent to Remoting, so there is no way to directly use Remoting to interact between .NET and COM applications or components.

Having said this, Remoting can still be a very attractive option, since it does provide features and performance that exceed XML Web Services. Fortunately, there are techniques we can use to allow the use of Remoting between a .NET client and a COM component. In particular, we can wrap the COM component within a .NET class on the server so our client can communicate with the .NET wrapper class, which in turn uses COM interop to invoke methods on the COM component itself. While this process incurs a certain level of overhead, it often offers less overhead – and thus better performance – than XML Web Services.

DCOM

We can also use the standard COM interop facilities we discussed in Chapter 2 to directly interact with remote COM components via DCOM. Remember that DCOM is transparent to a COM client application and, when we are using COM interop, our .NET application becomes a simple COM client. This means that we can invoke a component via DCOM just as though it were local to our client machine.

Of course, all the normal rules that govern the interaction between COM clients and components via DCOM apply to our .NET clients as well. Thus, the remote COM object must be registered appropriately on the client machine, using either DCOMCNFG or some other means to set up the registry entries so that COM invokes the component on the right machine. As with any other DCOM environment, the easiest way to do this is to put the server-side components in MTS or COM+ and use the client deployment facilities provided by those tools to handle the configuration.

It is also important to keep in mind that DCOM can be very difficult to work with over the Internet or even an intranet. Any time the clients are on opposite sides of a firewall from the server, DCOM becomes very complex to configure and work with from a security perspective. While there are some solutions to these issues, the fact is that XML Web Services and .NET Remoting are typically much better technologies when firewalls are involved.

We won't create an example of directly using DCOM within this chapter, as the topic is effectively covered in Chapter 2.

XML Web Services and Interop

Given the open XML-based SOAP standard and the fact that both .NET, through XML Web Services, and VB6, through the SOAP Toolkit, support this standard, we have a powerful technology on which to build applications that interoperate across the network between these two platforms.

> *Of course SOAP and XML are entirely cross-platform and cross-language technologies. This means that solutions developed along this line are useful not only for interop between VB6 and Visual Basic .NET, or between COM and .NET. They are equally useful for interoperation with any other platform or language we can imagine – including Unix, Linux, Java, COBOL, and so forth.*

In this section, we'll build a COM component and use the SOAP Toolkit to host it on a web server. We'll then build a .NET client application that invokes that component just as it would any other Web Service based on SOAP. We'll then do the reverse – building a VB6 client that invokes an XML Web Service built using Visual Basic .NET.

In both cases, we will need to have the SOAP Toolkit installed on our machine for the code to work. The XML Web Services support is built into .NET, but our VB6 code will require the Toolkit in order to function. SOAP Toolkit 2.0 SP2 is available at http://msdn.microsoft.com/downloads/default.asp under the Software Development Kits link.

The SOAP Toolkit requires IIS 4.0 or higher on the server. Windows NT 4.0 SP6 or higher will do the trick. On the client machines we need to have IE 5.0 or higher installed. On both client and server, MSXML 3.0 and the VB6 runtime DLLs are also required. The SOAP Toolkit install will add these to the systems as needed.

Calling COM from .NET

Visual Studio .NET provides integrated support that allows us to add a reference to a Web Service almost in the same way that we reference any local component on our system. This includes not only XML Web Services created by .NET, but also includes any SOAP-compliant services produced by other tools or platforms.

Creating the Web Service in VB6

We can create such a Web Service using VB6 and the SOAP Toolkit. In Chapter 2 we created a VB6 ActiveX DLL that we can use here to create a Web Service with a number of methods.

> *If you didn't create the project in Chapter 2, please do so now (or download it from www.wrox.com). The following steps assume that we have a compiled and registered version of* Chapter2COM.dll *on our system.*

The first thing we need to do to create a Web Service based on this DLL is set up a virtual root to hold the files that define our Web Service.

Creating the Virtual Root

To create a virtual root, we need a directory to hold the files that we want to make available via our web server. This directory can be created anywhere on our drive as long as it is publicly available to the IIS process. For this example, the directory we'll create is C:\inetpub\wwwroot\soap.

With the directory created, we can use the Internet Information Services management console to configure the directory as an application. To do this, bring up the console by selecting Start | Settings | Control Panel | Administrative Tools | Internet Services Manager, and then expand the nodes for the server and the Default Web Site in the left-hand pane. Select the soap directory:

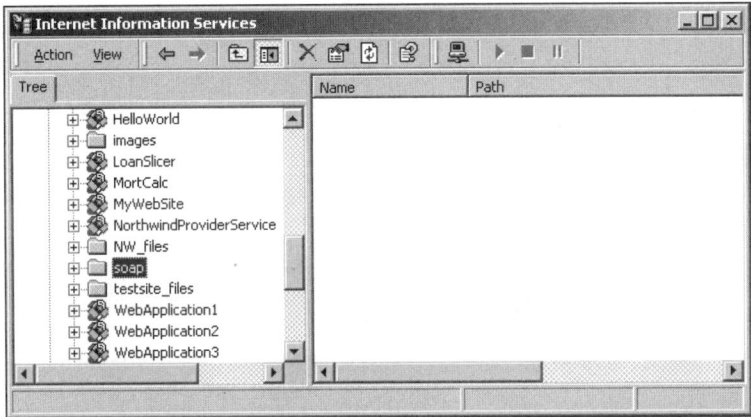

Right-click on the directory and choose Properties. Click the Create button to create an application for this directory:

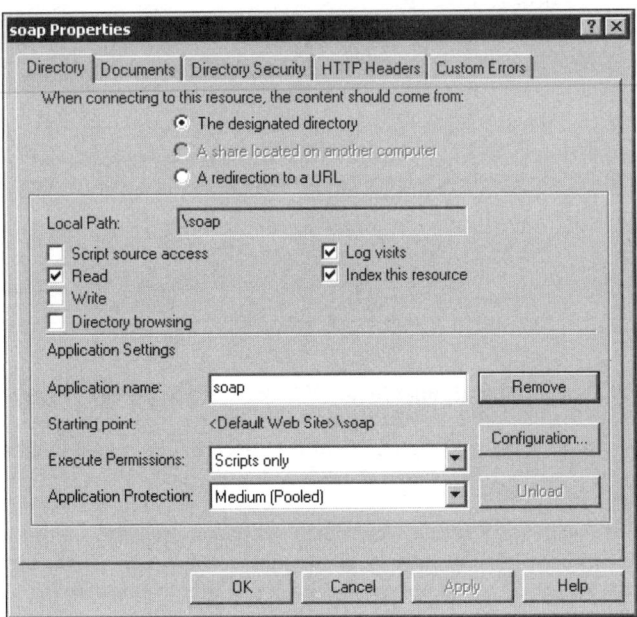

After clicking **OK**, we have a virtual root configured and ready to hold the files that will drive our Web Service. The default security settings for the virtual root will work fine for SOAP, since the client merely needs to be able to do regular GET and POST operations to the site just like it would with any simple web site implementation.

We can now move on to run the SOAP Toolkit 2.0 Wizard that will create our Web Service files.

Running the SOAP Toolkit 2.0 Wizard

A WSDL (Web Service Description Language) file contains an XML description of a Web Service and is used by client applications so they know the nature of our service and how to call it. The SOAP Toolkit provides a wizard that will generate an appropriate WSDL file based on the type library information about a COM component.

Run the SOAP Toolkit 2.0 Wizard by choosing Start | Programs | Microsoft Soap Toolkit | WSDL Generator.

The wizard requires that we provide our service with a name. In this case, we'll name it `Chapter2COM`, the same as our DLL, though any name will do. We must also provide the path to our COM DLL. The wizard will interrogate the DLL to find its classes and methods:

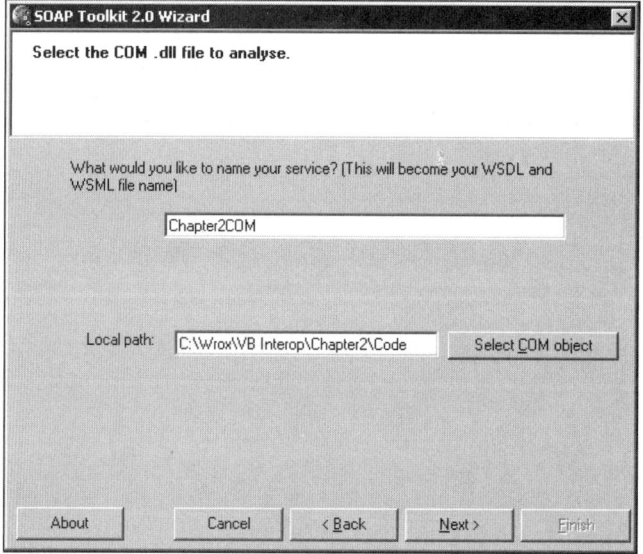

> Note that the COM component must be in a location accessible by IIS for our Web Service to work. This may or may not be in the `inetpub` directory tree – any directory will work as long as the security of the directory makes it available to IIS.

The next step in the process requires that we identify which classes and methods should be exposed for use by a SOAP client application. This allows us to expose only those methods that we choose. It also allows us to avoid exposing methods that return data types that are not supported by SOAP.

Remember that SOAP is a cross-platform, cross-language specification that only defines ways to format common data types. This means that on any given platform or programming language we will be likely to have data types that aren't defined within the SOAP specification. This is one of the drawbacks with any lowest-common denominator technology, as it precludes the use of many advanced features of any given platform or language.

Notice that both the `ISecondary` and `SimpleClass` interfaces are available. We can expose either or both of them as we choose. In our case, let's only expose the `SimpleClass` interface.

The `SimpleClass` interface has methods that return user-defined types and object references, neither of which will work with SOAP. Consequently, we need to uncheck `GetExternal`, `GetSimpleClass`, `GetObject`, and `GetComplex`:

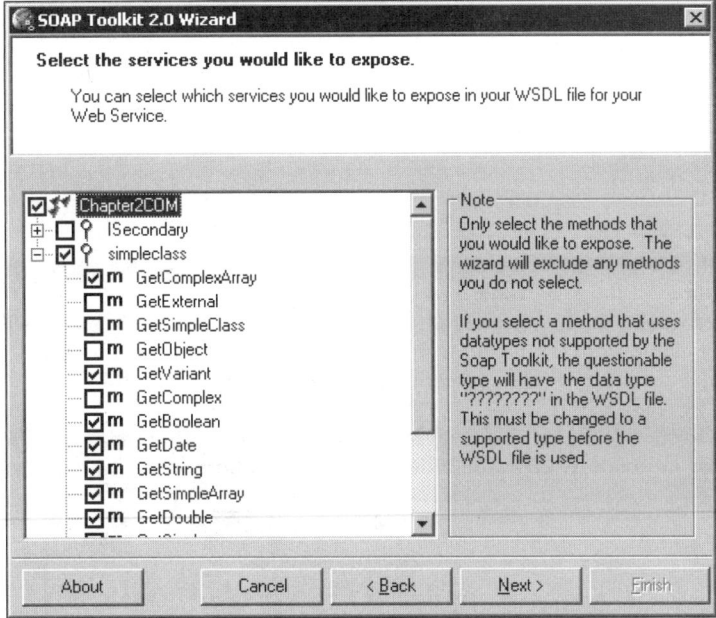

Technically, the wizard will run fine even if we leave these methods selected, but the resulting WSDL file will contain a set of question marks for each entry, requiring that we provide custom marshaling code to provide serialization to and from XML for these data types – something that is beyond the scope of this book.

The next page in the wizard asks us for the URI that will point to our Web Service. This is the web address that all clients will use when they access our service:

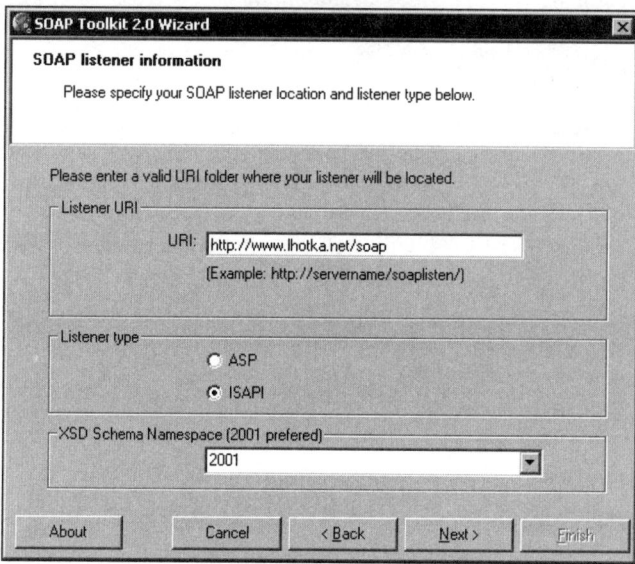

This address is stored in the WSDL file and it must point to a location that can be resolved by the client machine. In other words, if we use something like http://localhost/soap here, we will find that our Web Service is only available from the local machine – no other machines will be able to invoke our service since they'd resolve the address to themselves rather than to the real web server.

Finally, we need to specify the location where the Web Service definition files will be stored. To make the process as easy as possible, this should be the directory where we set up our virtual root:

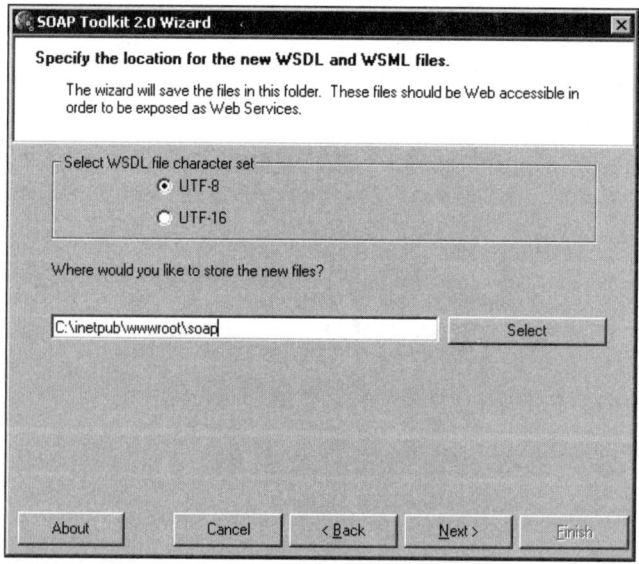

> *We're using the default character set of UTF-8. Unless our Web Service will be working with a lot of non-English data (such as data in Arabic or Asian languages) this is the best choice. If we'll be working with primarily non-English data then UTF-16 may be a better choice. See http://www.Unicode.org for more information on this topic.*

The wizard will now create the WSDL file along with a related WSML file in the directory we specified. Our Web Service is now ready for use.

Creating the .NET Client

Open the Visual Studio .NET IDE and create a new Windows Application named Chapter8NetClient. Add four labels and a button to the form:

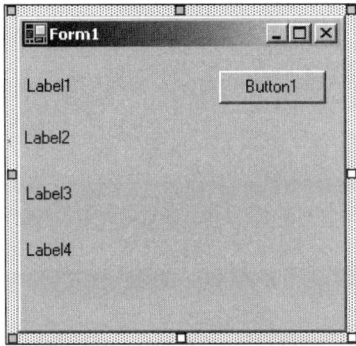

We'll set it up so that, when we click on the button, a series of methods will be called on our Web Service to populate the labels.

Before we can write code, we need to add a reference to the Web Service. This is done by choosing Project | Add Web Reference – just like we would if the Web Service had been written in .NET. Enter the URL of the virtual root where the Web Service files are located, followed by the name of the WSDL file:

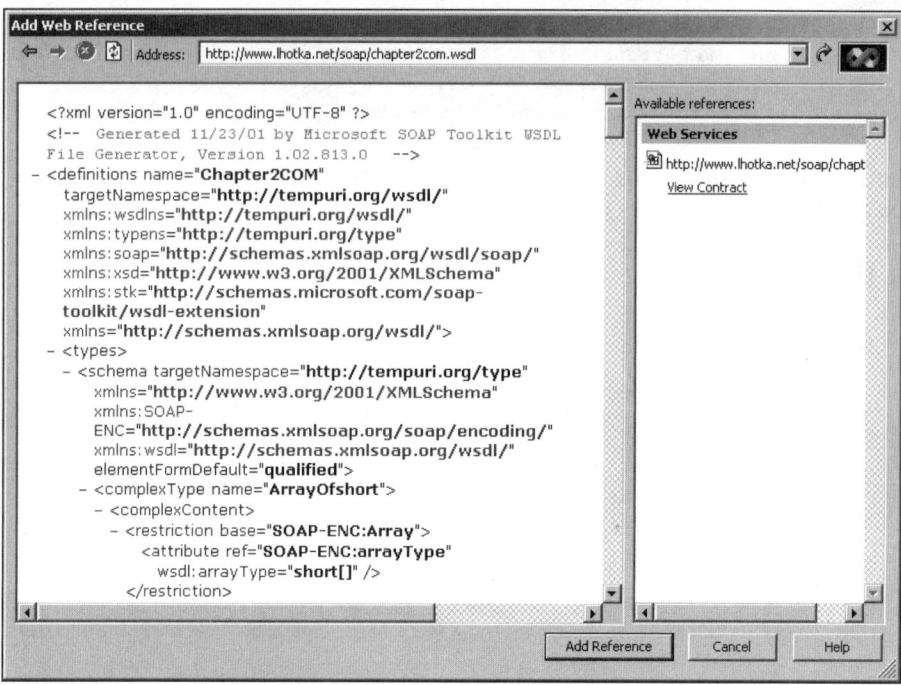

This will cause the WSDL file to be retrieved, telling Visual Studio .NET everything it needs to know in order to add a reference to the Web Service for use within our project. Click the **Add Reference** button to add the reference.

The reference is always added using the name of the web server that is hosting the service. Typically it is a good idea to rename the entry in the Solution Explorer to be something more descriptive. Click on the entry in the Solution Explorer and set the **Folder Name** property in the **Properties** window to **ch8**.

Now that we've added a reference to the Web Service, we can add our code. Double-click on the button to bring up the code window and enter the following:

```
Private Sub Button1_Click(ByVal sender As System.Object, _
    ByVal e As System.EventArgs) Handles Button1.Click

    Dim obj As New ch8.Chapter2COM()

    Label1.Text = obj.GetString
    Label2.Text = obj.GetDate
    Label3.Text = obj.GetVariant
    Dim ar() As Short = obj.GetSimpleArray
    Label4.Text = ar(0)
End Sub
```

At this point we can run the application. When the button is clicked, the application will invoke the Web Service to retrieve the information and populate the labels.

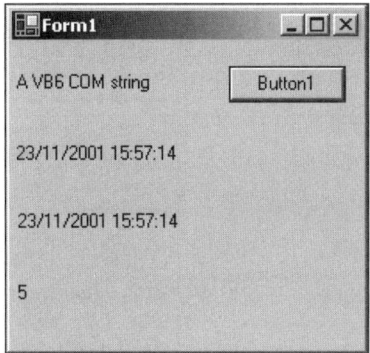

> **Note that the Web Service is invoked separately for *each method call*. This means that our code is invoking the Web Service four times.**

This technique allows us to easily invoke a COM component from a .NET application, but the cost is that each method call is a separate invocation, each one causing the creation of a new server-side object to do the work. Obviously, it is very important that our COM component be designed to minimize the number of method calls required to do any work, since there is a large amount of overhead in making each call via SOAP.

To minimize the overhead in this example, we could redesign the interface of our COM component to have a method that returns all four data elements as the result of a single method call. This would have the benefit of being much faster and more efficient, but there is the serious drawback of changing the COM component's interface.

We could also create a COM 'wrapper' object that is exposed via SOAP. That wrapper object could expose a method that returns all four data elements at once, but makes four individual calls to Chapter2COM behind the scenes. Since these four calls would happen through normal COM on the server they'd be very efficient. This technique gives us better performance and efficiency over SOAP, while avoiding any need to alter the interface of the original COM component.

Calling .NET from COM

SOAP and XML Web Services allow a .NET client to invoke a COM component. The reverse is also true – we can create a COM client in VB6 that invokes a .NET XML Web Service created in Visual Basic .NET. The process for doing this is similar to the work we just did, but several of the steps are simpler and more automated due to the Web Service support built into Visual Studio .NET.

Creating the XML Web Service

In Visual Studio .NET, create a new ASP.NET Web Service project named Chapter8Net:

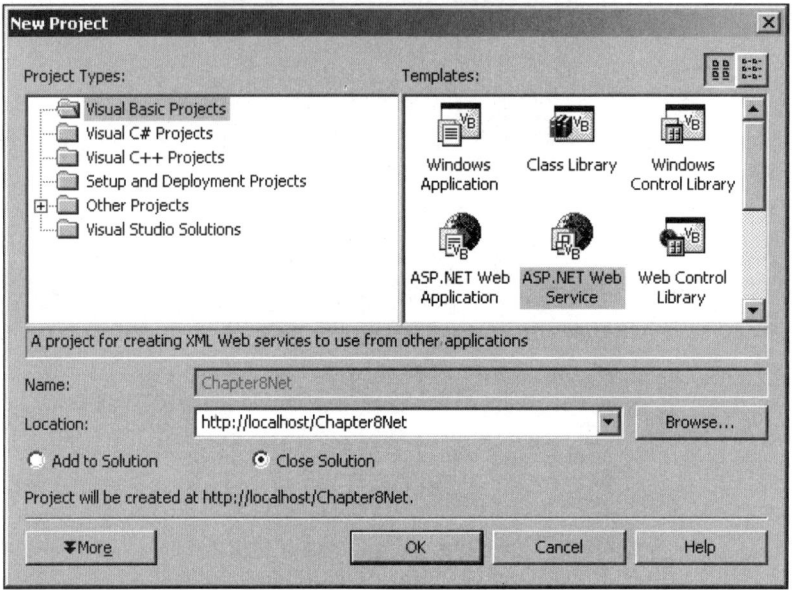

We will construct this Web Service to be similar in function to the .NET assembly we created in Chapter 2 – exposing a set of common data types that can be retrieved by the VB6 client.

Rename the Service1.asxm file to NETService.asmx using the Solution Explorer. Open the code window for this file and change the name of the class to NETService:

```
Imports System.Web.Services

<WebService(Namespace:="http://tempuri.org/")> _
Public Class NETService
    Inherits System.Web.Services.WebService
```

These changes mean that we are now creating an XML Web Service named Chapter8NET.NETService.

Add the following code to the class:

```
' Blittable types
<WebMethod()> _
Public Function GetByte() As Byte
    Return 65
End Function
```

```
<WebMethod()> _
Public Function GetShort() As Short
  Return 42
End Function

<WebMethod()> _
Public Function GetInteger() As Integer
  Return 4242
End Function

<WebMethod()> _
Public Function GetSingle() As Single
  Return 42.42
End Function

<WebMethod()> _
Public Function GetDouble() As Double
  Return 4242.4242
End Function

<WebMethod()> _
Public Function GetSimpleArray() As Short()
  Dim ar(5) As Short

  ar(0) = 5
  ar(1) = 4
  ar(2) = 3
  ar(3) = 2
  ar(4) = 1
  ar(5) = 0
  Return ar
End Function

' Non-blittable types
<WebMethod()> _
Public Function GetString() As String
  Return "A .NET string"
End Function

<WebMethod()> _
Public Function GetDate() As Date
  Return Now
End Function

<WebMethod()> _
Public Function GetBoolean() As Boolean
  Return False
End Function
```

This code can be copied from the SimpleClass.vb file we created in Chapter 2, as it is a subset of that code. Note that we are no longer attempting to return a few data types that were supported in Chapter 2 because they aren't supported by Web Services. The following methods have been removed:

```
GetObject
GetVariant
GetComplex
GetComplexArray
```

Now build the solution and we're all set. It's time to move on and build a VB6 client that can make use of this .NET service.

Creating the VB6 Client

To create a VB6 client application that makes use of the Web Service, we will utilize the SOAP Toolkit. Create a new VB6 Standard EXE project and then use the project properties window to change its name to Chapter8VB6Client.

Click on Project | References and add a reference to the Microsoft Soap Type Library:

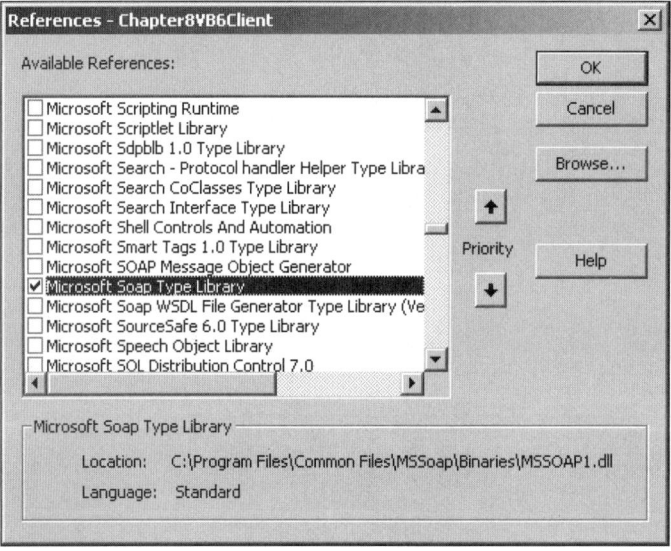

This library provides us with support for SOAP, allowing us to call Web Services from within our code. Of course this is all COM-based code, having nothing to do with .NET at all.

We can now add some labels and a button to the form:

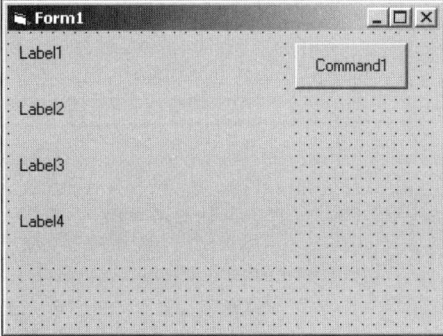

As in the .NET client, the button will invoke the Web Service methods to populate the Label controls. Double-click on the button to bring up the code window and enter the following:

```
Option Explicit

Private Sub Command1_Click()
   Dim obj As SoapClient
   Dim ar() As Integer

   Set obj = New SoapClient

   obj.mssoapinit "http://localhost/Chapter8NET/NETService.asmx?WSDL"

   Label1 = obj.GetString
   Label2 = obj.GetDate
   Label3 = obj.GetDouble
   ar = obj.GetSimpleArray
   Label4 = ar(0)

   Set obj = Nothing
End Sub
```

To invoke a Web Service using the SOAP Toolkit, we create an instance of a SoapClient object. This object will act as a proxy for the Web Service object itself, allowing us to call the server-side methods. In order to make the SoapClient object aware of the remote object, we call its mssoapinit method, passing it the URI to the WSDL that defines the Web Service:

```
obj.mssoapinit "http://localhost/Chapter8NET/NETService.asmx?WSDL"
```

In this example we are using a host name of localhost. You may need to change this to match the host name in your environment.

The interesting thing here is that there is no WSDL file on disk – instead the information is dynamically generated when our VB6 client invokes this URL. If we look in the directory where the Visual Basic .NET XML Web Service project was created we'll find a number of files, but no WSDL file. As we recall from creating a VB6 web service, the WSDL file contains XML that describes the web service. This same type of XML is created dynamically by .NET when our asmx file is invoked with the ?WSDL parameter as shown here.

Now that the `SoapClient` proxy object is initialized with information about the Web Service, we can call methods on it that correspond to the server object's methods.

In our Visual Basic .NET client we got IntelliSense support when writing code against the web service object. This is not the case in VB6, however, because the `SoapClient` object is invoked using late binding rather than early binding. It is not possible to call it using early binding, because its interface is generated dynamically at run time when the WSDL information is processed. This means that the `SoapClient` object doesn't know about the server object's methods at design time when we are writing our code. This has the unfortunate side effect of precluding IntelliSense as well, and so we must live without it when writing web service client applications in VB6.

Now save the project and run it. When the button is clicked, the .NET Web Service will be invoked to populate each `Label` control.

Note that our code goes across the network five times – once to get the WSDL data, and then once for each method call. Just like when calling from .NET to COM, it is very important that our Web Services be designed to minimize the number of method calls required to do any work, as each method call requires a separate call across the network and thus incurs a large amount of overhead.

> *Since our .NET client retrieved the WSDL information at design time, it didn't need to retrieve it at run time like the VB6 implementation. To avoid this extra call in our VB6 implementation, we could choose to manually retrieve and store a copy of the WSDL information at design time and then use that copy from within our program to initialize the `SoapClient` object. This would avoid a network call at run time, but prevents our application from dynamically updating the WSDL when the client is run.*

At this point, we've walked through the process of interoperating between .NET and COM bi-directionally by using XML Web Service and SOAP technology. This approach is nice because it leverages the open SOAP and XML standards, but it has the drawback of being somewhat slow – certainly slower than DCOM and also slower than the related .NET Remoting technology. Let's take a look at .NET Remoting from an interop perspective.

.NET Remoting and Interop

.NET Remoting is a faster and more feature-rich technology than XML Web Services. Remoting provides the ability to call methods across the network in a connectionless and stateless manner just like Web Services – including using a single TCP port, even port 80. However, Remoting also allows multiple method calls to the same server-side object, a feature unavailable with Web Services, but one that is supported today by DCOM. Because it supports both models – single call or multiple calls – Remoting is a more complete replacement for DCOM than Web Services.

Remoting also supports two types of data formatting, using SOAP and XML or using a proprietary binary format. The SOAP format serializes our data by following the XML format and thus is more open, but suffers from many of the same performance issues as Web Services. The binary format is proprietary to .NET, but is faster both in terms of serializing the data into the format and in terms of network bandwidth, since the binary data is smaller than the text-based XML data.

Finally, where Web Services require a web server to host the service objects, Remoting can optionally be hosted by an application of our own design – such a server is created with just a handful of lines of code. This means that we do not need IIS to host an object via Remoting, so we can host such objects on Windows 98, ME, or NT 4.0. However, if our server is a Windows 2000 machine, we can choose to use IIS as a Remoting host, saving us from having to write our own host application.

Remoting is often the obvious choice for .NET to .NET communication and is typically the obvious replacement for DCOM. However, it does not have the same focus on interoperability as Web Services and may not be as ideal when we need to interact with COM components. This is because we can't directly expose a COM component to a client application via Remoting. Neither can we create a COM client application that directly uses Remoting to invoke server-side .NET assemblies.

In order to use Remoting with COM components, we must create our own .NET wrapper class around any COM components to be invoked on the server. Likewise, if a COM client wishes to use Remoting to reach a .NET server-side object, we'll need to build our own .NET proxy object to run on the client. We'll explore each of these scenarios in the following sections.

Calling COM from .NET

Since a server-side COM object can't be directly exposed via Remoting, we need to wrap the COM object in a .NET object of our own design. This .NET object can then be exposed to the client through Remoting, as illustrated by the following diagram:

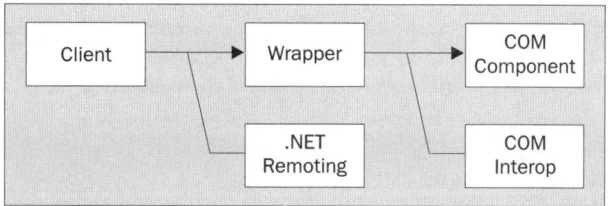

In Chapter 2, we discussed how COM interop services creates a wrapper (RCW) object through which our .NET code can invoke methods on a COM object. Unfortunately, that wrapper object can not be directly exposed via Remoting, which is why we must create our own wrapper object that, in turn, uses the RCW generated by COM interop services to invoke the COM component.

This doesn't require us to create a new RCW. In fact, from Chapter 2 we should still have our primary interop assembly that allows .NET client applications to interact with the COM component. All we are going to do here is create another .NET DLL that is a regular Class Library assembly. This new wrapper assembly can be exposed via Remoting because it is a normal .NET DLL. The trick is that behind the scenes it will delegate each method call to the COM component. We know that each of those method calls will actually go through the primary interop assembly as we discussed in Chapter 2, but this will be entirely transparent to anyone using this new .NET wrapper DLL.

To see how this works, we'll again use the Chapter2COM ActiveX DLL, along with its primary interop assembly, that we created in Chapter 2. This should already be installed and waiting for our use.

Creating the Wrapper Project

Creating a wrapper class is not difficult; unfortunately, it can be rather tedious. To be a wrapper, our class will need to create an instance of the real COM class, and then we will have to implement a method that corresponds to each method in the COM class. This is a technique known as **delegation**, since our wrapper class will delegate each method call to its underlying COM object.

For instance, if our COM object has a method named GetInteger, we would create the following code in our wrapper class:

```
Public Function GetInteger() As Short
   Return objCOMobject.GetInteger()
End Function
```

Notice how the method doesn't do any real work on its own – instead it delegates to the underlying COM object to do the work. Our wrapper class will be composed of a series of methods just like this – each one corresponding to a method from the COM object.

Open Visual Studio .NET and create a new Class Library project named Chapter8NetWrapper.

In order to interact with the COM component we'll need to reference it, so add a reference to the primary interop assembly we created for Chapter2COM.dll in Chapter 2. At this point we should be able to utilize the classes and methods contained in the COM component.

The wrapper class can expose any number of methods – so we can choose which specific methods or properties of the COM object we want to make available to any .NET client application. In the Class1.vb file, remove the template class code and add the following:

```
Public Class SimpleClass
   Inherits MarshalByRefObject

   Dim objCOM As New ch2com.SimpleClass()

   Public Function GetDate() As Date
      Return objCOM.GetDate
   End Function

   Public Function GetSimpleArray() As System.Array
      Return objCOM.GetSimpleArray
   End Function

   Public Function GetString() As String
      Return objCOM.GetString
   End Function

   Public Function GetVariant() As Object
      Return objCOM.GetVariant
   End Function
End Class
```

There are some key lines of code here. First off, notice that this class inherits from `MarshalByRefObject`.

```
Inherits MarshalByRefObject
```

This is critical for any server-side object that we'll be accessing via Remoting. By default, an object is not accessible over the network. In order to make an object available, we must either mark it as serializable so it can be passed by value, or inherit from `MarshalByRefObject` so it can be passed by reference. In our case, we want the object to run on the server with the client having a reference to that object. By inheriting from `MarshalByRefObject` we have indicated that our wrapper class should be passed by reference.

The next line of code creates an instance of the COM object that our client is trying to invoke.

```
Dim objCOM As New ch2com.SimpleClass()
```

Though we cannot make this RCW object directly available via Remoting, we *can* make our wrapper class available and it can, in turn, invoke methods on the COM object via the RCW.

The remainder of the code does exactly that – invoking specific methods on the underlying COM object and returning the results to the client. In this case, we've only implemented four of the methods available on the COM object. Obviously, we could just as easily create the code to delegate calls to all the methods of the underlying object.

> *One advantage to this approach is that our wrapper class could do more than merely delegate the calls. We could choose to have it add extra functionality or provide a friendlier interface to the underlying object if we so desire. This may make our application easier or faster to use when called from a client via Remoting.*

At this point, we have a .NET assembly that can be used by any .NET application in order to invoke methods on the underlying COM component. This assembly can be used just like any other .NET assembly – meaning it can be referenced directly by a .NET client application, or it can be invoked via .NET Remoting.

Hosting the Wrapper Assembly for Remoting

There are two ways we can choose to make the wrapper assembly available via Remoting. We can create our own Remoting host application that can run on any machine where the .NET runtime is installed. We can also choose to host the assembly within IIS, which requires that our machine be running IIS 5.0 or higher (available on Windows 2000 or higher). Let's take a look at both options.

Creating a .NET Remoting Host

Any .NET executable can act as a Remoting host. This includes Windows Applications, Console Applications, and Windows Service application types in Visual Studio .NET. The simplest application type is the console application, so we'll create our host application using that approach.

Add a new Console Application project to our solution by using the File | Add Project | New Project menu option. Name it Chapter8Host.

Add a reference to the `Chapter8NetWrapper` assembly by using the **Project | Add Reference** menu option and the **Projects** tab. By adding this reference, we are making not only the wrapper class available but, by extension, we are also making the underlying COM component available.

Also add a reference to the `System.Runtime.Remoting.dll` assembly from the **.NET** tab in the dialog:

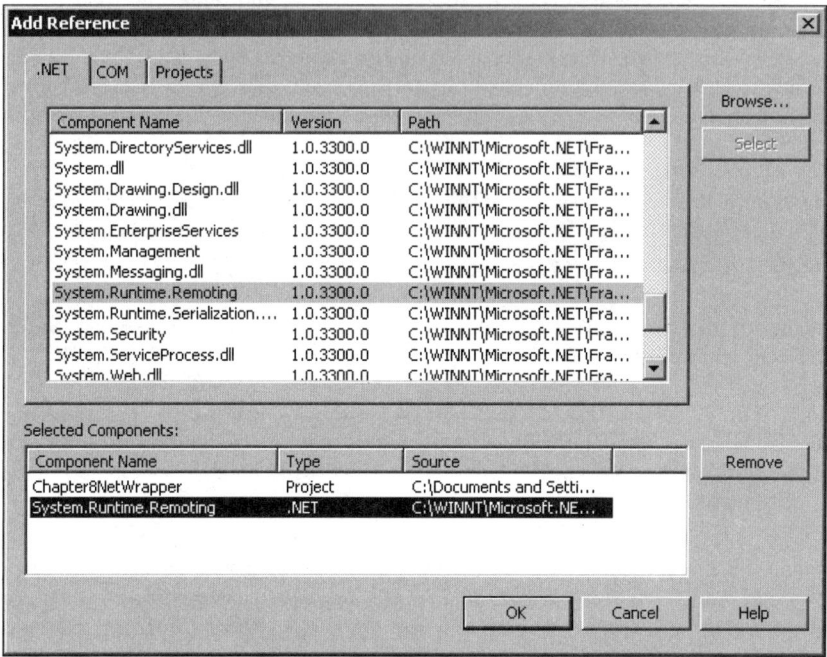

Now we are ready to configure .NET Remoting to expose the wrapper class to any client applications. The first step is to add a couple `Imports` statements to the top of our code module:

```
Imports System.Runtime.Remoting
Imports System.Runtime.Remoting.Channels
```

Then we can move on to add the lines of code to configure the channels to be used by the Remoting subsystem. A channel indicates whether the client can use raw TCP socket or HTTP communication formats, and also specifies the TCP port number on which our host will be listening for client requests:

```
Module Module1

  Sub Main()
    ChannelServices.RegisterChannel(New Tcp.TcpServerChannel(40000))
    ChannelServices.RegisterChannel(New Http.HttpServerChannel(40001))
  End Sub

End Module
```

In this case, the code specifies support for both TCP and HTTP communication, specifying a different port for each channel. This means that a client application can use port 40000 to invoke objects via a TCP socket, or 40001 to invoke objects via HTTP.

It is critically important that we choose a port number that is not already in use on our server. Here are some guidelines for choosing port numbers:

- ❏ 0-1023 are well-known ports reserved for specific applications such as web servers, mail servers, etc.

- ❏ 1024-49151 are registered ports that are reserved for various widely-used protocols such as DirectPlay

- ❏ 49152-65535 are intended for dynamic or private use – such as for applications that might be performing remoting with .NET

Now add the following code to register our wrapper class so that it is known to the Remoting subsystem, and will thus be exposed for use by client applications:

```
Sub Main()
    ChannelServices.RegisterChannel(New Tcp.TcpServerChannel(40000))
    ChannelServices.RegisterChannel(New Http.HttpServerChannel(40001))

    RemotingConfiguration.RegisterWellKnownServiceType( _
        GetType(Chapter8NetWrapper.SimpleClass), "SimpleClass.rem", _
        WellKnownObjectMode.SingleCall)
End Sub
```

The `RegisterWellKnownServiceType` method takes the type of the class to be exposed, the URI by which it can be accessed, and whether the object should be exposed such that a new instance is created for each method call (`SingleCall`) or a single instance of the object should be used for all method calls by all client applications (`Singleton`).

The second parameter, the URI, has the value `SimpleClass.rem` which is entirely arbitrary. It is important, in that this is part of the URL that the client will use to access our server, but there is nothing magic about the use of this particular text, or the `rem` extension. This is not true if we are hosting our DLL directly from within IIS – as then either a `rem` or `soap` extension is required. We're using the `rem` extension here to be consistent with the IIS requirement.

In the third parameter we are specifying that we want this object to use the `SingleCall` mode. `SingleCall` indicates that each method call will get a new and independent instance of the object to service that call. Whether the methods are called from a single client or many clients, each method call gets a whole new object all to itself. This mode is best for objects that don't hold a lot of data, which is the case for us.

Our other option is `Singleton`. In the `Singleton` mode, all method calls go to the same object. Even calls from different clients all go to the same object. A `Singleton` object is valuable when the object will hold a large amount of data, since that data can be reused for all the method calls rather than having to be loaded or created for each individual method call as would be the case with a `SingleCall` object.

A third option exists, called **Activation**. With `Activation` each client gets its own object, and all method calls from each client are handled by the object associated with that client. This is most similar to the way DCOM works today.

The URI we specified here, `SimpleClass.rem`, is combined with the host computer name and port number to invoke the object. In this case, we've just defined the following two URIs:

```
tcp://localhost:40000/SimpleClass.rem
http://localhost:40001/SimpleClass.rem
```

The last thing we need to do is add a line of code to keep the application running until we are ready to close it:

```
Sub Main()
  ChannelServices.RegisterChannel(New Tcp.TcpServerChannel(40000))
  ChannelServices.RegisterChannel(New Http.HttpServerChannel(40001))

  RemotingConfiguration.RegisterWellKnownServiceType( _
    GetType(Chapter8Wrapper.SimpleClass), "SimpleClass.rem", _
    WellKnownObjectMode.SingleCall)

  Console.Read()
End Sub
```

The Remoting subsystem works in the background, meaning that our application's code continues to run. If we don't do something to keep our application running, it will simply terminate – meaning that it won't be listening for client requests. The `Console.Read` method waits until the user presses the *Enter* key, so our application will remain alive until we press enter in the console window.

In a production environment we'd almost certainly build our Remoting host as a Windows Service. This would cause it to run in the background on the server even when no user was logged into the computer at all. Microsoft SQL Server and IIS are examples of Windows Service applications that always run as long as the computer is running – and this is the kind of thing we'd want for a Remoting host application as well. In this case we've implemented it as a simple Console Application for simplicity.

To listen for client requests, simply open a command window, navigate to the `bin` directory that contains the EXE, and run the application.

Hosting via IIS

Instead of creating our own host application, IIS can be used to host an assembly for Remoting. This can be done in either an ASP.NET Web Forms application or an ASP.NET Web Service application. We need to do is make the DLL available to the web application or web service and add a section to web.config file to configure the Remoting subsystem appropriately.

Add a new ASP.NET Web Service application to the solution using the File | Add Project | New Project menu option, hosted at http://localhost/Chapter8Remote.

Next add a reference to the Chapter8NetWrapper assembly by using the Project | Add Reference menu option and the Projects tab. Again, by adding this reference, we are not only making the wrapper class available but, by extension, we are also making the underlying COM component available.

All we need to do now is configure the Remoting subsystem. This is done by adding some lines to the `web.config` file:

```xml
<?xml version="1.0" encoding="utf-8" ?>
<configuration>
  <system.runtime.remoting>
    <application>
     <service>
       <wellknown mode="SingleCall" objectUri="SimpleClass.rem
       type="Chapter8NetWrapper.SimpleClass, Chapter8NetWrapper"  />
     </service>
    </application>
  </system.runtime.remoting>

    <system.web>
```

With our own custom host we were able to define both TCP and HTTP channels. When hosting in IIS only the HTTP channel is available for use. Notice that we don't specify the port number on which we'll listen – that is handled by IIS and is 80 by default.

Other port numbers can be used. To change the port number, change the configuration of the web server by using the Internet Services Manager administrative tool. If the port number is changed on the server, obviously our client code will need to be changed to use the same port.

There is also a <wellknown> node which defines the class to be made available – `Chapter8NetWrapper.SimpleClass`. It also defines that the class is available in `SingleCall` mode, though we could also specify `Singleton`, and it defines the URI to be used when accessing the class.

The result is that we've defined the following URI:

```
http://localhost/Chapter8Remote/SimpleClass.rem
```

Build the project to complete the process. Our `Chapter8NetWrapper` project is now exposed via Remoting and can be called by client applications.

Creating a Remoting Client

A Remoting client is relatively easy to create. Any .NET application can be a Remoting client. All we need to do is configure the Remoting subsystem before attempting to invoke a remote object.

Supporting Client Initialization

For a client application to use Remoting, it must be configured by registering the remote class with the Remoting subsystem and by linking it to a URI where it can be found. This code can be included directly in the client application, or it can be included in our wrapper project to consolidate the Remoting code away from the client application.

Open the `Chapter8NetWrapper` project and add a new class named `Client`. Add the following code to this class:

```
Imports System.Runtime.Remoting

Public Class Client
    Public Shared Sub InitRemoting()
        Dim wt As WellKnownClientTypeEntry = _
            RemotingConfiguration.IsWellKnownClientType( _
            GetType(Chapter8NetWrapper.SimpleClass))
        If wt Is Nothing Then
            RemotingConfiguration.RegisterWellKnownClientType( _
                GetType(Chapter8NetWrapper.SimpleClass), _
                "tcp://localhost:40000/SimpleClass.rem")
        End If
    End Sub
End Class
```

This class contains a single shared method that can be called by the client to initialize the Remoting subsystem by registering the `SimpleClass` type and associating it with a specific URI where the server code will be running.

It also checks to see if the class is already registered as a remote class – in which case we don't reconfigure Remoting, as that would result in a run-time error. Using the `IsWellKnownClientType`, we can easily determine whether the class has already been configured for Remoting.

Notice that we aren't configuring a channel but, instead, we're just registering the `SimpleClass` type for use by our client. The channel is implied in the URI that is specified in the method call – in this case we're specifying the TCP channel for our custom host application.

We could also opt to use the HTTP channel if we desired. To do this we'd simply change the URI to use HTTP instead of TCP. The client must choose one or the other for each object – a given object can't be bound to both at the same time. However, we could have one object being referenced via TCP and another remote object referenced via HTTP if we so desired – though it is difficult to see how this would make sense.

Though the `Chapter8NetWrapper` assembly now contains both `SimpleClass` and `Client`, it is important to note that we are only configuring the Remoting subsystem to invoke `SimpleClass` remotely. We can pick and choose which classes in our DLL should be invoked remotely and which should be invoked locally by only configuring Remoting for those classes that should run on the server.

If the Remoting host is IIS instead of the custom application we need to use the URI that points to the IIS host instead of the custom host. To do this, use the following code instead:

```
Imports System.Runtime.Remoting

Public Class Client
    Public Shared Sub InitRemoting()
        Dim wt As WellKnownClientTypeEntry = _
            RemotingConfiguration.IsWellKnownClientType( _
            GetType(Chapter8NetWrapper.SimpleClass))
        If wt Is Nothing Then
```

```
        RemotingConfiguration.RegisterWellKnownClientType( _
          GetType(Chapter8NetWrapper.SimpleClass), _
          "http://localhost/Chapter8Remote/SimpleClass.rem")
      End If
    End Sub
End Class
```

By configuring Remoting, we have told the .NET runtime that any attempt to create an instance of `Chapter8NetWrapper.SimpleClass` should cause the Remoting subsystem to kick in to handle the request. This means that we can write our code to use this class just as we normally would, and .NET will transparently make sure it is invoked across the network.

Creating the Client Application

Create a new Windows Application project in Visual Studio .NET and name it Chapter8Client. Add four labels and one button to the form, as shown:

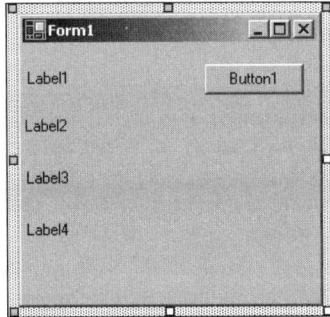

In order to access the type information about the wrapper class, we need to add a reference to the `Chapter8NetWrapper` project.

Even though `Chapter8NetWrapper.SimpleClass` will be running on the server, the client needs a reference to the DLL to get type information about the class. Additionally, this DLL contains our `Client` class, which we will directly be using *on the client* machine.

This can be confusing, so let's be clear. Though the DLL contains both `SimpleClass` and `Client`, they will run on different machines. We'll use the `Client` class directly from our client application – on the client workstation. The `SimpleClass` object will exist on the *server* and will be accessed via Remoting.

We can then use our new `Client` class from `Chapter8NetWrapper` to initialize the Remoting subsystem within our client. This can only be done once and so it is best handled in the form's `Load` event:

```
    Private Sub Form1_Load(ByVal sender As System.Object, _
      ByVal e As System.EventArgs) Handles MyBase.Load

    Chapter8NetWrapper.Client.InitRemoting()

    End Sub
```

This initializes the Remoting subsystem and tells the .NET runtime to automatically direct any calls to `SimpleClass` to the appropriate server by using the URI we specified in the `Client` class.

Now add code behind the button to invoke the object and populate the label controls:

```
Private Sub Button1_Click(ByVal sender As System.Object, _
   ByVal e As System.EventArgs) Handles Button1.Click

   Dim obj As New Chapter8NetWrapper.SimpleClass()

   Label1.Text = obj.GetString
   Label2.Text = obj.GetDate
   Label3.Text = obj.GetVariant
   Dim ar() As Short = obj.GetSimpleArray
   Label4.Text = ar(0)
End Sub
```

Since Remoting transparently handles the remote invocation of the object, our code here is no different from that if we were invoking the `SimpleClass` object locally.

> *Since `SimpleClass` is set up on the server for `SingleCall` mode, each method call in our code will result in a separate instance of the remote object being created – the same behavior we had with Web Services earlier in this chapter. We could have marked the server-side object as `Singleton` mode to avoid this or we could use `Activation`, which would mean that each client would have a long-lived instance of the object on the server for its own use – just like we have in DCOM.*

Run the application and click the button to invoke the remote COM object. If using a custom host, make sure that the host application is running before clicking the button, otherwise the host won't be listening for the client requests.

Calling .NET from COM

We may want to use .NET Remoting to allow a VB6 client application to invoke a server-side object. This is attractive because it allows a VB6 application to gain the benefits of Remoting – getting DCOM-like capabilities over a simple IP port, and thus moving easily through firewalls. While we could also use SOAP to achieve a similar effect, Remoting can often provide better performance and gives us more options for how we interact with the server-side object.

Unfortunately, there is no direct support for using .NET Remoting from a VB6 client application. In order to make use of the technology, we need to create a .NET assembly that can run on the client workstation and then use COM interop to invoke that client-side proxy assembly from VB6. This is illustrated in the following diagram:

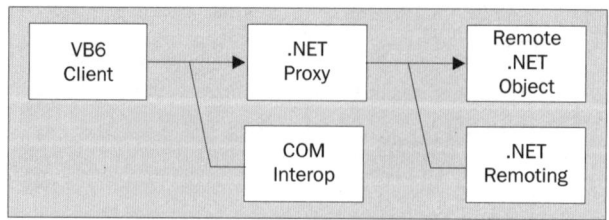

Both the VB6 client application and the .NET proxy object will run on the client workstation, with the server-side object being accessed via .NET Remoting. The drawback to this approach is that both the .NET runtime and a proxy DLL must be installed on the client workstation, but the advantage is that the VB6 client application gains the ability to use .NET Remoting.

It is important to realize the amount of complexity we're introducing here just to give VB6 access to Remoting. This approach may not be appropriate in all cases, so it is important to test carefully and evaluate the overhead for your particular situation. The client machine not only runs the VB6 client, but also a .NET proxy object and the .NET runtime. The .NET proxy object on the client uses Remoting to invoke .NET objects running on the server. By the time we've gone to the work of installing the .NET runtime and our .NET proxy object on the client workstation it is valid to question why we didn't simply rewrite the VB6 client application into Visual Basic .NET – thus avoiding the COM Interop overhead of calling from VB6 into the .NET proxy object.

Though great caution and serious thought should go into the application design before using this technique, we'll walk through it to see how it all works.

To start, we'll create a VB6 client application that makes use of the `Chapter8NetWrapper.SimpleClass` object that we created in the previous section. This is about as complex as we can get, since we are going from a VB6 COM client to a .NET proxy object, through .NET Remoting to a .NET server-side object that then invokes a server-side COM object. Whew!

The `Chapter8NetWrapper` class is already set up and ready for use by any .NET Remoting client, so all we need to do is build a client application.

Creating the .NET Proxy

The proxy assembly will be a regular .NET DLL, and will be constructed much like the .NET wrapper class we built to encapsulate the COM component in the previous section. The wrapper class will need to expose any methods that we want the VB6 client to use, and it will need to be made available to VB6 through COM Interop as we discussed in Chapter 3.

Create a new Class Library project in Visual Studio .NET and name it Chapter8Proxy.

Add a reference to the `Chapter8NetWrapper` class so we can make use of the remote class, just as we did with our `Chapter8Client` application earlier. Then change the name of `Class1` to `RemotingProxy` and add the following code:

```
<ComClass()> _
Public Class RemotingProxy
  Dim objRem As Chapter8NetWrapper.SimpleClass

  Public Sub New()
    Chapter8NetWrapper.Client.InitRemoting()
    objRem = New Chapter8NetWrapper.SimpleClass()
  End Sub
End Class
```

As in Chapter 2, we are making use of the `<ComClass()>` attribute to indicate that we want this class exposed for use by COM clients such as VB6. The code also declares a variable to hold a reference to the remote object and a constructor method that initializes Remoting and creates an instance of the remote object.

Of course, it doesn't really create an instance. As we know, `SimpleClass` is marked for `SingleCall` mode, so an instance will be created and destroyed for each method call.

Now add the code to implement the methods we want available for use by the VB6 client application. In this case, we'll implement only those methods that we made available on the server-side wrapper class earlier in the chapter. Obviously, we could implement any methods that are available on the server-side object as needed, including adding new methods that may provide valuable functionality to our client application:

```
<ComClass()> _
Public Class RemotingProxy
  Dim objRem As Chapter8NetWrapper.SimpleClass

  Public Sub New()
    Chapter8NetWrapper.Client.InitRemoting()
    objRem = New Chapter8NetWrapper.SimpleClass()
  End Sub

  Public Function GetDate() As Date
    Return objRem.GetDate
  End Function

  Public Function GetSimpleArray() As Short()
    Return objRem.GetSimpleArray
  End Function

  Public Function GetString() As String
    Return objRem.GetString
  End Function

  Public Function GetVariant() As Object
    Return objRem.GetVariant
  End Function
End Class
```

The final thing we need to do is bring up the project's properties dialog and check the **Register for COM Interop** option:

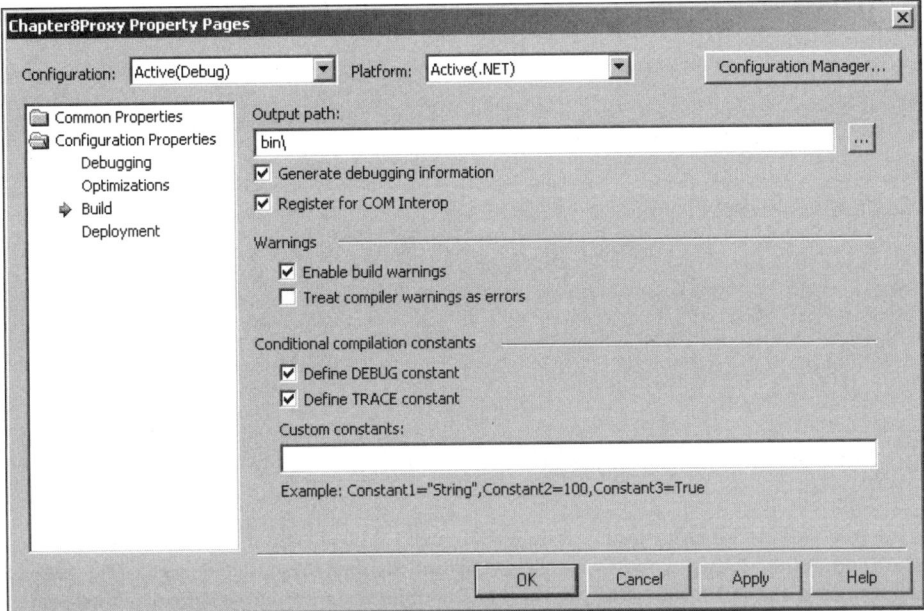

Now build the project to create the DLL and we are ready to move on to build a VB6 client application that utilizes this proxy class in order to tap into the power of Remoting.

Creating the VB6 Client

At this point we have the server-side COM object, `Chapter2COM`. We have the server-side wrapper that we created to make it available via Remoting, `Chapter8NetWrapper`. We now have a client-side proxy that can be called by a VB6 application that will use Remoting to call the server-side objects, `Chapter8Proxy`. All that remains is to create a new VB6 client application that makes use of this new client-side proxy object.

Open the VB6 IDE and create a new Standard EXE project. Use the project's properties dialog to set the name to Chapter8VB6Client2. Also bring up the project's references dialog and add a reference to `Chapter8Proxy`. It should be listed as a regular COM component in the references dialog.

As we saw in Chapter 3, this will make the .NET assembly available for our use within VB6. Now – as usual – add four labels and a command button control to the form:

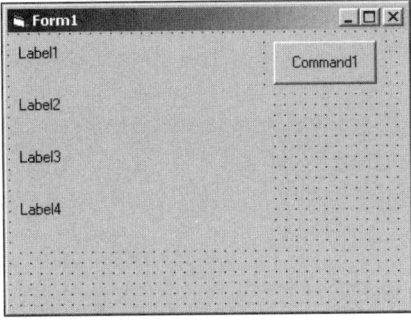

At this point, we're ready to write some code. Double-click on the button to bring up the code window and add the following code:

```
Option Explicit

Private Sub Command1_Click()
   Dim ar() As Integer
   Dim obj As Chapter8Proxy.RemotingProxy
   Set obj = New Chapter8Proxy.RemotingProxy

   Label1 = obj.GetString
   Label2 = obj.GetDate
   Label3 = obj.GetVariant
   ar = obj.GetSimpleArray
   Label4 = ar(0)

   Set obj = Nothing
End Sub
```

First we declare and create an instance of the .NET proxy object, which automatically invokes the constructor code in the RemotingProxy class. This means that the code we wrote to initialize .NET Remoting and to create an instance of the server-side object is automatically run at this point.

With the object created, we can simply call the methods on the object to populate the label controls on our form.

Though it requires extra work to create the proxy object that runs on the client machine along with the VB6 application, this technique does provide a form of support that allows VB6 to take advantage of .NET Remoting.

Summary

If we view COM and .NET as two different platforms, we can look at interoperability between the two as an exercise in cross-platform communication. XML and SOAP can be used as a very effective mechanism for cross-platform communication and so it is no surprise that they can be used to interoperate effectively between the .NET and COM platforms.

SOAP provides us with a powerful technology that enables easy communication across the network between VB6 and Visual Basic .NET applications and components in a bi-directional manner. Since SOAP is an open standard, this same technique can be used to communicate with other platforms and other programming languages in the same way.

SOAP support is built into .NET and so it is very easy to create client applications in Visual Basic .NET that call SOAP services, and it is equally easy to create SOAP services by simply creating an XML Web Service project.

In VB6 the story is a bit different, since there SOAP is an add-on that comes via the SOAP Toolkit. This freely downloadable add-on gives VB6 the ability to create SOAP services that can be consumed by clients – including Visual Basic .NET. It also gives VB6 client applications the ability to invoke methods exposed by SOAP services, including .NET XML Web Services.

Because of the support built into .NET and easily added to VB6, using SOAP and Web Services for interoperability is relatively straightforward and can be quickly implemented.

As powerful as SOAP and XML Web Services are, they are not as flexible or fast as DCOM, and so we may want to also consider the use of .NET Remoting. Remoting is a more obvious replacement for DCOM, but it doesn't offer the same cross-platform simplicity as SOAP.

.NET Remoting uses simple TCP or HTTP socket-level communication, and so it works very well over the Internet, just like Web Services. However, Remoting can use a binary protocol for moving the data over the network and thus can be much faster and more efficient than using XML. Remoting also provides advanced features such as the ability to pass objects across the network by value as well as by reference, and it does not require IIS 5.0, so any machine with the .NET runtime can act as a Remoting server.

Unfortunately, neither COM nor VB6 have any native support for Remoting. To expose a COM component for use by a Remoting client requires that we create a wrapper assembly on the server that delegates each method call that comes in through Remoting to the underlying COM component. While not difficult to create, this is tedious code to write.

For a COM client to use Remoting is even trickier. For this to happen, we need to create a .NET DLL that runs *on the client*. This client-side proxy is exposed to the COM clients through regular COM Interop, and then it uses Remoting to communicate with the server-side objects. By the time we've gone through all this work, it is worth wondering if the client application itself shouldn't be written using Visual Basic .NET.

In this chapter, we have explored all these concepts – SOAP and XML Web Services and the various wrapper techniques that we can use to make Remoting work with COM components and applications. With this knowledge we should be ready not only to interoperate between COM and .NET, but to do it across the network or even the Internet.

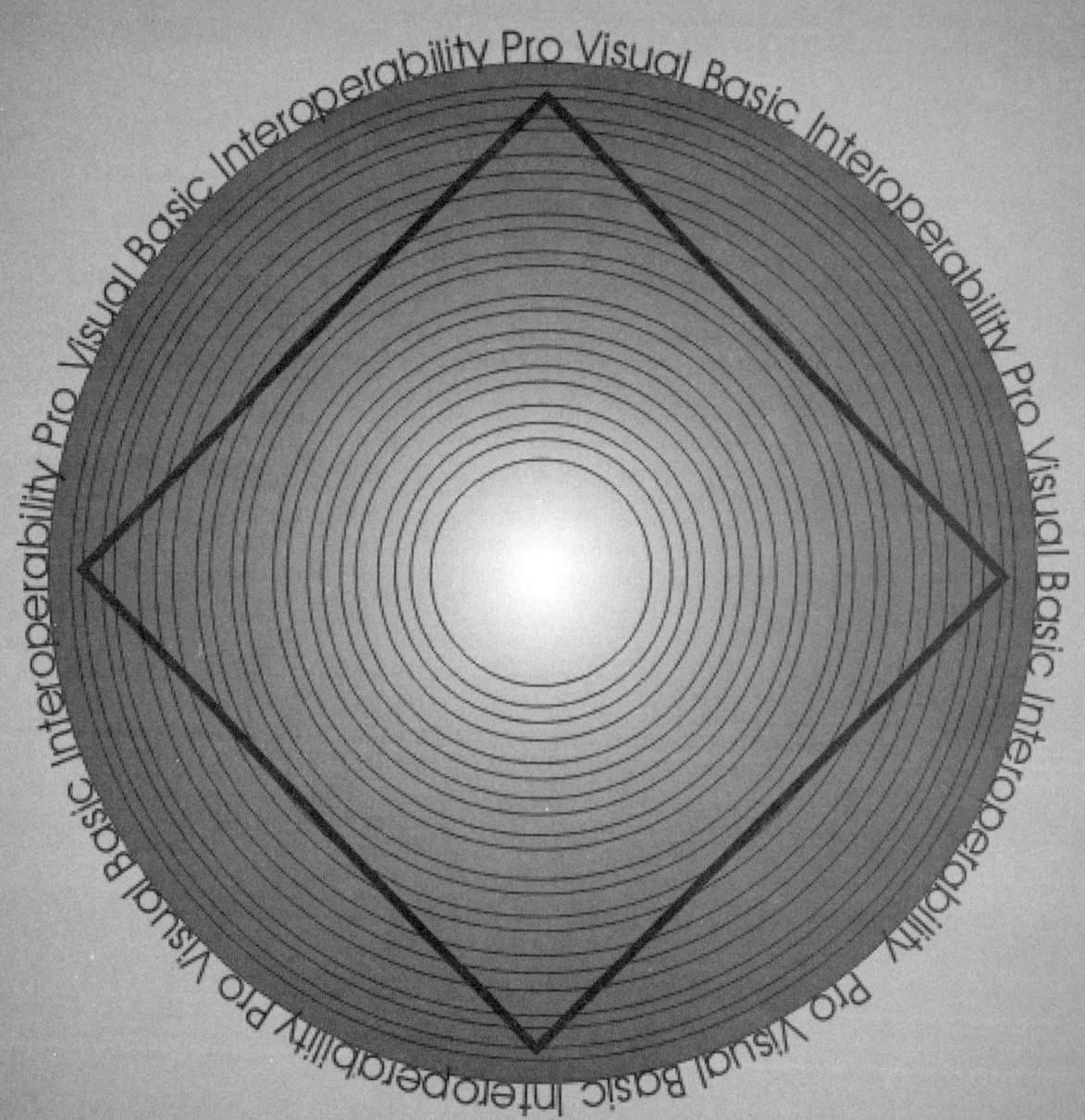

Sharing Configuration Information

For programs to interoperate, it is often necessary for them to share configuration information. For example, the information needed to establish a connection to a database may need to be used by both older VB6 programs and new Visual Basic .NET programs.

There are three common techniques for storing configuration information in VB programs. They are:

- ❑ Private INI files
- ❑ The Windows Registry
- ❑ XML-based configuration files

Of course, it is possible to store configuration information in any location that provides a permanent data store, such as a database. However, configuration information is often customized to a particular user or client machine, and so it is common for it to be local.

Until three years ago, the first two methods predominated. Each has advantages. Private INI files are easy to change with a text editor, and can be located in an application's directory. The Registry has the advantage of centralization, making it easy to back up or find configuration information for many different applications. Both have been used for a number of years. INI files go back to the early versions of Windows, and the Registry was introduced with Windows 95.

More recently, some development teams have shifted to using configuration files with an XML format. These are often used to replace INI files because they have the same advantages, but eliminate one key disadvantage: INI files cannot store any hierarchical data. For example, if you would like to include the names of several reports that the user accesses, but the actual number varies from user to user, an INI file would typically hold the information like this:

```
[Reports]
Report1=AccountsReceivableByClient
Report2=AccountsReceivableByDate
Report3=RecentPayments
Report4=NewCustomers
```

This requires extra logic to parse, because it is necessary to embed a number in the key for the report name (Report1, Report2, etc.). An XML-based configuration can represent this information much more cleanly. A section of an XML file to represent the reports above might look like this:

```
<Reports>
    <Report>AccountsReceivableByClient</Report>
    <Report>AccountsReceivableByDate</Report>
    <Report>RecentPayments</Report>
    <Report>NewCustomers</Report>
</Reports>
```

It would also be possible to store information for each report in a hierarchical fashion with XML. These advantages, plus the fact that the standard XML format is easily accessible in several ways, are encouraging many development shops to move to XML configuration files.

Any of these configuration stores can be shared between VB6 and Visual Basic .NET. This chapter covers the techniques to access each of these types of configuration stores from both languages.

Private INI Files

The standard INI file format was created for use in early versions of Windows. Those of us who used Windows 3.0 and 3.1 will recall the need to manually edit Win.INI and System.INI, which were two of Windows' main configuration files. (Most of the information in these files was moved to the Windows Registry starting with Windows 95.)

The Windows API includes the capability to read and write information in the INI format, so it became common for the format to be used to store application configuration information. The most typical scenario is that an application includes an INI file in its own application directory to hold configuration information specific to that application.

The Structure of an INI File

In case you are not familiar with how INI files work, here is a quick overview. Information is stored in sections, with the name of each section shown in square brackets at the top of the section. Then the information in a section is stored in the form of key-value pairs (sometimes called name-value pairs). A key is just a string that describes the information, such as MaxPages, which might be the maximum number of pages that a user can print for a report (to keep them from starting up 5000 page reports by accident). The value would be an appropriate number, such as 100.

Here is a typical example of information in an INI file:

```
[UserInfo]
MaxPages=100
LastReportRun=NewCustomers

[Config]
ProgramsDir=C:\MyApp\Programs
HelpDir=C:\MyApp\Help
DataDir=C:\Programs\Data

[Reports]
Report1=AccountsReceivableByClient
Report2=AccountsReceivableByDate
Report3=RecentPayments
Report4=NewCustomers
```

Naturally, the information in these files can be inserted with a text editor, and the information can be read or written with typical flat file access using techniques such as those discussed in Chapter 10. However, the easiest and best way to get information into and out of INI files is by using the Windows API, which has two functions called `GetPrivateProfileString` and `WritePrivateProfileString` to do the work. We will now turn to using those functions in both VB6 and Visual Basic .NET. (By the way, there are similar functions for working specifically with the WIN.INI file. They are called `GetProfileString` and `WriteProfileString`. If you understand the following section, it's easy to translate the examples to use `GetProfileString` and `WriteProfileString` instead.)

Accessing INI Files in VB6

Manipulating private INI files from VB6 requires you to declare the two API functions needed (`GetPrivateProfileString` and `WritePrivateProfileString`). The arguments for these functions are mostly self-explanatory, but there are a couple that are not obvious, so let's take a quick look at the arguments for each function. The argument names used are those that are included when the API Text Viewer is used in VB6 to create the Declare statement.

Argument for `GetPrivateProfileString`	Description
`lpApplicationName`	The section in the INI file.
`lpKeyName`	The key for the key-value pair desired.
`lpDefault`	A substitute to use for the return value for the key-value pair if the pair is not present in the INI file.
`lpReturnedString`	The value for the key-value pair.
`nSize`	The length of the buffer being passed in to hold the value. This is normally the length of the variable for `lpReturnedString` before the API call is made.
`lpFileName`	The name of the INI file.

Table continued on following page

Argument for GetPrivateProfileString	Description
lpApplicationName	The section in the INI file.
lpKeyName	The key for the key-value pair to be written.
lpString	The value to write for the key-value pair.
lpFileName	The name of the INI file.

It's also necessary to do a bit of extra work to handle the value returned by GetPrivateProfileString. The extra work is to compensate for the fact that Windows API functions do not handle VB variable length strings very well. API functions work with C++ style strings, and GetPrivateProfileString cannot place the returned string value in a standard VB string. The solution is to pass a fixed-length string as the argument to hold the returned value. GetPrivateProfileString can work with that, and it will place the value in the string followed by an ASCII zero, which serves as the terminator of the string. All that's necessary back in VB6 is to examine the fixed length string and strip out the characters before the ASCII zero as the returned value.

Here is the code that writes to and reads from an INI file using API functions, in VB6. The code should be placed in a BAS module to use it.

```
' declares to read/write INI files
Declare Function WritePrivateProfileString Lib "kernel32" _
            Alias "WritePrivateProfileStringA" _
            (ByVal lpApplicationName As String, _
            ByVal lpKeyName As Any, _
            ByVal lpString As Any, _
            ByVal lpFileName As String) As Long

Declare Function GetPrivateProfileString Lib "kernel32" _
            Alias "GetPrivateProfileStringA" _
            (ByVal lpApplicationName As String, _
            ByVal lpKeyName As Any, _
            ByVal lpDefault As String, _
            ByVal lpReturnedString As String, _
            ByVal nSize As Long, _
            ByVal lpFileName As String) As Long

Public Function GetINIEntry(sSection As String, sEntry As String, _
            sDefault As String, sINIFile As String) As String

Dim sValue As String
Dim sReturnedValue As String * 128
Dim nReturnCode As Long
Dim nSize As Integer

' Assume a max size of 128 (length of sReturnedValue declared above)
nSize = 128
nReturnCode = GetPrivateProfileString(sSection, sEntry, sDefault, _
                            sReturnedValue, nSize, sINIFile)
' Look for the ASCII zero that terminates the string, and
' get everything to the left of it.
```

```
Dim nPos As Integer
nPos = InStr(sReturnedValue, Chr$(0))
If nPos <> 0 Then
    sValue = Left$(sReturnedValue, nPos - 1)
Else
    sValue = ""
End If
GetINIEntry = sValue
End Function

Public Sub WriteINIEntry(sSection As String, sEntry As String, sValue As String,
sINIFile As String)

Dim nReturnCode As Integer
nReturnCode = WritePrivateProfileString(sSection, sEntry, sValue, sINIFile)

End Sub
```

For simplicity, this code leaves out error handling and validation of the input parameters. None of the input parameters to either of the functions should be blank, for example, except for sDefault in GetINIEntry, which can be an empty string. You could also examine the return value of the API functions to check for errors.

You can test this code with the following code behind a button in a VB6 form:

```
WriteINIEntry "MySection", "MyFirstEntry", _
        "Value for the first entry", "C:\test.ini"
WriteINIEntry "MySection", "MySecondEntry", _
        "Value for the second entry", "C:\test.ini"

Dim sValue As String
sValue = GetINIEntry("MySection", "MySecondEntry", _
                    "Default value", "C:\test.ini")
MsgBox sValue
```

You do not have to create the test.ini file before running this code. The API function WriteINIEntry is smart enough to create the file if it does not exist, and to insert a new section into the file if does exist.

After running the above code, the INI file will look like this:

```
[MySection]
MyFirstEntry=Value for the first entry
MySecondEntry=Value for the second entry
```

The message box displayed by the last line will look like this:

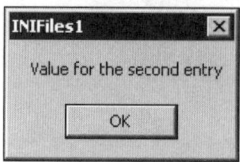

Notice that all values for key-value pairs in INI files are manipulated as strings. The API functions only return string representations. If the values are supposed to represent anything besides strings, it is the responsibility of the calling code to translate the types as necessary.

Accessing INI Files in Visual Basic .NET

Performing equivalent operations in Visual Basic .NET is easier in some ways, and slightly more complex in others. The Declare statements have to be more complex for the data marshaling to be done correctly, and a StringBuilder has to be used to contain the value returned from GetPrivateProfileString. However, once that is done, the rest of the data marshaling is automatic, so there is no need to worry about the ASCII zero delimiter.

Here is the equivalent code to the previous VB6 example, done in Visual Basic .NET. As with the VB6 code, this version of the code is for a BAS module.

```
Imports System.Text
Imports System.Runtime.InteropServices

Module INIFiles
    ' API declares to read/write INI files
    Declare Auto Function WritePrivateProfileString Lib "kernel32" _
                Alias "WritePrivateProfileStringA" _
 (<MarshalAs(UnmanagedType.LPStr)> ByVal lpApplicationName As String, _
  <MarshalAs(UnmanagedType.LPStr)> ByVal lpKeyName As String, _
  <MarshalAs(UnmanagedType.LPStr)> ByVal lpString As String, _
  <MarshalAs(UnmanagedType.LPStr)> ByVal lpFileName As String) As Integer

    Declare Auto Function GetPrivateProfileString Lib "kernel32" _
                Alias "GetPrivateProfileStringA" _
 (<MarshalAs(UnmanagedType.LPStr)> ByVal lpApplicationName As String, _
  <MarshalAs(UnmanagedType.LPStr)> ByVal lpKeyName As String, _
  <MarshalAs(UnmanagedType.LPStr)> ByVal lpDefault As String, _
  <MarshalAs(UnmanagedType.LPStr)> ByVal lpReturnedString _
  As StringBuilder, _
  ByVal nSize As Integer, _
  <MarshalAs(UnmanagedType.LPStr)> ByVal lpFileName As String) As Integer

    Public Function GetINIEntry(ByVal sSection As String, _
                        ByVal sEntry As String, _
                        ByVal sDefault As String, _
                        ByVal sINIFile As String) As String
```

```
            Dim sValue As String
            Dim sReturnedValue As New StringBuilder(128)

            Dim nReturnCode As Integer
            Dim nSize As Integer = 128
            nReturnCode = GetPrivateProfileString(sSection, sEntry, _
                        sDefault, sReturnedValue, nSize, sINIFile)

            sValue = sReturnedValue.ToString
            Return sValue
        End Function

        Public Sub WriteINIEntry(ByVal sSection As String, _
                            ByVal sEntry As String, _
                            ByVal sValue As String, _
                            ByVal sINIFile As String)

            Dim nReturnCode As Integer
            nReturnCode = WritePrivateProfileString(sSection, sEntry, _
                                        sValue, sINIFile)

        End Sub

End Module
```

Notice the difference in the Declare statements. It is necessary to tell .NET exactly how to marshal the string data so that the API function will be able to manipulate it properly. Chapter 12 has a more complete discussion of declaring API functions in Visual Basic .NET, so we won't go into any more detail on that here.

The code to test the functions is almost the same as VB6. It looks like this:

```
WriteINIEntry("MySection", "MyFirstEntry", _
        "Value for the first entry", "C:\test.ini")
WriteINIEntry ("MySection", "MySecondEntry", _
        "Value for the second entry", "C:\test.ini")

Dim sValue As String
sValue = GetINIEntry("MySection", "MySecondEntry", _
                    "Default value", "C:\test.ini")
MsgBox(sValue)
```

Note that you can use exactly the same INI file for access from both VB6 and Visual Basic .NET. You may wish to vary the values placed in the code by the Visual Basic .NET code to satisfy yourself that it is working properly.

Using the Windows Registry to Store Configuration Settings

As an alternative to using private INI files, the Windows Registry can also hold key-value pairs. The Registry has a hierarchical structure, which looks like a hierarchy of folders when you look at it in the Registry editor. The Registry contains "base keys" that are major folders, and "sub-keys" that further divide the information into categories.

Each folder (or sub-key, if you prefer that designation) in the Registry can hold key-value pairs, and thus acts much like a single section of an INI file.

VB6 has commands to read and write a special application section of the Registry. The commands are `GetSetting` and `SaveSetting`. They take parameters much like the API functions that write to INI files, and even more like the wrapper functions we created named `GetINIEntry` and `WriteINIEntry`. Here is an example of using the functions to store a couple of key-value pairs:

```
SaveSetting "MyAppName", "MySection", "MyFirstEntry", _
        "Value for the first entry"

Dim sValue As String
sValue = GetSetting("MyAppName", "MySection", "MyFirstEntry", "Nothing")
MsgBox sValue
```

This looks almost exactly like the code to use `GetINIEntry` and `WriteINIEntry`, except that the functions do not need to supply an argument for the INI file name (since the system knows where the Registry is), but they do need to supply something for the application name so that the values are placed in an area of the Registry for a specific application.

There is also a command to delete all the settings in an application area. It is called `DeleteSetting`. The following line of code will remove the settings entered by the code above:

```
DeleteSetting "MyAppName"
```

`GetSetting`, `SaveSetting`, and `DeleteSetting` are also available in Visual Basic .NET, and they work in exactly the same way. The only difference in code is that `SaveSetting` and `DeleteSetting` both require parentheses around their arguments, as all subroutines do in Visual Basic .NET.

However, `GetSetting` and `SaveSetting` have a limitation in both VB6 and Visual Basic .NET. You can only read and write to a specific sub-section of the Registry (which is specifically intended to hold application configuration data for VB applications) using these functions. The area is separate from the area used for other applications on the system (it's not even in the same base-key area). Its location is `HKEY_CURRENT_USER\Software\VB and VBA Program Settings`.

If you want to read from or write to other areas of the Registry, that can be done with a number of Windows API functions that were created for that purpose. The API functions all begin with "Reg" and include functions like `RegConnectRegistry` and `RegDeleteKey`.

Using these API functions in VB6 is beyond the scope of this chapter. It is complex and requires using the API functions to navigate the Registry hierarchy. If you are already doing it in VB6, then you know how, so a tutorial is unnecessary. If for some reason you don't know how to do it in VB6 and need to learn, check this web page for sample code: http://www.xploiter.com/programming/vb/visual2.shtml.

If you need interoperability in .NET for those Registry settings, however, the preferred way to get at the information is changed, so we will discuss the .NET way to access arbitrary Registry locations.

We can get to any location in the Registry hierarchy in .NET by using the `Registry` class, which is in the `Microsoft.Win32` namespace. It wraps the API functions, allowing us to read and manipulate registry values anywhere in the Registry by manipulating an object model.

The `Registry` class does not need to be instantiated because we use only shared members of it. It contains members to give access to the main base keys of the Registry. There is a member for each base key, and the names of the members correspond to the base key names. The member returns a reference to a `RegistryKey` object that is then used to manipulate values in that part of the Registry.

Here is a table showing the base key names in the Registry and the associated `RegistryKey` members of the `Registry` class:

Base key in Registry	Corresponding member of Registry class in .NET
HKEY_CLASSES_ROOT	ClassesRoot
HKEY_CURRENT_CONFIG	CurrentConfig
HKEY_CURRENT_USER	CurrentUser
HKEY_DYN_DATA	DynData
HKEY_LOCAL_MACHINE	LocalMachine
HKEY_PERFORMANCE_DATA	PerformanceData
HKEY_USERS	Users

To use these `RegistryKey` classes, you must be familiar with the hierarchy of Registry information it contains. But it you know the location in the base key for the information you want, getting to it is quite easy. Here is an example of getting the current user's location for application data:

```
Dim key As RegistryKey = _
        Registry.CurrentUser.OpenSubKey("Volatile Environment")
Dim sFileLoc As String = key.GetValue("APPDATA")
```

The first line of code gets an object that points to the HKEY_CURRENT_USER part of the Registry, and opens a sub-key called "Volatile Environment". That sub-key contains several settings, and one of them is named "APPDATA". The second line of code places the value in the APPDATA setting into a string variable named sFileLoc.

If the area we want access to is further down in the hierarchy, we just indicate that in the argument for the OpenSubKey method. This example gets the current user's wallpaper name. The location of that setting is two levels down. The first level is the "Control Panel" sub key of HKEY_CURRENT_USER, and the second level is the "Desktop" sub key of "Control Panel". The setting name is "ConvertedWallpaper"

```
key = Registry.CurrentUser.OpenSubKey("Control Panel\Desktop")
Dim sWallPaper As String = key.GetValue("ConvertedWallpaper")
```

Writing a piece of information to the Registry is similar, though you must have appropriate permissions to write the information, and you must specify when you create your RegistryKey object that you want permission to write (the default is read-only access). Here is some code to read and write a value in the HKEY_LOCAL_MACHINE base key area. It contains a sub-key name "Software" that has settings for applications. In this example, assume that the application named MyApp already has a sub-key area for its settings:

```
Dim Key As RegistryKey
key = Registry.LocalMachine.OpenSubKey("Software\MyApp")
Label1.Text = key.GetValue("MyConfigSetting")

key.SetValue("MyConfigSetting", "Altered value for configuration setting")
```

XML-Based Configuration Files

The preferred storage format for application-specific configuration files has switched from INI format to XML in the last few years. The prevalence of XML parsers has made that format a natural one to use for just about any data-storage need, including configuration information. Newer projects, even some done in VB6, have begun to use XML format for configuration files.

It is not possible to show all the ways that XML files can be used to store configuration information. Because of the flexibility of XML, it is possible to use many different techniques, each with their own sets of XML tags and meanings for those tags.

To show XML-based configuration storage at a base level, we will use the format Microsoft uses in its XML-based configuration files for .NET. In this format, the root element is named Configuration and the first-level elements correspond to the sections in an INI file. Each section can then have attributes that correspond to the key-value pairs in an INI file. There is also a section called configSections that names the other sections that will be used in the configuration file.

Here is an example configuration file using this format:

```
<configuration>
    <configSections>
        <section name="MySection"
                 type="System.Configuration.SingleTagSectionHandler" />
    </configSections>
    <MySection MyFirstEntry="Value for First Entry" MyLastEntry="Value for last
entry" />
</configuration>
```

More complex configuration files are possible. It is possible to do hierarchical storage of configuration information, for example. However, the simple form above will be sufficient for our discussion and examples.

Such a configuration file is named, by convention, with the name of the application's EXE file plus the suffix "config", and the file is located in the application's \bin directory. For example, if the application is named MyApp.exe, the configuration file should be MyApp.exe.config, and it should be in the same \bin directory in which MyApp.exe is located. This is not critical for some of the examples we will show, in which you are able to specify the location of the config file. However, to use the .NET Framework classes that work with application configuration information, this naming convention must be followed. The main ConfigurationSettings class, seen in the example below, only loads configuration information from a file with the appropriate name. ConfigurationSettings does not have a method to load from any other source.

In the sections below, we will just look at the basics of reading and storing key-value pairs in attributes as shown above. Examples in both Visual Basic .NET and VB6 will show the actual code to access files with Microsoft's configuration format.

Accessing XML Configuration Info with the .NET Framework Classes

If you just want to read the information in these configuration files from Visual Basic .NET, there is a set of classes in the .NET Framework to do that. However, those classes don't let you set up your own sections in the configuration file and write to them, and of course they are not available from VB6. The classes are in the System.Configuration namespace.

We will not look at those classes in complete detail, but we will do a simple example of reading key-value pairs for an application section. Here is some code to read the application configuration file above and display the value that is in the MyFirstEntry attribute of the MySection element:

```
' The module will need these lines at the top:
Imports System.Configuration
Imports System.Collections

' This code goes further down in the module, e.g. behind a button
Dim MyTable As IDictionary
Dim sValue As String
Dim value2 As String
Dim value3 As String

MyTable = CType(ConfigurationSettings.GetConfig("MySection"), IDictionary)
sValue = CType(MyTable("MyFirstEntry"), String)
MsgBox(sValue)
```

This code uses the ConfigurationSettings class and retrieves a table of key-value pairs in MySection, storing them in MyTable. Then the item in MyTable for MyFirstEntry is fetched and placed in a message box.

If all you want to do is read configuration information from a Visual Basic .NET application, this is a clean way to do it. However, it is more common to need to change configuration settings, or even add new ones. The following sections show code to do that.

329

Accessing Settings Using System.XML in Visual Basic .NET

Getting complete access to configuration settings (for adding and changing as well as reading) at this point requires manipulating the XML file. There are various ways to do this. Using the XMLDocument class in the .NET System.XML namespace is preferred in most circumstances.

We cannot give a complete tutorial here on manipulating XML files using the XMLDocument class and associated classes (you can consult *Professional XML Second Edition*, Wrox Press, ISBN 1-861005-05-9 for complete coverage of XML techniques). However, we can go over a simple example that reads, writes, and adds key-value pairs to a configuration file with the same format as above.

This example is not production ready. It lacks error handling, for example. It also does not allow creation of new sections in the XML configuration file, nor does it handle any hierarchical storage of configuration information. However, someone who is knowledgeable about manipulating the XML Document Object Model (DOM) can add these capabilities.

The example is in the form of a class. This is necessary because the XML file must be read into memory before it can be manipulated, and you typically don't want to read the file in for every separate setting you get. So the class loads the XML file in the constructor, and holds on to it as long as the instance of the class exists.

Changes made to key-value pairs via the class are not automatically saved to disk. The class has a Save method to place the changes back into the original XML file that the configuration information was read from. Here is the complete code for the class:

```
Imports System.Xml

Public Class XMLConfigFile
    Dim mXMLConfigDoc As XmlDocument
    Dim msXMLFile As String

    Public Sub New(ByVal sXMLFile As String)
        mXMLConfigDoc = New XmlDocument()
        mXMLConfigDoc.Load(sXMLFile)
        msXMLFile = sXMLFile
    End Sub

    Public ReadOnly Property XMLFileName() As String
        Get
            XMLFileName = msXMLFile
        End Get
    End Property

    Public Function GetXMLEntry(ByVal sSection As String, _
                        ByVal sEntry As String) As String
        Dim SectionNode As XmlNode

'       Get the node containing the section of key-value pairs we want.
        SectionNode = mXMLConfigDoc.GetElementsByTagName(sSection).Item(0)

'       Get the attributes of the section node. Each attribute is one
'       name-value pair.
        Dim SectionAttributes As XmlAttributeCollection = _
                            SectionNode.Attributes
        Dim sValue As String
```

```
'    Find the name-value pair we want. If it exists, get its value
     Dim EntryNode As XmlNode = SectionAttributes.GetNamedItem(sEntry)
     If EntryNode Is Nothing Then
         sValue = ""
     Else
         sValue = SectionAttributes.GetNamedItem(sEntry).Value
     End If
     Return sValue

 End Function

 Public Sub WriteXMLEntry(ByVal sSection As String, _
                          ByVal sEntry As String, _
                          ByVal sValue As String)
     Dim SectionNode As XmlNode

'    Get the node containing the section of key-value pairs we want.
     SectionNode = mXMLConfigDoc.GetElementsByTagName(sSection).Item(0)

'    Get the attributes of the section node. Each attribute is one
'    name-value pair.
     Dim SectionAttributes As XmlAttributeCollection = _
                          SectionNode.Attributes

'    Check to see if a value already exists for this setting
     Dim EntryNode As XmlNode
     EntryNode = SectionAttributes.GetNamedItem(sEntry)

'    If setting does not exist, create a new attribute for it,
'    set its value and add it to the attributes collection.
     If EntryNode Is Nothing Then
         Dim NewEntry As XmlAttribute
         NewEntry = mXMLConfigDoc.CreateAttribute(sEntry)
         NewEntry.Value = sValue
         SectionAttributes.SetNamedItem(NewEntry)
     Else

'        If setting already exists, just set the value
         EntryNode.Value = sValue
     End If

 End Sub

 Public Sub Save()
     mXMLConfigDoc.Save(msXMLFile)
 End Sub
End Class
```

The two main members are GetXMLEntry and WriteXMLEntry. By design, these methods look a lot like the corresponding function and subroutine in the earlier example of reading and writing an INI file. The same arguments are passed in for both cases.

GetXMLEntry gets the correct section by using the GetElementsByTagName method of the XMLDocument, and then by finding the first element with the right tag name. This is a fairly simplistic way of getting hold of the section. If multiple elements with the same section name existed, for example, the code would just ignore all of them after the first one. It should also have better error handling. For example, it should check to see if the section is actually there. But this example is sufficient to show the principle involved.

After getting the relevant section, the required attribute is fetched with the GetNamedItem method of the element's attributes collection. Then, if the attribute exists, the value of the attribute is fetched and returned. If the attribute does not exist, an empty string is returned.

WriteXMLEntry uses some similar code to get the XML element containing the section, and to get the attribute within the section if it exists. However, it contains code to create a new attribute if one with the correct name does not yet exist.

To test out this code, you can start a new Windows Application, place a button on it, and put the following code in the button's Click event.

```
    ' Need project reference to VB compatibility DLL for this line to work.
    Dim sXMLFile As String = _
       Microsoft.VisualBasic.Compatibility.VB6.GetPath & "/MyAppName.exe.config"
    Dim myXMLConfigFile As New XMLConfigFile(sXMLFile)

    Dim sValue As String
    sValue = myXMLConfigFile.GetXMLEntry("MySection", "MyLastEntry")
    MsgBox(sValue)

    sValue = "New Value for Last Entry"
    myXMLConfigFile.WriteXMLEntry("MySection", "MyLastEntry", sValue)
    sValue = myXMLConfigFile.GetXMLEntry("MySection", "MyLastEntry")
    MsgBox(sValue)
    myXMLConfigFile.Save()
```

Don't forget that the config file must first be created, named with the application name plus the suffix "config", and placed in the application's \bin directory. The code just above assumes you are using a config file based on the example configuration file in Microsoft format shown earlier.

The results of this code will be two message boxes, with the first displaying the value "Value for last entry" and the second displaying the value "New Value for Last Entry". Notice that the last line of code saves the change in the value for MyLastEntry to disk so, if the code is run again, the results will be different.

Accessing Settings Using MSXML in VB6

The MSXML libraries that are installed with Internet Explorer contain very similar functionality to that in the System.XML namespace in .NET. This means that the Visual Basic .NET code above can be translated for use in VB6 without too many changes.

After creating a project to hold the VB6 class for accessing the configuration information, the project must be given a reference to the MSXML library. For the code below, the reference was made to version 3.0 of the library. The version will vary depending on what Internet Explorer version you have, but if you have installed Visual Studio .NET, then Internet Explorer 6.0 was installed and you have MSXML version 3.0, possibly along with some earlier versions.

Here is the class in VB6 that corresponds to the Visual Basic .NET class above. The class name in the properties window should be set to XMLConfigFile, since the class name is not in the source code as in Visual Basic .NET.

```
Option Explicit

Dim mXMLConfigDoc As MSXML2.DOMDocument30
Dim msXMLFile As String

Private Sub Class_Initialize()
    Set mXMLConfigDoc = New MSXML2.DOMDocument30
End Sub

Public Sub Load(sXMLFile As String)
    mXMLConfigDoc.Load (sXMLFile)
    msXMLFile = sXMLFile
End Sub

Public Property Get XMLFileName() As String
    XMLFileName = msXMLFile
End Property

Public Function GetXMLEntry(ByVal sSection As String, _
                            ByVal sEntry As String) As String
    Dim SectionNode As MSXML2.IXMLDOMNode

    Set SectionNode = mXMLConfigDoc.getElementsByTagName(sSection).Item(0)
    Dim sValue As String
    Dim EntryNode As IXMLDOMNode
    Set EntryNode = SectionNode.Attributes.getNamedItem(sEntry)
    If EntryNode Is Nothing Then
        sValue = ""
    Else
        sValue = EntryNode.nodeValue
    End If
    GetXMLEntry = sValue

End Function

Public Sub WriteXMLEntry(ByVal sSection As String, _
                         ByVal sEntry As String, _
                         ByVal sValue As String)
    Dim SectionNode As MSXML2.IXMLDOMNode
    Set SectionNode = mXMLConfigDoc.getElementsByTagName(sSection).Item(0)

    Dim EntryNode As IXMLDOMNode
    Set EntryNode = SectionNode.Attributes.getNamedItem(sEntry)
    If EntryNode Is Nothing Then
        Dim NewEntry As IXMLDOMAttribute
        Set NewEntry = mXMLConfigDoc.createAttribute(sEntry)

        NewEntry.Value = sValue
        SectionNode.Attributes.setNamedItem NewEntry
```

333

```
    Else

            EntryNode.nodeValue = sValue

        End If

    End Sub

    Public Sub Save()
        mXMLConfigDoc.Save (msXMLFile)
    End Sub
```

This code is very much like the Visual Basic .NET version, except for:

- ❏ Syntax changes between VB6 and Visual Basic .NET
- ❏ Different class names for the XML classes used
- ❏ Different method names for some of those XML classes
- ❏ A new Load event to take the place of the Visual Basic .NET constructor

Since the code is so similar, we won't repeat the discussion of it.

The code to test the class is also similar to the Visual Basic .NET version, and it is shown below. Since VB6 applications have no /bin directory, we are assuming the config file is in the application directory.

```
Dim sXMLFile As String
sXMLFile = App.Path & "/MyAppName.exe.config"
Dim myXMLConfigFile As New XMLConfigFile

myXMLConfigFile.Load (sXMLFile)

Dim sValue As String
sValue = myXMLConfigFile.GetXMLEntry("MySection", "MyFirstEntry")
MsgBox (sValue)

sValue = "New Value for Last Entry"
myXMLConfigFile.WriteXMLEntry "MySection", "MyLastEntry", sValue
sValue = myXMLConfigFile.GetXMLEntry("MySection", "MyLastEntry")
MsgBox (sValue)

myXMLConfigFile.Save
```

The differences here are very minor and all have to do with syntax differences between the VB versions.

Concurrency Problems

Notice that all of the techniques presented assume only one application is changing configuration settings at a time. If several applications (or users) are simultaneously making changes, then the last one to save gets precedence, and the changes made by others may not be preserved. This problem is not unique to the techniques presented in this chapter, of course. And since most configuration information is user or client-machine specific, concurrency is usually not a big problem. But you should be aware of this potential issue if several programs are simultaneously accessing configuration information.

Summary

Sharing configuration information is one of the necessities for interoperable systems. No one wants to maintain two copies of configuration information, nor try to keep them in synchronization. Using the techniques in this chapter, which should cover the vast majority of configuration scenarios, can prevent these difficulties.

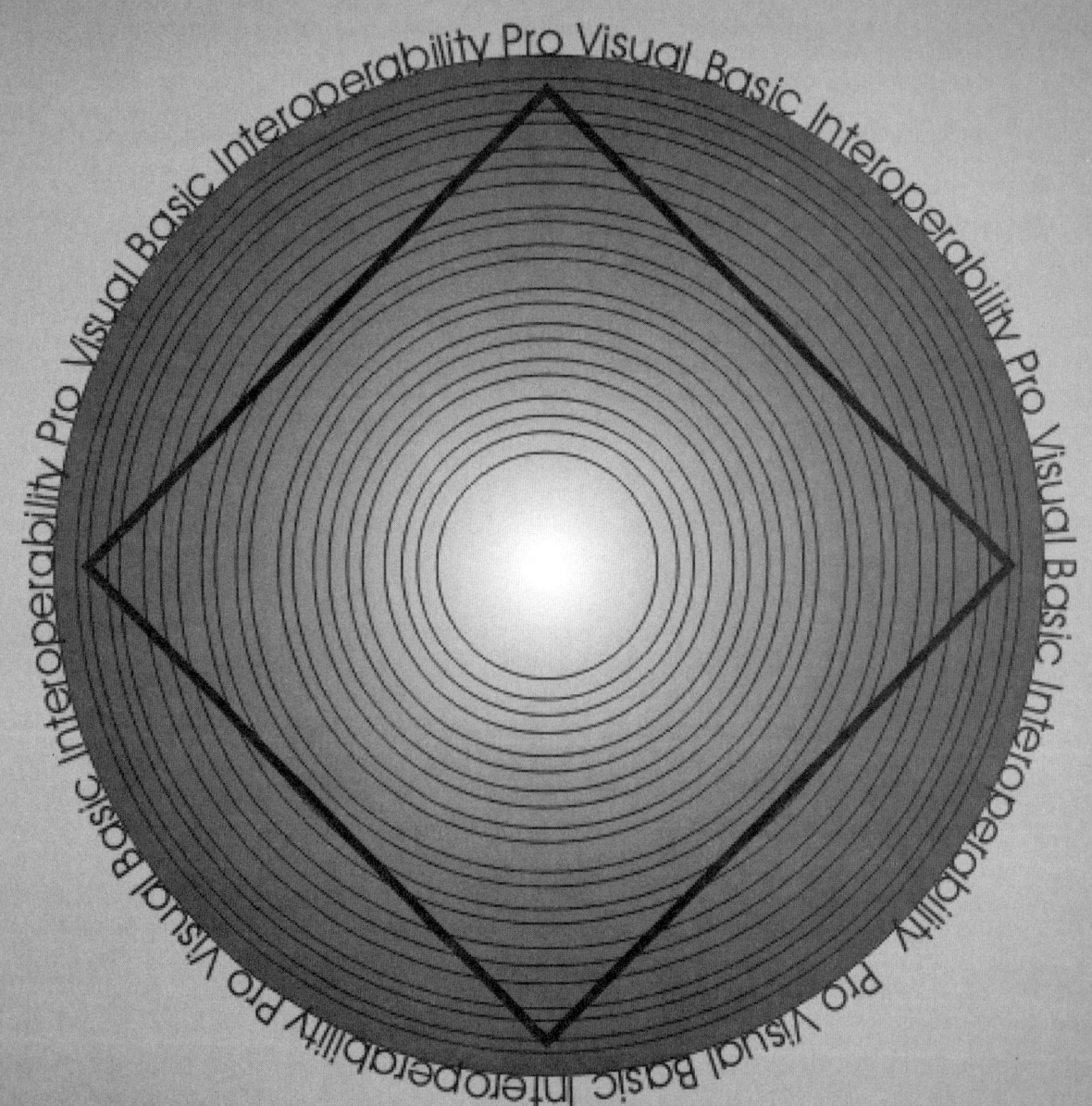

10

Flat File Access in .NET

In its role as the glue that holds many corporate systems together, Visual Basic sometimes needs to use data capabilities that pre-date relational access. Mainframes and other existing systems may need to communicate data as **flat files**, from which data must be read in and interpreted by Visual Basic code. While XML is becoming a more common way to communicate such data, some older systems still need to interoperate via these flat files.

VB6 and its ancestors have been good tools for working with data in flat files. Besides having the ability to manipulate strings more easily than other mainstream languages, VB has also had good access to flat files since version 1. Keywords in the language support three different types of flat file access:

❑ **Random** access to fixed length records in a flat file, using `Get` and `Put` keywords

❑ **Binary** access to arbitrary positions within a file, using the `Get` and `Put` keywords

❑ **Sequential** reading and writing of files using the `Input`, `Line Input`, `Write`, and `Print` keywords

These types of access are also available in Visual Basic .NET but, in keeping with the way that .NET works, many of the keywords that provide the functionality have been replaced by members of classes. In some cases, such as in random access, this results in only minor syntax changes for new code. In other cases, such as sequential access to files using `Stream` objects, the preferred method in .NET is radically different from equivalent techniques in VB6.

This chapter will go over each of the types of flat file access above, and show how syntax must change in .NET to accommodate the access. Most of this information will be presented by first showing how the access would be accomplished in VB6, and then showing the equivalent functionality in Visual Basic .NET.

Random Access to Flat Files

Before relational databases were common, many data files had a structure in which each data record was a fixed length. Mirroring the punched cards common in early systems, it was originally usual to make the records 80 bytes, but later it became possible to make the records any necessary length. Because of the way that file systems fetch data, record lengths of 128 and 256 bytes were often used to get the most efficient access to disk, although record lengths up to various limits (depending on the platform) were available.

In such a fixed length record, groups of bytes were set aside to represent certain fields in the record. For example, if a record represented a customer, the first 10 bytes might be considered the record ID, the next 20 might hold the name, the next 10 might contain the phone number, and so on. Diagrammatically, a record could be represented like this:

Total record length - 80 bytes		
1234567890ABC Company, Inc.	6155554321 more fields as needed...	
ID	Customer Name	Phone

Writing these records required constructing a string of the appropriate length, with pieces of the string representing each field. Reading the record required getting an entire record and then decomposing the record to get the individual fields.

It was often common for the last field to be a "filler" field that did not hold data. Such fields were used to round out the record to a desired total length, and were also included to provide space for fields to be added in the future.

Random Access in VB6

The most common way to handle the process in VB6 is to construct a User-Defined Type (UDT) with fields that are fixed length strings. Thus, a UDT for the example above would be defined like this in VB6 code:

```
Type FlatCustomer
    sID As String * 10
    sCustomerName As String * 20
    sPhone As String * 10
    ' other fields as necessary
    sFiller As String * 40        ' fill up the record for the example
End Type
```

It is important when constructing such a record that the total length of all the fields should be exactly the record length needed. In this case, the total is 80 bytes, which will be used as the record length when a random access file is opened in the example code below.

The records contained in such UDTs can be written into or read out of flat files with Put and Get statements, respectively. The code in VB6 to put data in a customer record and place it into the file as the fifth record looks like this:

```
' Assume our file name is "C:\custfile.dat"
' Open the file
Open "C:\custfile.dat" For Random As #1 Len = 80

Dim FifthCustomer As FlatCustomer
FifthCustomer.sID = "1234567890"
FifthCustomer.sCustomerName = "ABC Company, Inc."
FifthCustomer.sPhone = "6155554321"
FifthCustomer.sFiller = ""

' Write the record into the file as record 5
Put #1, 5, FifthCustomer
Close #1
```

This code places the record into the position for the fifth record, even if some or all of records 1 through 4 do not exist. Such "assumed" records will contain null data – that is, each byte of the records will be an ASCII zero.

The read operation in VB6 is basically the inverse of this. Here is code to read the fifth record and put it into a `FlatCustomer` UDT, and then place the data into text boxes:

```
' Assume our file name is "C:\custfile.dat"
' Open the file
Open "C:\custfile.dat" For Random As #1 Len = 80

Dim ReadCustomer As FlatCustomer
' Write the record into the file as record 5
Get #1, 5, ReadCustomer

txtID.Text = ReadCustomer.sID
txtName.Text = ReadCustomer.sCustomerName
txtPhone.Text = ReadCustomer.sPhone
Close #1
```

The example above used only strings, but numeric data can be part of the record as well. Suppose we change our UDT to the following:

```
Type FlatCustomer
    sID As String * 10
    sCustomerName As String * 20
    sPhone As String * 10
    nCode As Long
    ' other fields as necessary
    sFiller As String * 36        ' fill up the record for the example
End Type
```

Here we have added a field named `nCode` and declared it as a `Long`. Since a long is 4 bytes, the length for `sFiller` is then reduced to 36, still giving us a total record length of 80 bytes.

Now we can include the `nCode` field when writing the data:

```
' Assume our file name is "C:\custfile.dat"
' Open the file
Open "C:\custfile.dat" For Random As #1 Len = 80

Dim FifthCustomer As FlatCustomer
FifthCustomer.sID = "1234567890"
FifthCustomer.sCustomerName = "ABC Company, Inc."
FifthCustomer.sPhone = "6155554321"
FifthCustomer.nCode = 654321
FifthCustomer.sFiller = ""

' Write the record into the file as record 5
Put #1, 5, FifthCustomer
Close #1
```

and reading it:

```
' Assume our file name is "C:\custfile.dat"
' Open the file
Open "C:\custfile.dat" For Random As #1 Len = 80

Dim ReadCustomer As FlatCustomer
' Write the record into the file as record 5
Get #1, 5, ReadCustomer

txtID.Text = ReadCustomer.sID
txtName.Text = ReadCustomer.sCustomerName
txtPhone.Text = ReadCustomer.sPhone
txtCode.Text = ReadCustomer.nCode
Close #1
```

The only practical difference is that the data is not stored in ASCII, but is stored in binary. The format used for binary storage is an Institute of Electrical and Electronics Engineers (www.IEEE.org) standard, so many other systems can read the binary data in such flat files if they know the data type that the binary data is supposed to represent. Any of the numeric types (Integer, Long, Single, Double) can be handled this way. There are some systems and languages that do not use the IEEE spec, and this method of writing binary data will not work with them.

Using FreeFile to Get the File Number

The above example used a hard-coded file number for simplicity but, in most practical applications, the file number is obtained with the VB6 keyword FreeFile. This keyword returns the next available free file number, guaranteeing that the file number used will not conflict with other file operations already in progress. Thus, the code for the first write operation above would more commonly be written like this:

```
' Assume our file name is "C:\custfile.dat"
' Open the file
Dim nFileNum As Integer
nFileNum = FreeFile
Open "C:\custfile.dat" For Random As nFileNum Len = 80

Dim FifthCustomer As FlatCustomer
FifthCustomer.sID = "1234567890"
```

```
FifthCustomer.sCustomerName = "ABC Company, Inc."
FifthCustomer.sPhone = "6155554321"
FifthCustomer.nCode = 654321
FifthCustomer.sFiller = ""

' Write the record into the file as record 5
Put nFileNum, 5, FifthCustomer
Close nFileNum
```

For systems that use fixed-length records, this random access technique is usually preferred. While it is possible to use other techniques – such as the binary access discussed later in the chapter – and then do custom parsing of the record, that would take a good deal more code. However, it is important when using this technique to ensure that all records are precisely the right length. A difference of one byte anywhere in the file can throw off all subsequent records.

Random Access in Visual Basic .NET

There are several differences that need to be noted when doing the equivalent operations in Visual Basic .NET. They include:

❑ The Open, Close, Get, and Put keywords are replaced by equivalent functions in the .NET Framework

❑ Structures replace UDTs in Visual Basic .NET

❑ Fixed length strings are not a native type in Visual Basic .NET, and so can't be used in a structure

Let's look at how we deal with each of these issues.

Replacements for File Access Keywords

Each of the keywords used above for random access (Open, Close, FreeFile, Get, and Put) have equivalent functions in Visual Basic .NET, and the arguments to the functions correspond to the parameters for the VB6 keywords. Here are the keywords and their replacement functions:

VB6 keyword	Visual Basic .NET replacement function
Open	FileOpen
Close	FileClose
FreeFile	FreeFile
Get	FileGet
Put	FilePut

All of these functions are intrinsic to Visual Basic .NET. That is, you don't have to refer to a particular library to make them available – they are automatically available in every Visual Basic .NET project.

While the functions are operational equivalents, and take the same information as arguments, the order of the arguments can be different in the Visual Basic .NET equivalents from the original VB6 keywords. Here are examples of each, showing the VB6 form and the Visual Basic .NET equivalent to compare how the parameters are specified:

Open and FreeFile

```
'VB6 Open Statement
Dim nFileNum As Integer
nFileNum = FreeFile
Dim nRecLength As Integer
nRecLength = 80
Open "C:\custfile.dat" For Random As nFileNum Len = nRecLength
```

```
'Visual Basic .NET FileOpen function
Dim nFileNum As Integer
nFileNum = FreeFile()
Dim nRecLength As Integer
nRecLength= 80
FileOpen (nFileNum, "C:\custfile.dat", OpenMode.Random, , , nRecLength)
```

The only difference for the `FreeFile` function is that it now requires empty parentheses following it. However, the `FileOpen` function shifts the order of the parameters around a bit from the `Open` keyword. It also has two optional parameters, which can be placed between `OpenMode.Random` and `nRecLength`, and that are not shown in the example above.

The first optional parameter specifies an access mode. In VB6, random access always implies both read and write access. However, the access parameter of `FileOpen` can be set to `Read`, `Write`, or `ReadWrite`. The default is `ReadWrite`, which gives the same capability as random access in VB6.

The second optional parameter specifies a sharing mode. The default is that the file can be shared with other processes (which is the only mode available in VB6). The other possible settings are to lock the random access file for reading, lock it for writing, or lock it for both.

To illustrate, if we wanted our random access file to be opened only for writing, and to be locked so that no other program can write to it (but others can read from it), then the last line in the example above would become:

```
FileOpen (nFileNum, "C:\custfile.dat", OpenMode.Random, _
          OpenAccess.Write, OpenShare.LockWrite, nRecLength)
```

Get and Put

```
'VB6 Get Statement
' We already have nFileNum for file number. Assume record number is in
' nRecNum and record to write is in CustomerRec
Get nFileNum, nRecNum, CustomerRec
```

```
'Visual Basic .NET FileGet Function
' We already have nFileNum for file number. Assume record number is in
' nRecNum and record to write is in CustomerRec
FileGet(nFileNum, CustomerRec, nRecNum)
```

Note that the order of the last two parameters is reversed for `FileGet` versus `Get`. The same is true of `FilePut` versus `Put`, as we see in the following code :

```
'VB6 Put Statement
' We already have nFileNum for file number. Assume record number is in
' nRecNum and record to hold data from file is CustomerRec
Put nFileNum, nRecNum, CustomerRec


'Visual Basic .NET FilePut Function
' We already have nFileNum for file number. Assume record number is in
' nRecNum and record to hold data from file is CustomerRec
FilePut(nFileNum, CustomerRec, nRecNum)
```

This all shows that the keyword replacements don't cause much trouble in creating Visual Basic .NET code to read random records, since there are equivalent replacements in Visual Basic .NET for each of the necessary VB6 keywords. However, there is one difference not obvious from the code above. The record being read or written is named CustomerRec in both VB6 and Visual Basic .NET, but it is handled differently internally. Let's discuss this next.

Structures Replace UDTs in Visual Basic .NET

In VB6.0, a UDT is declared using the Type...End Type construct, as we saw in the example above:

```
Type FlatCustomer
    sID As String * 10
    sCustomerName As String * 20
    sPhone As String * 10
    nCode As Long
    ' other fields as necessary
    sFiller As String * 36      ' fill up the record for the example
End Type
```

In Visual Basic .NET, the Type statement is no longer available. In its place, a structure can be declared using the Structure...End Structure syntax. Furthermore, every member of a structure must be declared as one of the following: Dim, Public, Protected, Friend, Protected Friend, or Private. Dim and Public both indicate public access and the others give various restrictions on access. A similar structure in Visual Basic .NET for the UDT in the preceding example might look like this:

```
Structure FlatCustomer
    Public sID As String
    Public sCustomerName As String
    Public sPhone As String
    Public nCode As Integer
    ' other fields as necessary
    Public sFiller As String
End Structure
```

Another change is that public structure definitions can be made inside a class. In VB6, they had to be in a module.

The syntax for accessing a structure is object syntax, and looks the same as the syntax for accessing UDTs in VB6 and earlier.

Handling Fixed Length Strings in Visual Basic .NET

The definition above has one huge difference from the VB6 equivalent. The constituent elements of the structure that were fixed-length strings in VB6 are simply strings in Visual Basic .NET. That's because fixed-length strings are not a native type in .NET, and so structures cannot include them.

There is a replacement for a fixed-length string that works in many contexts. It is a "compatibility class" that performs similarly to a fixed-length string variable in VB6. However, since it is an object and not a native type, it *cannot* be included in structures.

However, there is a way to tell .NET to treat strings in a structure as fixed-length for the purposes of input and output. The functionality is part of the ability of .NET to *marshal* data across interfaces in various ways, which is discussed at various points in this book.

The marshaling capability we need is invoked with a .NET attribute called VBFixedString. It takes an argument to specify the length desired. To make the Visual Basic .NET structure above behave like its VB6 equivalent for random access, it must be changed to look like this:

```
Structure FlatCustomer
    <VBFixedString(10)> Public sID As String
    <VBFixedString(20)> Public sCustomerName As String
    <VBFixedString(10)> Public sPhone As String
    Public nCode As Integer
    ' other fields as necessary
    <VBFixedString(36)> Public sFiller As String
End Structure
```

Now, variables declared as type FlatCustomer in Visual Basic .NET will behave in the same way as the equivalent UDT in VB6 when performing random access I/O.

Putting It All Together

To see all of these changes in action, let's see the complete example in Visual Basic .NET corresponding to the VB6 code presented earlier:

```
' Assume our file name is "C:\custfile.dat"
' Open the file
Dim nFileNum As Integer
nFileNum = FreeFile()
Dim nRecLength As Integer
nRecLength= 80
FileOpen(nFileNum, "C:\custfile.dat", OpenMode.Random, , , nRecLength)

Dim FifthCustomer As FlatCustomer
FifthCustomer.sID = "1234567890"
FifthCustomer.sCustomerName = "ABC Company, Inc."
FifthCustomer.sPhone = "6155554321"
FifthCustomer.nCode = 654321
FifthCustomer.sFiller = ""

' Write the record into the file as record 5
FilePut(nFileNum, FifthCustomer, 5)
FileClose(nFileNum)
```

```
' Open the file
Dim nFileNum As Integer
nFileNum = FreeFile()
Dim nRecLength As Integer
nRecLength = 80
FileOpen(nFileNum, "C:\custfile.dat", OpenMode.Random, , , nRecLength)
Dim ReadCustomer As FlatCustomer
' Write the record into the file as record 5
FileGet(nFileNum, ReadCustomer, 5)

txtID.Text = ReadCustomer.sID
txtName.Text = ReadCustomer.sCustomerName
txtPhone.Text = ReadCustomer.sPhone
txtCode.Text = ReadCustomer.nCode
FileClose(nFileNum)
```

Binary Access to Flat Files

Both random access and sequential access (covered later in this chapter) assume that the data file to be accessed is in the form of "records". In random access, the records have a predefined length. In sequential access, the records are variable length and are delimited by CrLf characters. In both cases, access is to a particular record.

In binary access, it is possible to read or write data down to the level of a single byte. In some applications, this access is similar in some respects to stream access discussed in the section below on sequential access. In other cases, this byte-level access is used to do things that do not resemble anything we've described anywhere else in this chapter.

To prevent confusion, it's important to understand that "binary access" is different from "binary storage". Binary access means that you can get to any arbitrary position in the file. Binary storage means that the data is stored in some binary format. You may be doing binary access using only string data, or you can use binary access with binary data. It's your responsibility when you read the data to determine how to interpret it.

Binary Access in VB6

Opening a file for binary access looks much like opening a file for random access. The difference is that the phrase For Random is replaced by the phrase For Binary, and the record length setting is left off.

The Get and Put keywords are used to do binary access in VB6 in addition to their use in random access. The arguments that they take are different for binary access, however. The record number is left off, leaving only the string argument. The length of this string argument indicates how many bytes of information there are in the file to read or write.

For example, the following code opens a file for binary access, writes a six character string, and then writes a ten character string:

```
'VB6 Open Statement
Dim nFileNum As Integer
nFileNum = FreeFile
Open "C:\custfile.dat" For Binary As nFileNum

Dim sSixCharString As String
sSixCharString = "123456"

Dim sTenCharString As String
sTenCharString = "1234567890"

Put nFileNum, ,sSixCharString
Put nFileNum, ,sTenCharString

Close nFileNum
```

At this point, the file contains sixteen bytes: 1234561234567890. The fact that the strings being written are different lengths does not matter – binary access allows any amount of data to be placed in the file during a Put operation.

Similarly, reading the file is done by creating a string with the desired number of bytes, and using it in a Get statement. If the code above had been run, then this code would get the first eight bytes out of the file:

```
'VB6 Open Statement
Dim nFileNum As Integer
nFileNum = FreeFile
Open "C:\custfile.dat" For Binary As nFileNum

Dim sEightCharString As String
sEightCharString = space$(8)

Get nFileNum, ,sEightCharString
Close nFileNum
```

At this point, the variable sEightCharString would contain 12345612.

It is also possible to go to a particular place in the file with the Seek keyword. We can modify the above example to get the eight characters beginning at position 3 in the file like this:

```
'VB6 Open Statement
Dim nFileNum As Integer
nFileNum = FreeFile
Open "C:\custfile.dat" For Binary As nFileNum

Dim sEightCharString As String
sEightCharString = space$(8)

Seek nFileNum, 3
Get nFileNum, ,sEightCharString
Close nFileNum
```

At this point, the variable sEightCharString would contain 34561234.

This example has demonstrated that we can read and write arbitrary amounts of data at arbitrary positions with VB6's binary access. Here is an example of using these capabilities to do a search and replace in a file. We will use this file as our test case:

```
This is test file for the binary access in VB6 and Visual Basic .NET.

The file has several places where the string "XXX" appears. We want to replace all
of these with six Zs. Except for replacing XXX everywhere it appears, the rest of
the file should be unchanged.

XXX

XXX

We're done.
```

Save it as C:\SampleFile.txt. The following code will examine this file and find all of the places where the characters XXX appear. This string will then be replaced with ZZZZZZ. Note that this changes the length of the file.

For simplicity, we will just read the entire file at once into a string variable. This works fine as long as the file is not too large. Then we will write out the changed file into a new file name, with the replacements. Here is the code:

```
' Get the input file
Dim sFileName As String
sFileName = "C:\SampleFile.txt"
Dim nFileNum As Integer
nFileNum = FreeFile
Open sFileName For Binary As nFileNum

Dim sFileContents As String
sFileContents = Space$(LOF(nFileNum))
Get nFileNum, , sFileContents
Close nFileNum

' Set the output file
sFileName = "C:\SampleFileOut.txt"
Dim nOutputFileNum As Integer
nOutputFileNum = FreeFile
Open sFileName For Binary As nOutputFileNum

Dim sTextToFind As String
sTextToFind = "XXX"

Dim sTextToInsert As String
sTextToInsert = "ZZZZZZ"

Dim nCurrentPosition As Integer
Dim nNextPosition As Integer
Dim sNextPieceToInsert As String
nCurrentPosition = 1

nNextPosition = InStr(nCurrentPosition, sFileContents, sTextToFind)
```

```
    Do While nNextPosition <> 0
        sNextPieceToInsert = Mid$(sFileContents, nCurrentPosition, _
                             nNextPosition - nCurrentPosition)
        Put nOutputFileNum, , sNextPieceToInsert
        Put nOutputFileNum, , sTextToInsert
        nCurrentPosition = nNextPosition + Len(sTextToFind)
        nNextPosition = InStr(nCurrentPosition, sFileContents, sTextToFind)
    Loop

    ' Now need to write the last piece
    sNextPieceToInsert = Right$(sFileContents, _
    Len(sFileContents) - nCurrentPosition + 1)
    Put nOutputFileNum, , sNextPieceToInsert

    Close nOutputFileNum
```

Binary Access in Visual Basic .NET

As with random access, the same functionality is available in Visual Basic .NET, though keywords have been replaced with equivalent functions. Open, Close, and FreeFile are replaced as before, with the only difference being that the mode to open the file in the FileOpen function changes from OpenMode.Random to OpenMode.Binary. FileGet and FilePut also replace Get and Put, as before. However, the extra comma used in Get and Put in the VB6 code to indicate random access usage is not present in Visual Basic .NET. The fact that the value being passed in is a variable length string, plus the fact that the file was opened in Binary mode, gives FileGet and FilePut all the information they need to work in binary mode.

Here is the first binary access example above, changed to Visual Basic .NET:

```
'Visual Basic .NET Open Statement
Dim nFileNum As Integer
nFileNum = FreeFile()
FileOpen(nFileNum, "C:\custfile.dat", OpenMode.Binary)

Dim sSixCharString As String
sSixCharString = "123456"

Dim sTenCharString As String
sTenCharString = "1234567890"

FilePut(nFileNum, sSixCharString)
FilePut(nFileNum, sTenCharString)

FileClose(nFileNum)

nFileNum = FreeFile()
FileOpen(nFileNum, "C:\custfile.dat", OpenMode.Binary)

Dim sEightCharString As String
sEightCharString = Space$(8)
```

```
    Seek(nFileNum, 3)
    FileGet(nFileNum, sEightCharString)
    FileClose(nFileNum)
```

Again, the string `sEightCharString` will contain the value `34561234`.

Now, let's see the more complex example that did searching and replacing in Visual Basic .NET:

```
' Get the input file
Dim sFileName As String
sFileName = "C:\SampleFile.txt"
Dim nFileNum As Integer
nFileNum = FreeFile()
FileOpen(nFileNum, sFileName, OpenMode.Binary)

Dim sFileContents As String
sFileContents = Space$(LOF(nFileNum))
FileGet(nFileNum, sFileContents)
FileClose(nFileNum)

' Set the output file
sFileName = "C:\SampleFileOut.txt"
Dim nOutputFileNum As Integer
nOutputFileNum = FreeFile()
FileOpen(nOutputFileNum, sFileName, OpenMode.Binary)


Dim sTextToFind As String
sTextToFind = "XXX"

Dim sTextToInsert As String
sTextToInsert = "ZZZZZZ"

Dim nCurrentPosition As Integer
Dim nNextPosition As Integer
Dim sNextPieceToInsert As String
nCurrentPosition = 1

nNextPosition = InStr(nCurrentPosition, sFileContents, sTextToFind)
Do While nNextPosition <> 0
    sNextPieceToInsert = Mid$(sFileContents, nCurrentPosition, _
                             nNextPosition - nCurrentPosition)
    FilePut(nOutputFileNum, sNextPieceToInsert)
    FilePut(nOutputFileNum, sTextToInsert)
    nCurrentPosition = nNextPosition + Len(sTextToFind)
    nNextPosition = InStr(nCurrentPosition, sFileContents, sTextToFind)
Loop

' Now need to write the last piece
sNextPieceToInsert = Microsoft.VisualBasic.Right (sFileContents, _
                    Len(sFileContents) - nCurrentPosition + 1)
FilePut(nOutputFileNum, sNextPieceToInsert)

FileClose(nOutputFileNum)
```

349

Sequential File Access

Another way that files from other systems may need to be accessed is by reading or writing them sequentially. In a read operation, that means starting at the beginning of the file and stepping through it line by line, processing data as necessary. On a write operation, it means creating the file from the beginning and writing each line of data sequentially. It is also possible to append data to an existing sequential file.

Examples of files from other systems that may have to be read sequentially are report files and various kinds of file dumps. Also, some older systems may produce comma-delimited files and sequential access is the appropriate way to read and write this data as well.

Sequential Access in VB6

The basic read and write operations for sequential access in VB6 use these keywords:

Keyword	Description
Open	Open the file for sequential access, which means either opening it for Input mode (to read the file), Output mode (to write the file), or Append mode (to append the data to an existing file)
Write	Write data to the file, automatically inserting commas for delimiters as necessary
Print	Write data to the file without inserting delimiters
Input	Read the data field by field, with commas as the usual delimiters (delimiters can also be tabs and carriage returns)
Line Input	Read an entire line of data, regardless of any delimiters in it

Here is a simple example in VB6 illustrating the use of most of these keywords.

```
Dim sFileName As String
sFileName = "C:\SequentialIO.txt"

Open sFileName For Output As #1
Write #1, "Clark", "Kent", 37, 6.1
Print #1, "He fights for Truth, Justice, and the American Way"
Close #1

Open sFileName For Input As #1
Dim sFirstName As String
Dim sLastName As String
Dim nAge As Integer
```

```
Dim sngHeight As Single
Dim sDescription As String

Input #1, sFirstName, sLastName, nAge, sngHeight
Line Input #1, sDescription

MsgBox sFirstName & " " & sLastName & " is " & _
       Str$(nAge) & " years old and is " & _
       Str$(sngHeight) & " feet tall. " & sDescription
```

The file that is written out by this code, `SequentialIO.txt`, will look like this:

```
"Clark","Kent",37,6.1
He fights for Truth, Justice, and the American Way
```

Running this code in VB6 will result in the following message box being displayed:

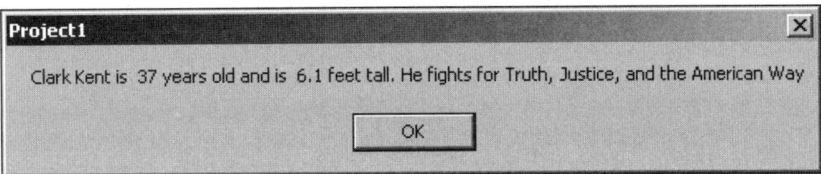

Notice that the first line has quotes around the strings because it was written with the `Write` keyword. The second line does not have quotes because it was written with the `Print` keyword. In general, if you are going to read the data with `Input`, it should be written with `Write`. If you will read with `Line Input`, the data should be written with `Print` because `Print` will not insert any quotes.

Sequential Access in Visual Basic .NET

As before, there are replacements for the VB6 keywords used in sequential I/O:

VB6 keyword	Visual Basic .NET replacement function
Open	FileOpen
Close	FileClose
FreeFile	FreeFile
Write	Write, WriteLine
Print	Print, PrintLine
Input	Input
Line Input	LineInput

The first three of these work in the same way as in the previous types of access. It is only necessary to change the access mode to `OpenMode.Output`, `OpenMode.Input`, or `OpenMode.Append` in the `FileOpen` function.

The `Write` and `Print` functions also work similarly to the corresponding `Write` and `Print` statements in VB6. The differences are cosmetic and only involve adding parentheses around the arguments, reflecting the change from a statement to a function. `WriteLine` and `PrintLine` work like `Write` and `Print` respectively, except that they add a carriage return-line feed to the file after writing their data.

`Input` has the largest difference. The `Input` statement in VB6 allows multiple variables to be input with one line. There is no corresponding capability in Visual Basic .NET. Such a statement has to be replaced with multiple `Input` functions, each fetching one piece of data from the file. `Line Input` in VB6 only takes a single argument, however, so the `LineInput` function in Visual Basic .NET is quite similar.

Here is code similar to the VB6 example above, showing these keywords in action. This example performs exactly as the VB6 example:

```
Dim sFileName As String
sFileName = "C:\SequentialIO.txt"

FileOpen(1, sFileName, OpenMode.Output)

Write(1, "Clark", "Kent", 37, 6.1)
PrintLine(1, "He fights for Truth, Justice, and the American Way")

FileClose(1)

FileOpen(1, sFileName, OpenMode.Input)

Dim sFirstName As String
Dim sLastName As String
Dim nAge As Integer
Dim sngHeight As Single
Dim sDescription As String

Input(1, sFirstName)
Input(1, sLastName)
Input(1, nAge)
Input(1, sngHeight)
sDescription = LineInput(1)

MsgBox(sFirstName & " " & sLastName & " is " & _
       Str$(nAge) & " years old and is " & _
       Str$(sngHeight) & " feet tall. " & sDescription)
```

Streams as an Alternative in Visual Basic .NET

While sequential file I/O and binary access to files is possible in Visual Basic .NET in the same way as in VB6, there is a new capability, which will be preferred for most new development – **streaming I/O**.

Since streaming I/O is not an interoperability topic, we won't go into extensive detail here. We will, however, cover two examples that show analogs in streaming I/O to simple sequential access and simple random access.

You should be aware that streams are the recommended method for reading and writing data in files in .NET for most new development projects. The techniques covered earlier in this chapter are more applicable to situations that require interoperability.

Streaming shares some common characteristics with sequential I/O, and has similarities to binary I/O. There are a variety of stream objects in .NET. Some are for writing to files and objects, while others are for reading. In the following examples, we will show the most frequently used objects – the `FileStream`, `StreamReader`, and `StreamWriter` classes. Use of these requires an `Imports System.IO` statement.

Sequential Access with Streaming Techniques

In this Visual Basic .NET example, we will write three lines of data to a text file, and then read them back in. This will demonstrate both directions for data access.

Because we are trying to compare streaming to techniques presented earlier in the chapter, we will do our stream access in ASCII encoding. Because .NET strings are Unicode, standard ASCII encoding is not the default, and we must specify it when we declare our objects to read and write to the file. Here is the code:

```
' create a FileStream object pointing to the output file
Dim fs As FileStream = New _
        FileStream("C:\LinesOfData.txt", FileMode.Create)

' Create a stream writer to write to the file in ASCII format
Dim swOut As StreamWriter = New _
        StreamWriter(fs, System.Text.Encoding.ASCII)

' Write three lines to the file and flush the output
swOut.WriteLine("This is the first line in the file")
swOut.WriteLine("This line has fields, separated by commas, & a number, 22")
swOut.WriteLine("This is the third and last line")
swOut.Flush()

' Set the pointer to the beginning of the file using the FileStream
fs.Seek(0, SeekOrigin.Begin)

' Now read the lines back again
' First create a stream reader that reads in ASCII
Dim InputStreamReader As StreamReader = New _
        StreamReader(fs, System.Text.Encoding.ASCII)

Dim sLines(2) As String
Dim iLineIndex As Integer
For iLineIndex = 0 To 2
    sLines(iLineIndex) = InputStreamReader.ReadLine()
Next

' Now show the lines in a message box
Dim sOutput As String
sOutput = sLines(0) + vbCrLf + sLines(1) + vbCrLf + sLines(2)

MsgBox(sOutput)
```

As in binary access, streams have a "current position" that is a pointer to the place where the next operation will take place. Both `StreamWriter` and `StreamReader` objects update the pointer after every operation they perform.

Notice that the `FileStream` object is used for both the reader and the writer. The repositioning of the `FileStream` object `fs` affects the position for both the `StreamReader` and the `StreamWriter`.

Stream objects have a variety of methods for reading and writing different types of data. Using the `WriteLine` and `ReadLine` methods with strings resembles the sequential access presented earlier in the chapter, which is why they were used in this example.

There is one big limitation in using stream access rather that the sequential access presented earlier. There is no built-in capability in stream access to read delimited data (as there is in the Visual Basic .NET `FileInput` function covered earlier). If you need to process delimited data with streams, it is your responsibility to parse the data.

Binary Access with Streaming Techniques

We can use the same stream objects to perform file access that resembles the binary access we demonstrated earlier. For this example, we will modify the code used in the second example of binary access in Visual Basic .NET above:

```
' Get the input file
Dim fsIn As New FileStream("C:\TestData\SampleFile.txt", FileMode.Open)
Dim InputStreamReader As New StreamReader(fsIn, System.Text.Encoding.ASCII)

Dim sFileContents As String
sFileContents = InputStreamReader.ReadToEnd()

' Set the output file
Dim sFileName As String = "C:\TestData\SampleFileOut.txt"
Dim fsOut As New FileStream(sFileName, FileMode.Create)
Dim OutputStreamWriter As New _
        StreamWriter(fsOut, System.Text.Encoding.ASCII)

Dim sTextToFind As String
sTextToFind = "XXX"

Dim sTextToInsert As String
sTextToInsert = "ZZZZZZ"

Dim nCurrentPosition As Integer
Dim nNextPosition As Integer
Dim sNextPieceToInsert As String
nCurrentPosition = 1

nNextPosition = InStr(nCurrentPosition, sFileContents, sTextToFind)
Do While nNextPosition <> 0
    sNextPieceToInsert = Mid$(sFileContents, nCurrentPosition, _
                             nNextPosition - nCurrentPosition)
    OutputStreamWriter.Write(sNextPieceToInsert)
    OutputStreamWriter.Write(sTextToInsert)
```

```
        nCurrentPosition = nNextPosition + Len(sTextToFind)
        nNextPosition = InStr(nCurrentPosition, sFileContents, sTextToFind)
Loop

' Now need to write the last piece
sNextPieceToInsert = Microsoft.VisualBasic.Right(sFileContents, _
                    Len(sFileContents) - nCurrentPosition + 1)
OutputStreamWriter.Write(sNextPieceToInsert)

OutputStreamWriter.Close()
```

This example shows that there are comparable operations available with stream objects to the binary access functions examined earlier in the chapter. The previous example showed the same objects used for sequential access.

This demonstrates one of the strengths of stream-based access – its flexibility. You have the ability with stream objects to manipulate bytes in the stream and channel them from one stream to another (including streams that are based in memory or console devices instead of files).

Summary

Older systems produce data in a variety of non-standard formats. From fixed-length records, to report files, to comma-delimited data, it will be necessary to interoperate with these systems and, thus, read and write this data for quite a while.

Standards such as XML will lessen the demand for such operations over time but, in the mean time, Visual Basic .NET is still positioned to provide all of the functionality needed to work with these older formats.

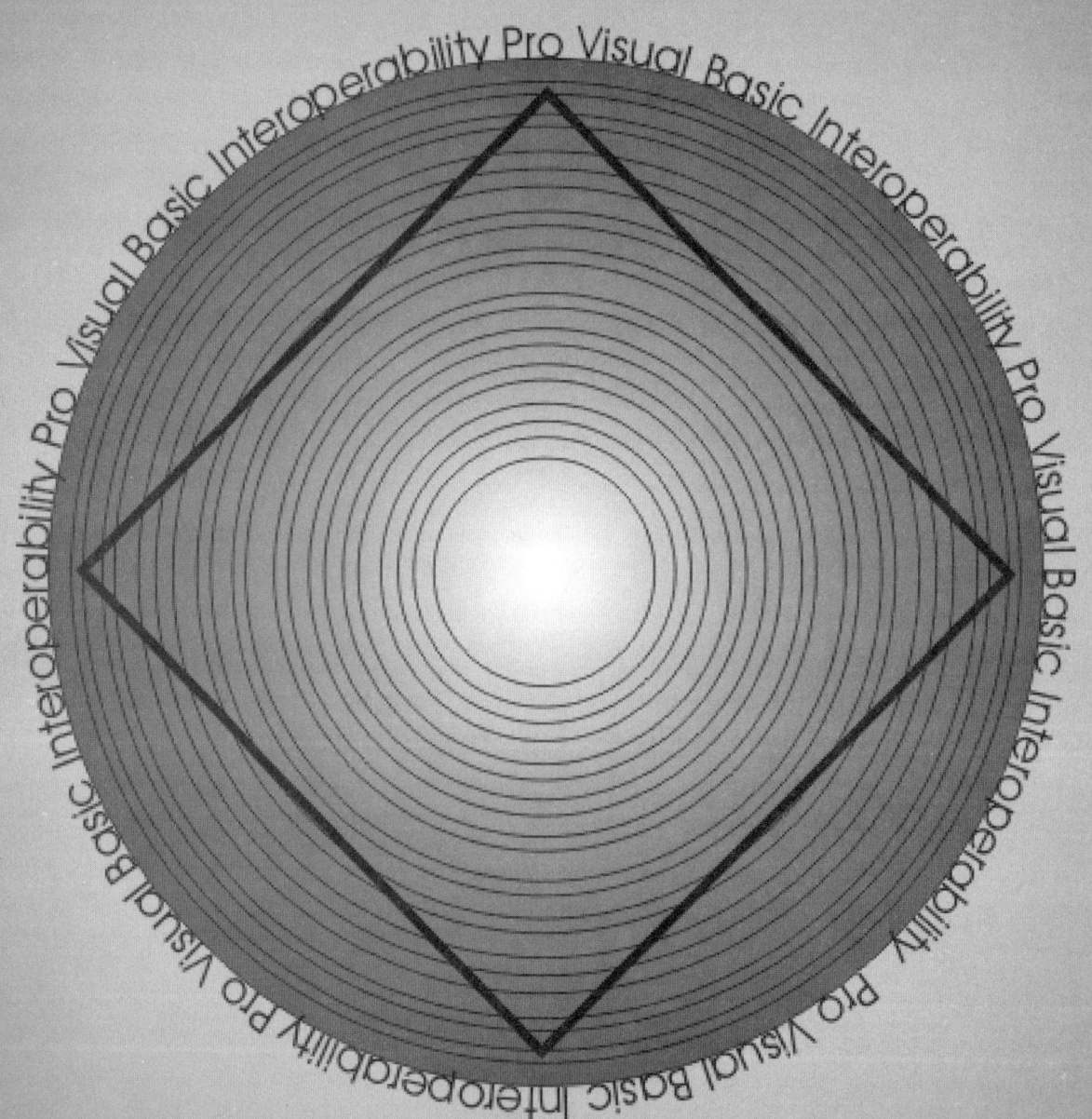

11

Using ADO in .NET

Much of the attention on data access in .NET has been focused on the new data technologies in ADO.NET. While ADO.NET does have some exciting capabilities and allows some interesting new architectures, it is not a complete replacement for ADO.

This chapter will compare ADO and ADO.NET and, based on that comparison, will talk about situations where ADO should still be used, even for new projects in Visual Basic .NET. We'll also discuss some of the implications of using ADO in .NET, including some minor differences from using it in VB6.

The chapter concludes with a brief look at data interoperability with DAO and RDO.

Comparison Between ADO and ADO.NET

Data access techniques in have evolved quickly in the last few years. This has caused some consternation among developers, but many of the changes have been necessary to adapt to evolving application architectures. We have gone from local access to client-server access to Internet access, all in about seven years.

The first data access model specifically for Visual Basic was called Data Access Objects (DAO). It was the first object model that made getting to data easy, offering an alternative to lower-level access methods like ODBC. DAO was created for access to *local databases* in the Access Jet format. It could also be extended to use databases on a server, such as SQL Server or Oracle, but was less than ideal for this function because its performance was optimized for local databases.

The successors to DAO were Remote Data Objects (RDO) and ActiveX Data Objects (ADO). Both were designed primarily for *client-server* use. RDO didn't hang around too long, but ADO is by far the most used data access model in VB6 projects. It has been extended to the Internet world, with capabilities such as Remote Data Services (RDS). ADO is still the easiest to use for client-server projects, but is more cumbersome for the highly distributed environment of the Internet.

The .NET Framework includes a new data access model created specifically for *distributed Internet* use. Called ADO.NET, it uses the same access methods for all kinds of data access, in which a local container of data is manipulated in a disconnected mode. While ADO.NET has some significant similarities to ADO, it also has some major differences.

For more information on ADO.NET, see Professional ADO.NET *(Wrox Press, ISBN 1-861005-27-X).*

Like ADO, ADO.NET can be used for accessing many kinds of data stores. In ADO, data is accessed through an OLE DB provider, and such a provider can be written for all kinds of data sources, such as file systems, spreadsheets, and flat files, in addition to traditional relational stores. ADO.NET can also go through an OLE DB provider to get to the same data sources. However, it also includes some customized capabilities to get to SQL Server (version 7.0 and above), yielding better performance than access through OLE DB.

ADO Advantages and Disadvantages

ADO was designed for tightly-coupled, connected architectures and, by default, passes data around in a binary, proprietary format through COM interfaces. As a "third-generation" client-server data access model, ADO is flexible and can be used for a wide variety of data access needs.

Newer requirements have forced ADO to evolve to be usable in Internet applications. While ADO is arguably still the best data access technology for connected access to data, the legacy and evolution of ADO have led to several issues for today's Internet-based development:

❑   Maintaining a connection to a database, as done in vanilla ADO, is resource intensive and limits scalability of applications. Such architecture is unsuitable for most Internet applications. Instead, using ADO on the server for Internet applications requires us to create a connection for a page and then dispose of it as soon as possible, after rendering the page. This architecture leaves no ability to persist the data between pages.

❑   The main alternative for disconnected access is Remote Data Services (RDS). This exposes new Internet functionality by providing persistence on the client, but introduces additional complexity. Developers have a tough learning curve before being able to use the right features of ADO for a given application architecture.

❑   XML support is not built-in, so accessing XML means going through the MSXML libraries and accessing the XML DOM. Later versions of ADO (version 2.6 and later) can export XML, but XML integration is still primitive in ADO.

ADO.NET is specifically designed to solve these limitations:

❑   A set of data in ADO.NET can be passed to any appropriate application tier in XML, so no continuous connection to the database is necessary.

❑   The same access techniques in ADO.NET can work for local, network, or Internet access.

❑   XML support is built in. This makes ADO.NET a flexible alternative, suitable for many different kinds of data access in Visual Basic .NET.

So we see that ADO.NET is the preferred data access technique for most Internet-based applications. However, it is not suitable for all types of data access. There are capabilities of ADO that are not present in ADO.NET.

To give developers access to these capabilities, the .NET Framework includes support for traditional ADO as well as ADO.NET. In most cases, it will not be necessary to change the ADO data access logic in old code to use it in .NET.

When is ADO Still Needed in .NET?

Existing data access code using ADO still works in .NET, and one reason to use ADO would be to import such code from older projects. This would apply, for example, if a VB6 project containing ADO code were being upgraded to Visual Basic .NET.

However, in new applications there is a choice. For the majority of situations, ADO.NET will prove to be preferred. This is especially true of disconnected applications.

However, there are several limitations of ADO.NET that can show up in certain programming situations. These limitations are consequences of the intended target for ADO.NET – disconnected scenarios – so most of them occur in applications that need connected access to data.

ADO.NET Only Has Optimistic Concurrency

ADO.NET implements an **optimistic concurrency** model. Data in a disconnected `DataSet` is checked for changes when updates are attempted. If the data has changed in the mean time, an exception is thrown and the developer must have code to decide what to do with the changes.

This makes complete sense in a disconnected environment. Maintaining a lock on records requires an open connection to the database, and disconnected scenarios have no easy way to maintain such a connection.

ADO Supports Pessimistic Concurrency

Some scenarios, particularly for client-server systems, require a different type of control over changes to data. Some applications need to access certain records, and lock the records so that no other application can get to the record (except in a read-only mode). Locking a record while making a change – to make sure that no one else can alter it in the mean time – is called **pessimistic concurrency**.

There is no capability in ADO.NET to lock records in a database and maintain the lock until the application is through with the data. That is, ADO.NET does not support pessimistic concurrency. That means that those .NET applications that need pessimistic concurrency must either use ADO to get it, or do significant extra work to implement a custom locking scheme that will lock the records as they are being placed in an ADO.NET `DataSet`.

For example, if a client-server application for a credit-card company supports operators that change credit-card data for customers, normally such an application would use pessimistic concurrency. When one operator opens a customer record for changes, that operator does not want any other operator to be able to alter the record until it is released. If another operator attempts to access the record, that operator knows immediately that the data cannot be changed. That eliminates the possibility that data may be entered by one operator and then accidentally over-written by another. An application such as this should not normally use ADO.NET for a data access model – ADO would typically be used instead.

ADO.NET Does Not Support Most Cursors

Cursors are a means of accessing a particular record in a set of records. They can be thought of as a "pointer" to an active record in the set.

The only cursor available in ADO.NET is for an object called a `DataReader`. This object is used for forward-only, read-only access to data, and it strongly resembles a forward-only, read-only `Recordset` in ADO. The other container for data in ADO.NET – the `DataSet` – accesses rows by using indices of row collections. There is no active row in such data access, and no pointer is maintained. The developer can manipulate the index and jump around in the collection as much as desired.

Furthermore, the `DataSet` is always local to the running application because it is an in-memory representation of the data. While this architecture works well for disconnected scenarios, there are other situations in which it is not suitable. In particular, working with large volumes of data is inadvisable in ADO.NET, because all the data is transferred to the client and stored in memory.

ADO Supports a Variety of Cursors, Including Server-Side

There are various types of cursors. Static cursors do not reflect changes made to the underlying database after the cursor was established. Dynamic cursors do reflect such changes. And there are "hybrid" types like the `KeySet` cursor, which reflects updates in the `Recordset`, but not insertions, and needs less memory than a dynamic cursor.

In addition, cursors can manipulate result sets on the client (client-side cursor) or on the server (server-side cursor). Using a client-side cursor means moving all the data in the result set down to the client, so there are situations involving large amounts of data in which a server-side cursor is much more suitable and gives better performance.

As mentioned earlier, ADO.NET only supports the forward-only, read-only cursor in a `DataReader`. The local, index-based access to a `DataSet` can be used as a replacement for client-side cursors in many situations. However, ADO.NET has no capability to implement a server-side cursor.

This leaves an important niche for ADO. If an application requires a server-side cursor, ADO will be required in the application.

Note that such situations are not overly common. You should always look at alternatives before using a cursor, because they are resource intensive. However, sometimes nothing else will do. For example, we mentioned that working with large volumes of data can often be done more effectively with a server-side cursor than an ADO.NET technique. The server-side cursor makes it unnecessary to transfer large amounts of data to the client and store it in memory there.

Other situations in which server-side cursors are helpful or essential are those in which the underlying data is changing a lot, and the changes must be reflected in the data immediately for all consuming clients. For example, a reservation system for airlines has constantly changing availability of seats, and an operator needs to know immediately if a seat becomes unavailable because another customer has just reserved it.

Using ADO in .NET

Using ADO in .NET is rather simple. However, note that you must have ADO 2.6 or above. The .NET Framework installs ADO 2.7 by default.

To begin using ADO in a project, first you have to establish a reference to the ADO library. .NET already has an interop assembly created for it, so it will show up on the .NET tab in the references. You should reference it there instead of the COM tab, because the reference on the COM tab will cause another interop assembly to be generated. The one that ships with .NET is specially tweaked to deal with ADO, and it is preferable to a generic one created by Visual Studio .NET.

To see this in action, start a new Windows Application in Visual Basic .NET. Then select the menu option Project | Add Reference. The dialog for adding a reference will look something like this:

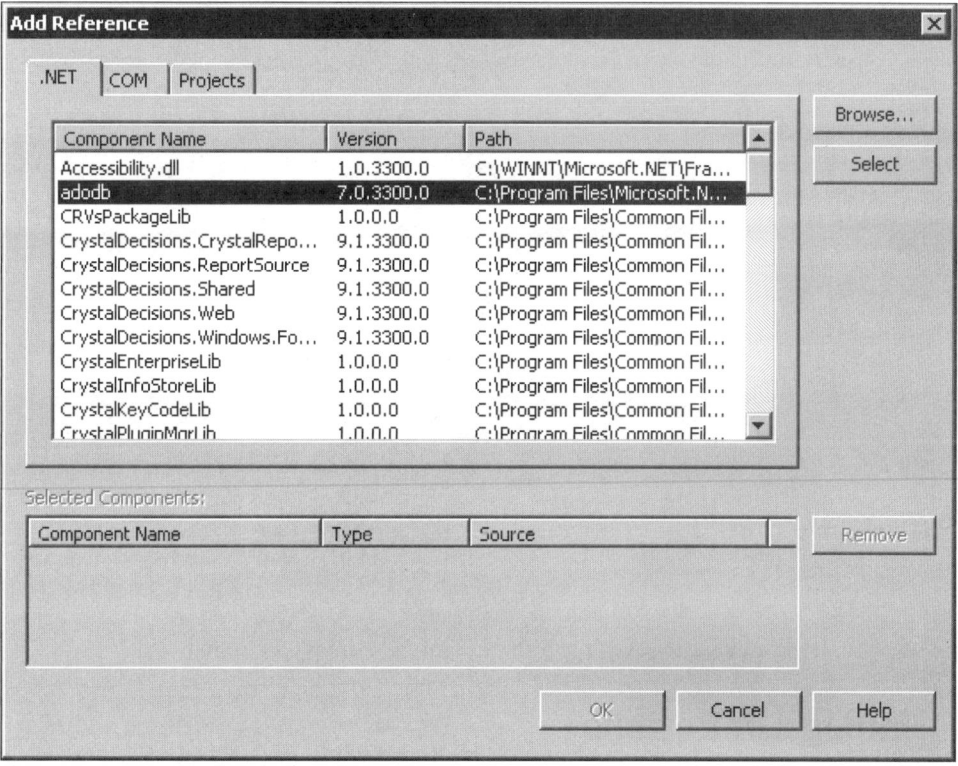

The adodb library will be close to the top. Highlight it, press the Select button and OK, and you're ready to use ADO in the .NET project. By default, you'll be using version 2.7. The version number shown in the dialog box is a .NET assembly version, not the ADO version.

ADO Code in Visual Basic .NET

The ADO code you write looks almost exactly like ADO code you would write in VB6. We refer to the classes with the ADODB prefix unless we add an "Imports ADODB" statement at the beginning of our module. Also, enumerations are indicated differently. The enumeration "adBookMarkCurrent" in VB6 ADO code, for example, would become BookMarkEnum.adBookMarkCurrent in Visual Basic .NET.

Here is some typical ADO code to access the Customers table in the Northwind sample database (installed with SQL Server). The records in the Recordset that is returned are then used to place some text in a TextBox (set its Multiline property to True). Here's the code:

```
' ADO usage in Visual Basic .NET
Dim adoConn As ADODB.Connection
Dim rs As New ADODB.Recordset()
Dim sConnectString As String
sConnectString = "uid=sa;pwd=;driver={SQL Server};" & _
        " server=MyServer;database=Northwind;dsn=,,connection=adConnectAsync"
adoConn = New ADODB.Connection()

With adoConn
    .ConnectionString = sConnectString
    .ConnectionTimeout = 10
    .Open()
End With

Dim sSQL As String
sSQL = "SELECT * FROM Customers ORDER BY CompanyName"

rs.Open(sSQL, adoConn, ADODB.CursorTypeEnum.adOpenKeyset,
ADODB.LockTypeEnum.adLockPessimistic)

While Not rs.EOF
    TextBox1.Text &= rs.Fields("CompanyName").Value & " - " & _
                     rs.Fields("ContactName").Value & " - " & _
                     rs.Fields("Phone").Value & vbCrLf
    rs.MoveNext()
End While
```

From this point, it's just like using ADO in VB6, except for a couple of limitations.

Data Binding Limitations

The standard .NET controls (DataGrid and TextBox, for example) are designed to bind to a DataSet. They can also bind to objects that implement certain required interfaces. However, ADO Recordsets do not have the required interface and so cannot be directly data bound to these controls.

ADO Recordsets can still be bound to ActiveX controls that are imported into Visual Basic .NET. (Chapter 13 discusses using ActiveX controls in Windows Forms.) However, it is not a good idea to use ActiveX controls unless there are no alternatives.

This is not as big a limitation as it might seem at first, for two reasons:

1. Data binding is not used much in advanced VB6 applications, so it won't be missed that badly when using ADO in .NET. Managing the placement of data into and out of controls with code still works fine, and that's the way most developers do it in VB6 anyway.

2. One of the most common ADO data binding needs is to data bind a `ListBox`, `DataGrid`, or similar control to a list derived from a `Recordset`. Fortunately, this can be done by importing a `Recordset` into a `DataSet`, and then binding the control to the `DataSet`. The control then shows the same data as if it were bound to the `Recordset`. This technique works best if the data is read-only and changes very infrequently, because it's difficult to manage concurrency if the data has been placed in a `DataSet`. We'll show that technique a little later on in the chapter.

Problems in Setting Some ADO Properties to Strings

In ADO, some properties can be set to either a string value or an object reference. An example is the `ActiveConnection` property of a `Recordset`. It can accept a connection object or a connection string (in which case it will establish a connection based on the string).

This works fine in VB6. However, it does not work in .NET because of the way .NET handles interfaces. You can only set the `ActiveConnection` property for an ADO `Recordset` to an object in .NET. Trying to set it to a string will result in an error.

However, the interop assembly for the ADO library has a workaround in place. You can use a new method implemented by the interop assembly called `let_ActiveConnection`. Here is an example in code:

```
Dim myConnString As String = _
    "Provider=SQLOLEDB.1;User ID=sa;password=;" & _
    "Initial Catalog=pubs;" & _
    "Data Source=mySQLServer"
Dim mySelectQuery As String = "SELECT * FROM Authors"
Dim myConnection as New ADODB.Connection()
Dim myRecordset As New ADODB.Recordset()

Try
    myConnection.ConnectionString = myConnString
    myConnection.open

    'Setting the ActiveConnection to a Connection object works fine.
    myRecordset.ActiveConnection = myConnection

Catch ex As Exception
    MessageBox.Show(ex.ToString())
Finally
    myConnection.Close()
End Try
```

This will *not* work, however:

```
...

Try
    myConnection.ConnectionString = myConnString
    myConnection.open

        'Setting the ActiveConnection to a Connection string will fail.

        ' This line will not work - generates an exception
        myRecordset.ActiveConnection = myConnString

Catch ex As Exception
    MessageBox.Show(ex.ToString())
Finally
    myConnection.Close()
End Try
```

We get a System.Runtime.InteropServices.COMException saying that the "Arguments are of the wrong type, are out of acceptable range, or are in conflict with one another." Here's the workaround:

```
...

Try
    myConnection.ConnectionString = myConnString
    myConnection.open

        ' This line works fine.
        myRecordset.let_ActiveConnection(myConnString)

Catch ex As Exception
    MessageBox.Show(ex.ToString())
Finally
    myConnection.Close()
End Try
```

This technique works for all of the properties of ADO objects that take either a string setting or an object setting. In each case, the object version works but the string version does not, and there is a work-around method for the string version named with a "let_" prefix plus the name of the property.

Converting an ADO Recordset into an ADO.NET DataSet

It is possible to get data from an ADO Recordset into an ADO.NET DataSet. One of the objects in ADO.NET, the OleDbDataAdapter, provides this capability.

If you are not familiar with DataAdapters in ADO.NET, you should know that they are the object used to transfer data into DataSets, and they take care of writing changes back to the database out of the DataSet. DataAdapters have a Fill method to place data from a database into a DataSet.

There are different `DataAdapters` for different types of database access. The one needed to import an ADO `Recordset` is in the `System.Data.OleDb` namespace and is called the `OleDbDataAdapter`. The `Fill` method for this `DataAdapter` has an overloaded version to accept a `Recordset` as the source of the data instead of fetching it directly from the database. (The other `DataAdapter`, in the `System.Data.SQLClient` namespace, does not work through OLE DB, and so cannot interface to ADO.)

We can change our earlier ADO example (the one that fetched customers from the `Northwind` database) to place the `Recordset` in a `DataSet`, and then we can bind the `DataSet` to a `DataGrid`. Here is how the code would change:

```
' ADO usage in Visual Basic .NET
Dim adoConn As ADODB.Connection
Dim rs As New ADODB.Recordset()
Dim sConnectString As String
sConnectString = "uid=sa;pwd=;driver={SQL Server};" & _
        " server=MyServer;database=Northwind;dsn=,,connection=adConnectAsync"
adoConn = New ADODB.Connection()

With adoConn
    .ConnectionString = sConnectString
    .ConnectionTimeout = 10
    .Open()
End With

Dim sSQL As String
sSQL = "SELECT * FROM Customers"

rs.Open(sSQL, adoConn, ADODB.CursorTypeEnum.adOpenKeyset,
ADODB.LockTypeEnum.adLockPessimistic)

Dim ds As New DataSet()
Dim da As New OleDb.OleDbDataAdapter()
da.Fill(ds, rs, "Customers")

DataGrid1.DataSource = ds.Tables("Customers")
```

This operation is one-way, however. There is no automatic way to get the data back into the `Recordset`. You could write your own code to do that, but you would have to loop through both the `Recordset` and the `DataSet`, matching up rows to change. This is probably not an appropriate technique.

Instead, you should use the capabilities of ADO.NET to write any changes back to the database. The same `DataAdapter` object that was used to fill the `DataSet` can also be used to write the changes in the `DataSet` back to the database, using its `Update` method.

However, this technique is most effective when the data is read-only. As discussed in the section on data binding, if the data is read-only and does not change much, this technique can be used to overcome the fact that .NET controls cannot data-bind to ADO `Recordsets`.

For more information on ADO.NET, see Professional ADO.NET *(Wrox Press, ISBN 1-861005-27-X).*

DAO and RDO Implications

To finish up the chapter, let's briefly look at data interoperability with DAO and RDO.

You can import and use the DAO and RDO libraries also. There are few good reasons for doing this – normally you should use the ADO library. But if you already have some DAO or RDO code you need to use, you can run it in .NET with minor changes. There is no pre-packaged interop assembly for these libraries, so you will have to refer to them under the **COM** tab of the **Add Reference** dialog.

From there, old code will work as expected, except for minor issues. For example, since .NET does not support default non-indexed properties, if your code uses any of them, it will need to be changed.

Here is a short example showing DAO support in .NET. First, start a new Visual Basic .NET Windows Forms Application. Then add a reference to the DAO library with **Project | Add Reference**. Here is how the dialog looks with the latest DAO library highlighted:

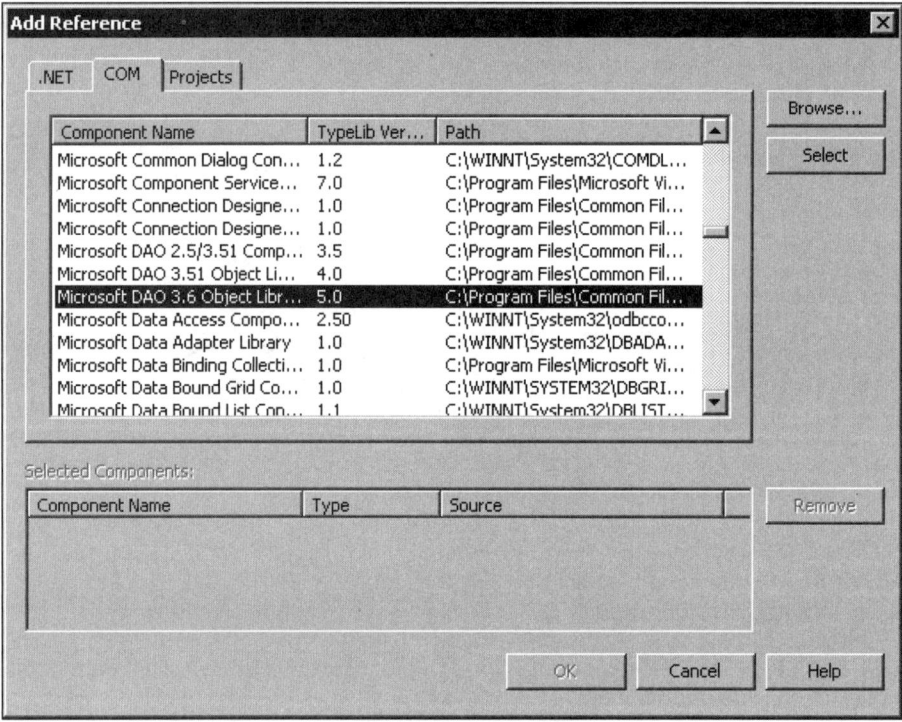

Press the **Select** button and then **OK**. You'll now have a reference to the DAO library.

Put a button on the form and this code behind the button:

```
Dim MainDatabase As DAO.Database
Dim wsMyWorkspace As DAO.Workspace
Dim myDBEngine As New DAO.DBEngineClass()
```

```
' Get workspace based on DBEngine
wsMyWorkspace = myDBEngine.Workspaces(0)

' Open database
MainDatabase = _
    wsMyWorkspace.OpenDatabase("C:\testdata\northwind.mdb")

' create a DAO recordset and place some
' of its data in a message box
Dim rs As DAO.Recordset
Dim sSQL As String
sSQL = "SELECT * FROM Customers"
rs = MainDatabase.OpenRecordset(sSQL)

MsgBox("Company Name - " & rs.Fields("CompanyName").Value)
```

This is standard DAO code except for the line that creates the database engine. This line is unnecessary in standard DAO – the DBEngine construct is always available without instantiating it. But in .NET we do have to instantiate the class.

You can change the line that points to the database (northwind.mdb) to point to its actual location, or you can use a different MDB file and change the SQL statement and the name of the field used later in the code.

Once you run the code, you'll see a message box that looks like this:

Summary

You can access relational stores in Visual Basic .NET via ADO, with close to full functionality. There are ADO features like pessimistic concurrency and server-side cursors that have no matching capability in ADO.NET. This makes it appropriate to use ADO in applications that need these features. The biggest limitation is that ADO cannot be used for data binding to standard controls in .NET.

It is possible to pump an ADO Recordset into an ADO.NET DataSet. In addition, you can use DAO and RDO in Visual Basic .NET, though it's not recommended that you do so unless you have a very good reason.

The relational data interoperability features of Visual Basic .NET are sufficient for most of the needs you will probably have. While you will want to learn ADO.NET for most database access in new systems, don't shy away from using ADO to get the level of data interoperability you need.

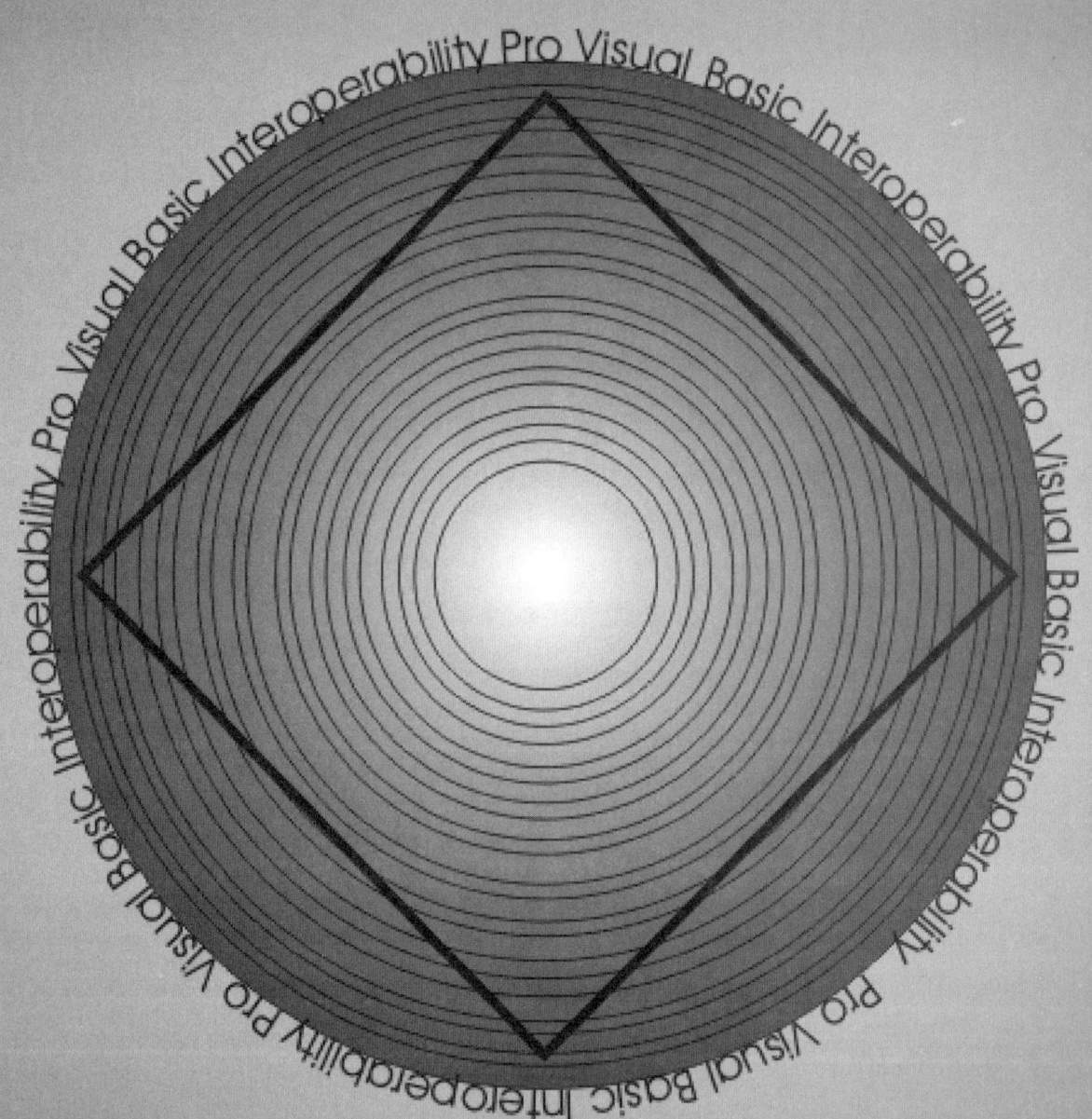

12

Calling API or Static DLL Functions from .NET

Much of this book has concentrated on interoperability with recent technologies such as COM and ADO. Most organizations are expected to need these types of interoperability. However, there will be some cases in which interoperability with older (pre-COM) software is necessary. Typically, that will mean allowing .NET software to use functionality packaged in DLLs that do not have a COM interface.

In previous versions of Visual Basic, a `Declare` statement is used to access such DLLs. The `Declare` statement contains a function declaration that is often called a **static method declaration** or **static entry point**, to differentiate it from a method in a COM interface. It merely consists of the name of the function that is needed from the DLL. That function name is then mapped to a particular entry point (address) in the DLL, based on information that the DLL supplies about the functions that it contains.

At one time, this type of interfacing was common in VB programming, but it has been mostly replaced by COM-based interfaces. The most prevalent use of this type of interfacing in recent years has been to allow VB programs to work with the Windows API. This API is contained in a number of DLLs that have static entry points with no COM interface. `kernel32.dll`, `user32.dll`, and `gdi32.dll` are some of the system DLL file names that may look familiar to experienced VB developers.

However, this interfacing technique is also used to work with DLLs (typically written in C or C++) that were developed before COM became popular. There is less need for such DLLs each year, but some organizations still have both 32-bit and 16-bit DLLs that contain important functionality.

This chapter covers the basic aspects of interoperating .NET with DLLs that functions access through static entry points. As with the COM interoperability chapters, the focus here is on the common cases. There are, however, a number of unusual cases that require more advanced techniques. While the documentation on .NET interoperability with such DLLs is less than ideal, it should be sufficient to help you tackle the unusual cases once you understand the basics.

Reduced Need for Using DLLs with Static Entry Points in .NET

In general, .NET programs will not need to interface with legacy, non-COM based DLLs as frequently as VB6 programs. There are a couple of reasons for this.

Reduced Need for Access to Windows API

First, programs written in Visual Basic .NET have a dramatically reduced need to work directly with the Windows API. A wide variety of functions in the API have been wrapped by .NET classes that serve as intermediaries and expose a true .NET interface. For example, printing slanted text on a form or control in VB6 requires using the Windows API. The following code snippet should demonstrate just how complicated this typically is:

```
' Types and Declares needed for API functions to work (these go elsewhere
' in the project.)

Public Type LOGFONT
        lfHeight As Long
        lfWidth As Long
        lfEscapement As Long
        lfOrientation As Long
        lfWeight As Long
        lfItalic As Byte
        lfUnderline As Byte
        lfStrikeOut As Byte
        lfCharSet As Byte
        lfOutPrecision As Byte
        lfClipPrecision As Byte
        lfQuality As Byte
        lfPitchAndFamily As Byte
        lfFaceName(1 To LF_FACESIZE) As Byte
End Type

Public Type RECT
        Left As Long
        Top As Long
        Right As Long
        Bottom As Long
End Type

Public Declare Function GetClientRect Lib "user32" _
Alias "GetClientRect" (ByVal hwnd As Long, lpRect As RECT) As Long
```

```
Public Declare Function TextOut Lib "gdi32" _
Alias "TextOutA" (ByVal hdc As Long, ByVal x As Long, _
ByVal y As Long, ByVal lpString As String, ByVal nCount As Long) As Long

Public Declare Function SelectObject Lib "gdi32" _
Alias "SelectObject" (ByVal hdc As Long, ByVal hObject As Long) As Long

Public Declare Function CreateFontIndirect Lib "gdi32" _
Alias "CreateFontIndirectA" (lpLogFont As LOGFONT) As Long

Public Declare Function DeleteObject Lib "gdi32" _
Alias "DeleteObject" (ByVal hObject As Long) As Long

' This is VB6 code to place text on a form at an angle. This code is
' usually run in a Paint event.

Dim lf As LOGFONT
Dim nOldWindowHandle
Dim TempByteArray() As Byte
Dim nReturnValue As Long
Dim nArrayIndex As Integer
Dim nByteArrayLimit
Dim rc As RECT
Dim sngRotation As Single

' Set rotation angle and font.

sngRotation = 45
If FontToUse <> 0 Then dl = DeleteObject(FontToUse)          ' API call
lf.lfHeight = mnHeight
lf.lfWidth = mnWidth
lf.lfEscapement = Int(sngRotation * 10)
lf.lfWeight = mnWeight

Dim sFontName As String
sFontName = Me.FontName
TempByteArray = StrConv(sFontName & Chr$(0), vbFromUnicode)
ByteArrayLimit = UBound(TempByteArray)
For nArrayIndex = 0 To nByteArrayLimit
    fntFont.lfFaceName(nArrayIndex) = TempByteArray(nArrayIndex)
Next nArrayIndex
FontToUse = CreateFontIndirect(fntFont)                      ' API call
If FontToUse = 0 Then Exit Sub
nOldWindowHandle = SelectObject(frmFormName.hdc, FontToUse)  ' API call

' For example, put text in center of form.

Dim nLeftPos As Long
Dim nTopPos As Long
nLeftPos = Me.Width / 2
nTopPos = Me.Height / 2

' Get the client rectangle in order to place the text midway down the
' box - these are all API calls.
```

371

```
nReturnValue = GetClientRect(frmFormName.hwnd, rc)
nReturnValue = TextOut(frmFormName.hdc, nLeftPos, nTopPos, msText,
    Len(msText))
nReturnValue = SelectObject(frmFormName.hdc, nOldWindowHandle)
```

We will not explain this code – it is just an example to demonstrate the number of lines of code and calls to the API that are necessary for this simple operation. The code is not easy to understand unless you are quite familiar with the Windows API.

In .NET, there is no need to use the API for this purpose. The Graphics object in the System.Drawing namespace is completely capable of painting text to the screen at any angle. Exactly the same functionality as the previous VB6 example can be obtained with this code in .NET:

```
' This is the Visual Basic .NET version for drawing text at an angle.
' This code is usually run in a Paint event. We can get the Graphics
' object directly from the PaintEventArgs parameter of the event.

Dim grfGraphics As Graphics = e.Graphics

' Declare a brush and a font to use.

Dim bshBrush As Brush
Dim fntFont As Font

' Set the brush to the form's foreground color.

bshBrush = New SolidBrush(Me.ForeColor)

' Set the font to the form's default font.

fntFont = Me.Font

' Set the coordinates of the text's starting point - in this case,
' dead center on the form.

Dim sngHorizontalPos As Single
Dim sngVerticalPos As Single
sngHorizontalPos = Me.Size.Width * 0.5
sngVerticalPos = Me.Size.Height * 0.5

' Now draw some rotated text.

Dim nRotationAngle As Integer = 45
grfGraphics.RotateTransform(nRotationAngle)
grfGraphics.DrawString(Me.Text, fntFont, bshBrush, _
    sngHorizontalPos, sngVerticalPos)
grfGraphics.ResetTransform()
```

As you can tell, this code is considerably more concise and easier to understand than the VB6 version. This demonstrates the power of the .NET Framework base classes, and should convince you not to use the API in .NET unless you really need to because there is no .NET equivalent for what you want to do.

Retirement of Older Code

The second reason why access to DLLs with static entry points will be needed less in .NET is the retirement of older software. While there's no reason to replace code that works well, in many cases changing requirements over time make older code obsolete. New development projects are often an opportunity to replace such functionality in older modules, especially those using technologies no longer in favor.

If it is desirable to keep using the same code, there is another alternative to consider. Most DLLs that are not based on COM were originally made in C or C++. If the sourcecode is available, it can usually be imported into .NET using Visual C++ .NET.

Platform Invocation Services

Despite the fact that .NET reduces the need to get to older DLLs, there will still be some custom-written legacy, non-COM-based DLLs that need to be used with .NET. There are also a handful of situations where it is still helpful to access the Windows API from .NET. The capability to do both of these is part of what .NET calls **Platform Invocation Services**. This is often abbreviated as **PInvoke** (sometimes written as P/Invoke).

Declaring the API

For VB developers, the PInvoke capability is wrapped up in the .NET version of the `Declare` statement. This is the way that VB developers are accustomed to dealing with DLLs using static entry points, and the .NET syntax is quite similar to VB6. However, it is often used differently because the recommended way to handle such declarations in Visual Basic .NET is inside a class. (The only other allowed technique in Visual Basic .NET is to use a BAS module, which is actually implemented as a class behind the scenes.)

The class that contains the declaration then automatically exposes the function that was declared as a shared member of the class. Here is a simple example to show the general structure.

First, we need to set up a class to hold the declaration. We'll call it `Win32API` (several of the examples in the documentation use this convention). Then, inside the class, we declare the function. For the example, we will use the `GetWindowText` API call, because it will be familiar to many VB developers and is relatively simple to use. Here is the `Win32API` class:

```
Imports System.Text
Public Class Win32API
    Public Declare Auto Sub GetWindowText Lib "User32.Dll" _
        (ByVal nWindowHandle As Integer, _
        ByVal sWindowText As StringBuilder, _
        ByVal nMaxCharCount As Integer)
End Class
```

The reason why this example is relatively simple is that the data passed to the API call is made up of basic types – in this case Integer and String. In such a case, the Declare statement looks very much like the equivalent in VB6. However, there are two significant differences. The first is the Auto keyword, which tells .NET how to handle the data marshaling of strings for this function. The other is declaring the text as a StringBuilder instead of a String. (The use of StringBuilder is also the reason for the first line that imports the System.Text namespace, where the StringBuilder class resides.) We'll discuss both of these differences in more detail in the section below, entitled *Data Marshaling Issues.*

As with VB6, the reference to the DLL that occurs after the Lib keyword can be a complete pathname. In fact, if you are using one of your own DLLs (that is not part of the Windows API), then you must supply the full pathname. However, for DLLs in the Windows API, only the file name is required.

If you have several API functions that you need to access, you can put them in the same class. Each of them becomes a separate shared method of the class (even though they are not marked as Shared in the code). It is good practice to group related API calls into the same class, though there's nothing to stop you from putting each API call into a separate class if you want to.

It is common for functions to expect certain integer arguments to correspond to pre-defined values with various meanings. For example, the Windows API function MessageBox accepts an integer argument that controls how the MessageBox control is displayed, and which takes values such as the hexadecimal value &H20 to tell it to display an icon for a question mark. These values often are encoded as constants with names such as MB_ICONQUESTION.

If you need such constants in your .NET class, you will have to declare them in your code, just as you would need to do in VB6.

Calling the API Function

Once the class is declared as shown above, you are ready to use the API function by calling it as a member of the Win32API class. Here is some code to use the GetWindowText function declared above:

```
'Place "Imports System.Text" at top of Module.
Dim sbWindowText As New StringBuilder(256)
Dim nMyWindowHandle As Integer

' Get a window handle from the form and convert it to 32-bit integer.

nMyWindowHandle = Me.Handle.ToInt32

Win32API.GetWindowText(nMyWindowHandle, _
                       sbWindowText, _
                       sbWindowText.Capacity)
Label1.Text = sbWindowText.ToString()
```

Since the API function is created in the class as a shared method by the Declare statement, it is not necessary to create an instance of the Win32API class. You can just call the shared method GetWindowText directly.

You can try this code out by creating a form in a Windows Forms project that has a Label1 control on it, and then placing the code behind a button. The window text will be equivalent to the Text property of the form (which shows up in the window's title bar).

Of course, normally, `GetWindowText` is used to get the window text from some other window after obtaining a handle for the window. We will not go into getting window handles here, since VB developers who use API calls will be familiar with the techniques for doing that.

Aliasing a Function

In most cases, it is fine to use the original name of the function in the DLL to declare and call it. But occasionally the name conflicts with something else, or is not a legal VB function name, or needs to be abbreviated for ease of use. In that case, the function name can be replaced with another declared name, and the `Alias` keyword is used to indicate the real name of the function in the DLL. For example, the declaration for GetWindowText above can be changed to use an alias of `GetTitle` with the following code:

```
Imports System.Text
Public Class Win32API
    Public Declare Auto Sub GetTitle Lib "User32.Dll" _
        Alias "GetWindowText" _
            (ByVal nWindowHandle As Integer, _
            ByVal sWindowText As StringBuilder, _
            ByVal nMaxCharCount As Integer)
End Class
```

In this case, the calling code just changes to use the new name, like this:

```
Dim sbWindowText As New StringBuilder(256)
Dim nMyWindowHandle As Integer

' Get a window handle from the form and convert it to 32-bit integer.

nMyWindowHandle = Me.Handle.ToInt32

Win32API.GetTitle(nMyWindowHandle, _
                    sbWindowText, _
                    sbWindowText.Capacity)
Label1.Text = sbWindowText.ToString()
```

Now that we have looked at a simple example, we need to cover techniques used in more complex cases.

Passing Structures as Parameters

Many Windows API functions have arguments that are actually structures. For example, many API functions dealing with drawing to the screen take what's called a `Rect` structure, which represents the position and size of a rectangle.

To use such an API function from .NET, it is necessary to create a structure declaration that matches the structure used in the API call. This can be tricky because you must tell .NET exactly how to lay out the structure in memory so that the API function can use it properly. The default way that .NET lays out structures in memory will not marshal correctly to API functions.

Specifying the memory layout of the structure is done with .NET attributes. The two attributes used to lay out structures are the `StructLayout` attribute and the `FieldOffset` attribute.

The `StructLayout` attribute takes an enumeration for the type of layout that you want. The two layout types that you should use in .NET are:

❑ `LayoutKind.Sequential` – tells .NET to lay out the memory exactly as the elements of the structure are specified, with no automatic adjustment of any kind. This only works properly for PInvoke if each element of the structure has the precise number of bytes that it needs in the structure. Otherwise, the memory layout of the structure will not be correct for use by API functions.

❑ `LayoutKind.Explicit` – tells .NET that you will be giving exact offsets from the beginning of the structure for each element. This provides some flexibility to place fields exactly where you need them in the structure.

There is also `LayoutKind.Auto`, but this layout option should not be used with PInvoke because it usually does not layout the memory for the structure in such a way that the data can be used by an API function.

If you are using `LayoutKind.Explict`, then you must specify the offset for each element in the structure using the `FieldOffset` attribute. `FieldOffset` takes a single argument, which is the number of bytes for the offset.

Here is an example that shows declarations for each type:

```
<StructLayout(LayoutKind.Sequential)> Public Structure Point
    Public x As Integer
    Public y As Integer
End Structure

<StructLayout(LayoutKind.Explicit)> Public Structure Rect
    <FieldOffset(0)> Public left As Integer
    <FieldOffset(4)> Public top As Integer
    <FieldOffset(8)> Public right As Integer
    <FieldOffset(12)> Public bottom As Integer
End Structure
```

In the first example, since the `Integer` type needs four bytes, the structure will be assembled by .NET as eight bytes in total, with the first four for the element x and the second for the element y. In the second example, the offsets start at zero and go up by four for each element (which gives a result functionally equivalent to `LayoutKind.Sequential` for this particular case). This example is only shown to demonstrate the syntax of the `FieldOffset` attribute, because it would be easier to use the `LayoutKind.Sequential` option and leave off the `FieldOffset` attributes.

Note that the structure declarations must be `Public` so that code in other modules can declare a variable of the structure type to use in the API call (assuming that the API calls are in a class of their own and a module separate from application code, as is recommended).

Remember that you can only use attributes if they have been referenced appropriately. For the attributes above, the DLL containing them is automatically referenced by Visual Basic .NET, but you do need an `Imports` statement for the `System.Runtime.InteropServices` namespace at the top of the module.

Example of an API with a Structure Parameter

To show an example of using a structure in an API call, here is the entire class containing the API declaration for an API call (PtInRect) that needs both a Point structure and a Rect structure:

```
Imports System.Runtime.InteropServices

Class Win32API

    <StructLayout(LayoutKind.Sequential)> Public Structure Point
        Public x As Integer
        Public y As Integer
    End Structure

    <StructLayout(LayoutKind.Explicit)> Public Structure Rect
        <FieldOffset(0)> Public left As Integer
        <FieldOffset(4)> Public top As Integer
        <FieldOffset(8)> Public right As Integer
        <FieldOffset(12)> Public bottom As Integer
    End Structure

    Declare Auto Function PtInRect Lib "user32.dll" _
        (ByRef r As Rect, p As Point) As Boolean
End Class
```

This API call determines if a point is inside a rectangle. A form could use it, with the following code inside the form:

```
Dim MyPoint As New Win32API.Point()
MyPoint.x = 10
MyPoint.y = 100

Dim MyRect As New Win32API.Rect()

MyRect.left = Me.Left
MyRect.top = Me.Top
MyRect.bottom = Me.Top + Me.Height
MyRect.right = Me.Left + Me.Width

Dim bInRect As Boolean
bInRect = Win32API.PtInRect(MyRect, MyPoint)

Label1.Text = bInRect.ToString
```

If you test this code, notice that bInRect will be True if the code is executed while the form is very close to the upper left portion of the screen, but False if the form is displaced even a small distance from the upper left corner.

Notice that you must explicitly specify that you want to declare a structure of type Win32API.Point instead of just Point. There is a Point type already in .NET that will be used if you don't.

Data Marshaling Issues

The engine used to do data marshaling for PInvoke is the same as the engine used to do data marshaling for COM Interop. That means that the discussion of data marshaling in the chapters on COM Interop is applicable to PInvoke, except for the parts on COM-specific marshaling types.

By far the biggest data marshaling issues in PInvoke that vary from COM Interop are those related to strings. Most of the complexities in passing strings back and forth to functions in DLLs have to do with the fact that strings in .NET are **immutable**. That is, .NET strings cannot be changed in their current memory location. Whenever a string is changed in .NET (even if the change does not affect the length), .NET creates a new memory location for the string and copies the changes into that location. When the operation is done, .NET then switches the reference to the string variable to the new location.

This means that .NET cannot pass a memory reference to a string in a call to a function in a DLL if the string's value needs to be changed and passed back. Such an operation will generate an exception because .NET will not allow the string to be changed in place.

Dealing with Strings

There are actually several different ways that functions in DLLs might expect to receive strings in arguments. We will cover the most common cases. There are additional minor cases that you can find out about in the .NET documentation, but these are rarely needed.

Here is a description of the major scenarios for passing strings to an unmanaged function in a non-COM DLL.

1. The function expects the string to be passed by value, and will not need to return a value in the string

2. The function needs to pass a result back in the string parameter

3. The function needs the string as part of a structure, and will not need to return a value in the string element of the structure

4. The function needs the string as part of a structure, and will change the string to pass back a value

Case 1 is straightforward to deal with. The `Declare` statement for the function can just use a `String` type for the string parameter. Since it will not be passed back, the .NET data marshaling engine will take care of getting the value of the string into the function.

Case 2 is usually dealt with by using a `StringBuilder` class instead of a `String` data type. The `GetWindowText` example earlier in the chapter demonstrates this scenario.

Case 3 is also straightforward, because the string part of the structure can just be declared as type `String`. It is important to make sure that the layout of the structure is correct, as covered in the topic above on *Passing Structures as Parameters*. For common cases, the layout type of `LayoutKind.Sequential` will work. However, the strings in the structure need an attribute to specify the length for marshaling. Here is an example of such a structure:

```
<StructLayout(LayoutKind.Sequential)> Structure Example1
    <VBFixedString(10)> Public sTenCharacterString As String
    <VBFixedString(5)> Public sFiveCharacterString As String
    Public nNumber As Integer
    ' Other fields as necessary.
End Structure
```

The attribute `<VBFixedString(n)>` tells the marshaling engine to lay out the string as n characters.

Case 4 involves complex issues that are beyond the scope of this chapter. However, this situation does not arise as often as the others. The complexity arises from the fact that the DLL may be expecting the string in the form of a buffer of characters, or it may be expecting a reference to the string's location, along with another parameter that holds the length of the string. These cases are handled quite differently, and there are examples of each in the .NET documentation. (In the Visual Studio .NET Help Index, look at the platform invoke index entry, marshaling data subentry, Marshaling Strings topic.)

Using Automatic ANSI/Unicode Location

Another string marshaling issue is making sure strings passed into a function in a DLL are of the right format (ANSI versus Unicode). Internally, all .NET strings are Unicode, so it is necessary for .NET to know whether or not to change the format of the string when doing data marshaling to the function.

Most custom DLLs with static entry points use ANSI strings for their arguments, though it is possible for them to use Unicode strings. But Windows API functions can actually have implementations for both ANSI and Unicode strings. In many cases, the Unicode version is named by appending a "W" to the regular function name, so that `GetComputerName` is the ANSI version while `GetComputerNameW` is the Unicode version.

This all leads to several ways to tell .NET how to marshal strings in a `Declare` statement. The keyword to specify the type of string marshaling, if present, comes right after the `Declare` keyword. The three possible options for the string marshaling keyword are:

Marshaling	Description
ANSI	Marshal strings to the function as ANSI format (this is the default if no option is specified).
Unicode	Marshal strings to the function as Unicode. This should only be chosen if you know that the function expects Unicode strings, since they are stored very differently from ANSI strings, using two bytes per character instead of one.
Auto	Lets .NET choose how to marshal strings based on its own internal information and the arguments passed to it. This only works for Windows API functions.

All of the examples in this section are Windows API calls, and so they all use the `Auto` option. Most Windows API calls can be either `ANSI` or `Auto`. As mentioned above, most custom DLLs will require ANSI strings. You should not use `Auto` with your declarations for functions in your own DLLs, but you can use `Unicode` if you know that the DLL expects a Unicode string as a parameter.

You can see another example of marshaling strings for an API call in Chapter 9 on *Sharing Configuration Information*. The API calls used to get to Windows INI files are used in examples in that chapter, and these APIs have string arguments.

Getting More Control

If the automatic capabilities of PInvoke covered above are not sufficient for your needs, there are a couple of other options to pursue.

Control Over Data Marshaling

You can specify attributes that tell .NET to use specific types of data marshaling. The `MarshalAs` attribute can be used to explicitly specify unmanaged data types that an API expects. Here is an example of a parameter that has been labeled with the `MarshalAs` attribute:

```
Public Declare Sub MyUnmanagedSub Lib "MyDLL.Dll" _
    (<MarshalAs(UnmanagedType.LPStr)> s As String)
```

This allows the parameter that is passed in to be a normal .NET string, but tells the data marshaling engine to format it as the C type `char*`. Note that this only works if the string will not be changed by the DLL function because .NET strings are immutable, as previously discussed. The marshaling attribute in this case only fixes up the string to be acceptable to the DLL.

The permitted enumerations for the `MarshalAs` attribute include several different types of strings that are used in unmanaged DLLs. Here are the C++ string types and the related enumerations:

C++ string type	Corresponding enumeration
BStr	MarshalAs(UnmanagedType.BStr)
LPStr	MarshalAs(UnmanagedType.LPStr)
LPTStr	MarshalAs(UnmanagedType.LPTStr)
LPWStr	MarshalAs(UnmanagedType.LPWStr)

Using DLLImport Instead of Declare

There is an advanced alternative to using the `Declare` statement in a class to perform the declaration of a function in an unmanaged DLL. An attribute named `DLLImport` can be applied to the function, and it has parameters to give precise control over the declaration instead of using the automatic features of the `Declare` statement.

To see how `DLLImport` compares to using the `Declare` statement, let's look at a simple example. This is a function created with `DLLImport` that duplicates the functionality of the example shown earlier under the heading *Aliasing a Function*. That example accessed the `GetWindowText` API call, and aliased the function as `GetTitle`. This example accesses the same API function, but uses the alias of `GetTitle2`:

```
<DllImport("User32.dll", EntryPoint:="GetWindowTextW", _
    SetLastError:=True, CharSet:=CharSet.Unicode, _
    ExactSpelling:=True, _
    CallingConvention:=CallingConvention.StdCall)> _
Public Shared Function GetTitle2(ByVal nWindowHandle As Integer, _
    ByVal sWindowText As StringBuilder, _
```

```
            ByVal nMaxCharCount As Integer) As Integer
                ' Leave function empty - DLLImport attribute forwards calls
                ' for the function to GetWindowTextW in User32.DLL.
    End Function
```

The `EntryPoint` setting for `DLLImport` shows the entry point as `GetWindowTextW`, which is actually the Unicode version of the `GetWindowText` API function. The `CharSet` option specifies that we are working in Unicode.

This code can be tested with very similar code to that used in the earlier example:

```
Dim sbWindowText As New StringBuilder(256)
Dim nMyWindowHandle As Integer
nMyWindowHandle = Me.Handle.ToInt32

Dim iReturn As Integer
iReturn = GetTitle2(nMyWindowHandle, _
                    sbWindowText, _
                    sbWindowText.Capacity)
Label1.Text = sbWindowText.ToString()
```

You will need to import the `System.Runtime.InteropServices` namespace, as well as `System.Text` for this example.

This is a simple demonstration, but there are many settings available to control the way that such functions are declared. If you like having more control than the `Declare` statement gives you, `DLLImport` is a nice alternative.

Performance Considerations

The performance impact of using PInvoke is similar to that of using COM Interop. Each time that a function in an unmanaged DLL is accessed, there is a small performance hit to transition from managed to unmanaged code. However, the impact of this is minor. The noticeable performance impact of PInvoke involves certain types of data marshaling.

Parameters that are exact matches for .NET types do not cause significant performance impact because the marshaling is just a memory-to-memory copy. Numeric types, such as `Short`, `Integer`, `Long`, `Single`, and `Double`, are good examples.

However, we've seen that strings may require significant marshaling, including conversion from Unicode to ANSI. If a .NET application calls an unmanaged DLL function that uses strings extensively, and the function is used a lot (say in a loop that calls it hundreds or thousands of times), then the .NET application may be slower than an equivalent VB6 application that makes the same number of calls to the DLL.

Summary

If you have been accustomed to doing a lot of API access in VB6, you need to make an adjustment in .NET. API access is not needed nearly as much. You will need to learn the .NET classes that provide the functionality that you want, and then you can dispense with most of your API access.

Most, but not all. This chapter covers the basics for using those API functions that you still need to access from Visual Basic .NET. The same techniques can also work with legacy DLLs that do not have COM interfaces, but instead must be used by declaring a static entry point in your code. This Platform Invoke (PInvoke) capability is built into .NET, and takes care of most of the system-level interfacing required to use these functions from .NET.

Gaining access to these functions is similar to the way that it's done in VB6 except for data marshaling issues. In some respects, .NET does even more for you than VB6 in that area, but you have to understand how to tell .NET what you need it to do for data marshaling.

It's also important to understand how structures in Visual Basic .NET vary from user-defined types in VB6. From an interoperability standpoint, the differences are minor, mostly having to do with data marshaling.

If you want complete control over the way that API functions and other non-COM functions are declared, `DLLImport` can be used. But for common cases, the `Declare` statement will give you all that you need to use these functions.

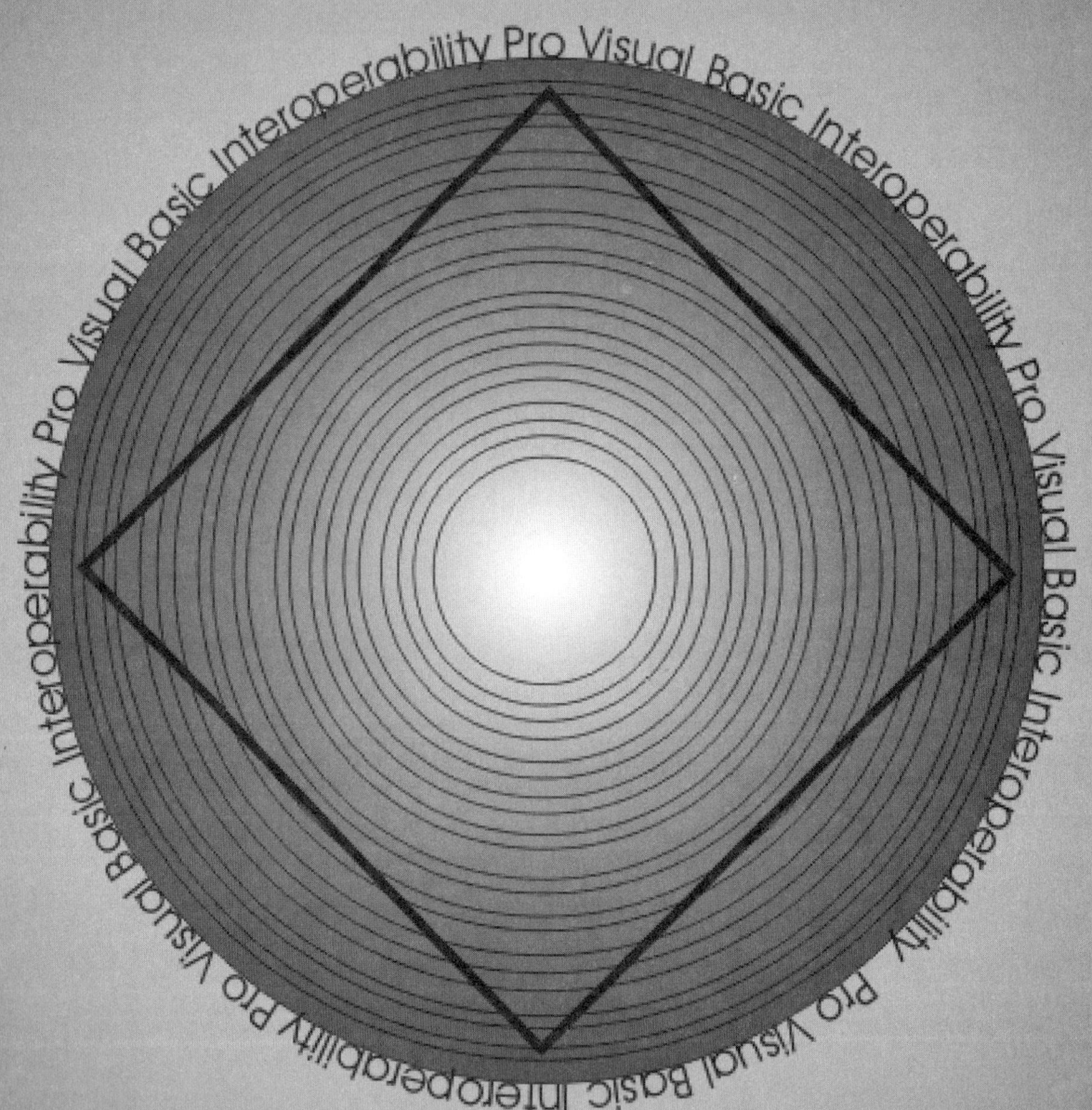

13

Interoperability of ActiveX Controls in .NET

The chapters in this book on COM interoperability have discussed using generic COM components inside .NET. There is one special kind of COM component that requires special treatment – ActiveX controls.

Experienced VB developers are quite familiar with ActiveX controls as the visual elements used on VB forms. They are stored in files with an OCX extension, and can be represented in the VB6 toolbox with an icon from which they can be dragged onto a VB6 form surface.

The replacement for VB forms in .NET is Windows Forms. The designer for Windows Forms looks superficially much like the VB forms designer, but it operates very differently underneath. For visual elements, Windows Forms uses .NET components that inherit from specific classes in the System.Windows.Forms namespace. Windows Forms cannot use ActiveX controls directly.

However, a hosting program is included in .NET to allow ActiveX controls to be exposed as Windows Forms controls, so the controls can be placed on Windows Forms in this way. As with other types of COM interop, there are performance implications due to data marshalling, but overall the technique works well for most ActiveX controls. This chapter covers the details of using the hosting program, which is known as AxHost.

We will first discuss when it is appropriate to use ActiveX controls in .NET, and go over the main differences between ActiveX controls and .NET Windows Forms controls. That will make it possible to discuss how the hosting program compensates for those differences.

When to Use ActiveX Controls in .NET

Windows Forms contain a set of controls that duplicates almost all the functionality in the controls that come with VB6. That means it is unnecessary to use ActiveX controls for most routine work in Windows Forms – you can use the .NET replacements instead.

There are a couple of exceptions. .NET does not have a masked edit control or a charting control, such as those on this sample VB6 screen:

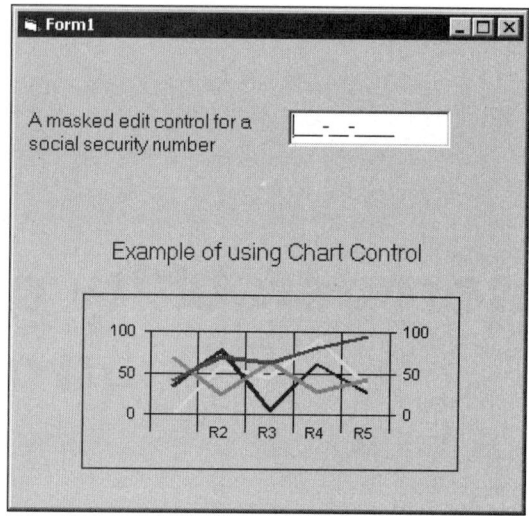

The ActiveX versions of these controls can be imported into .NET if needed. Note, however, that there are alternatives to using the masked edit control, such as inheriting a `TextBox` and equipping it with your own custom editing.

The most likely situation that will require the use of ActiveX controls is to get third-party control functionality. It will be some time before tools vendors can produce .NET equivalents of their controls, and some controls may not be ported to .NET at all. In most cases, the ActiveX versions of these can be imported and used in .NET, as described below.

If a development organization has created its own controls (either composite UserControls in VB6 or more general controls in C++), these are also candidates to use within .NET. While the source code for the UserControls can be upgraded from VB6 to Visual Basic .NET, such an upgrade may not be feasible in some cases. C++ controls based on unmanaged COM code may also be difficult to migrate to .NET.

The Differences Between Windows Forms Controls and ActiveX Controls

ActiveX controls are usually created using C++. VB6 can create composite controls called UserControls, but there are limitations on what these controls are able to do. ActiveX controls expose a classic COM interface and their properties, events, and methods are manipulated via that interface.

Windows Forms controls can be created in any .NET-compliant language. There are a variety of techniques used to create Windows Forms controls, but they all involve exposing a .NET interface for the control's members. Using a control in Windows Forms requires manipulation of a .NET interface rather than a COM interface.

A good resource to review Windows Forms control creation techniques is Chapter 10 of Professional VB.NET *from Wrox Press (ISBN 1-861004-97-4).*

Comparison of Properties

Windows Forms use a more consistent naming scheme for properties. For some ActiveX controls, text is displayed in the control with a `Caption` property. For others, a `Text` property is used. All standard Windows Forms controls use a `Text` property to get text in and out.

Windows Forms also uses a different convention for properties containing the position and size of a control. ActiveX controls have four properties for position and size – `Top`, `Left`, `Height`, and `Width`. In standard Windows Forms controls, position is contained in the `Location` property, which has two sub-properties named `X` and `Y` that correspond to the old `Left` and `Top` properties, respectively. Size is contained in the `Size` property, which exposes `Height` and `Width` sub-properties.

Hosting an ActiveX Control in .NET

As we discussed in the introduction to the chapter, Windows Forms only know how to manipulate controls with a .NET interface, and cannot use ActiveX controls directly. We can get around this with a wrapper class, however, much as the Runtime-Callable Wrapper (RCW) does for COM components (as discussed in Chapter 2), and the technical issues and limitations are the same as discussed for the RCW. The base class for this wrapper is already included with .NET. It is a class in the Windows Forms namespace – `System.Windows.Forms.AxHost`. .NET creates a separate wrapper class for every ActiveX control you want to use, but they all derive from `AxHost`.

`AxHost` in turn inherits from the `Windows.Forms.RichControl` class. This gives the ActiveX wrappers a lot of the built-in functionality of .NET controls. In addition to providing appropriate cosmetic settings such as `ForeColor` and `BackColor`, `RichControl` also has properties for `Anchor` and `Dock`, so imported ActiveX controls receive that functionality (even though it is not present in the original ActiveX control).

The wrapper also manipulates older properties to expose them ".NET style". The `Top`, `Left`, `Height`, and `Width` properties of the ActiveX control are exposed as `Location` and `Size` properties, using the same conventions as other Windows Forms controls.

Of course, AxHost can only expose these legacy properties (for size, position, and color) if the original ActiveX control has them. Almost all ActiveX controls do, so that's usually not an issue. However, to emphasize, the Anchor and Dock properties are not dependent on the imported ActiveX control.

Here is a diagram of the class hierarchy involved in creating wrappers from AxHost:

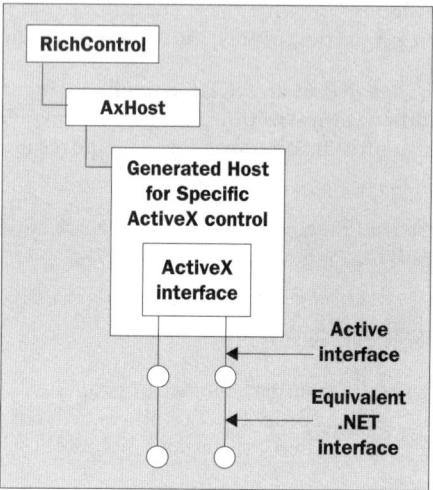

As you might expect, the individual wrapper classes are created automatically by Visual Studio .NET when you request a reference to an ActiveX control from inside the environment. We'll go through the process of doing this in the next section. When we do so, you will notice that the dialog used does not refer to them as ActiveX controls. They are simply referred to as COM Components in Visual Studio .NET.

You can also generate a wrapper with a command-line utility aximp.exe (which is found in the C:\Program Files\Microsoft Visual Studio .NET\FrameworkSDK\Bin folder by default). The wrapper can be customized by generating source for it, or by supplying options to the utility (as described in the example below), but this is seldom necessary. The automatically generated wrappers work properly for most of the typical controls you would want to import. The aximp.exe utility is also used behind the scenes by the Visual Studio .NET environment to create the wrapper, as described in the previous paragraph.

Let's look at examples of both of these techniques.

Example – Windows Media Player Control

Let's go through the process of importing an ActiveX control to use in a Windows Form. We will import the Windows Media Player control, since it is available on most systems (or can be downloaded from Microsoft if you don't have it), and since there is not yet a .NET equivalent for it.

Start a new Visual Basic .NET Windows Application in Visual Studio. While looking at the design surface for the blank Form1 that is created, right-click on the Windows Forms tab in the Toolbox. One of the available options is Customize Toolbox. Select that option and you'll see a dialog box much like this one:

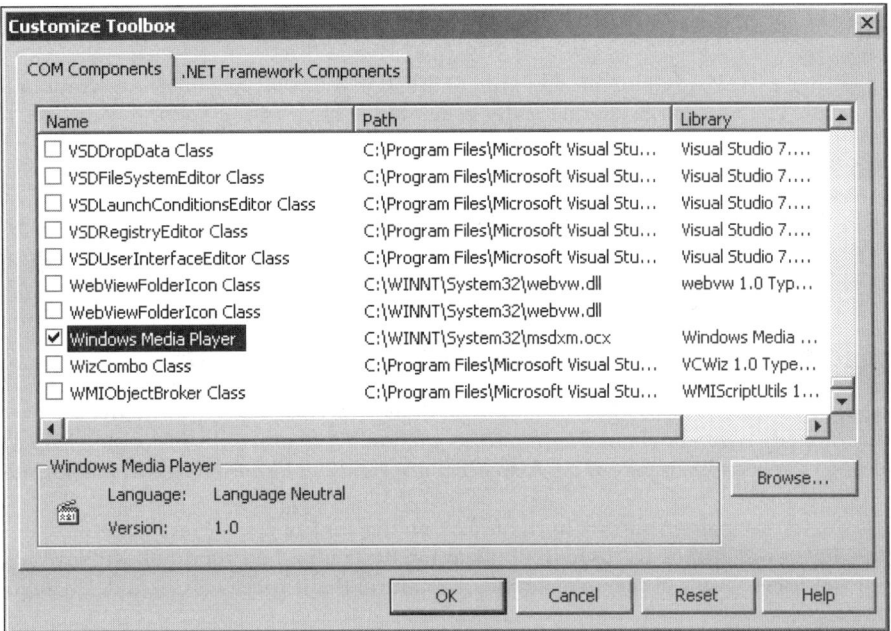

Check the box next to the **Windows Media Player** control and press **OK**. If you now scroll to the bottom of the controls in the **Windows Form** tab of the Toolbox, you will see the MediaPlayer control there.

Drag this control onto Form1 and drop it. You'll see it appear just as any other .NET control would appear.

Notice that the **Properties** window for the control contains an **Anchor** property. Set the **Anchor** property to anchor the control to all four sides of the form.

Now let's test it to see that it works. Place a button on the form and place this code behind it:

```
Private Sub Button1_Click(ByVal sender As System.Object, _
                 ByVal e As System.EventArgs) Handles Button1.Click
'For Windows XP, change file name to C:\Windows\Media\town.mid.
    AxMediaPlayer1.FileName = "C:\WINNT\Media\canyon.mid"
    AxMediaPlayer1.Play()
End Sub
```

If you have a typical installation of Windows 2000, this should start some music playing. (For Windows XP, you'll need to change the path of the file name the player is using to `"C:\Windows\Media\town.mid"`.) Note that the stop, pause, and play buttons on the control are now active. Also note that if you resize the form, the MediaPlayer control will automatically resize with it.

Notes on the Example

Unlike importing a COM component, you are not asked if you want to generate a wrapper for an ActiveX control. The wrapper is automatically generated as soon as you add the control to the project.

If you check the Solution Explorer, you'll see that adding the MediaPlayer control onto the form adds three references to the project. The references are AxMediaPlayer, MediaPlayer, and stdole. These point to specific DLLs. The first two are newly generated DLLs that are stored in the bin directory for your project, and are named Interop.AxMediaPlayer.dll and Interop.MediaPlayer.dll, respectively. The third is a standard interop library from the global assembly cache.

Custom Property Moved from Properties List

A minor change that can be puzzling is the relocation of the Custom property for ActiveX controls. In VB6, the Custom property is listed right in the Properties window along with other properties. When selected, it causes a dialog to appear that is part of the ActiveX control and can be customized to manipulate it.

In .NET, to get to this dialog you should right-click on the control and select Properties. In some cases, the Custom dialog will also be exposed as a link at the bottom of the Properties window labeled ActiveX – Properties. You can see an example of a control that exposes such a link by importing the VB6 TabStrip control.

Creating a Wrapper with Aximp.exe

The import utility aximp.exe is used by the Visual Studio .NET environment to automatically generate a wrapper, as described in the example above. However, we can also generate a wrapper manually using aximp.exe. It is a command-line utility, so you must type it into a command window to use it.

Aximp.exe is easy to use. In the simplest case, we would generate a wrapper for the Media Player with this command:

```
aximp c:\winnt\system32\msdxm.ocx
```

This generates the same two DLLs as the previous example. The DLLs are compiled and ready to use. However, if you wish, you can generate source for them instead (in C#, not Visual Basic .NET) with the following command:

```
aximp c:\winnt\system32\msdxm.ocx /source
```

Other command line options allow you to assign a different name to the DLLs that are generated, and to perform actions such as signing the resulting control with a publisher's name. These optional actions would be the most likely reason to use aximp.exe directly instead of having Visual Studio .NET invoke it automatically. For example, if you have a public-private key pair in a file named C:\Keys\Mainkey.key, then you can sign the generated assembly with the key pair using this command:

```
aximp c:\winnt\system32\msdxm.ocx /keyfile:C:\Keys\MainKey.Key
```

Importing VB6 UserControls

The above techniques work just as well on VB6 UserControls as they do on other types. You simply refer to the control in the Customize Toolbox dialog and use it, or create a wrapper with `aximp.exe`.

Of course, such UserControls require the VB6 libraries on the client. If such a control is imported into a .NET project, when that project is deployed, the VB6 runtime and associated DLLs must be deployed along with it.

Controls that Cannot be Imported

Some controls cannot be imported with `AxHost`. There are different reasons why these controls don't fit into the `AxHost` wrapper, but fortunately the list of such controls is short.

Windowless Controls

These are "windowless" controls that don't actually manipulate a rectangular window (using an `HWnd`). Examples are the `Line` and `Shape` controls from VB6. Because they don't actually manipulate a window, they don't support all the ActiveX capabilities that `AxHost` expects.

The alternative to these controls in .NET is to use GDI+ to draw directly to a form or control.

The UpDown Control

The `UpDown` control in VB6 is used to manipulate the value of an associated `TextBox`. The `TextBox` that works with the `UpDown` control is called the "buddy" control.

`AxHost` does not have the capability to associate a buddy control with an `UpDown`, so the `UpDown` control cannot be hosted in `AxHost`. This is not a major issue, since the `UpDown` control is replaced in .NET by the `NumericUpDown` and `DomainUpDown` controls, which have the `UpDown` and the associated buddy control wrapped up in one control.

SSTab Control

VB6 has two tab controls that operate quite differently. One of them is the `SSTab` control. Because of the way the `SSTab` control manages the controls that appear on its tabs, `AxHost` is not able to work with it. (The other type of tab, the `TabStrip`, can be imported.)

As with the `UpDown` control, this is not a major issue because .NET contains a new tab control (with the straightforward name of `TabControl`).

Security

Since ActiveX controls run unmanaged code, they do not observe .NET's code-access security restrictions. A .NET application with restricted permissions cannot enforce those permissions in an ActiveX control. This opens the possibility that ActiveX controls can create security holes in an application, allowing such capabilities as read/write permission to directories that are restricted from the hosting application.

There is one level of security that affects ActiveX controls. In order to host an ActiveX control at all, an application must have permission to run unmanaged code. This is controlled with the `SecurityPermissionAttribute.UnmanagedCode` property. Under certain default conditions, such as code downloaded automatically from a web server, this permission will not be available and will need to be granted explicitly. Otherwise, an application in these circumstances that attempts to run a hosted control will generate a security exception.

> *The default for local applications is to allow unmanaged code permissions, so the applications you develop locally will host ActiveX controls with no changes to default security settings.*

Once that permission is granted, however, the door is wide open. So the ability to secure applications that contain ActiveX controls is limited.

.NET Windows Forms Controls in VB6

This chapter has discussed how OCX controls can be imported and used in Windows Forms and Visual Basic .NET. In some beta versions of .NET, it was also possible to go the other way and expose Windows Forms with COM-based control interfaces to be used in VB6.

This capability is not included in the first release version of .NET. Windows Forms controls can be exposed as .NET components (because they are a .NET class), but the additional mechanisms to allow these classes to function as controls in OCX containers are not present.

However, note that you can compile a .NET form into a class library and have the form shown from a VB6 form. For details on how to do that, check out the sample project at the following address, which is installed with Visual Studio .NET:

C:\Program Files\Microsoft Visual Studio
.NET\FrameworkSDK\Samples\Technologies\Interop\Basic\WinForms

Summary

As with general COM components, most ActiveX controls are interoperable with .NET. They can be imported and hosted in Windows Forms, and act like a Windows Forms control from the developer's standpoint. The import process is transparent, and covers the vast majority of common cases without any difficulty. The imported controls even gain new functionality, by receiving the `Anchor` and `Dock` properties.

There are a few controls that cannot be imported. Besides the ones from Microsoft (windowless controls, `SSTab`, `UpDown`), there are likely to be some third-party controls that have the same difficulties. However, these should be a small minority.

As with a COM component, imported ActiveX controls run as unmanaged code within .NET. This means that there are performance considerations, and some implications for security. However, these considerations should not cause significant problems in using most ActiveX controls inside Windows Forms.

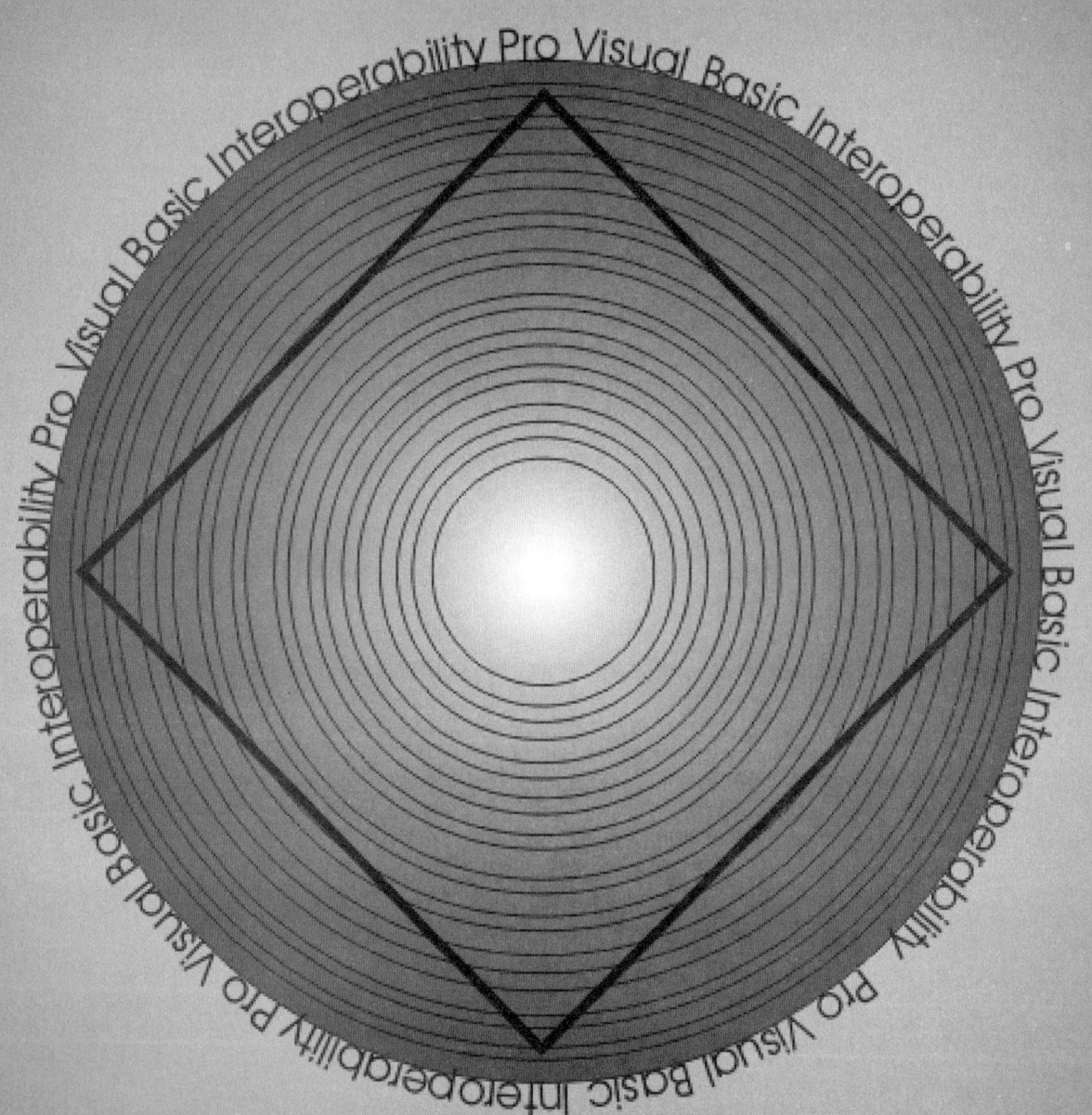

14

How Do I Prepare VB6 Code for Migration?

As we discussed in the introduction to this book, many organizations will need interoperability for an extended period. The replacement of older VB6 programs by new Visual Basic .NET programs will be a gradual process for these development shops.

One implication is that the VB6 code will require maintenance and possibly some enhancement during this period. There are two long-term possibilities for this code:

1. The code will eventually be completely scrapped and rewritten from scratch in Visual Basic .NET.

2. The code will eventually be migrated to Visual Basic .NET.

If the code fits into the first category, then there's not much to be said about it. Your only consideration is to keep maintenance to a minimum, since the code will eventually be thrown away. In this case, the only hard part is choosing when to do the rewrite.

However, if the code falls into the second category, you may be able to make the eventual migration easier by following certain guidelines in your maintenance and enhancement of the code. This chapter covers some of the most important guidelines.

There have been a number of changes during the beta cycle that impacted on the appropriate guidelines to prepare code for migration. There may well be more such changes in future versions of Visual Basic .NET. That means some of the guidelines presented below may become obsolete at some point in the future.

Some of the guidelines refer to capabilities of the Visual Basic .NET Upgrade Wizard, which converts projects in VB6 to Visual Basic .NET code. This wizard does a pretty good job overall, but it does have limitations (which may be fixed in future) and some of them are noted in this chapter.

Stop Using Default Properties and Methods

VB6 and earlier versions allow you to write code like this, where `lblTitle` is a `Label` control:

```
lblTitle = "My Summer Vacation"
```

This works because the label control has a default property, which is `Caption`. So the preceding line really means this:

```
lblTitle.Caption = "My Summer Vacation"
```

Visual Basic .NET does away with the concept of default properties unless the property has an index, so the first form won't work in Visual Basic .NET. You *must* use the second form.

Many development shops have long frowned on using default methods and properties anyway, because they make code more difficult to read. The change in Visual Basic .NET gives you another reason to avoid them.

The indexed form of default properties is considered acceptable, even in professional shops, for data access coding. Here's an example, where `rsCustomers` is a `Recordset`:

```
rsCustomers("City") = sCity
```

This line actually means:

```
rsCustomers.Fields("City") = sCity
```

In this case, the `Fields` collection is the default for the `Recordset` object. This works in Visual Basic .NET, so there's no need to change this programming convention if your shop uses it.

Avoid Non-Zero Lower Bounds for Arrays

As was mentioned in the book's introduction, one of the changes necessary to make VB work with the .NET Framework was to remove support for arrays that started at any index other than zero. The VB syntax in the following line is not available in .NET:

```
Dim nMyNumbers(1000 To 1050) As Integer
```

During maintenance of VB6, it's best to avoid such code because converted code will require manual intervention. Usually, that means using a base number for the array element and adjusting the actual element used by subtracting the base, like this:

```
Dim nBaseElement As Integer
nBaseElement = 1000
```

```
Dim nMyNumbers(50) As Integer
' Intervening code here.
Dim nIndex As Integer
nIndex = 1023    ' I want the array element at position 1023.
                 ' That's really at position 23 in the new array
                 ' so need to subtract the base (1000) to compensate.
Debug.Print nMyNumber(nIndex - nBaseElement)
```

It should be noted, however, that providing support for non-zero lower bounds on arrays is one of the most commonly requested enhancements to Visual Basic .NET. That means it is possible that Microsoft will find a way to provide this capability in .NET, making VB6 code with such syntax easier to migrate.

Make All Parameters Explicitly ByRef or ByVal

In VB6, if you fail to make a parameter `ByRef` or `ByVal` explicitly, then it's `ByRef` by default. Such parameters can be changed by subroutines or functions that take them as arguments, and the changes are passed back to the calling code. There are a few good reasons to use such `ByRef` parameters, and declaring them explicitly as `ByRef` is considered acceptable coding practice. But many developers just leave off the `ByRef` or `ByVal` on all parameters and let the parameters be `ByRef` by default.

This practice is often considered sloppy and error-prone, and now there's an even better reason for not doing it. If parameters are not explicitly declared `ByRef` or `ByVal` in Visual Basic .NET, they become `ByVal` by default – the opposite behavior to that in VB6.

There are a few situations where this can result in subtle bugs when a value is being changed in an underlying routine, and the programmer is expecting the changes to be passed back, but they are not. The solution is simply to always explicitly declare parameters `ByRef` or `ByVal`, and this is a good habit to get into.

Place Default Values on All Optional Parameters

While Visual Basic .NET still has support for optional parameters, there is a new requirement in using them – you must supply a default value for each optional parameter in the declaration of a routine that uses them.

The reason is that Visual Basic .NET is dropping support for the `IsMissing` keyword. This keyword is almost always used to supply a default value for a missing `Variant` parameter – in fact, it doesn't even work with non-variant types. This style of programming was the only way to use optional parameters in VB4 (which was the first version of VB to support optional parameters). It then became a habit with some developers.

An alternative way of supplying default values has been available since VB5. You can supply a default value for an optional parameter when you declare the parameter, like this:

```
Function PhoneLookup(sName As String, sAge As Integer, _
                  Optional bVitalStatus As Boolean=True)
```

This procedure assumes that the person involved in this operation is alive, unless `bVitalStatus` is passed in as `False`. You should use such default values in all code using optional parameters, and `IsMissing` should be removed wherever it appears.

Declare All Variables on a Separate Line

Visual Basic .NET has slightly different variable declaration rules from VB6. In particular, this line will work in both versions, but the effect will be different in Visual Basic .NET:

```
Dim nFirstNumber, nSecondNumber As Long
```

In VB6 and earlier, nFirstNumber actually becomes declared as a Variant. In Visual Basic .NET, both will be declared as Long. This brings VB's syntax in line with that of other languages.

The easy way to avoid this problem is to declare all variables on their own separate line. This works now and later, and also makes code easier to read.

Be Careful Where You Declare Variables

In VB6, it doesn't matter where in a routine you declare a variable. You can declare a variable inside a For loop or an If block, and it's available anywhere in the routine, including outside the loop or the block. Here's an example:

```
Do
    Dim nIndex As Integer
    nIndex = nIndex + 1
Loop Until nIndex > 10
MsgBox nIndex
```

This code works fine in VB6 and the message box displays the value 11 after execution exits the loop. However, Visual Basic .NET introduces the concept of **block scope**. If you declare a variable inside a block, then it is available only inside that block. The code shown above fails in Visual Basic .NET because nIndex is declared inside the "Do loop" block. The last line (which is outside the block) attempts to use nIndex, and the block scope of nIndex makes this a syntax error. In fact, the Until clause is also considered to be outside the block and also generates an error.

The fix for this problem is simply to declare variables in VB6 outside of Do loops, For loops, While loops, If statements, and other block constructs. Doing so will ensure that the code works the same way in VB6 and Visual Basic .NET.

> *If you're absolutely sure that the variable is not used outside of the loop, it's OK for its declaration to be inside. But, if even one reference is outside of the loop, the code will fail and need manual adjustment when it is converted to Visual Basic .NET.*

Many shops adopt the convention that you declare all variables at the top of the routine, which takes care of the problem. This will allow VB6 code to migrate without any possibility of errors due to the new block scope in Visual Basic .NET.

Avoid Fixed Length Strings in UDTs

Fixed-length strings are not a primitive data type (one natively supported by the compiler) in Visual Basic .NET as they are in VB6. In .NET, a compatibility class makes fixed-length strings available for most situations, and you only need to make a declaration change. For example, a declaration in VB6 might look like this:

```
Dim sTwelveCharacterID As String*12
```

In Visual Basic .NET, you need to change it to this:

```
Dim sTwelveCharacterID As VB6.FixedLengthString(12)
```

The module needs an `Imports` statement that refers to the VB6 compatibility classes for this declaration to work but, otherwise, the variable – which is now actually an object – behaves as a VB6 developer would expect.

Unfortunately, this change presents one big problem: user-defined types (UDTs) in VB6 are replaced by a concept called **structures** in Visual Basic .NET. Only primitive data types are allowed in Visual Basic .NET structures, which means that you can't use fixed-length strings in them. For example, a UDT in VB6 might look like this:

```
Type TransferRecord
RecID As Integer
Description As String*20
Status As Boolean
End Type
```

The closest equivalent in Visual Basic .NET is this:

```
Structure TransferRecord
Public RecID As Integer
Public Description As String
' Note! Variable length string!!
Public Status As Boolean
End Structure
```

Using this structure, you're completely responsible for controlling the length of the `Description` part of the `TransferRecord` structure. If `Description` has to be exactly 20 characters, you need to write code to ensure that. One way to do that is to make `Description` 20 characters immediately after a structure element is declared, and then use the new replacement for `LSET` (named `PadRight`) to put data into it:

```
Dim stcRecord As TransferRecord

stcRecord.Description = Space$(20)
' At this point, the Description string is exactly 20 characters.

' This code would occur further down.
stcRecord.Description =
"Some description"
stcRecord.Description.PadRight(20)
' The Description string is now exactly 20 characters long.
```

Another way to handle this situation is to switch in Visual Basic .NET from fixed length strings to character arrays, which *are* a primitive type in .NET. However, the logic changes needed for that alternative are even more extensive than those above for using variable length strings instead.

So, avoid using fixed length strings in UDTs in current code if you expect to migrate the code to Visual Basic .NET. This is a problem that the migration tool can't completely fix for you. Some manual intervention will be required.

Get Rid of Obsolete Keywords

In the *Introduction*, we discussed the fact that VB is descended from earlier versions of the BASIC language. The most proximate ancestor was QuickBASIC, which was a DOS-based compiler from Microsoft very popular in the 1980s. Going back further, QuickBASIC itself was descended from even earlier BASIC implementations.

To retain some backward compatibility with QuickBASIC, VB has always supported a number of obsolete syntax elements. All of them have more modern replacements and most are no longer used, so Microsoft is taking this chance to clean them out of Visual Basic.

We saw the list of obsolete keywords in the introduction, but it is appropriate to repeat them here:

- ❑   `Gosub`
- ❑   `On x GoTo` ... (computed `GoTo`'s)
- ❑   `Let` (as in "`Let i = i + 1`")
- ❑   `VarPtr, ObjPtr, StrPtr`
- ❑   `DefBool, DefByte, DefInt, DefLng, DefCur, DefSng, DefDbl, DefDec, DefDate, DefStr, DefObj, DefVar` (keywords used to implicitly declare the type of a variable based on the first letter in the name)

If some of these are so old that you don't even know what they do, that's OK – ignore them. But if you're working with code that uses any of these keywords, then you'll need to change the logic to replace them. The exception to that is `Let`, which you can just delete. The migration tool won't help you with any of these, except to mark them as unsupported.

Note that `Return` has a different usage. It was used in VB6 to return from a `Gosub` back to the calling code. In Visual Basic .NET, it is used to return the value for a function. With this incompatibility in usage, it's best if your VB6 code does not use `Return` at all.

Remove Implicit Object Instantiation

VB6 offers two ways to declare and instantiate an object. Here's the most commonly used way:

```
Dim objSomeObject As MyClass
Set objSomeObject = New MyClass
```

This technique is used the most because the second line immediately instantiates the object. This action removes the uncertainty about when the object is instantiated. The code still works in Visual Basic .NET, with the following minor changes:

```
Dim objSomeObject As MyClass
objSomeObject = New MyClass()
```

In the second line, the `Set` is removed because it is no longer used in Visual Basic .NET, and `MyClass` requires parentheses to indicate that the constructor has no arguments.

Here's the second way to declare and instantiate an object in VB6:

```
Dim objSomeObject As New MyClass

' Some intervening code goes here...

' This is the first reference to a property or method of the object.
objSomeObject.SomeProperty = "A string value"
```

In this case, the object is actually not instantiated by the first line. The first time a property or method of the object is referenced, the object is instantiated before carrying out the operation. So, in this case, for VB6, the last line in the example instantiates the object.

Things work differently in Visual Basic .NET. If you declare an object with "`Dim... As New...`", then the instantiation is immediate. This change normally doesn't matter. However, if the instantiation of the object is lengthy, and the developer is counting on the object not getting instantiated until the code references it, the behavior of the program changes. In that case, the user might notice the delay due to instantiation at a different point in the program. If the logic is sufficiently sloppy that the intervening code is counting on the object *not* being instantiated – say if the object creates a file, but the logic assumes that the file is not there yet – then the code will not work properly in Visual Basic .NET.

It has long been considered good programming practice in VB6 to use the first technique above, which avoids implicit instantiation. This technique also works in Visual Basic .NET, so it's probably best to continue using that technique in your VB6 code. However, after moving to Visual Basic .NET, for new code you might prefer the more concise second form, in which the declaration and instantiation take place in the same line.

Stop Implicit Loading of Forms

It's always been possible in versions of VB prior to Visual Basic .NET to load a form by just referring to it in code. This is called implicit instantiation. For example, if you have a form in a project named `frmDialog` then, in VB6 and earlier, this line causes the form to load:

```
frmDialog.Show
```

This kind of behavior does not work with objects based on class modules in VB6 – only with forms. Class instances must be declared in a declaration statement before they can be used.

Forms can be declared in the same way as classes in VB6 and earlier. (The reason is that a form is actually just another class in Visual Basic .NET, as we discuss a little later.) That's done by declaring a form variable, instantiating it, and then showing the form – like this:

```
dim frmNewDialog As Form
set frmNewDialog As New frmCustomer
frmNewDialog.Show
```

This VB6 technique to show a form works fine in Visual Basic .NET, but the first way (using implicit instantiation in VB6) does not. In Visual Basic .NET, a form is actually a class module that inherits from a class in `System.Windows.Forms` to get forms capabilities. Classes that happen to be forms must be instantiated just like any other class.

The Upgrade Wizard will actually fix this problem, using a method of the `Form` class called `DefInstance`. The line of code we looked at above:

```
frmDialog.Show
```

will be converted to:

```
frmDialog.DefInstance.Show
```

All later references that would just be `frmDialog` in VB6 are converted to `frmDialog.DefInstance` in Visual Basic .NET. Your migrated code will actually work OK, but this syntax is an obvious kludge. To avoid such syntax in your migrated code, it's a good idea to have a programming convention in VB6 to use the second technique above. You'll have to change your habits for Visual Basic .NET anyway, so you might as well start now.

Switch Data Binding to ADO

If you use data binding, be aware that Visual Basic .NET supports data binding only for ADO, not for DAO or RDO. If you expect to convert projects with data binding, you might want to convert the binding to ADO first. The migration tool will not assist by changing DAO or RDO code to ADO during the conversion. Also note that data binding to ADO in .NET is limited to ActiveX controls.

Use Intrinsic Constants Whenever Possible

It's a good programming convention to use VB's intrinsic constants whenever possible. Code is more readable, less prone to bugs, and easier to modify. Here are typical lines that use intrinsic constants:

```
Me.WindowState = vbNormal
MsgBox "Error!", vbCritical
```

In VB6, these lines are equivalent to the previous ones, as far as the compiler is concerned:

```
Me.WindowState = 0
MsgBox "Error!", 16
```

The Visual Basic .NET migration tool doesn't change any of the lines in either of these examples. *However, some of the underlying intrinsic constant values might change.* If you use intrinsic constants, as in the first example, you won't notice the change and your code will continue to work fine. But, if you habitually use the hard-coded constant values, as in the second example, your code will break if any of the constant values are different in Visual Basic .NET.

Stop Writing DHTML Pages and WebClasses

In *Chapter 1*, we touched on the fact that the Upgrade Wizard won't handle DHTML pages and WebClasses very well. Converting existing DHTML pages is a completely manual process. The Upgrade Wizard will perform some conversion on WebClasses, but the results will need manual intervention to work.

Web Forms replace the functionality in both DHTML pages and WebClasses in Visual Basic .NET. Since DHTML pages and WebClasses are structured completely differently from Web Forms, it's more effective in most cases to recreate the pages with Web Forms, and possibly cut and paste logic from old VB6 code.

For any programming situations where you might expect to use DHTML pages or WebClasses, using Active Server Pages that call on COM components is probably a better choice for any new development. Projects done this way will be much easier to convert to Visual Basic .NET code later.

Wrap Your API Calls

Doing API calls in VB has always been a bit messy, so most developers have wrapped the calls in VB functions. Now there's another good reason to do that.

Many API calls should ideally be replaced with different techniques when going to Visual Basic .NET. While such code will work in Visual Basic .NET, there are very few cases in which calling the API is really necessary. There are .NET Framework classes for most of the functionality that the API supplies in VB6. These classes simplify code, and can also improve performance and portability of the code for the future. Centralizing API calls makes it easier to replace them manually with their .NET equivalents in converted programs.

There's one additional way that such centralization helps. We saw in *Chapter 1* that VB is changing several data types. For API calls, the important changes involve Integers and Longs. These changes can have an impact on Win32 API calls because most of them take 32-bit arguments. You declare these arguments as Long in VB6. However, a Long in Visual Basic .NET will be 64 bits, so arguments declared as Long won't work with these API calls. You'll need to re-declare such arguments as Integer in Visual Basic .NET.

The Upgrade Wizard supplied with Visual Basic .NET will translate old types to new. But it only works on whole projects. So, if you are cutting and pasting API-related code, you'll have to fix all of the Declare statements to take the right data type. By isolating API calls into their own functions, and centralizing the API calls into a small number of modules, you can reuse such code more easily.

Get Your Logic Out of the UI and Into Components and Classes

We discussed in *Chapter 1* the fact that components will often be better candidates for migration than user interface modules. Many current VB user interface apps won't be good candidates for migration. That's especially true of fat VB clients, in which business logic is indiscriminately mixed with presentation logic. Such code is difficult to maintain, will be just as bad in Visual Basic .NET, and does not fit the object-based philosophy of .NET very well.

The more logic your system places in components and classes, the better the chance that it can be cleanly converted. So, look for opportunities to encapsulate your logic in classes. Even if the classes are compiled into VB forms-based executables rather than as separate components, they'll still be easier to salvage in Visual Basic .NET.

Avoid Late Binding

The late binding capability in VB6 makes programming objects for which you don't know the exact type until run time easy. However, late binding hurts performance. So it's always a good idea to avoid it when you can.

Visual Basic .NET offers another reason to do so. Some Visual Basic .NET experts have concluded that using a capability in Visual Basic .NET called `Option Strict` is a good idea. `Option Strict` disallows certain types of implicit object conversions, which can avoid bugs. But it also disallows late binding. So, if your organization decides to adopt use of `Option Strict` as a best practice, converted code with late binding will need manual adjustment.

Conclusion

Preparing for Visual Basic .NET doesn't require a lot of changes to your VB6 code. Many of the guidelines in this chapter have been a part of good coding conventions for quite a while, so you may already be using them. Others are new, but in no case is the adjustment major. The tradeoff of making an ultimate migration easier is well worth the effort.

In addition to the material presented in this chapter, there are a number of resources on Microsoft's web site that deal with migration and upgrade issues. Here are some good ones to start with:

❑ http://msdn.microsoft.com/vbasic/technical/upgrade/vbupgrade.asp

❑ http://msdn.microsoft.com/library/default.asp?url=/library/en-us/dnvb600/html/vb6tovbdotnet.asp

❑ http://msdn.microsoft.com/vbasic/technical/upgrade/roadmap.asp

As more companies attempt to upgrade their code to Visual Basic .NET, it is likely that more resources will appear. It's a good idea before you make any migration effort to check the latest resources for ideas on how to do it effectively.

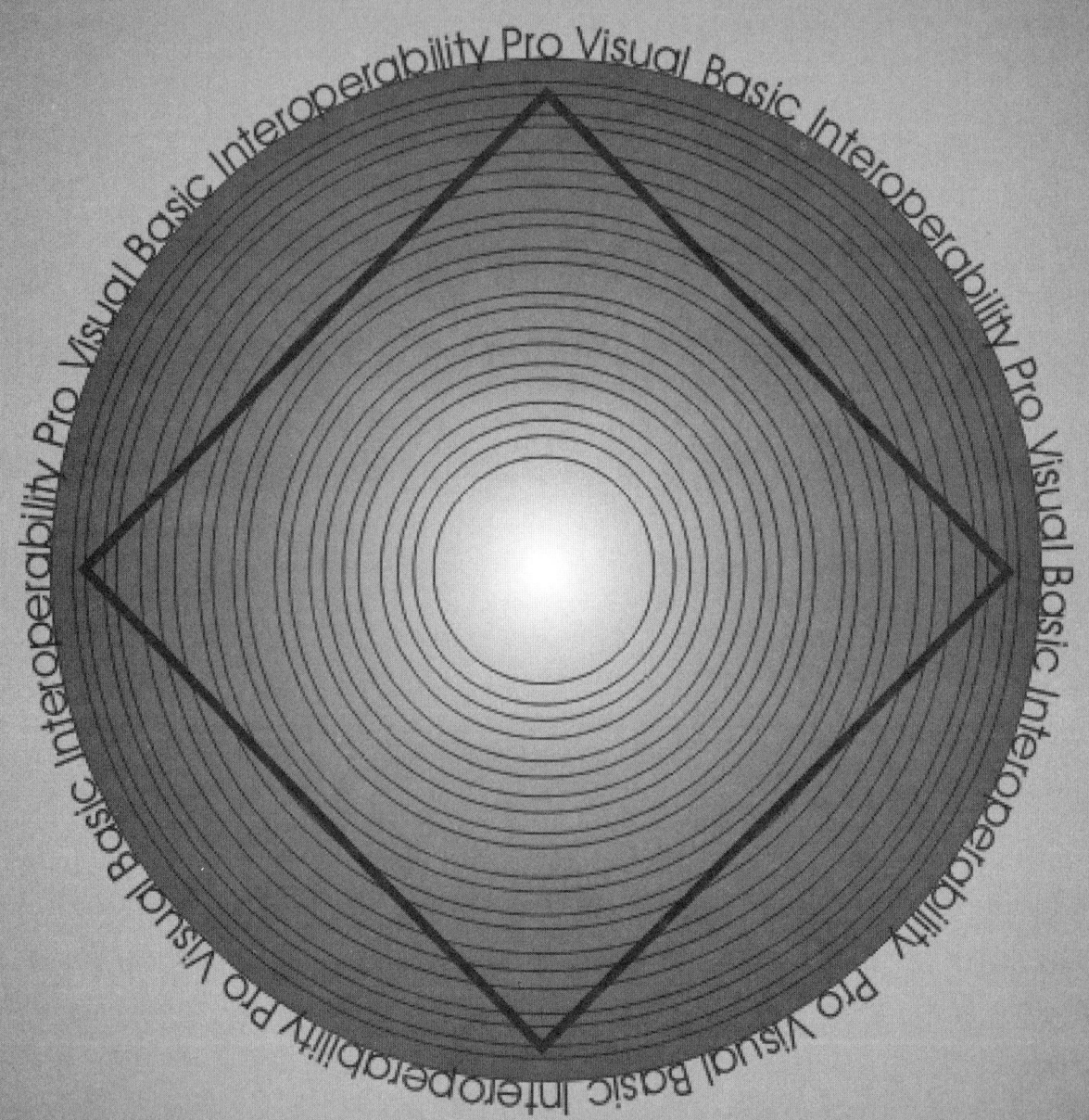

Index

A Guide to the Index

The index is arranged hierarchically, in alphabetical order, with symbols preceding the letter A. Most second-level entries and many third-level entries also occur as first-level entries. This is to ensure that users will find the information they require however they choose to search for it.

X

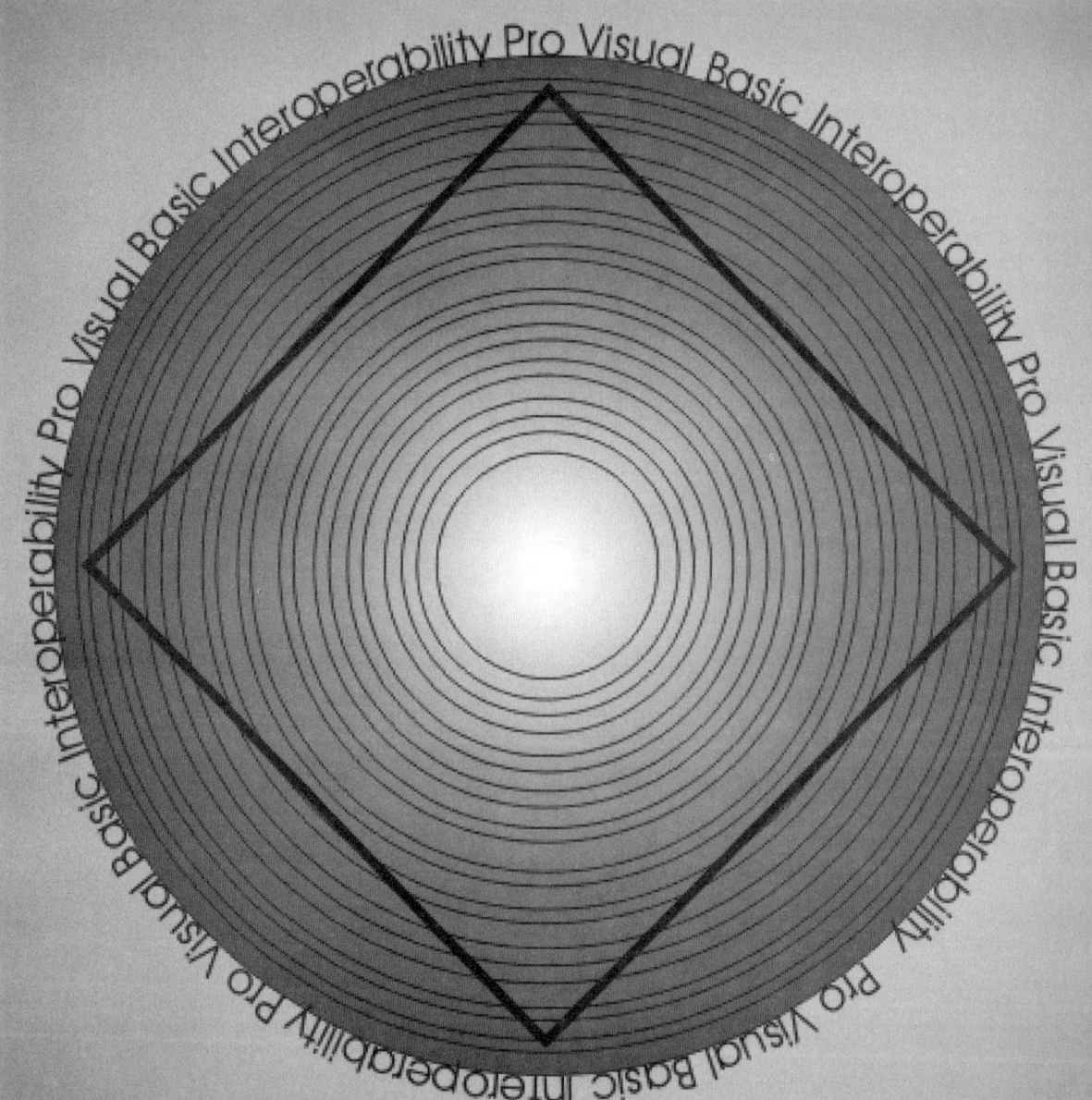

wrox

Programmer to Programmer™

Wrox writes books for you. Any suggestions, or ideas about how you want information given in your ideal book will be studied by our team. Your comments are always valued at Wrox.

Free phone in USA 800-USE-WROX
Fax (312) 893 8001

UK Tel.: (0121) 687 4100   Fax: (0121) 687 4101

Pro Visual Basic Interoperability – Registration Card

Name _____

Address _____

_____

_____

City _____ State/Region _____

Country _____ Postcode/Zip _____

E-Mail _____

Occupation _____

How did you hear about this book?

❏ Book review (name) _____

❏ Advertisement (name) _____

❏ Recommendation _____

❏ Catalog _____

❏ Other _____

Where did you buy this book?

❏ Bookstore (name) _____ City _____

❏ Computer store (name) _____

❏ Mail order _____

❏ Other _____

What influenced you in the purchase of this book?

❏ Cover Design   ❏ Contents   ❏ Other (please specify):

_____

How did you rate the overall content of this book?

❏ Excellent   ❏ Good   ❏ Average   ❏ Poor

What did you find most useful about this book? _____

_____

What did you find least useful about this book? _____

_____

_____

Please add any additional comments. _____

_____

What other subjects will you buy a computer book on soon?

_____

What is the best computer book you have used this year?

_____

Check here if you DO NOT want to receive support for this book ■

wrox

Programmer to Programmer™

Note: If you post the bounce back card below in the UK, please send it to:

Wrox Press Limited, Arden House, 1102 Warwick Road,
Acocks Green, Birmingham B27 6HB. UK.

Computer Book Publishers